Mental Illness, Discrimination and the Law

Mental Illness, Discrimination and the Law

Fighting for social justice

Felicity Callard, BA (Hons) MA, PhD

Health Service and Population Research Department, Institute of Psychiatry, King's College London, UK

Norman Sartorius, MD, PhD, FRCPsych

Association for the Improvement of Mental Health Programmes, Geneva, Switzerland

Julio Arboleda-Flórez, MD, PhD, FRCPC

Queen's University, Kingston, Ontario, Canada

Peter Bartlett, BA, MA, LLB, PhD

School of Law and Institute of Mental Health, University of Nottingham, UK

Hanfried Helmchen, Prof, Dr Med

Charité – University Medicine Berlin, Germany

Heather Stuart, BA (Hons) MA, PhD

Queen's University, Kingston, Ontario, Canada

Jose Taborda, MD, PhD

Federal University of Health Sciences of Porto Alegre, Porto Alegre, Brazil

Graham Thornicroft, FRCPsych, PhD, FAcadMed

Health Service and Population Research Department, Institute of Psychiatry, King's College London, UK

WILEY-BLACKWELL

A John Wiley & Sons, Ltd., Publication

Wiley-Blackwell is an imprint of John Wiley & Sons, formed by the merger of Wiley's global Scientific, Technical and Medical business with Blackwell Publishing.

Registered office: John Wiley & Sons, Ltd, The Atrium, Southern Gate, Chichester, West Sussex, PO19 8SQ, UK

Editorial offices: 9600 Garsington Road, Oxford, OX4 2DQ, UK
The Atrium, Southern Gate, Chichester, West Sussex, PO19 8SQ, UK
111 River Street, Hoboken, NJ 07030-5774, USA

For details of our global editorial offices, for customer services and for information about how to apply for permission to reuse the copyright material in this book please see our website at www.wiley.com/wiley-blackwell

Library of Congress Cataloging-in-Publication Data

Mental illness, discrimination, and the law : fighting for social justice / Felicity Callard ... [et al.].
p. : cm.
Includes bibliographical references and index.
ISBN 978-1-119-95354-8 (cloth)
I. Callard, Felicity.
[DNLM: 1. Mentally Ill Persons–legislation & jurisprudence. 2. Mental Health Services–legislation & jurisprudence. 3. Patient Rights–legislation & jurisprudence. 4. Prejudice. 5. Social Justice. WM33.1]
344.04'4–dc23

2011043533

A catalogue record for this book is available from the British Library.

Wiley also publishes its books in a variety of electronic formats. Some content that appears in print may not be available in electronic books.

Set in 9.5/13pt Meridien by Aptara Inc., New Delhi, India
Printed and bound in Singapore by Markono Print Media Pte Ltd

First Impression 2012

Contents

Acknowledgements

The authors wish to acknowledge the support of the Association for the Improvement of Mental Health Programmes. We also wish to thank Mrs Josette Mamboury (who sadly passed away before publication) and Mrs Lydia Kurk for their assistance. We are very grateful to Jane Smith, who made superb editorial contributions to this book as it reached its final stages, as well as to Kevin Dunn, who ably copy-edited the manuscript once it had been submitted to Wiley-Blackwell.

Felicity Callard and Graham Thornicroft acknowledge financial support from the National Institute for Health Research (NIHR) Specialist Biomedical Research Centre for Mental Health award to the South London and Maudsley NHS Foundation Trust and the Institute of Psychiatry, King's College London.

Felicity Callard thanks Constantina Papoulias for her advice, as well as her critical engagement with the book's substantive issues. She also thanks Lynne Friedli and Oliver Lewis for inspiration as regards the role that legislative and policy transformation can have in improving the lives of people with mental health problems.

Norman Sartorius and Graham Thornicroft gratefully acknowledge the financial support that the Eli Lilly Company provided to the Association for the Improvement of Mental Health Programmes in order to facilitate the coordination of the project that led to the development of this publication and cordially thank Dr John Hayes, Vice-President Neurosciences, Eli Lilly for his interest in improving the lives of people with mental illness and for his help in this matter. Eli Lilly, however, played no role in developing the conceptual framework for and content of this book.

The authors thank and acknowledge the many individuals who have played an important role in the development of this book. They are listed below. Their diverse contributions have included: participation in interviews; the provision of country and/or regional case studies (in the form of responses to a questionnaire); the provision of background documents, journal papers, reports and references to relevant literature; suggestions for additional contacts and organisations; reflections and comments on the manuscript.

It should be emphasised that the authors – and not the individuals enumerated below – bear responsibility for the contents of the book. The authors have benefited from the content of the individuals' contributions, and many of the examples and insights presented in the book are indebted to them. Nonetheless, responsibility for the interpretation of those contributions rests with the authors and not with those who offered them. In addition, the views expressed by these individuals in their contributions were not necessarily those of their organisations. The book does not, furthermore, necessarily represent the views of all of these individuals in all respects.

Moshe Z Abramowitz, Eitanim Psychiatric Hospital, Jerusalem Mental Health Centre, Israel
Edgard Belfort, Asociación Psiquiátrica de América Latina (APAL), Venezuela
Wim van Brakel, KIT (Royal Tropical Institute), The Netherlands
Peter Byrne, Newham University Hospital, London, UK
Andrew Byrnes, University of New South Wales, Australia
Terry Carney, University of Sydney, Australia
Patrick Corrigan, Chicago Consortium for Stigma Research, USA
Natalie Drew, World Health Organization, Switzerland
Saïda Douki, Faculty of Medicine of Tunis, Tunisia
Mary Forde, Amnesty International, Ireland
Melvyn Freeman, South Africa
Wolfgang Gaebel, Heinrich-Heine-University Düsseldorf, Germany
Brigitte Gafa, Ministry of Health, Elderly and Community Care, Malta
Dolores Gauci, Richmond Foundation, Malta
Klementina Gecaite, Global Initiative on Psychiatry, Lithuania
Helen Gilbert, Mental Health Commission, New Zealand
Semyon Gluzman, Ukrainian Psychiatric Association, Ukraine
DS Goel, India
Michelle Gold, Canadian Mental Health Association – Ontario, Canada
Mona Gupta, University of Toronto & Women's College Hospital, Canada
Fuad Ismayilov, Azerbaijan Medical University, Azerbaijan Psychiatric Association, Azerbaijan
Sarojini Kadurugamuwa, National Council for Mental Health in Sri Lanka, Sri Lanka
Anirudh K Kala, North India Psychiatry Centre, India
Elie G Karam, St George Hospital University Medical Center, Balamand University, Lebanon
Christel Kirkøen, The Norwegian Equality Tribunal, Norway
Valery Krasnov, Moscow School of Psychiatry, Moscow, Russia

Nanna Margrethe Krusaa, Institute for Human Rights, Denmark
Alisher Latypov, Global Initiative on Psychiatry, Tajikistan
Oliver Lewis, Mental Disability Advocacy Center (MDAC), Hungary
Ros Lyall, Mental Welfare Commission for Scotland, UK
Donald Lyons, Mental Welfare Commission for Scotland, UK
Mihalis Madianos, University of Athens, Greece
Nino Makhashvili, Global Initiative on Psychiatry, Tbilisi, Georgia
James M Mandiberg, Columbia University School of Social Work, USA
David Mason, Australian Human Rights Commission, Australia
Driss Moussaoui, Université Psychiatrique, Centre Ibn Rushd, Casablanca, Morocco
Nalaka Mendis, University of Colombo, Sri Lanka
Ahmed Okasha, Institute of Psychiatry, Ain Shams University, Egypt
Jorge Luis Pellegrini, Vice Gobernador, San Luis, Argentina
Geneviève Pinet, World Health Organization, Switzerland
Cristina Ricci, Australian Human Rights Commission, Australia
John Saunders, Schizophrenia Ireland, Ireland
Liz Sayce, RADAR, United Kingdom
Maria Sciriha, Ministry for the Family and Social Solidarity, Malta
Mustafa Sercan, Bakırköy State Hospital for Psychiatric and Neurological Diseases, Turkey
Sigrid Steffen, EUFAMI (European Federation of Associations of Families of People with Mental Illness), Austria
Vesna Švab, University Psychiatric Hospital, Slovenia
Aslak Syse, The Norwegian Equality Tribunal, University of Oslo, Norway
Ryoko Takahashi, Kanazawa University, Japan
Javier Vásquez, Pan American Health Organisation/World Health Organization, USA
Robert van Voren, Global Initiative on Psychiatry, The Netherlands
Raymond Xerri, Ministry of Health, Malta
Harald Zäske, Heinrich-Heine-University Düsseldorf, Germany

Glossary

This comprises explanations of terms and concepts that are used frequently within the text. As is made clear in various parts of the book, there is significant debate about the use and meaning of many of these terms. The glossary clarifies how these terms are used and understood in the context of the arguments and the material that is presented in this book.

It should be further noted that mental health programmes have a low priority in many countries. The reasons for this are many: they include the stigma related to mental health problems, the multitude of other health problems competing for attention and resources and the scarcity of qualified staff. Among the reasons for the low priority given to mental health is also the vagueness of terms that are commonly used in the field. The lack of clear and universally agreed definitions of terms makes it difficult to compare the laws and regulations relevant to mental health and to the protection and promotion of the rights of people with mental health problems. It also interferes with the formulation of policies that govern mental health care and the education of health personnel.

Advocacy: The act of speaking or interceding for and on behalf of people (in this book, for and on behalf of people with mental health problems). Advocacy activities aim to empower and allocate resources to people in need of them. Advocacy – whether peer, citizen, professional or legal – should respect and promote the legal capacity of the person being supported.

Article: A numbered section of a legal document such as a convention, treaty or declaration.

Capacity and competency: Capacity in medicine refers to the necessary physiological, mental and emotional integrity required to make decisions, and hence to be considered legally competent. Competency is a legal construct referring to a person having the necessary capacity to engage in legally defined acts, such as entering into contracts, being a witness, being prosecuted, or agreeing to medical interventions. In some countries, capacity rather than competency is the legal term used.

Carer: A relative, friend or partner who provides (or intends to provide, or used to provide) a substantial amount of care to another person on a regular basis. They do not necessarily live with that person. The term 'professional carer' denotes people providing care through professional or formal channels.

Civil and political rights: The classic 'liberal' rights of citizens to, for example, liberty and equality. They include freedom to think and express oneself, to vote, to take part in political life and to have access to information.

Convention: A legally binding agreement between states, usually developed within the context of an intergovernmental organisation (see definition below). Conventions create international law that is intended to be binding on states that sign and ratify them. They are not mere guidance as to best practice. Examples include the Convention on the Rights of Persons with Disabilities (which is a United Nations convention) (Chapter 14.1.1.1) and the European Convention on Human Rights and Fundamental Freedoms (which is a Council of Europe convention, better known as the European Convention on Human Rights) (Chapter 14.2.1.1.1).

Disability: Disability is a term that is subject to considerable academic and political debate. The UN Convention on the Rights of Persons with Disabilities states that 'Persons with disabilities include those who have long-term physical, mental, intellectual or sensory impairments which in interaction with various barriers may hinder their full and effective participation in society on an equal basis with others'. It further recognises 'that disability is an evolving concept and that disability results from the interaction between persons with impairments and attitudinal and environmental barriers that hinders their full and effective participation in society on an equal basis with others'.

Disabled people's organisation (DPO): A disabled people's organisation is an organisation that is managed by a management or executive committee on which disabled people hold the majority of its voting membership. They will normally, in practice, have an advocacy role for people with a disability. While that role is likely to be particularly important in the context of this book, it will not necessarily be the only (or indeed the prime) function of these organisations.

Disease, disorder and illness: In terms of nosology (the classification of diseases), a condition can be considered to be a disease when there is sufficient knowledge about the risk factors and causes, about its pathogenesis, its clinical appearance, its reaction to treatment and its natural history. In psychiatry there are no such conditions. The World Health Organization has therefore decided to use the term disorder, which it defines as 'the existence of a clinically recognisable set of symptoms or behaviour associated in most cases with distress and with interference with personal functions' (WHO, 1993). An important corollary follows this definition: social dysfunction, without clinically recognisable sets of symptoms, should not be considered as a mental disorder.

The term 'illness' is often used as well, usually to indicate the individual's feelings about his or her state of health. The overlap between illness and disease is often minimal. Distress and a feeling of ill health are often not accompanied by a disease – and diseases can exist without causing a feeling of ill health. 'Sickness' is usually employed in relation to society's recognition of a state of disease (e.g. in 'sickness benefits').

Entry into force: The process through which a treaty becomes fully binding on the states that have ratified it. This occurs when the minimum number of ratifications called for by the treaty has been achieved.

General Comment: The interpretation by the international body charged with the implementation of a treaty or convention (the 'treaty body') of the content of human rights provisions, on thematic issues or on its methods of work. Thus, for example, General Comments on the UN Convention on the Rights of Persons with Disabilities will be issued by the UN Committee on the Rights of Persons with Disability, the organisation created by the Convention to oversee its implementation.

Global North: The Global North refers to the countries that have 'high human development', as reported by the United Nations Development Programme Report 2005. Most, but not all, of these countries are located in the northern hemisphere.

Global South: The Global South refers to the countries of the rest of the world, most of which are located in the southern hemisphere. It includes both countries with 'medium human development' and 'low human development'. Most of the Global South is located in south and central America, Africa and Asia.

Health: There are three main definitions of health: (i) health as the absence of disease; (ii) health as a state of full functional capacity; and (iii) health as a state of balance between the individual and the society and environment in which he or she lives. Notably, the often quoted definition provided in the constitution of the World Health Organization is that: 'Health is a state of complete physical, mental and social wellbeing (sic) and not merely the absence of disease or infirmity' (WHO, 1948). This definition includes mental well-being as one of the components of health.

Human rights: The rights people are entitled to simply because they are human beings, irrespective of their citizenship, nationality, race, ethnicity, language, gender, sexuality, or abilities. Human rights become enforceable when they are codified as conventions, covenants or treaties, or as they become recognised as customary international law. Human rights are frequently divided into 'civil and political' rights, and 'social and economic' rights – see definitions elsewhere in this glossary.

Instrument: A formal, written, official document that has legal meaning, such as a treaty, declaration or statute. The most relevant instruments in the current context are those in which a state or group of states expresses an intention to uphold certain human rights principles or norms. An instrument may be legally binding or non-binding. It may be global, regional, or domestic, depending on the legal nature of the instrument in question.

Intellectual disability: A disability that follows a significant impairment of a person's ability to learn and use information. It is a disability that is present during childhood and continues throughout that person's life.

Intergovernmental organisations (IGOs): Organisations sponsored by several governments that seek to coordinate their efforts (e.g. the World Health Organization, the International Labour Organisation (ILO)). Usually, but not necessarily, these will be given a legal form by a convention or treaty.

Mental health: Mental health is a contested concept that has been defined in numerous ways by different groups and by different cultures. Broadly speaking, a deficit model defines mental health as an absence of diagnosable disease or disorder. A positive, holistic model of mental health conceives of mental health as a state of physical, social and mental well-being. In this latter sense, mental health implies that the individual is emotionally and psychologically flourishing (see also **Health**).

Mental illness: This term is commonly used to describe a number of diagnosable disorders that significantly interfere with an individual's cognitive, emotional or social abilities (e.g. schizophrenia, anorexia nervosa, depression). Traditionally, mentally ill people are people who have a diagnosed mental disorder. A more restrictive – and perhaps less stigmatising – definition could be that people are mentally ill if their ability to behave in a meaningful and acceptable way in a given social context, as well as their competence to decide and to act in a self-determined way, is impaired by a disease or disorder. Also, people without disturbances of behaviour and competence may have a diagnosable mental disorder (see also **Disease, disorder and illness).**

Mental health problem: The term 'mental health problem' can be used to refer to the full range of mental health issues, from common experiences such as 'feeling depressed' to more severe clinical symptoms such as those seen in bipolar disorder and enduring problems such as schizophrenia. 'Mental health problem' has been used to refer to 'mental disorders' – that is diagnosed and/or clinical levels of mental health problems. It is also used to signify an approach to mental distress that is not based on current psychiatric or medical models. It is a phrase commonly used by many people who have received psychiatric diagnoses to describe their experiences.

National Human Rights Institutions (NHRIs): National Human Rights Institutions are bodies that promote and protect human rights and are established by countries under their national legislation or under their constitutions. NHRIs are responsible for promoting and monitoring the effective implementation of international human rights standards at the national level. The United Nations Paris Principles, which are internationally recognised standards, have been adopted by the United Nations General Assembly and specify the requirements for independence of NHRIs as well as their mandate.

Non-governmental organisations (NGOs): Organisations comprising people and groups who are independent of government. They vary enormously in size and geographical scope.

Non-binding: A document, such as a declaration, that carries no formal legal obligations. It may, however, carry moral obligations or indicate accepted good practice. It can also be used to interpret binding international law, and thus be more 'binding' than would first appear. A non-binding document sometimes may attain a binding status by becoming customary international law.

Ratify: The process by which the legislative body of a state confirms a government's action in signing a treaty; a formal procedure by which a state becomes bound to a treaty after acceptance.

Reasonable accommodation: Necessary and appropriate modifications or adjustments to a practice, programme or physical environment so that it becomes accessible, appropriate and usable for a person with disabilities on an equal basis with others. Article 2 of the UN Convention on the Rights of Persons with Disabilities defines reasonable accommodation as the 'necessary and appropriate modification and adjustments not imposing a disproportionate or undue burden, where needed in a particular case, to ensure to persons with disabilities the enjoyment or exercise on an equal basis with others of all human rights and fundamental freedoms'.

Right to health: The right to health refers to the enjoyment of a variety of goods, facilities, services and conditions necessary for the realisation of health. As articulated in most conventions that refer to it, it is the right to the highest 'attainable' standard of physical and mental health and not the right to 'be healthy'. The right to health is specified in Article 12 of the International Covenant on Economic, Social and Cultural Rights (Chapter 14.1.1.6), Article 25 of the UN Convention on the Rights of Persons with Disabilities (Chapter 14.1.1.1) and in many other international instruments.

Service user: Someone who uses, or has used, health and/or social care services because of illness or disability.

Social model of disability: This model regards disability as the loss or limitation of opportunities for people with physical, sensory or mental impairments to take part in the ordinary life of the community on an equal level with others owing to physical, structural and social barriers (see also **Disability**).

Social and economic rights: These are rights that give people social and economic security (e.g. the right to shelter, the right to health).

State Party: A State Party to a treaty is a state that has expressed its consent to be bound by that treaty by an act of ratification, acceptance, approval or accession, and so on, where that treaty has entered into force for that particular state.

Glossary References

WHO (1948) Preamble to the Constitution of the World Health Organization as adopted by the International Health Conference, New York.

WHO (1993) *The ICD–10 Classification of Mental and Behavioural Disorders: Diagnostic criteria for research*. World Health Organization, Geneva, Switzerland.

CHAPTER 1

Introduction

1.1 Using the law in the fight for social justice

Legislative action is indispensable in the fight to combat the discrimination, abuse and social injustice experienced across the world by people with mental health problems.

This book is intended to assist and speed up legislative and policy reform. It presents a range of conceptual and empirical material which documents the role that legislative actions – whether applying internationally, regionally, at country level, or to devolved regions within countries – can play in combating the discrimination and abuse experienced by people with mental health problems. At the same time, we emphasise that such reform will effect changes 'on the ground' only if it is buttressed by enforcement mechanisms as well as societal and discursive shifts in how people with mental health problems are perceived and treated by other members of society.

The relationship between legislative action on the one hand and experiences of discrimination, abuse and social injustice on the other, is undoubtedly complex. It has been argued that 'legislation has a limited capacity to achieve social transformation' – but legislation does have significant 'symbolic and authoritative power, particularly when enforced and publicised through litigation' (Watchirs, 2005). The book therefore seeks to maximise the 'symbolic and authoritative power' of legislation, by further disseminating knowledge of how it can be used to effect change in the lives of people with mental health problems.

There have already been important strides taken in many countries, both in terms of overturning legislation that explicitly discriminates against people with mental health problems and in developing new legislation that better protects and promotes their rights.

There is also a powerful new impetus in the form of the United Nations Convention on the Rights of Persons with Disabilities (CRPD). This Convention, which was adopted on 13 December 2006 and entered into

Mental Illness, Discrimination and the Law: Fighting for Social Justice, First Edition.
Felicity Callard, Norman Sartorius, Julio Arboleda-Flórez, Peter Bartlett, Hanfried Helmchen, Heather Stuart, Jose Taborda and Graham Thornicroft.

force on 3 May 2008, is a human rights instrument with an explicit social development dimension. The CRPD lays out a robust framework for promoting, protecting and ensuring the human rights and fundamental freedoms of people 'who have long-term physical, mental, intellectual or sensory impairments which, in interaction with various barriers, may hinder their full and effective participation in society on an equal basis with others'. By October 2011, there were 153 signatories to the CPRD and it had 105 ratifications. The Convention is legally binding on every State Party that ratifies it, and commits States Parties: 'to take all appropriate measures, including legislation, to modify or abolish existing laws, regulations, customs and practices that constitute discrimination against persons with disabilities.'

The CRPD has been heralded as a step-change in conceptualising disability and addressing discrimination on the grounds of disability (Lawson, 2008; Arnardóttir and Quinn, 2009; Bartlett, 2009). It has been seen as a document that 'might indeed mark the dawning of a new era' (Lawson, 2007). It was written with, and by, people with physical and mental disabilities and its development was characterised by the most significant involvement of civil society of any of the United Nations conventions. Fundamentally, it recognises the capacity of people with disabilities – that is people with mental health problems, people with intellectual disabilities and people with physical disabilities – and places the onus on society in terms of facilitating their full participation. In other words, the CRPD shifts away from a model of disability that is framed around individual dysfunction and culpability to a model in which disability is an issue of human rights and non-discrimination. The CRPD opens up the possibility of real transformation in legislation and policy relating to mental health, and offers new ways in which we might all think about disability and about the ways in which our societies are organised.

The coming into force of the Convention on the Rights of Persons with Disabilities indicates how much there is still to be done at a country level: to transform or abolish existing laws; to draft new laws that adhere to the CRPD; and to implement legislation in ways that have visible and enduring ameliorative impacts on the lives of people with mental health problems.

This book's focus then, is on how legislation can be used to advance the rights and entitlements that people with mental health problems have as citizens. We hope it will contribute to the significant shift that the CRPD heralds in relation to how we conceptualise and address disability.

Many people still frequently assume that the intersection of mental health and law indicates the specific terrain of mental health legislation. This has exacerbated the tendency to regard those with mental health problems simply as patients, rather than as citizens entitled to the full complement of rights (Sayce, 2000; Yamin, 2005). Many people who work in mental health services are accustomed to seeing those for whom they care primarily as (and, in fact, sometimes only as) patients. This book refocuses their attention – indeed, the attention of all of us – in order to address how legislation can be used to advance the rights and entitlements of people with mental health problems in their roles as citizens and members of communities and families (Sayce, 2000; Dhanda and Narayan, 2007). There is much talk about legislation intended to 'protect' society from people with mental health problems, but little debate about law that is designed to protect people with experience of mental illness from the wrongs that can be inflicted by society.

In approaching such legislation, it is helpful to consider what law can and cannot do. Overarching statements of principle – for example, those favouring non-discrimination – are to be found in many of the statutes and conventions we include and refer to throughout the book. Such overarching statements may be beneficial, as they may re-enforce social norms: law has, as we have already stated, a symbolic value, and that should not be underrated. It is much too simplistic to suggest that changing laws changes attitudes, however, and the overarching principles are likely to be difficult or impossible to enforce without much more specific, implementing legislation. Indeed, professions of 'formal equality' within statutes can act as a smokescreen if statutes are not backed up by significant efforts to ensure that laws are translated into real experiences of equality. 'Formal equality alone,' it has been argued, can end up simply 'giv[ing] an illusion that all are equal and that fairness exists, without addressing underlying inequalities in power, access, and socioeconomic and political circumstances' (Burns, 2010; see also Sayce, 2003). There is much still to be to be done conceptually – as well as in practice – to determine and to demonstrate how legislation can contribute to the diminution of social inequalities.

In the realm of enforcement, law is better at governing actions than ideas. It is difficult, for example, for the law to make people believe that people with mental health problems are fully-fledged citizens, but it is possible for the law to prohibit those people from harassing and abusing people with mental health problems, or from denying jobs to people with those problems when they are otherwise qualified to be hired. Law can similarly establish complaints mechanisms so that people with mental health problems who feel their rights have been violated can take concrete action for redress. And law can impose duties upon sectors and organisations to have due regard to the need to promote equality of opportunity and eliminate discrimination and harassment: this has the virtue of shifting emphasis away from the individual who has been wronged and placing the onus and responsibility on the body in terms of its facilitation of equality of opportunity.

But creating societies in which people with mental health problems can live their lives free from discrimination and abuse is not simply a matter for law: a non-discriminatory environment must become part of the lived experience of everyone in society – and that is a much bigger task than passing a statute. That is acutely clear in countries in which legislative frameworks are without significant power or authority. There is also a growing body of research from both low- and high-income countries that demonstrates the pernicious effects that can result from the close ties between poverty, disability and social exclusion. This research makes it clear that any use of legislation will need to dovetail with sustained social, structural and political action to address social and health inequalities, as well as social, political and economic marginalisation. To that end, we have included, where appropriate, sources detailing programmes for enhancing non-discriminatory environments that are not essentially legal in structure. Political and legal advocacy both by and on behalf of people with mental health problems is also an essential part of the required social change, and sources that provide advice on these matters are similarly referenced where appropriate. That said, we believe that legal change is one crucial part of this broader process and it is with the specifically legal aspects of reform that the book is concerned.

The book is titled *Mental illness, discrimination and the law: fighting for social justice*. We regard the nexus of discrimination, the law and mental illness as critical both in understanding why social injustice persists, and in mobilising for social justice. Social justice is, of course, based on the premise of the upholding of human rights and on equality of opportunity, but it also demands that individuals and groups within society have equal access to – and equal means of being able to enjoy – both the material and the psychosocial 'goods' that circulate within society (Harvey, 1975). Amartya Sen has argued in his recent work on justice that in judging the advantages and disadvantages that different people have in relation to one another, 'we have to look at the overall capabilities they manage to enjoy' (Sen, 2009). (Sen means by 'capabilities' the substantive freedoms that people have reason to value [e.g. to participate in community life, to appear in public without shame] – rather than income or financial assets.) For many social, economic, and cultural – as well as legal – reasons, people with mental health problems are often restricted in the capabilities they are able to enjoy. There is, additionally, increasing evidence of the unequal distribution of mental health problems within societies – and of its complex relationship with a range of indicators of material and psychosocial deprivation (Kelly, 2005, 2006; Melzer et al., 2004; Sheppard, 2002; WHO, 2010; Wilkinson, 2005; Wilkinson and Pickett, 2010). Improving the lives of people with mental health problems fundamentally demands pursuing social and structural – rather than individualised – solutions. A recent publication from the World Health Organization (European Region) has argued that: 'A focus on social justice may provide an important corrective to what has been seen as a growing overemphasis on individual pathology. Mental health is produced socially: the presence or absence of mental health is above all a social indicator and therefore requires social, as well as individual solutions. A focus on collective efficacy, as well as personal efficacy is required' (Friedli, 2009).

We regard legislation as part of a diverse palette of 'social solutions' that can and should be used to combat the unequal distribution of poor mental health within and across societies. Legislation has contributed substantially to the undermining of people's mental health – by removing people's rights, denying their capacity, and preventing them from participating in society. But the flourishing of disability rights legislation in a number of countries across the globe over the last quarter century indicates the impact that legislation can have in improving people's lives, as well as in enhancing community as well as individual self-efficacy (Lawson and Gooding, 2005; Quinn and Waddington, 2009; Waddington and Quinn, 2010). Indeed, the adoption of new legislation has often come after long and hard-fought advocacy by disabled people's organisations (DPOs) (as well as by the organisations that work alongside and in partnership with them). We draw attention to the fact that the quotation above from the World Health Organization speaks of the need for a focus on collective, as well as personal efficacy. While in lay parlance, engagement with the law is frequently imagined as a realm in which it is individuals who are centre stage – as plaintiffs, defendants, and attorneys – we want to draw attention to how engagement with the law can build and enhance collective knowledge and solidarity. In other words, the more that people with mental health problems – as well as those organisations and stakeholders who work with and alongside them – become aware of their rights and understand the potential within legislation for positive change, the greater the possibility that they will be able collectively to use the law in advocating more broadly for social justice in relation to mental health.

1.2 Whom are we addressing?

Challenging the discrimination and abuse experienced by people with mental health problems ought not be seen as the responsibility of those who are most directly affected by such discrimination and abuse. It is, rather, the responsibility of us all. The potential readership for this book is therefore diverse and wide-ranging. We have endeavoured to minimise the amount of specialised language and terms (whether from the fields of law, disability studies or mental health) to ensure that readers with little previous knowledge of the topics under consideration are able to map a clear path through the book. However, to assist clarity, a glossary of terms we use most regularly has been included in the Preliminary section of the book. We hope that the content of the book will be of interest to those with previous knowledge of and expertise in these issues as well as those new to them. We consider some of the key audiences to include:

- advocacy organisations and civil society organisations;
- clinicians dealing with mental disorders, allied health professionals and other health care staff;
- people with mental health problems – including people who use or have used mental health services, as well as people who have experienced mental health problems in the past;
- the families and friends of people with mental health problems;
- mental health service user organisations and disabled people's organisations (DPOs);
- legislators, parliamentarians and people working within government;
- people working in sectors (such as employment, housing, education and public health) that have a significant influence on the everyday lives of people with mental health problems;
- representatives of the media.

It is our intention that readers of this book will:

- become better acquainted with the range of issues and domains over which legislation has influence in relation to the lives of people with mental health problems;
- understand the shift from viewing mental illness and disability only through an individualised, medical lens, to addressing them as matters of human rights and social justice;
- become better acquainted with the international and regional instruments (conventions, recommendations, guidelines etc.) of use in protecting and promoting the human rights of people with mental health problems;
- achieve greater familiarity with legislative frameworks and conceptual innovations that have been pursued in other countries to address the discrimination, abuse and social injustice experienced by people with mental health problems;
- find inspiration from some of the approaches taken in other countries and sectors in order to consider how they might be used in readers' own countries and sectors.

We hope, indeed, that the book can be used in a number of contexts. These include:

- advocacy in a policy and/or legal context;

- the development of programmes to address discrimination against people with mental health problems at a variety of levels of action;
- the development of legislative and administrative frameworks to address the discrimination, abuse and social injustice experienced by people with disabilities;
- dissemination of the power that legislation can and does have in shaping the lives of those affected by mental health problems.

1.3 The history of this book

The Association for the Improvement of Mental Health Programmes (AIMHP) works to improve and promote mental health programmes worldwide. Its activities include support of academic studies and other theoretical and practical work that can contribute to improving treatment and quality of life of people with mental illness and of their families and raise the value given to mental health by individuals and societies (http://aim-mental-health.org).

In 2006, the AIMHP commissioned a review of legislative actions of use – or potential use – in protecting people with mental health problems from abuse and discrimination. This book is the culmination of that review.

The developmental phase of this book traced a sinuous course. This is indicative of the challenges that are posed by working within this field. These include:

- the relative rapidity with which the legislative environment can sometimes shift (at the moment of this project's conception, for example, the UN Convention on the Rights of Persons with Disabilities had not yet been adopted);
- the difficulties of ascertaining – given limited resources and personnel – the specifics of legislative environments in particular countries;
- the complexities of bringing together different kinds of expertise and conceptual frameworks when interpreting and ordering the material.

The phases of the project are briefly summarised below, so as to allow readers to have a clearer sense of how and why the book came to fruition in its present form.

1.3.1 Initial review of legislation

The review that was commissioned by the AIMHP aimed to:

- identify and analyse international and country-specific legislative actions that might be held up as successful examples of legislation that combats discrimination and/or abuse on the grounds of actual or perceived mental health problems;
- identify the key principles and characteristics that underlie these successful legislative actions.

The scope and objectives of the review were refined in light of other recently completed and ongoing projects on the use of legislation and policy to improve the lives of people with mental health problems (e.g. the mental health and legislation projects of the World Health Organization (Chapter 16.2).

The review sought to identify a linguistically and geographically diverse selection of current country-based legislation that could act as exemplars or possible models for the combating of discrimination experienced by people with mental health problems. Specifically, the review:

- endeavoured to represent all regions of the world;
- focused on legislative actions that advanced the rights and entitlements of people with mental health problems within civil society (i.e. focused neither on legislation addressing mental health settings, whether in the community or closed, nor on coercive measures);
- acknowledged that the complex categories of 'mental health problems' and/or 'mental disorders' are interpreted differently in different parts of the world and by different audiences. Nonetheless, the AIMHP specified that the review should, in determining the scope of relevant legislation, use the category of mental disorders as defined by the International Classification of Diseases (10th edition) (WHO, 1993) to define its area of interest;
- contextualised country-based legislation in light of existing international law, covenants, guidelines and recommendations that pertain to the protection of those with mental health problems and of those with disabilities from discrimination and abuse.

1.3.2 Contributions from key informants

In order to refine the scope and focus of the review, the lead author interviewed a select number of experts to discuss some of the current pressing issues associated with the use of legislative and administrative actions to combat the abuse and discrimination experienced by people with mental health problems. These experts were interviewed in person or by telephone. Key themes and lines of inquiry were distilled from those interviews to help structure the next phase of research, namely contact with a larger number of experts and country informants.

The lead author approached this larger group of key informants via email and/or telephone and asked them to respond to several short questions about legislative actions within their country or region of expertise. The material gathered from these responses did not necessarily represent the full range of relevant legislative/administrative actions available in any particular country. Informants often chose to focus on one or two legislative actions or mechanisms when identifying relevant or interesting material.

Experts and informants included:

- non-governmental organisations (NGOs) with a focus on legislative and/or policy reform and advocacy to protect and promote the rights of people with mental health problems; these included service-user led, family/carer-led and clinician-led organisations;
- researchers and academics with expertise in legislative approaches to combating discrimination and abuse experienced by people with mental health problems (and by people with disabilities more broadly);
- governmental and intergovernmental organisations concerned with protecting and promoting the rights of people with mental health problems (and of people with disabilities more broadly);
- independent regulators and monitors of health and social care services;
- psychiatrists and other mental health professionals with a strong interest and/or involvement in legislative and/or policy reform in their country.

The sampling of countries on which to focus initially was purposive to ensure that material was acquired from countries with a range of legal traditions and social, political and economic environments. Contacts were initially made via experts known to the AIMHP. Subsequent to this, snowball sampling was also used: the lead author followed up references, organisations and names of additional experts mentioned by existing contacts and generated additional material. She concurrently identified, acquired and analysed relevant legal and policy material, as well as literature from the field of mental health and disability studies, to complement and add depth to country-based submissions. This material comprised both published and grey literature (i.e. materials such as working papers and reports from government agencies that cannot be found easily through conventional channels such as publications).

The lead author also collated international and regional instruments (conventions, recommendations, guidelines etc.) of use in protecting and promoting the rights and entitlements of people with mental health problems (Chapter 14). She critically assessed and assembled the various material gathered in the course of the review into a composite document that contained conceptual arguments as well as a wealth of country-based material. This document was submitted to the AIMHP in July 2008.

1.3.3 Transformation into a book

A small group of experts (several of whom had been interviewed at the start of the review) gathered to assess the review and consider how it might best be transformed into a book. This group – the co-authors of the book – convened in person twice, once in the summer of 2009 and again in 2010, to discuss the scope, content and structure of the book and to draft some additional material.

What became clear at this stage was: (a) the difficulty of identifying examples of 'good practice' from the material that had been submitted (many of the informants had lamented the inadequacies and weaknesses of the legal frameworks they had described); and (b) the overemphasis on mental health law in many of the submissions.

At that point, it was decided to reaffirm the commitment made in the initial AIMHP review to focus on legislation that pertains to people with mental health problems in their role as citizens and not to focus on mental health laws. This decision was also made in light of the extensive guidance that the World Health Organization has been developing in relation to the reform of mental health law.

It was also decided that it would be invidious for the book to pick out examples of 'poor' legislation that had been submitted by our informants. We determined, instead, to contextualise the case examples that we did wish to use through setting them within chapters that addressed some of the domains (e.g. housing, civil and political participation) that are front and foremost when one considers the impact that legislation can have on people's everyday lives.

The adoption – and subsequent coming into force – of the UN Convention on the Rights of Persons with Disabilities (CRPD) during the course of the book's development gave added authority to its central purpose. The CRPD also provided a strong framework with which to address one of the aims of the initial review – namely, to identify the key principles of legislation that protects people with mental health problems from discrimination.

The CRPD can be regarded as a distillation of much of the progressive thinking that has been taking place internationally over a number of years vis-à-vis how we might best promote, protect and ensure the rights and fundamental freedoms of people with disabilities. The CRPD, therefore, should be regarded as the font of many of the key principles and concepts that are used within the book in the context of combating the discrimination experienced by many people with mental health problems in diverse legislative contexts – recognising however that mental health problems are not always linked to disability.

The book that has emerged out of the initial review for the AIMHP is characterised by a number of features. The initial review did not survey comprehensively and systematically existing legislation on an international scale, but rather sought to identify a linguistically and geographically diverse selection of current country-based legislative and administrative actions that might act as possible models or 'tools for thinking'. The book therefore provides a snapshot of some of the models and frameworks in use in the early part of the twenty-first century to address discrimination and rights violations against those with mental health problems. The examples that are mentioned draw on a variety of mechanisms and are embedded within diverse legal frameworks. We do not advocate a particular legal framework, and we of course acknowledge that specific legislative or administrative actions will need to bear in mind the political, economic, cultural – as well as, of course, legal – contexts into which they will be inserted. While sustained attempts were made to include examples from all regions of the world in the review, there are regions that are not represented in the book. This was both because of difficulty in acquiring material from certain regions and because informants in some countries provided material about which it was impossible – either for them, or for us – to feel optimistic.

Many of the examples that were submitted offered weak protection and promotion of the human rights of people with mental health problems, which meant that we were unable to use them. We are sorry, therefore, that we have not been able to represent all of the countries from which we received submissions. We would also stress that if a country is not represented in the book, this does not mean that it does not have examples of legislative and administrative action that would be worthy of inclusion.

Our selection of case studies is intended to be indicative of what is taking place internationally, rather than the result of a strict sampling frame. We were necessarily constricted by the limited number of countries that we could tap in the time and with the resources that we had. The book over-represents high-income countries (and, in particular, English-speaking countries within the Global North). This is for a number of reasons – one of which is the indisputable fact that certain countries that fall within this category (e.g. New Zealand and Scotland) have been at the forefront of developing robust legislative and administrative frameworks to address the discrimination, inequalities and abuse experienced by people with mental health problems. We have endeavoured as much as we can to include examples from middle- and low-income countries, and from countries outside of western Europe and north America.

The book does not provide readers with details about how to draft law. Nor does it provide substantive discussion of the complexities of legal judgments and of current disability law and of the philosophical debates within the field of disability studies. (Readers should turn for those to a growing number of excellent resources by disability law scholars and practitioners [e.g. see Quinn and Waddington, 2009; Waddington and Quinn, 2010 in relation to Europe].) Rather, it is intended to build the constituency of people and organisations for whom legislative reform and transformation is central in any attempt to address the discrimination, abuse and injustice experienced by people with mental health problems. The route it takes to build that constituency is one of demonstrating what is possible – through the use of brief country-based vignettes and case studies – in contexts that range significantly in their financial resources, their legal traditions and their social, cultural and economic specificities.

Material for the initial review was gathered over two years (June 2006–June 2008). Significant efforts have been made to check and, where necessary, update all material that was chosen from the initial review for inclusion within the book; we cannot guarantee that that has been possible in all cases. In addition, because the book has relied on submissions (many of which comprised translated material) from country-based informants and has made use of a range of literature (published and grey literature, as well as material available on and via the internet), we cannot directly vouch for the accuracy of all the material that is presented here.

The review largely focused on the specifics of legislation itself, rather than on how legislation has or has not been implemented. Country informants were asked to indicate what they considered to be the strengths and weaknesses of the legislation that they had identified. The majority of them specifically raised, unprompted, problems of implementation when addressing this question. This is cause for concern: legislation without implementation makes no change to people on the ground, and it would be naïve to think that this is not the fate of a number of the examples provided in this book. Nonetheless, implementation requires good legislative frameworks – and that is what we have focused on here.

1.4 How the book has been organised

In Chapter 2 (Principles and Concepts), we address key themes that clarify the context, constraints and opportunities characterising attempts to use legislation to improve the lives of people with mental health problems.

We present a brief history of the legislative frameworks that have shaped the lives of people who have been judged to be mentally ill; explain the distance between most mental health legislation and rights-based disability legislation; discuss the various ways in which discrimination has been conceptualised; comment on the use of general versus specific law; emphasise the indispensability of enforcement mechanisms; introduce the concepts of capacity and competence; provide a brief introduction to human rights; reflect on the relationship between the stigma, discrimination and 'structural violence' experienced by people with mental health problems; and clarify our central focus on social justice.

Chapters 3 to 11 cover a wide terrain. They consider some of the most important spheres in which legislation ought to be and is being used to combat discrimination and social injustice. Chapters focus on civil and political participation; private law and legal capacity; work and the workplace; education; housing; social security and social protection; and health, health care and the right to health. In addition, we consider protections against abuse in research that involves people with mental health problems. In Chapter 11 (Promotion of Mental Health and Prevention of Mental Illness), we discuss legislative and administrative efforts that are devoted to improving the mental health of all citizens, as well as to improving the lives of people with mental health problems specifically.

Chapter 12 (Implementation and Enforcement) discusses the range of tools and mechanisms to be considered when implementing and enforcing legislative transformations.

Chapter 13 (Summary and Conclusions) distils from the conceptual and empirical material presented elsewhere and summarises the journey that the book has taken. We hope that the arguments in this chapter will be in readers' minds when they turn to the question of how best to develop, transform and use legislation to address the discrimination, abuse and social injustice experienced by many people with mental health problems in their own country or region.

Chapter 14 comprises summaries – and, in certain cases, the full texts – of important instruments, standards and guidelines of relevance in combating the discrimination, abuse and social injustices experienced by people with mental health problems. We include binding United Nations treaties; non-binding international instruments; regional human rights systems, treaties, conventions, charters and standards; and non-binding standards, guidelines and declarations.

Chapter 15 lists examples of disability legislation from across the world and Chapter 16 (Organisations and Resources) points readers to relevant legislation libraries and databases and to literature and resources produced by the World Health Organization. It also includes a list (including addresses and relevant resources) of relevant and prominent intergovernmental organisations and non-governmental organisations (NGOs) that are working to protect and promote the rights of persons with mental health problems.

Readers can choose to make their way through the book from start to finish, or can pick out particular chapters and read them in the order they themselves decide. We do recommend, however, that readers unfamiliar with this literature gain a thorough grounding in the overarching principles and concepts by starting with Chapter 2, Principles and Concepts. All readers will find it useful to move to and fro between Chapters 2 to 13 and the material in Chapters 14, 15 and 16, since we refer episodically in the earlier chapters to instruments, standards and guidelines about which we provide more detailed information in these later chapters.

We have included relevant website addresses and these were checked for accuracy as the book was going to press.

1.5 Terms used to describe mental health problems

Existing international and country-based legislation and policy use a wide variety of terms when outlining procedures and frameworks that relate to people with mental health problems. People with long-term mental health problems are one of the groups comprising 'persons with disabilities' within the UN Convention on the Rights of Persons with Disabilities (CRPD) and the phrase 'persons with disabilities' is undoubtedly gaining political and discursive traction in a number of spheres and contexts to describe people with mental health problems.

Nonetheless, the international terrain is still characterised by heterogeneous terminologies and categories influenced by history, culture, legislative frameworks, social norms, organisational decisions, domains of expertise and so on. You will therefore find that the material that appears in this book uses an array of terms to describe mental ill health. In much of our main text, we have tended to use the phrase 'mental health problems', since this phrase is commonly accepted by many people who have received a psychiatric diagnosis and/or who have experienced mental distress. The term 'mental disability' includes people with intellectual disabilities (what used to be called 'mental retardation') as well as those with mental health problems and this term features substantially in legal literature. Many people within the disability rights movement prefer the term 'psychosocial disability' (rather than 'mental health problems') because it moves away from the medical model of disability and instead emphasises the interaction between psychological and social components of disability. The term adheres to the social model of disability (Chapter 2.6), through emphasising that a medical diagnosis becomes a disability when the individual experiences discrimination on account of that diagnosis. The term 'mental illness' is used in the title of the book and in some of its sections. 'Mental illness' – as well as the term 'mental disorder' – is commonly used by mental health clinicians, in health contexts and in many countries' policy documents.

The wide array of terms – many now considered stigmatising – that are used in case material and resources that were surveyed for inclusion within the book include:

- criminally insane (individuals)
- disabled person/disability/persons with disabilities
- handicap(ped) (person/people)
- intellectual(ly) disabled/disability
- learning disabled/disability

- mental(ly) disabled/disability
- mental disease
- mental(ly) disorder(ed)
- mental health consumer
- mental health issue/problem
- mental health service user/consumer/survivor
- mental ill health
- mental illness
- mental impairment/mentally impaired
- mental incapacity/mentally incapacitated
- mental patient
- mentally disordered offender
- mentally retarded
- mentally ill (person)/the mentally ill
- person(s) with disabilities
- psychiatric disability/psychiatrically disabled
- psychiatric disorder
- psychiatric illness
- psychiatric patient
- psychosocial disability

People who have received psychiatric diagnoses, and/or people have been categorised as disabled, have powerfully argued and demonstrated that both the specific terms used, as well as the concepts underlying those terms, have a profound effect on society's attitudes towards people with mental health problems and disabilities (Sweeney et al., 2009; Beresford, 2005; Oliver, 1996). Indeed there is a long history of people who have been described and categorised through the use of disparaging, paternalistic and/or stigmatising language working to transform the terms of political and societal debate. We emphasise that we do not – for the reasons just described – list the terms above in order to recommend any of them for use. We do so to alert readers to how they might, when doing further research of their own, need to expand the terms they use when searching for potentially relevant material.

It is also important to point out that the manner in which legislation defines both mental health problems and disability can have significant consequences for those who then fall under, or are categorised through, that legislation. For example, legislation can compound discrimination if, when establishing the criteria for involuntary psychiatric admission, the thresholds are set too low. In this respect, the World Health Organization has emphasised that: '[L]egislation that is primarily concerned with involuntary admission and treatment may restrict the category to only severe mental disorders. On the other hand, legislation concerned with positive rights may define mental disorder as broadly as possible to extend the benefits of legislation to all persons with mental disorders (WHO, 2005).

It should also be remembered that many mental health problems are intermittent and episodic. This implies that care should be taken when defining disability as 'long term', since this might unwittingly exclude some people with mental health problems from the protections one is wishing to provide through legislation (Lawson, 2008). Legislative efforts to counter discrimination on grounds of disability have thus far – and for a number of complex reasons – arguably been more effective in addressing the discrimination and exclusion of persons with physical impairments than those with mental health problems and intellectual disabilities. One contributing factor to this disparity may well be the way in which physical and mental impairments and resulting disabilities are defined and described.

We wish to point out that the primary focus within the book is on people with mental health problems. Legislation that is relevant will often encompass 'people with mental disabilities' – that is will include people with intellectual disabilities as well as people with mental health problems. The term intellectual disability is used increasingly often to avoid the term 'mental retardation' which has been found unacceptable by NGOs and individuals concerned and those working in this field. At particular moments in the book, therefore, you will find material that specifically refers to people with intellectual disabilities (e.g. Chapter 5.2: Intellectual disabilities and labour force participation). Please note, however, that our book does not claim to cover all legislative issues that are relevant to people with intellectual disabilities; these are covered elsewhere (Dimopoulos, 2010; Herr *et al.*, 2003).

1.6 Our authorial voice(s)

The book has been written by a number of authors who are differently located within the complex terrain of mental health and human rights. The authors' expertise includes mental health law, psychiatry, sociology, stigma and discrimination, service user research, epidemiology and socio-legal studies. There were, unsurprisingly, differences in terms of how authors approached the conceptual, legal, practical and political issues addressed by the book, and lively discussions and differences of opinion in the course of drafting some of the content. (Any of you who have participated in forums that bring together lawyers, psychiatrists, mental health service users, disability rights experts and sociologists, for example, will be familiar with the inevitable terminological tussles that characterise them!) The domain of mental health is undoubtedly a political and politicised one, not least because there is substantive and ongoing debate over the meaning, boundaries and very coherence of the central concepts – 'mental health', 'mental disorder', 'mental illness' – themselves (Bolton, 2008).

Different authors took overall responsibility for the development of and content within different parts of the manuscript, with the help of informants from a number of countries around the world (given in the Acknowledgements in the Preliminary section of the book). We have tried to ensure that the book that has emerged coheres in terms of its substance, register and rhetoric. Nonetheless, the book bears the imprint of the many discussions and viewpoints that contributed to its development, and careful readers will be able to find traces of more than one discourse concerning mental health and mental illness as the book progresses.

References

Arnardóttir, OM and Quinn, G (eds) (2009) *The United Nations Convention on the Rights of Persons with Disabilities: European and Scandinavian perspectives*. Martin Nijhoff, Leiden, The Netherlands.

Bartlett, P (2009) The United Nations Convention on the Rights of Persons with Disabilities and the future of mental health law. *Psychiatry*, **8**(12):496–498.

Beresford, P (2005) 'Service user': regressive or liberatory terminology? *Disability & Society*, **20**:469–477.

Bolton, D (2008) *What is Mental Disorder? An Essay in Philosophy, Science, and Values*. Oxford University Press, Oxford.

Burns, JK (2010) Mental health and inequity: a human rights approach to inequality, discrimination, and mental disability. *Health and Human Rights*, **11**(2):19–31.

Dhanda A and Narayan, T (2007) Mental health and human rights. *Lancet*, **370**:1197–1198.

Dimopoulos, A (2010) *Issues in Human Rights Protection of Intellectually Disabled Persons*. Ashgate, Farnham, UK.

Friedli, L (2009) *Mental Health, Resilience and Inequalities*. Mental Health Foundation/World Health Organization, Geneva, Switzerland 2009.

Harvey, D (1975) *Social Justice and the City*. Edward Arnold, London.

Herr, SS, Gostin, LO and Koh, HH (eds) (2003) *The Human Rights of Persons with Intellectual Disabilities*. Oxford University Press, Oxford.

Kelly, BD (2005) Structural violence and schizophrenia. *Social Science & Medicine*, **61**:721–730.

Kelly, BD (2006) The power gap: freedom, power and mental illness. *Social Science & Medicine*, **63**:2118–2128.

Lawson, A (2007) The United Nations Convention on the Rights of Persons with Disabilities: new era or false dawn? *Syracuse Journal of International Law and Commerce*, **34**(2):563–619.

Lawson, A (2008). People with psychosocial impairments or conditions, reasonable accommodation and the Convention on the Rights of Persons with Disabilities. *Law in Context*, **26**:62–84.

Lawson, A and Gooding, C (eds) (2005) *Disability Rights in Europe: From theory to practice*. Hart, Portland, OR.

Melzer, D, Fryers, T and Jenkins, R (2004) *Social Inequalities and the Distribution of Common Mental Disorders*. Psychology Press, Hove, UK.

Oliver, M (1996) *Understanding Disability: From Theory to Practice*. St Martin's, New York.

Quinn, G and Waddington, L (eds) (2009) *European Yearbook of Disability Law*, volume **1**. Intersentia, Antwerp and Oxford.

Sayce, L (2000) *From Psychiatric Patient to Citizen: Overcoming Discrimination and Social Exclusion*. Palgrave, Basingstoke and New York.

Sayce, L (2003) Beyond good intentions. Making anti-discrimination strategies work. *Disability & Society*, **18**(5):625–642.

Sen, A (2009) *The Idea of Justice*. Allen Lane, London.

Sheppard, M (2002) Mental health and social justice: gender, race and psychological consequences of unfairness. *British Journal of Social Work*, **32**:779–797.

Sweeney, A, Beresford, P, Faulkner, A, Nettle, M and Rose, D (eds) (2009) *This is Survivor Research*. PCCS Books, Ross-on-Wye, UK.

Waddington, L and Quinn, G (eds) (2010) *European Yearbook of Disability Law*, volume **2**. Intersentia, Antwerp and Oxford.

Watchirs, H (2005) Human rights audit of mental health legislation–results of an Australian pilot. *International Journal of Law and Psychiatry*, **28**:99–125.

WHO (1993) *The ICD–10 Classification of Mental and Behavioural Disorders: Diagnostic criteria for research*. World Health Organization, Geneva, Switzerland.

WHO (2005) *WHO Resource Book on Mental Health, Human Rights and Legislation*. World Health Organization, Geneva, Switzerland.

WHO (2010) *Mental Health and Development: Targeting people with mental health conditions as a vulnerable group*. World Health Organization, Geneva, Switzerland.

Wilkinson, R (2005) *The Impact of Inequality: How to Make Sick Societies Healthier*. Routledge, London.

Wilkinson, R and Pickett, K (2010) *The Spirit Level: Why Equality is Better for Everyone*. Penguin, London.

Yamin, AE and Rosenthal E (2005) Out of the shadows: using human rights approaches to secure dignity and well-being for people with mental disabilities. *PLoS Medicine*, **2**(4):e71.

CHAPTER 2

Principles and Concepts

The topics that this book addresses, and the terms that it uses to do so, can seem complex, difficult and perhaps confusing – especially to those not familiar with them. The complexity is in part due to the fact that a term might be used differently by groups with different kinds of expertise, and/or by people in different countries and contexts. We therefore devote some space in this chapter to clarifying some of the ways in which we shall be using the terms and concepts that lie at the heart of the book: disability, mental capacity, and discrimination.

The law was historically (and indeed on many occasions still is) used in the service of 'protecting' society from individuals deemed to pose a danger because of their mental illness or disorder, rather than used to protect and promote those individuals' human rights. Many training schemes for mental health professionals also place a significant focus on the issue of 'public safety' and 'risk' and do not devote adequate attention to promoting the human rights of people with mental health problems. It is therefore crucial to document the shift – which is hard won, and still unevenly implemented – towards using legislation to further the rights of people with mental health problems (Perlin and Szeli, in press).

The foundations of this book are the key precepts and frameworks that characterise current legislative and administrative approaches to combating discrimination and abuse experienced by people with mental health problems. We aim to provide a schematic, short and accessible account of these precepts and frameworks; to do so, we combine conceptual reflection with brief vignettes that we have taken from particular legislative contexts. We also point readers to key texts and other resources, both through the use of bibliographic citations and through indicating, where relevant, internet resources.

Mental Illness, Discrimination and the Law: Fighting for Social Justice, First Edition.
Felicity Callard, Norman Sartorius, Julio Arboleda-Flórez, Peter Bartlett, Hanfried Helmchen, Heather Stuart, Jose Taborda and Graham Thornicroft.

2.1 The tension between advancing the rights of people with mental health problems and attitudes in society

The balanced relationship between the individual and his or her social context is at risk in the case of mental illness. Mental illness may impair the capacity of individuals to live their lives in accordance with their intentions, objectives, wishes, needs and expectations. It may reduce their ability to use the social context to its optimal advantage and to adequately tackle its constraints. Social context will also affect an individual's mental health if it exceeds his or her capacity to cope with the multitude of stresses resulting from insults (e.g. bullying, harassment, stigmatisation), broken relationships, unsuitable company (e.g. friends who abuse drugs), overwork (e.g. 'workaholism'), social insecurity (unemployment, homelessness, poverty), war, persecution and many other social events. Such social events may influence the causes, the development, the manifestation and the course or outcome of mental illness (whether it remits, recurs, relapses or becomes chronic).

At least as important for the fate of people with mental illness are attitudes prevailing in a society – such as prejudice or negative stereotypes – which lead to exclusion, discrimination and stigmatisation, and which often make it impossible for people to rejoin or fully participate in society (Thornicroft, 2006; Link and Phelan; 2001; Sayce and Curran, 2007). The conviction that mental illness is untreatable can lead to the belief that people affected by mental illness are no longer of any value to society and – at its most extreme – that they should therefore be eliminated.

A rough indication of the attitudes that societies have towards people with mental illness may be found in the considerable differences in the nature of psychiatric care among European countries that recent studies have uncovered (Becker and Kilian; 2006; De Girolamo *et al.*, 2006). These differences are related to:

- the provision of mental health services;
- their appropriateness to meet the needs of people with mental illness;
- their use;
- the outcome for individuals.

Notwithstanding the methodological difficulties of these studies, these differences are likely to be related to cultural attitudes towards people with mental illnesses, as well as the priority that governments give to the development of mental health care.

Governments do not provide adequate resources for psychiatric care and they provide less for services for people with mental illnesses than for people with physical illnesses. This is a clear transgression against the principle of distributive justice (i.e. the socially just allocation of goods within a society) and a demonstration of discriminatory tendencies affecting the principle of solidarity (i.e. the union of interests or sympathies among members of a group or society).

People with mental illness often do not receive the care and social services they need for another reason: they often do not use services that are available. This is also a transgression against distributive justice, but by virtue of different mechanisms. Sometimes, those charged with directing people to services will not recognise the presence of mental ill health in the individual. Referrals, therefore, do not occur to relevant programmes. Furthermore, people often do not seek psychiatric care when it is available, because they are ashamed to do so in a society that stigmatises mental illnesses and people who suffer from them. They are also often unwilling and/or afraid to use the services because the services are often inadequate and patients' rights are not necessarily protected. In other words, mental health patients will at times find the competence, attitudes and behaviour of mental health service personnel insufficient (which is in part a remote effect of the negative selection of personnel entering psychiatry, which is itself a stigmatised discipline) (Schulze, 2005). Significant differences in rates of detaining people with mental illness compulsorily in mental hospitals (Commander *et al.*, 2003) suggest that psychiatrists are differentiated in their attitudes and habits towards people with mental illness. This is particularly so in the way in which psychiatrists judge the dignity and autonomy of the person with mental illness in relation to the safety of him/herself as well as to the safety of the community.

A long time will be needed to adequately inform, educate and enlighten all members of society in order to change the negative attitudes that contribute to the discrimination of people with mental illness. This is the responsibility of everyone in society, but those working in mental health services perhaps have a particular responsibility to support these changes of attitudes, not only by appropriately treating and caring for people with mental health problems (freeing them from the symptoms that trouble them), but doing so in way that helps to empower them (i.e. freeing them for) to meet the requirements of an independent and self-determined life.

2.2 Law relating to people with mental health problems: the historical context

Changes in some countries' mental health legislation in the last few decades can be interpreted as attempts to give greater emphasis to the dignity and autonomy of the person with mental illness.

In former times, people who could not be understood or who behaved strangely according to society's norms were separated from the community. This was particularly the case if they were thought to be disturbing the public order or posing a danger to others. When such behaviour began to be understood as an expression of mental illness, societies developed legal procedures that were intended to ensure referral of such people into institutions for custody and treatment (Shorter, 1997). Compassion towards those considered to be ill and helpless was an early and major component of the treatment of diseases. The discovery of effective psychiatric treatments during the last century gave psychiatrists the hope that they might help their patients. This went alongside a paternalistic application of these new treatments – paternalism being a manner that prevailed among physicians of that time. Psychiatrists justified this by imputing the inability of patients to decide for themselves what would be in their best interests. However, in contrast to other physicians, psychiatrists thought the treatment of mental illness was permitted without the consent of – and indeed at times against the will of – the patient.

Although the concept of consent to all medical interventions has been known in medicine for at least the last 200 years, the legal concept of informed consent is a newer one and was developed in practice only after World War II. With the emergence of this concept in psychiatry specifically, the expressed wishes of those diagnosed with mental illness began to be taken into account (Helmchen, 2010). Psychiatrists realised that the self-defined interest of the patient was not necessarily identical with what the psychiatrist thought to be in the patient's best interests. The move from an emphasis on the protection of society from people with mental illness towards the protection of the rights of people with mental illness within the framework of 'patient-oriented medicine' is still ongoing and is supported by legal regulations.

The emphasis on protection is gradually being replaced within psychiatry by the emphasis on helping the individual to overcome his or her illness (or at least to live with it as well as possible) and, in that way, minimising the risks associated with the mental illness while also empowering the individual.

Current psychiatric debates about 'consent to treatment' illustrate the intractable difficulties associated with transforming the emphasis on protecting society *from* the person with mental illness towards full respect for that person's self-expressed interests. 'Dangerous behaviour against others or oneself' is the only – or at least most important – justification for confining individuals with a mental illness involuntarily to a mental hospital and most legislative frameworks specify that this requires a court's decision, either because of immediate dangerousness or because of a request from the patient's legal guardian. If a person with mental illness has the capacity to consent, the psychiatrist should accept his or her refusal of treatment, unless a failure to treat would result in immediate dangerousness. The disadvantage of this way of proceeding is that confining persons to hospital and not providing treatment reduces the mental hospital to a pure instrument of social control like a jail – and increases the stigmatisation of psychiatry. Moreover, this procedure may not protect the patient from becoming delinquent by actions which he will regret after remission.

However, this may only rarely be the case: many people with mental illnesses who will be admitted compulsorily to a hospital owing to their ill-determined dangerousness will be judged not competent to consent. In such cases, what is referred to as a 'one-step' procedure will be performed, that is patients will be given treatment – including against their will – if that is considered necessary to empower him/her to control his/her dangerous behaviour. This is the case in Brazil and Germany (in Germany: Bundesgerichtshof (BGH) (Federal Supreme Court) 1.2.2006, BGH 23.1.2008 (Diekmann, 2010). This one-step procedure is gradually being replaced by a 'two-step' procedure (e.g. in The Netherlands, Switzerland and the Province of Ontario in Canada [Box 2.1]). In other words, legal control of the decision to treat the person with mental illness against his or her will is separated from the decision regarding involuntary confinement. This will apply to patients with mental illness no matter whether they are competent or incompetent to consent. However, in the latter case a legal guardian has to give the informed consent. Notably, the Council of Europe's European Committee for the Prevention of Torture and Inhuman or Degrading Treatment or Punishment (CPT) requires, in its CPT Standards (Box 2.2), a two-step procedure.

Box 2.1 Legislative Case Study: Canada, Province of Ontario

In Ontario's Consent to Treatment Act, SO 1992, c.31, superseded by the Health Care Consent Act, SO 1996, c.2, SCH.A, any person with capacity to consent has the right to consent or refuse any treatment. Therefore, compulsory admission is restricted (asides from a relatively narrow exception) to the criterion of dangerousness and involuntary admission does not provide a power to treat the individual. In this sense, Ontario has a non-discriminatory approach to treatment in that an individual with capacity is able to refuse psychiatric (and other) treatment whether he or she is an inpatient or an outpatient (Bartlett, 2003). An individual without capacity is treated on the basis of consent provided by a designated substitute for psychiatric or other treatment.

Box 2.2 Standards: Council of Europe

The European Committee for the Prevention of Torture and Inhuman or Degrading Treatment or Punishment (CPT) in its CPT Standards (Chapter 14.2.1.1.2) specifies that: 'The admission of a person to a psychiatric establishment on an involuntary basis should not be construed as authorising treatment without his consent. It follows that every competent patient, whether voluntary or involuntary, should be given the opportunity to refuse treatment or any other medical intervention. Any derogation from this fundamental principle should be based upon law and only relate to clearly and strictly defined exceptional circumstances.'

This change should oblige the psychiatrist to give reasons for the need, the benefits and the risks of the treatment and to find a way of demonstrating to their patients, and/or their guardians, that treatment is in their best interest (which sometimes may be almost impossible without subtle coercion). In the probably rare cases in which an involuntarily confined mentally ill individual stays in a mental hospital without treatment, further problems may be envisaged:

- such patients cannot be referred to another institution of social control (e.g. a jail) because they have not committed an offence and show only the potential ('risk') of committing an offence;
- the health insurance company (in countries where psychiatric hospital treatment is not free) may refuse to pay for the hospital stay of the patient without treatment;
- the freedom of all patients of the mental hospital may be restricted (e.g. by locked doors), owing to the need to impose security measures on all because one or a few patients refuse treatment. This may be particularly the case in some countries with insufficient psychiatric services.

In legal terms, psychiatrists have to justify the decision (before an independent review board or at least before a judge) through the need to protect the right to life (Article 10 of the UN Convention on the Rights of Persons with Disabilities, Chapter 14.1.1.1 and 14.4.1) in situations where they have to disregard the basic human right of individual freedom, as well as the ethical principle of respect for the autonomy of the patient.

2.3 Discrimination

The previous section has provided an historical contextualisation of the debates that have tended to dominate discussions of mental health in their articulation with the law – in other words, the strong focus on how to formulate legal frameworks for the involuntary detainment and treatment of psychiatric patients. But in the remainder of this book, we are not primarily concerned with the development or phrasing of mental health legislation involving involuntary hospital admission or involuntary psychiatric treatment. Mental health legislation (including how to draft it, how to ensure that it protects patients' rights and its philosophical and political implications) are already discussed in a variety of high-quality materials, most prominently in the *World Health Organization Resource Book on Mental Health, Human Rights and Legislation* (WHO, 2005), in McSherry and Weller's (2010) *Rethinking Rights-Based Mental Health Laws* and in Gostin and colleagues' (2010) *Principles of Mental Health Law and Policy*. This subject is also covered in some detail by the UN Mental Illness Principles of 1991 (Chapter 14.1.2.3 and 14.4.3). While the Mental Illness Principles are to some extent superseded by the UN Convention on the Rights of Persons with Disabilities (CRPD) (Chapter 14.1.1.1 and 14.4.1) they remain an extensive and helpful document

We turn, then, to the concept of discrimination. Discrimination means, at its most basic, the singling out of an individual or a group. It is overwhelmingly used in common parlance to imply that this singling out is done with adverse intentions and/or consequences. Within the law, discrimination usually refers to the practice of treating a group or an individual differently and unfairly. Countries' legislative frameworks commonly outline how such differential treatment in relation to certain protected characteristics – for example, gender, ethnicity, religion, disability, age, sexuality – is both discriminatory and unlawful (Box 2.3 identifies a useful resource that provides examples from across Europe).

Box 2.3 Resource

For a helpful and clear explication of the various ways in which discrimination has been conceptualised and operationalised in legal contexts, see the *Handbook on European Non-Discrimination Law* (Council of Europe, 2011). This is available for download at the FRA (European Union Agency for Fundamental Rights) web site: http://fra.europa.eu

While the handbook covers non-discrimination law in the context of Europe, its sections on principles, as well as discrimination categories and defences, have much wider relevance.

2.3.1 Definitions of direct and indirect discrimination

One of the most critical distinctions is that between direct and indirect discrimination.

Direct discrimination occurs when someone is treated less favourably than others because of his or her membership – or assumed membership – within a group. For example, in many countries, people with psychiatric diagnoses experience direct discrimination when they are explicitly prohibited – on grounds of their psychiatric diagnosis – from being members of a jury, from driving, or from travelling freely. If an individual is prohibited owing to his/her impaired functioning in dealing with a special task that relies on functions that are impaired, it can be acknowledged as a fair or justified discrimination, but this exception must be approached with care. Real and compelling connections must be shown between the impairment and the function to be performed and traditions of exclusion will not suffice.

Indirect discrimination occurs when improper or unnecessary barriers or burdens are placed on someone because of his or her membership – or assumed membership – within a group. This can occur when certain conditions, practices or requirements that are used by employers, service providers, education facilities and so on have a disproportionately negative impact on certain individuals. In other words, the condition or requirement – if applied equally to everyone – actually means that certain groups are unfairly disadvantaged. For example, if an employer demands that all job candidates give a public presentation for a job that in actuality does not require public speaking, this would indirectly discriminate against individuals with anxiety disorder diagnoses who were unable to speak in such settings.

The United Nations Committee on Economic, Social and Cultural Rights – the body of independent experts that monitors implementation of the International Covenant on Economic, Social and Cultural Rights (Chapter 14.1.1.6) – emphasised in 1994 the importance of addressing the indirect as well as the direct discrimination experienced by persons with disabilities. This Committee stated in General Comment 5 that: 'Both de jure [in law] and de facto [in practice but not necessarily ordained by law] discrimination against persons with disabilities have a long history and take various forms'. They range from invidious discrimination, such as the denial of educational opportunities, to more 'subtle' forms of discrimination, such as segregation and isolation achieved through the imposition of physical and social barriers. General Comment 5 further noted that: 'In order to remedy past and present discrimination, and to deter future discrimination, comprehensive anti-discrimination legislation in relation to disability would seem to be indispensable in virtually all States Parties. Such legislation should not only provide persons with disabilities with judicial remedies as far as possible and appropriate, but also provide for social policy programmes which enable persons with disabilities to live an integrated, self-determined and independent life'.

In other words, the General Comment emphasised that combating discrimination requires a comprehensive legislative approach – one that works to ensure that individuals with disabilities have equal opportunities to fully participate in civil society, as well as one that provides legal remedies for those individuals whose rights are abused. Such an approach has been further consolidated by the UN Convention on the Rights of Persons with Disabilities (CRPD), which specifies in Article 2 (Definitions) that: 'Discrimination on the basis of disability means any distinction, exclusion or restriction on the basis of disability which has the purpose or effect of impairing or nullifying the recognition, enjoyment or exercise, on an equal basis with others, of all human rights and fundamental freedoms in the political, economic, social, cultural, civil or any other field. It includes all forms of discrimination, including denial of reasonable accommodation'.

2.3.2 Reasonable accommodations

'Reasonable accommodations' (referred to as 'reasonable adjustments' in some countries) are adjustments or modifications provided by employers and/or providers of services, which are designed to ensure that people with disabilities can access these opportunities and/or services on an equal basis with others. The concept was legally first extensively fleshed out in the context of the United States' Americans with Disability Act (ADA) of 1990 (Box 2.4). (United States legislation regarding disability, particularly the ADA, has had a profound influence on the development of anti-discrimination legislation in other countries (Degener, 2005).)

Box 2.4 Legislative Case Study: United States of America

The Americans with Disabilities Act (ADA) requires an employer to provide reasonable accommodation to an employee or job applicant with a disability, unless doing so would cause significant difficulty or expense for the employer.

A reasonable accommodation is any change in the work environment (or in the way things are usually done) to help a person with a disability apply for a job, perform the duties of a job, or enjoy the benefits and privileges of employment.

Reasonable accommodation might include: job restructuring, part-time or modified work schedules, or changing tests, training materials or policies.

For further information: www.ada.gov

Reasonable accommodations will vary depending on the needs of an individual. It is important that employers think carefully – and do so in discussion with people with mental health problems – about which reasonable accommodations might be appropriate, since people often find it harder to enumerate potential accommodations for people with mental disabilities, as opposed to physical disabilities (Guidance on how employers might make reasonable accommodations is indicated in Box 2.5.). Also, some mental health problems can fluctuate, and therefore appropriate adjustments or accommodations might vary over time. Lawson (2008) has provided a clear explanation of reasonable accommodations for people with psychosocial impairments (mental health problems) in the context of the UN Convention on the Rights of Persons with Disabilities.

Box 2.5 Guidance: Example from Scotland

The Scottish Association for Mental Health (SAMH) has developed a guide for employees on making reasonable adjustments in the workplace for people with mental health problems (n.d.). Its suggestions include:

- adjust recruitment processes, for example by providing more time for assignments or interviews and providing a quiet area for applicants to wait in;

- amend induction processes; for example, discuss with the new employee the possibility of a mentor, arrange additional support for the first few months, agree a longer induction process;
- allow variations in working hours. There are many reasons why someone might need to adjust their hours; for example, to access a service that is only available during working hours – or they might find it difficult to function in the morning, perhaps as a result of prescribed medication;
- allow several short breaks instead of one main lunch break, since some people might have difficulty in concentrating for long periods;
- permit more breaks at certain times, for example if someone is doing particularly stressful work;
- allow the person to change their workplace, for example if a noisy environment might undermine their mental health;
- provide a quiet space for breaks, since a quiet place away from the main workspace is helpful for many people.

The guide is available from the SAMH web site: www.samh.org.uk

While much of the existing discussion about reasonable accommodation – in terms of both legal and administrative actions – has been within the field of employment, it is important to bear in mind that reasonable accommodation extends well beyond that sphere. For example, it might well include the provision of support for people with depression or learning difficulties in filling out social services applications, or might encompass the provision of social housing that takes into account the individual's disability. In Chapter 7.2, an example is provided from Ontario's Human Rights Code, which applies to landlords and tenants. Under this Code, housing providers have a duty to accommodate the Code-related needs of tenants and this duty might include being flexible when enforcing rules and requirements. The policy attached to the Human Rights Code explicitly provides the example of a tenant with a mental disability – someone who is usually punctilious over fulfilling requirements and meeting deadlines who fails to meet a deadline for filing information on a change in income on account of a change in psychiatric medication. The policy encourages the housing provider to use his/her discretion to extend the deadline in such a case.

2.3.3 Legislation to address discrimination

The development of legislation specifically to address discrimination on the basis of disability has been a notable feature of the global legal landscape in the last two decades. By 2005, more than 40 out of 189 UN Member States had adopted some form of anti-discrimination legislation for disabled people. The adoption of the UN Convention on the Rights of Persons with Disabilities (CRPD) has provided an additional spur for countries – particularly those who have ratified the CRPD – to develop new disability legislation or transform their existing legislation. Box 2.6 contains resources that provide extensive data on disability legislation and policy within Asia and the Pacific, as well as within Europe.

Box 2.6 Resources

Disability Policy Central for Asia and the Pacific

Disability Policy Central for Asia and the Pacific is an internet database run by the United Nations Economic and Social Commission for Asia and the Pacific (ESCAP) about disability policy in 58 countries in Asia and the Pacific. It provides detailed information on disability legislation, statistics, definitions, policies and practices for policy-makers, researchers, persons with disabilities and other stakeholders.

For further information:
www.unescap.org/sdd/issues/disability/policycentral/index.asp

Academic Network of European Disability Experts (ANED)

One of the functions of ANED is to establish a mechanism for monitoring and evaluating European laws and policies that affect disabled people (e.g. European legislation, communications and resolutions of the Council of Europe etc.). The resulting summaries and details on laws and policies are made available via the ANED web site for the benefit of the research community, policy-makers and other stakeholders. The web site thereby contains extensive resources and analyses (at both country and European level) concerning legislation and policy addressing disability.

For further information: www.disability-europe.net

2.3.4 Discrimination on what grounds?

In considering the use of legislation to address discrimination, it is important to think through the concrete objectives of that legislation, as well as how it will define what constitutes discrimination. There are many ways in which people can be discriminated against in relation to their mental health (or presumed mental health) – and good legislation will need to capture this complexity. Discrimination on the grounds of mental health status can occur in relation to:

- an individual's current mental health problems;
- an individual's past mental health problems;
- an individual's possible future mental health problems;
- the imputation of mental health problems, even where such problems do not actually exist;
- an individual's association with someone with current, past or imputed mental health problems.

Discriminatory behaviour can occur, moreover, through knowledge of an individual's psychiatric diagnosis and/or through his or her use of psychiatric services. It can overlap with – and/or exacerbate – other forms of discrimination. For example, individuals with a psychiatric diagnosis who also have refugee status and/or who are lesbian, gay, transsexual or transgender and/or who have physical disabilities can experience 'multiple discrimination' (Crenshaw, 1989; Fredman, 2005). The term 'multiple discrimination' is actually an umbrella term: in effect it points to three different ways in which people can experience discrimination on more than one ground.

> 'Multiple (or additive) discrimination' takes place on the basis of several grounds that operate separately. For example, a lesbian who also uses mental health services may in certain contexts experience discrimination because of her sexuality and in other contexts because of her use of mental health services.
>
> 'Compound discrimination' means a person experiences discrimination on the basis of two or more grounds at the same time, where one ground adds to discrimination on another ground.
>
> 'Intersectional discrimination' means several grounds operate and interact inseparably with each other at the same time' (definitions: European Commission, 2007).

Some groups of people with mental health problems are particularly at risk of experiencing compound and/or intersectional discrimination. A black man, for example, who is experiencing psychotic symptoms (and/or side effects from antipsychotic medication) may be the recipient of discriminatory acts that are driven by particular prejudicial attitudes around 'dangerousness', in which ethnicity, gender and mental health status are all enmeshed (i.e. the discrimination would not occur in quite the same way in relation to a black woman or in relation to a white man who is experiencing psychotic symptoms and/or side effects from anti-psychotic medication).

Multiple discrimination raises additional complexities for the law, and many statutory regimes addressing anti-discrimination are inadequate in dealing with multiple discrimination claims (European Commission, 2007; Hannett, 2003; Schiek and Lawson, 2011). Notably, there has been little legislation that attempts to address multiple/intersectional discrimination outside of the contexts of employment and education. The European Commission publication (European Commission, 2007) quoted in the paragraphs above about tackling multiple/intersectional discrimination included the following legislative recommendations to the European Commission and Member States:

- EU and national anti-discrimination and equal treatment legislation should cover grounds that include disability outside employment and education – that is also in the fields of:
  - **(a)** social protection, including social security and health care;
  - **(b)** social advantages;
  - **(c)** access and supply of goods and services available to the public (including housing).

- New legislation should provide provisions to address intersectional discrimination.
- National equality bodies should have a mandate to assist victims of discrimination on all grounds within and outside employment and occupation, with the appropriate financial resources to assist victims of multiple discrimination.
- There should be the promotion and development of 'positive duties' and 'equality mainstreams' in the public and private sector, which should take into account multiple grounds of discrimination. (Positive duties have the advantage of shifting emphasis away from the individual who has been – or might be – discriminated against and placing the onus and responsibility on organisations/sectors for their facilitation of equality of opportunity. 'Equality mainstreaming' comprises the systematic integration of an equality perspective into the everyday operations of organisations/sectors.)

It is not solely people with a current psychiatric diagnosis who experience discrimination on mental health grounds. A good law will be able to protect people with no current mental health problems or disability (Rosenthal and Sundram, 2004), as well as people associated with individuals with mental health problems (or presumed mental health problems). A wide definition can be used to specify the grounds for protection against discrimination. The examples in Boxes 2.7 to 2.10 provide case studies that demonstrate the use of wide definitions and extensive protections.

Box 2.7 Legislative Case Study: Ireland

Equality Act 2004
www.irishstatutebook.ie

The Act amended Section 6 of the Employment Equality Act of 1998 and specifies that discrimination shall be taken to occur where:

(a) a person is treated less favourably than another person is, has been or would be treated in a comparable situation on any of the grounds specified in subsection (2) [which specifies disability] . . . which
  - **(i)** exists,
  - **(ii)** existed but no longer exists,
  - **(iii)** may exist in the future, or
  - **(iv)** is imputed to the person concerned.

(b) a person who is associated with another person
  - **(i)** is treated, by virtue of that association, less favourably than a person who is not so associated is, has been or would be treated in a comparable situation, and
  - **(ii)** similar treatment of that other person on any of the discriminatory grounds would, by virtue of paragraph (a), constitute discrimination.

For contextualisation of the situation vis-à-vis mental health, discrimination and human rights in Ireland, see also Crowley, 2003; Expert Group on Mental Health Policy, 2006; Lyons and Rush, 2004; MacGabhann *et al.*, 2010; Russell *et al.*, 2008; Tobin, 2007.

Box 2.8 Legislative Case Study: New Zealand

New Zealand Human Rights Act 1993 No 82 (as at 3 March 2010), Public Act www.legislation.govt.nz

Disability is among the prohibited grounds of discrimination, which includes:

- psychiatric illness;
- intellectual or psychological disability or impairment;
- any other loss or abnormality of psychological, physiological, or anatomical structure or function.

Each of the grounds specified is a prohibited ground of discrimination within the Act if:

(a) it pertains to a person or to a relative or associate of a person; and

(b) it either:

  (i) currently exists or has in the past existed; or

  (ii) is suspected or assumed or believed to exist or to have existed by the person alleged to have discriminated.

See also: Human Rights Commission, 2010.

Box 2.9 Legislative Case Study: Norway

Act June 20 2008 No 42 relating to a prohibition against discrimination on the basis of disability (the Anti-Discrimination and Accessibility Act)

Section 4, Prohibition against discrimination specifies:

> 'Direct and indirect discrimination on the basis of disability is prohibited. By direct discrimination is meant that the objective or effect of an act or omission is that persons are, on the basis of a disability, treated in a worse fashion than other people are, have been or would have been treated in a similar situation. By indirect indiscrimination is meant any apparently neutral act, provision, practice, act or omission that leads to persons, on the basis of a disability, being placed in a worse position than other people.'

The prohibition against discrimination relates to discrimination on the grounds of a present disability, assumed disability, past disability and possible future disability, as well as discrimination of a person due to their relationship with a person with a disability.

Taken from the unofficial English translation, available at: www.regjeringen.no/upload/BLD/Diskriminering/Engelsk/Lovteksten%20eng-22.09%20ELR.CBK.doc

The Act can be read in Norwegian at: www.regjeringen.no

Further background documents about the approach taken to disability in this new Act, as well as the Act's history, are available at: www.regjeringen.no/en/dep/bld/Topics/disabled-people.html

See also: Syse (2006).

Box 2.10 Legislative Case Study: Hong Kong

Disability Discrimination Ordinance (Chapter 487, Gazette Number LN 222 of 2008)

www.eoc.org.hk/eoc/graphicsfolder/showddo.aspx?id = 7926

The definition of 'disability' (in Section 2) includes:

'a disorder, illness or disease that affects a person's thought processes, perception of reality, emotions or judgment or that results in disturbed behaviour, and includes a disability that:

(i) presently exists;
(ii) previously existed but no longer exists;
(iii) may exist in the future; or
(iv) is imputed to a person'.

Protection under the Disability Discrimination Ordinance also extends to associates. An associate includes a spouse, another person living with a person with a disability, relative, carer and a business, sporting or recreational partner.

In 2000, the Hong Kong Equal Opportunities Commission helped three young men to take their claims of disability discrimination against the Fire Services Department and the Customs and Excise Department to the District Court. The departments admitted that the plaintiffs did not have schizophrenia themselves and that they were capable of discharging the duties of the jobs they applied for, except that they each had a parent who had, or who was believed to have had, a history of schizophrenia. The departments had assumed that the plaintiffs possessed an unacceptably high risk of developing schizophrenia sometime in the future and withdrew the job offers to these three young men.

The Court's judgment found that the departments' policy of screening out first degree relatives of people with schizophrenia to be discriminatory, and awarded damages to the three young men.

An assessment of the first decade of Hong Kong's Disability Discrimination Ordinance is given in Byrnes (2008).

2.3.5 What kind of equality?

Anti-discrimination legislation attempts to redress the consequences of unfair treatment in the past and prevent unfair treatment in the future. While it is commonly understood as working towards societal equality, we should note that there are a number of different models of equality, as well as lively debates amongst legal experts and philosophers concerning the implications of pushing for one model of equality over another. (Yamin (2009) provides a powerful interrogation of these complexities.) When developing legislation, therefore, one needs carefully to consider what exactly it is trying to achieve in pushing for non-discrimination and equality. Degener and Quinn (2000) have usefully sub-divided anti-discrimination legislation into three kinds, each depending upon a different model of equality.

1 Formal/juridical equality. With this approach, differences between people (e.g. between people with and without mental health problems) are ignored on the grounds of not discriminating. The difficulty with such

an approach is that it makes it difficult to address the structural reasons that contribute to inequalities between those with and without mental health problems.

2 Equality of results. The aim here is to achieve equality in outcomes; for example, having the same proportion of people with mental health problems employed as people without mental health problems. This is frequently the aim of legislation that uses a 'quota' approach. Such an approach is admittedly difficult within market economies.
3 Equal opportunity/structural equality. This approach aims to provide equal chances without ensuring equal results. It attempts to address both the stereotypes and the structural barriers that maintain and consolidate inequalities and discrimination.

It is this third model – equal opportunity/structural (sometimes 'substantive') equality – that arguably has the greatest potential in combating discrimination on the grounds of disability. This is because the structural equality model 'includes a commitment to the view that society must change in order to guarantee true equal opportunity for disabled people' (Degener, 2005). It is this model, for example, that underpins the concept of 'reasonable accommodations' that was first spearheaded in the United States in the 1970s and then formulated in detail in the Americans with Disabilities Act of 1990, and which now appears in a number of disability discrimination laws worldwide (Section 2.3.2). It is also the equal opportunity/structural equality model that lies at the heart of the new UN Convention on the Rights of Persons with Disabilities, which specifies, in Article 5, that: 'Specific measures which are necessary to accelerate or achieve de facto equality of persons with disabilities shall not be considered discrimination under the terms of the present Convention'.

Such a model emphasises that making adaptations or modifications to ensure that those with disabilities are able to participate fully in society is not an act of charity but a matter of social justice – and, indeed, a legally enforceable right.

The Philippines has an extensive, rights-based legislative approach to disability discrimination that operates within the equal opportunity/structural equality model (Box 2.11).

Box 2.11 Legislative Case Study: The Philippines

The Philippines Magna Carta for Persons with Disabilities contains guarantees of rights in a range of areas of life. Some provisions are expressed as guarantees of rights or in terms of the state's obligation to recognise particular rights. There are also provisions for programmes, which include:

- incentives for employers who employ persons with disability;

- obligations for the state to adopt appropriate rehabilitation and vocational training measures;
- obligations for the state to provide assistance for students with disabilities;
- obligations for state universities to conduct research on disability issues.

For further details and elaboration of the Magna Carta, see Byrnes, 2009.

The Magna Carta, as well as other legislative and policy actions relating to disability, are available on the web site of the Philippines' National Council on Disability Affairs: www.ncda.gov.ph

The relevant Acts are: Republic Act 9442 and Republic Act 7277.

For disability discrimination laws to be effective in moving towards structural/substantive equality, they will need to be buttressed by other laws, regulations and policy-making. These should provide a number of mechanisms, as well as a coherent and multi-sectoral framework, through which to push towards structural/substantive equality. Without other laws, regulation and policy, it is unlikely that there will be much progress made in addressing the significant structural inequalities and barriers that prevent many people with disabilities from being able to access opportunities (Bagenstos, 2004; Burns, 2009; Sayce, 2003). A background paper for the Economic and Social Commission for Asia and the Pacific Office of the United Nations High Commissioner for Human Rights (Expert Group Meeting on the Harmonization of National Legislation with the Convention on the Rights of Persons with Disabilities in Asia and the Pacific in 2009, Bangkok) draws on the experiences of disability discrimination legislation in a number of countries. The paper recommends a number of elements that should be taken into account by policy-makers, legislators and civil society in the development or review of disability legislation; these are summarised in Box 2.12.

Box 2.12 Guidance

Elements that should be taken into account by policy-makers, legislators and civil society in the development or review of disability legislation include:

- Legal regulation of disability discrimination and the promotion of equality for persons with disabilities must go beyond disability discrimination laws and also include appropriate laws and regulation in other legal and regulatory frameworks (for example, building regulations, transport regulations, telecommunications rules) – equality can only be achieved by a combination of legislative guarantees of the fundamental principle of equality with detailed specifications in particular sectors.
- Excessive complexity in definitions and procedures should be avoided.
- When formulating disability discrimination or equality law, a traditional equality or non-discrimination model which mandates equal treatment of similarly situated persons should be used with care.

- Any guarantee of equality must be formulated so as to take into account the fact that very often persons with disabilities must be treated differently in order for them to be treated equally and thereby given the same opportunities as others (for example, by reasonable adjustment to the workplace or working conditions) – a substantive equality approach must inform legislative guarantees and their interpretation.
- Disability discrimination or equality legislation must cover not only direct discrimination on the basis of disability, but also indirect discrimination.
- Any law must provide effective remedies for individuals who have had their rights denied on account of disability, as well as providing for procedures that can contribute to bringing about systemic change.
- While an individual complaint-based mechanism can be useful for redressing individual wrongs, it is not in itself sufficient for bringing about systemic change in many areas.
- Effective institutions must be set up, or existing institutions mandated and resourced, to publicise, to help implement and to monitor implementation of any such law, and these bodies should also have the right to take up issues and institute investigations or inquiries on its own motion.
- Access to affordable and readily available procedures for the consideration of complaints of discrimination is an important component of effective anti-discrimination legislative schemes.

(Taken from: Burns, 2009).

2.4 General versus specific law

It is important that we understand that legislation intended to combat the discrimination and abuse experienced by people with mental health problems can take a number of forms. In some contexts, traditional mental health legislation will address these issues. Abuse that occurs within psychiatric institutions, for example, is relevant both to the laws that we discuss in this book and to traditional mental health law. Rights to treatment and to standards of service are similarly relevant in both contexts.

The way in which relevant legal provisions are incorporated into the law of an individual state will flow from the legal and political traditions of each state. Sometimes, as we have seen in Section 2.3, States pass specific statutes devoted to disability in general, or indeed mental disability in particular. These statutes are sometimes part of mental health legislation.

Each format has advantages and disadvantages. A law dedicated to a specific topic (such as mental disability specifically) can more easily take into account the particularities of the specific condition(s). Any resources devoted to enforcing such a statute will much more likely be directed towards the actual issues raised by specific legislation and mental disability issues may be more directly addressed as a result. On the other hand, there is the possibility that legislation that specifically addresses mental disability might carry in its wake stigmatisation effects by singling out a specific group. At the same time, such an approach loses the sense of unity that a more all-encompassing statute may bring: if human rights are meant to be universal, there is perhaps a principled or presentational advantage to including all groups together. Victories for some become victories for all. Such an inclusion does, however, decrease the visibility of specific mental disability issues.

Furthermore, enforcement agencies for such legislation are likely to be permitted to allocate within themselves how much of their funding will be spent on mental disability related issues and how much on other groups. The possibility of discrimination within such organisations cannot be ignored. The risk is that other groups are accorded priority and mental disability becomes the poor relation whose needs are never properly addressed. Boxes 2.13 to 2.16 provide examples of how countries address discrimination on grounds of disability through the use of a variety of legislative mechanisms.

Box 2.13 Legislative Case Study: United Kingdom

In the United Kingdom, the law that protects people with mental health problems from discrimination is the Disability Discrimination Act 1995 (also amendments contained within the Disability Discrimination Act 2005 and The Equality Act 2010, which replaces a significant part of the Disability Discrimination Act).

The Equality Act 2010 introduced new protections for disability-related harassment in services – i.e. unwanted behaviour related to disability that has the purpose or effect of violating a person's dignity or creating an intimidating, hostile, degrading, humiliating or offensive environment. This would include such behaviour as staff at a day centre mimicking a person with mental health problems.

Both Acts are available at: www.legislation.gov.uk (www.legislation.gov.uk/ukpga/2005/13/contents and www.equalities.gov.uk/equality_act_2010.aspx).

Box 2.14 Legislative Case Study: South Africa

The Republic of South Africa protects against discrimination on grounds of disability as part of a general right in its Constitution to be free from discrimination (Article 9(3)). It also specifies in its Mental Health Care Act, 2002, Chapter III Section 10, 'Unfair discrimination' that: 'A mental health care user may not be unfairly discriminated against on the grounds of his or her mental health status'. There is no general disability discrimination law.

Box 2.15 Legislative Case Study: Fiji

The Constitution of the Republic of the Fiji Islands (Article 38) provides for equality before the law. Article 38(2) prohibits discrimination:

'A person must not be unfairly discriminated against, directly or indirectly, on the ground of his or her: (a) actual or supposed personal characteristics or circumstances, including race, ethnic origin, colour, place of origin, gender, sexual orientation, birth, primary language, economic status, age or disability'.

These rights are enforced through the Fiji Human Rights Commission. The Human Rights Commission Act 1999 expressly defines where discrimination is prohibited and states that affirmative action to achieve social justice is permitted (Harpur and Bales, 2010).

Box 2.16 Legislative Case Study: Germany

The Act on the Equalisation of Disabled Persons (BGG) of 2002 is an example of a general disability anti-discrimination law. Not withstanding some general weaknesses, such as barriers for reporting and claiming cases for discrimination, it has generally been appreciated.

Further discussion of the German Act is given in Kock (2004) and Degener (2006).

Equally significant is the general law of countries, which if equitably enforced, may provide considerable protection to people with mental health problems. Thus while many countries include specific provisions protecting people with mental disabilities from physical abuse, these are often in addition to general laws prohibiting such abuse against anyone. In this sense, the specific provisions may be superfluous: hitting a person with mental health problems is assault, just as hitting anyone else is assault. Advocates should thus remember to look to the general law of their nations and press for its equitable enforcement to protect people with mental health problems. There is much in existing law that they will find helpful.

Examples included in this book therefore demonstrate that several kinds of legislative and administrative structures can be, and have been, used to combat the discrimination experienced by people with mental health problems. These include:

- a country's constitution;
- human rights legislation;
- anti-discrimination legislation (on grounds of disability);
- social protection/social services legislation;
- employment legislation;
- mental health legislation – which can embed strong principles of anti-discrimination and/or social inclusion;
- national disability strategies;
- national mental health policies/plans.

One important example of mental health legislation being used to support social development as well as mental well-being is that of Scotland (Box 2.17).

Box 2.17 Legislative Case Study: Scotland

The Mental Health (Care and Treatment) (Scotland) Act 2003 introduces under Sections 25–31 a duty for local authorities to provide services designed to promote well-being and social development.

The Mental Welfare Commission has a duty to monitor the Act and to promote best practice in its use. It does this through a number of mechanisms, including meeting with people in the community who have a mental illness, learning disability or personality disorder to determine the types and quality of services that they are assessing. Feedback from people to the Mental Welfare Commission may help inform the knowledge base of the ways in which local authorities are meeting their duties under the Act.

The guidance published by The Scottish Government (2007) also indicates how local authorities might implement their duties under this Act to promote well-being and social development; see also Lyons (2008).

Note in the Scottish example that the duty is to promote 'well-being' in every aspect of life: Section 26 of the Act addresses mental health and not just mental disorder/mental illness. Well-being, rather than merely the alleviation of symptoms, therefore extends much more widely than the traditional domain of health and public health.

2.5 Importance of enforcement

Throughout the research that led to this book, the response most frequently heard from country informants as well as other experts was a need to ensure proper enforcement of legal provisions. Law without enforcement is of, at best, marginal relevance (Box 2.18). While it may send a broadly positive message, it may also occasionally be counter-productive, allowing national governments to adopt the appearance of social progressiveness while real problems 'on the ground' go unnoticed. The legal tools and frameworks discussed in this book must be devoted to real change in the lives of people with mental health problems and that means that meaningful structures to ensure implementation and enforcement are indispensable when developing legislation.

Box 2.18 Legislative Case Study: United Kingdom

When the Disability Discrimination Act (DDA) was passed in the United Kingdom in 1995, it was much criticised for not having an enforcement body – only a council to advise and encourage good practice. In 1999, therefore, the National Disability Council was abolished and the Disability Rights Commission (DRC) was installed in its place. The DRC had powers to support individuals taking cases under the Act, and to formally investigate organisations and sectors where discrimination might be occurring.

In October 2007, the functions of the DRC were subsumed within the new Equality and Human Rights Commission, a broader statutory human rights/anti-discrimination body that has the responsibility to protect, enforce and promote equality across seven 'protected' grounds (age, disability, gender, race, religion and belief, sexual orientation and gender reassignment).

For further information: www.equalityhumanrights.com

Certainly, part of that will involve introducing structures to ensure that people with mental health problems can enforce their rights, when they choose to do so (Box 2.19). Proper systems of advocacy, backed with proper funding, are thus of considerable importance. These are not sufficient methods of enforcement, however. The reality of life for many people with mental health problems is that they do not feel able to retain and instruct counsel to litigate on their behalf. This may because they are unaware of the rights that are being violated, or because they are sufficiently vulnerable in their current situation that they do not feel they can institute change – for fear of reprisal, for example. Even if the individual is able to litigate for his or her rights, the result may only be a victory for that individual. If the problem is widespread, or there is systemic failure to implement legislation, a more systemic approach to ensuring enforcement is needed. Inspectorates independent of both the person with mental disability and the service being offered – for example organised through service user or human rights organisations – are an important way to ensure that the rights protected by law are reflected in practice. These are discussed in greater detail in Chapter 12 (Implementation and Enforcement).

Box 2.19 Legislative Case Study: Korea

The Republic of Korea has an explicitly rights-based statute, the Anti-Discrimination against and Remedies for Persons with Disabilities Act (Public Law No. 8341, enacted April 10, 2007).

People who allege that they have been subject to unlawful discrimination are able to lodge complaints with the National Human Rights Commission of Korea, which has the power to undertake investigations into such a complaint and may also institute an investigation on its own initiative into grave acts of discrimination. Failures by any party to implement recommendations made by the Commission following its investigation of a complaint may be the subject of a remedial order by the Minister of Justice (Byrnes, 2009).

An English translation of the Act is available at:
www.humanrights.go.kr/english/information/legal_materials_05.jsp

National Human Rights Commission of Korea: www.humanrights.go.kr/english

2.6 Social model of disability

The preceding discussions of discrimination, structural/substantive equality and reasonable accommodations have implicitly depended upon a particular conceptualisation of disability. This conceptualisation comprises what is termed the social model of disability. It is important at this point to formulate explicitly the components of this model, since it differs substantially from some of the medical models of disability that many people still adhere to – wittingly or unwittingly – when thinking about disability issues. The social model of disability underpins much of the thinking in the last few decades vis-à-vis how legislation might be developed and used to address the discrimination and abuse experienced by people with disabilities. (It has not, however, been immune from critique or contestation – see, for example, Terzi (2004) and Thomas (2002).)

Concepts of disability have a complex history. In the 1980s, for example, the World Health Organization used a classification of disability (WHO, 1980) based on the notion that impairment of function (whether mental or physical) could lead to disability, which is dependent on the physical and social context in which the individual lives. That disability (expressed in terms of failing to perform in personal or social roles) could lead to handicap (which was described as the disadvantages imposed on the individual with a disability by society). Thus, an accident could lead to an amputation of a limb (leading to the difficulty in walking – a functional impairment), which could lead to disability unless arrangements were made (e.g. to provide the individual with a job that will not require much walking) and to a handicap (e.g. in some countries, entry into medical school was not allowed to individuals with an amputated leg).

More recently, the World Health Organization has updated the original classifications (WHO, 1997, 2001), providing a detailed description of body systems and possible impairments that could be linked to them, a detailed description of disability that could ensue and difficulties in participation in various activities of daily living in the community. The World Health Organization paid particular attention to the language used in the classification, avoiding terms that could be stigmatising.

Disability rights scholars and activists were, at the same time, formulating and utilising models of disability that took as their starting point not the question of impairments (as most models used in the health sphere do), but rather societal responses to individuals considered to have impairments. These disability rights activists took inspiration from the civil rights movement in the 1960s, and in the 1980s began explicitly formulating a social model of disability (Oliver, 1983, 1996, 1998).

The model argued that the exclusion and segregation of people with disabilities are tied not to the fact of the impairments themselves, but to sociocultural responses *to* those impairments. More recently, mental health service user scholars and activists have begun to develop the social model of disability specifically in relation to mental health problems (in their terms: 'a social model of madness and distress') (Beresford, 2002; Beresford *et al.*, 2010). These various writings that have emerged from the disability rights movement have challenged the medical model of impairment, disability and handicap historically offered by the World Health Organization (Carson, 2009). This social model of disability moves away from a conceptualisation in which disability is solely attached to the individual and turns our focus on to how the social environment fails to respond appropriately to human difference (in the form of impairments/disability) – and hence on how legislative actions can address these failures and barriers in the social environment. (A fascinating analysis of the conceptual, epistemological and political issues raised by the disjunctions between the World Health Organization classificatory systems and those that emerged from disability scholarship and activism is given in Bickenbach *et al.* (1999).)

Such a shift from a medical to a social model of disability is widely regarded as helping to install disability (including mental disability) as a question of human rights. The medical model was frequently used to underpin legislative approaches that focused on 'compensating' people with impairments – for example by providing them with special welfare benefits or by providing segregated facilities and services. This had the effect of positioning such legislation as an act of charity. In contrast, the social model of disability regards social exclusion and segregation as instances of disability-based discrimination (Sayce, 2000; Center for International Rehabilitation, 2005).

Legislation addressing disability therefore increasingly advances the social model of disability when defining what such legislation is designed to achieve. The UN Convention on the Rights of Persons with Disabilities (CRPD) explicitly draws on the social model when it states (in Preamble (e)) that: 'Disability is an evolving concept and that disability results from the interaction between persons with impairments and attitudinal and environmental barriers that hinders their full and effective participation in society on an equal basis with others'.

It also states in Article 1 (Purpose) that: 'Persons with disabilities include those who have long-term physical, mental, intellectual or sensory impairments which in interaction with various barriers may hinder their full and effective participation in society on an equal basis with others'.

The CRPD has given impetus to country-based legislative measures – including those relating to the definition of disability and discrimination –

that are designed to effect appropriate implementation of the CRPD in those States Parties which have signed it (Boxes 2.20 to 2.22).

Box 2.20 Legislative Case Study: Chile

In 2010, Chile, subsequent to ratifying the CRPD, acquired a new legislative framework (an Act on the 'Social Integration of Persons with Disabilities') through which to approach disability.

Act 20.422 (que Establece Normas sobre Igualdad de Oportunidades e Inclusión Social de Personas con Discapacidad) changes the focus of state action from providing assistance to providing quality of life. It also:

- establishes a new definition of persons with disabilities;
- modifies the concept of prevention, rehabilitation and technical assistance and emphasises independent living;
- considers the necessary legal modifications to mainstream disability;
- reinforces the principle of non-discrimination;
- defines the state as the grantor of the right to equality and equalisation of opportunities and prevention and rehabilitation.

The Act also creates a Committee of Ministers on Disability, an Advisory Council on Disability and a multi-sectoral National Disability Service.

For more information:
www.un.org/disabilities/documents/COP/COP3/chile_statement_english.pdf

For the law, see: http://el-observatorio.org/2010/02/ley-20-422-que-establece-normas-sobre-igualdad-de-oportunidades-e-inclusion-social-de-personas-con-discapacidad-chile

Historical contextualisation of the situation in Chile prior to the new Act can be found in Farmer (2008), Letelier and Bedregal (2006), Stewart (2004) and WHO (2007).

Box 2.21 Legislative Case Study: Jordan

Jordan was the first country in the Middle East to institute disability-specific legislation (Persons with Disabilities Care Law (no. 12 of 1993)). This was superseded by the Law on Disabled People's Rights (no. 31 of 2007). When Jordan ratified the CRPD in March 2008, its Higher Council of the Affairs of Disabled Persons formed a national team, including a legislative committee, to amend Law no. 31 of 2007 so that it complies with the CRPD. The National Centre for Human Rights in Jordan has been active in pushing for realisation of the goals of the CRPD, including the need for legislative amendments to law no. 31 of 2007.

See: Axelsson and Barrett (2009) and National Centre for Human Rights [of Jordan] (2010).

Box 2.22 Legislative Case Study: Vietnam

In 2010, Vietnam enacted its National Disability Law – its first comprehensive national law guaranteeing the right of people with disabilities. This replaces the Ordinance on People with Disabilities (1998).

UNICEF (which is mandated by the United Nations General Assembly to advocate for the protection of children's rights) and the government of Vietnam commissioned Eric Rosenthal and Mental Disability Rights International (MDRI) – now Disability Rights International (Chapter 16.4.4) – to compile a report that would assist the government of Vietnam in bringing its laws and policies into conformity with the CRPD. The report focuses on the rights of children. It is particularly attentive to mental disability issues – not least because it states that much of the language of the draft law 'seem[ed] primarily tailored to the concerns of people with physical disabilities' (Rosenthal, 2009).

2.7 Capacity and competence

If the history of jurisprudence is studied, it is immediately apparent how much weight has been placed on a person's 'mental capacity' or 'mental competence'. The determination of a person's mental incapacity or mental incompetence has had great effect on the rights they have been able to exercise under the law (Dhanda, 2007). Definitions of 'capacity' and 'competence' – as well as the ways in which such concepts have been mobilised within the law – have had profound effects on the lives of people with mental disabilities, since people with mental disabilities have had to endure multiple occasions on which they have been designated incompetent or without capacity.

Capacity and competence are discussed in greater detail in Chapter 4 (Legal capacity, decision-making, discriminatory statutes and practice). For now, a brief introduction is provided to the history of these terms as they have been employed within psychiatry, so as to allow the reader to be familiar with them as and when they are used in a number of other chapters. Readers should also beware: the terms mental capacity and mental competence are used differently in different countries. In some countries there is no difference between the two terms; however in others, mental capacity is understood as a medical term and has to be differentiated from the legal term 'competence'.

In relation to medicine, specifically, respect for the autonomy of the individual is one of the youngest but currently most important ethical principles. Autonomy will be realised as well as recognised by the mental capacity to consent to medical procedures, or in relation to decisions regarding medical and/or social services. Such capacity is commonly defined as the capacity to understand information, to appreciate it according to one's own value system and to make decisions accordingly. (This is an example of a rather high threshold for assuming capacity.) This cognitive aspect of mental capacity may be influenced by emotional and motivational components as well. Outside of the medical sphere, the manifestation of capacity is a frequent criterion in relation to undertaking acts such as the opening of a bank account, the signing of legal documents and voting.

Doubts about mental capacity will arise much more frequently when individuals have a mental disorder than when they have a physical disease and may be experienced as a form of discrimination by the individuals concerned, for example by older people with mild cognitive deficits. Doubts will arise especially if a patient refuses a treatment that the physician regards as imperative to overcome a life-threatening or dangerous morbid condition. It is, therefore, the obligation of the psychiatrist to assess this capacity both sensitively and validly. Wrongly to presume (in)capacity may either overburden the mentally ill person with a responsibility which he or she cannot at that point bear, or will deprive them of a basic human right and so discriminate against them.

Capacity to consent to medical treatment can be impaired by both physical and mental illnesses. However, since this impairment is more frequently manifest in persons with a mental illness, some people erroneously think that all people with mental illness lack the capacity to consent. Moreover, incapacity to consent may be of a transient nature. Most important is the understanding that capacity to consent is not a global characteristic of an individual but is related to the issue in question, i.e. a mentally ill individual may have the capacity to consent to a specific intervention but not to another, perhaps more complicated one. Box 2.23 shows a legislative example from Argentina that recognizes the need to assess capacity in different domains.

Box 2.23 Legislative Case Study: Argentina

The Ley de Desinstitucionalización 2006 (Deinstitutionalisation Law) of the Argentine Province of San Luis elaborates on capacity in Article 5. Incapacity in one domain does not necessarily indicate incapacity in other domains (5(f) below).

Article 5 specifies that:

'The Provincial State will guarantee medical and psychological assistance to people with mental disorders across the state, based on academic, health and professional principles, which are inspired by the Federal Constitution and by the human rights listed below.

(a) Consider mental illness as an episode and not a state.

(b) Ensure that everyone has the right to life, liberty and security of person.

(c) Ensure equal protection against any discrimination and against any incitement to such discrimination, which violates human rights.

(d) Ensure that no mentally ill person shall be subjected to arbitrary interference with his privacy, family, home or correspondence, nor to attacks upon his honour and reputation, nor be arbitrarily deprived of his property.

(e) Presume that patients are able to make decisions unless proven otherwise. Even with evidence to the contrary, one must obtain the voluntary consent of the patient except in exceptional cases and if necessary.

(f) Consider that incompetence to behave in one situation does not mean incompetence in relation to the exercise of self-determination with respect to other situations.

(g) Preserve the dignity of the patient.'

[translated by the authors]

The Ley de Desinstitucionalización can be downloaded from: www.catedramarielanger.com.ar/component/option,com_remository/Itemid,62/func,fileinfo/id,41

Most mental health legislation contains provisions for what to do when an individual does not have the capacity to consent. However, there is often no legal regulation of when, how and by whom a state of incapacity to consent should be assessed. The Mental Capacity Act (2005) in England and Wales, however, does specify certain procedural requirements (Box 2.24).

Box 2.24 Legislative Case Study: England and Wales

The Mental Capacity Act 2005 specifies Deprivation of Liberty Safeguards (MCA DoLS). MCA DoLS must be used if people who lack capacity need to have their liberty taken away in order to receive care and/or treatment that is in their best interests and protects them from harm. If a person working in a hospital or care home considers that a person for whom they are caring cannot be cared for and/or treated without having their liberty taken away, the relevant health authority (for hospitals) or the local authority (for care homes) must be asked to carry out an assessment to decide if it is right to take away the person's liberty.

This comprises a mental health assessment and a 'best interests' assessment and they must be carried out by different assessors. The mental health assessment must be carried out by a doctor; the best interests assessor must also be independent from the managing authority, or not involved in the care of the individual in question. The best interests assessor must ensure that the individual in question has a representative appointed to support them. Anyone who does not have family or friends who can be consulted will have an Independent Mental Capacity Advocate (IMCA) instructed to support and represent them during the assessment process.

An IMCA is a specialist advocate trained to advise and represent individuals in relation to mental capacity issues.

Available at: www.dh.gov.uk (www.dh.gov.uk/en/Publicationsandstatistics/Publications/PublicationsPolicyAndGuidance/DH_091868)

Many legal provisions are less developed or clear with regard to mental capacity to consent. This situation raises the risk that the threshold for establishing mental incapacity may be influenced not only by a patient's urgent need of help in treating his severe mental disorder but also by other objectives such as, for example, social control. It is undoubtedly the case that any judgment regarding an individual's lack of capacity to consent is fraught with ethical, political and pragmatic intractabilities. For example, it has been argued that it is preferable to have a relatively low threshold of capacity – with the consequence of some non-consensual treatment of those who have capacity – than to set a high threshold of capacity with the risk that many would never qualify as having it. Indeed this issue is arguably currently one of the most highly contested and discussed issues amongst those in the fields of mental health, disability and discrimination.

2.8 Human rights

Human rights are rights enjoyed by humans simply by virtue of their being human. They are universal and egalitarian. The first inkling of these rights is often located in primitive form in the city states of ancient Greece and in Roman law and, later, in the English Magna Carta and in the Twelve Articles of the Black Forest in Europe. More recently, they also appeared in the United States Declaration of Independence and in the French Declaration of the Rights of Man and of the Citizen. These rights have been further articulated after the World Wars in the last century – in international human rights law and especially through the United Nations, firstly in its Universal Declaration of Human Rights adopted by the General Assembly in 1948 (14.1.1.8), and in subsequent treaties. (A good introduction to international human rights law is given by Krause and Scheinin (2009).)

The United Nations Universal Declaration of Human Rights, 1948, is explicit about four freedoms: speech, association and freedom from fear or want. Articles 1 and 2 focus on dignity, liberty, equality and brotherhood; Articles 3–11 address rights such as the right to life and the prohibition of slavery; Articles 12–17 deal with rights of the individual and civil and political society; Articles 18–21 concern spiritual, public and political freedoms (religion and association); and Articles 22–27 set out social, economic and cultural rights.

2.8.1 Negative and positive rights

Human rights are commonly divided between positive rights and negative rights.

Negative rights are those held by the individual on a guarantee that the state has no right to prevent him/her from their enjoyment, to interfere with them in any way or form, or to abrogate them unless there are good legal reasons. Negative rights include, among others, the right to life, autonomy, and freedom of association.

Positive rights permit or oblige action. For example, positive rights include the state's provision of a good or service (for example, the right to social protection/social services).

Many civil and political rights are considered negative rights (freedom of speech, freedom of worship) and many economic, social and cultural rights are positive rights (the right to education, the right to social services). This distinction has served to emphasise that many positive rights require governments explicitly to set up programmes of implementation for their realisation. It should, nonetheless, be emphasised that a distinction on such grounds between positive and negative rights is in some ways a moot one – for example, many so-called negative rights arguably also require government or state action.

One example of a constitution that endorses social (i.e. positive) rights is that of South Africa (Box 2.25).

Box 2.25 Legislative Case Study: South Africa

The Bill of Rights in the Constitution of the Republic of South Africa, 1996 states:

- 'Section 12: Everyone has the right to bodily and psychological integrity, which includes the right ... (b) to security in and control over their body ...
- Section 27: (1) Everyone has the right to have access to: health care services, including reproductive health care; sufficient food and water; and social security, including, if they are unable to support themselves and their dependents, appropriate social assistance.'

The state must take reasonable legislative and other measures, within its available resources, to achieve the progressive realisation of each of these rights.

A discussion of welfare rights in state constitutions, including that of South Africa, is given in Pascal (2008).

International human rights law addresses both negative and positive rights – as indicated above in the description of the United Nations Declaration of Human Rights. Nonetheless, there has arguably been much more attention paid to the protection of negative rights than to consideration of how effectively to uphold positive rights. In 2005, Louise Arbour, the former United Nations High Commissioner for Human Rights, underscored the importance of expanding our vision, both nationally and internationally, of fundamental human rights, so that the upholding of economic, social and cultural rights is given as much attention as the upholding of civil and political rights. She argued that: '[r]ecognising the status of economic, social and cultural rights as justiciable entitlements is crucial to honouring the political, moral and legal commitments undertaken by States when the international Bill of Rights was adopted' (Arbour, 2005).

Her comments reaffirmed that positive social entitlements should be regarded as justiciable human rights (i.e. capable of being decided by legal principles or by a court of justice) under international law, as enshrined in such conventions as the International Convention on Economic, Social and Cultural Rights (Chapter 14.1.1.6). Her comments also pointed to the failure of many states to give meaningful effect to many social, economic and cultural rights. Arbour, as a former Justice of the Supreme Court of Canada and a frequent dissenter with respect to the ambit of social rights under the Canadian Charter of Rights and Freedoms (Constitution Act, 1982), has gauged the shortcomings of national legal systems in this respect.

2.8.2 Human rights in relation to people with mental health problems

The framework of human rights is becoming an increasingly powerful tool both internationally and at a country-based level for combating the discrimination and abuse experienced by people with mental health problems (Dhanda and Narayan, 2007). As we have already noted in our discussion of the United Nations Convention on the Rights of Persons with Disabilities (CRPD), the fundamental shift in the last two decades has been towards addressing people with mental health problems as equal citizens with the full complement of rights and fundamental freedoms (Parker, 2007).

As Yamin and Rosenthal (2005) have argued: 'The starting point for the development of a human rights-based policy on mental health is that mentally ill individuals are full human beings who are entitled to rights.... In a rights framework, "mental health needs" are not analysed (as they are in many studies) in terms of the application of given diagnostic criteria in isolation from the social context that leads to use of the mental health sector and mentally disabled persons are treated as more than patients who need services'.

However, it remains the case that many laws that address disability do so not through the framework of rights, but through non-rights-based social security and welfare legislation, health law or guardianship. Much of this legislation installs people with disabilities not as individuals with legal rights but as 'objects of welfare, health and charity programs' [sic] (Degener and Quinn G, 2000). A human rights approach serves to move us beyond a focus simply on the quality of care and the level of welfare entitlements. (We should emphasise that many of the specifications surrounding welfare have frequently resulted in discriminatory social policy through the installation of segregated housing and inadequate sheltered workshops.) The human rights-based approach to disability fundamentally regards people with disabilities as subjects – not objects – of law and sees legislation as a tool through which to ensure the participation of people with disabilities in all social spheres, in a way that is respectful towards and accommodating of their differences.

A human rights focus also makes it clear that legislative and administrative efforts to address the discrimination and abuse that people with mental health problems experience must be multi-sectoral: for people with mental disabilities to exercise their rights as citizens will require the involvement, for example, of the education, housing, social care and employment sectors (Sayce, 2003). Human rights comprise both rights and obligations, and human rights law conceives the duties of government to be broad. The state not only has an obligation not to infringe upon human rights and to prevent violations (e.g. anti-discrimination laws), but also an obligation to realise positive rights as well as actively to promote human rights (e.g. via education and awareness raising) (Gostin, 2000).

The framework of human rights is crucial both for countries with developed democratic and judicial systems and for those without. This is particularly the case where socio-cultural, ideological and political reasons are given to justify abuse, discrimination or the denial of rights. The framework of human rights is, after all, 'the only source of law that legitimises international scrutiny of mental health policies and practices within a sovereign country' (Gostin, 2000). Global enforcement of human rights has, nonetheless, to consider regional morals as the backbone of societal attitudes. The change of such norms may be experienced as an attack on an society's identity and hence this might provoke strong resistance (Ernst and Sellmaier, 2010).

Advancement of human rights for individuals with mental health problems has taken the form of both binding instruments (such as the Convention on the Rights of Persons with Disabilities and other UN conventions) and non-binding international norms. It has also taken place through domestic legislative reform, via treaties such as multilateral conventions promulgated by international organisations, particularly the United Nations, or through customary norms, which have their origins in state practice and *opinio juris* (i.e. the legal opinion of experts on law and jurisprudence) (Kinney, 2001). United Nations conventions are subject to the limitation that, in order to be effective for citizens domestically, they have to be given expression in the national law of the country whose citizens seek to enforce such rights. In Canada, for example, these rights are covered under several Acts, including the Canada Health Act (RS, 1985, c. C–6). Furthermore, a significant development with respect to the development of positive rights to health and health care is found in both the Principles for the Protection of Persons with Mental Illness and the Improvement of Mental Health Care (UN General Assembly, 17 December 1991) (Chapter 14.1.2.3 and 14.4.3) and in the Convention on the Rights of Persons with Disabilities (CRPD) (Chapter 14.1.1.1 and 14.4.1). The most significant international source of a 'right to health' is found in Article 12 of the International Covenant on Economic, Social and Cultural Rights (Chapter 14.1.1.6).

Notably, then, the CRPD contains both civil and political rights (which States that have ratified the CRPD have an 'immediate obligation' to respect, protect and fulfil) and economic, social and cultural rights (which may be 'progressively realised' – i.e. they may not be immediately fulfilled because of the limits of available resources, but States must work towards their realisation). The CRPD fundamentally recognises the intimate interconnection of civil and political rights on the one hand, and economic, social and cultural rights on the other. In so doing, it gives new energy to human rights law and discourse as vehicles for social change (Weller, 2009) (Box 2.26).

Box 2.26 Legislative Case Study: European Union

The European Union (EU) ratified the United Nations Convention on the Rights of Persons with Disabilities (CRPD) as a legal entity in December 2010. This binds the European institutions (the European Commission, Parliament, Council and Court of Justice) to uphold the rights of persons with disabilities. It is hoped that this will create added impetus for those countries within the EU that have not yet ratified the CRPD to do so.

In relation to health care specifically, national systems in countries with advanced mental health legislation, such as Canada, have provided substantial protections for patients receiving psychiatric treatment in institutions, so that they are infrequently abused in their bodily integrity or their freedoms abrogated. Similarly, many countries have provided significant civil and constitutional protections with respect to the negative rights of its citizens, including people with psychiatric diagnoses. The same, however, cannot be said with respect to many positive rights (Hirschl, 2000).

Louise Arbour's observations are particularly apposite with respect to the human rights of people with mental illness. Although there have been significant advances with respect to the negative rights of such persons over the last 20 years, positive rights have – in practice – not fared so well. Most agree that national legislatures have tended to be far better at protecting negative rights for people with mental illness than ensuring positive rights (Weisstub and Arboleda-Flórez, 2005). The development of robust legislative and administrative frameworks for the protection of positive rights is, therefore, currently a key arena for reform. These positive rights are central to ensuring the social inclusion of people with mental health problems, given the grave inequalities and structural barriers they so frequently experience in the domains of health care, housing and education (Kelly, 2005, 2006) (Chapters 6, Education; 7, Housing; and 9, Health, health care and the right to health).

The reverse of human rights could be conceived of as coercion. Persons in authority seek consensus and support for their orders, but there is no doubt that if orders are not followed or requests are not acquiesced to or obeyed, there will be negative consequences. Coercion works either through persuasion or through imposition and it is the opposite of freedom, however defined (whether in positive or negative terms). In psychiatry, for example, even when the patient enters into treatment voluntarily, there is commonly the open or veiled threat that imposition of coercive measures is a possibility. Coercion is a characteristic of many psychiatric interventions (Szmukler, 2010). Any limitation on freedom to choose has an impact on a person's ability to exercise individual rights and may have negative consequences on the patient's recovery. Hence, the need to go to the limit in explaining to patients and their families the need, where absolutely unavoidable, for coercive measures, their extent and their duration and what avenues are open for patients to appeal the application of such measures. Psychiatric treatment and interventions will be better received if practitioners use freedom as the default mode and invoke coercive measures in only extreme circumstances within the constrictions of the law.

Mental health legislation in many countries does not mention any rights for people with mental illness. There are growing efforts to ensure that mental health legislation is developed or overhauled so as to ensure that they adequately protect the negative and positive rights of psychiatric patients.

2.9 Stigma, discrimination and 'structural violence'

While stigma and prejudice are attitudes, discrimination is the direct or indirect denial of entitlements and rights that are ordinarily enjoyed by most citizens (Section 2.3). Stigma, prejudice and discrimination are closely related and tightly interwoven social constructs that are observed across all classes and social groups. Stigma and prejudice are important social attitudes that hinder the reintegration of people who have received inpatient psychiatric care within their communities (Arboleda-Flórez, 2005). It is, however, discrimination, which leads to the denial of rights and causes the most difficulties.

Stigma develops within a social matrix of relationships and interactions and can be understood within a three-dimensional axis labelled: perspective, identity and reaction (Crocker *et al.*, 1998). Perspective refers to an initial perception of threat and separateness; identity pertains to the identification of members of the group perceived as threatening and the consensual sharing of the belief in the perceived threat; and reaction is the way in which those under threat seek to protect themselves (Arboleda-Flórez, 2002). People with mental illness usually score highly in these dimensions. In addition, the public tends to have stereotypical views of people with mental illness as violent and unpredictable. The association between mental illness and violence helps to perpetuate stigmatising and discriminatory practices against people with mental illness and is only one of the many negative stereotypes and prejudicial attitudes held by the public about them (Stuart and Arboleda-Flórez, 2001). Furthermore, because many severe mental illnesses are long term and can be incapacitating, it is difficult for some people with mental illness to migrate out of the grip caused by negative social attitudes. The result can be social annihilation: they may be prevented from re-integrating into their communities and from participating in social activities.

Kelly (2005) describes 'structural violence' as an insidious condition of discrimination and abuse that, in essence, translates into 'anti-rights' for the mentally ill. For example, people with mental illness have the anti-rights to remain homeless in the streets where they might freeze to death on winter nights, to be unemployed, or to be confined to a permanent condition of poverty and dependency on charity. They may also be disproportionately robbed, mugged, raped, beaten up or murdered. Should they react violently, many times in self-defence, they are labelled dangerous and sent to prison. Many psychiatric patients have, in effect, been granted the anti-right to be criminalised and to receive treatment, if any, in prisons and penitentiaries, as opposed to hospitals, where most citizens expect to go if they fall ill (Appelbaum, 1997). The facile manner in which people with mental health problems have been criminalised reinforces the stigmatising attitudes in society. This has fuelled further fears that they are dangerous and unpredictable and has led to further calls for expansion of controls via commitment legislation (the use of mental health law to commit a person to a mental hospital) (Appelbaum, 1997).

Unfortunately, many individuals with mental illness, by virtue of the discrimination they experience on account of their disabilities, often lack the knowledge, power and motivation to know how to seek redress to their problems. There are also high rates of poverty among people with mental health problems. Many do not hold a job or work at menial occupations, many times below their level of knowledge, training, or abilities (Chapter 5, Work and the workplace). For those with severe mental health problems, the nature of the symptoms can often mean that it is difficult to raise one's voice to participate or even to complain. Poverty, lack of voice and lack of participation eventually lead to disenfranchisement, a condition that renders the individual invisible and powerless to champion his or her own cause in the political arena, or to seek successful champions to fight his or her battles. Those who take on the cause of such individuals are frequently clinicians, who in turn may be seen to be advancing their own careers or using people with mental illness to improve their own situation. The person with mental illness is, therefore, caught in a vicious circle of unwelcome social constructs and circumstances that conspire to deny his or her human rights – a spiral of despair.

Joblessness, homelessness, poor physical health and other undesirable circumstances have been cited both as risk factors for and consequences of long-term mental illness. It may be that unemployment, homelessness and poor physical health result from prolonged neglect of people with mental illness, thus constituting an abuse of their rights and a form of systemic discrimination.

2.10 Social justice

The previous sections have made it clear that legislative approaches to improve the lives of people with mental health problems will need to attend as much to their positive rights as to their negative rights. In light of the high levels of poverty, structural discrimination and disenfranchisement experienced by many, social justice for people with mental health problems will be impossible without adequate efforts being devoted to housing, social protection, social services and employment (Russell, 2002; Stein and Stein, 2007). A growing body of literature within the field of mental health (as well as research within disability studies and human rights) emphasises that if we are to improve the lives of people with mental health problems, we need fundamentally to understand that adverse outcomes – in terms of poverty, social exclusion and marginalisation – cannot be understood, let alone addressed, through an individual lens (assuming they arise from an individual's psychological deficits, illness or lack of assets etc.). Instead, we need to recognise that unequal distributions of mental health – and of disabilities – within communities and across groups are themselves a result of social injustice. At the same time, the use of human rights in the service of improving people's mental health and well-being must gain traction not solely by protecting the rights of a series of individuals, but by working to extend social rights and lessen social inequalities across communities and groups and within populations (Burns, 2009; Friedli, 2009; Isaac *et al.*, 2010; Kelly, 2005, 2006). The discrimination and social injustices that many people with mental health problems experience operate through a complex articulation of social, economic and political – as well as legal – forces; combating that discrimination and social injustice demands grappling with that web of inter-related forces rather than imaging that legal tools will effect transformation on their own.

This is acutely apparent when attempting to use legislation as a social development and human rights tool in low-income countries. Here, the mental health of communities can be undermined by profound economic and social marginalisation, at the same time as an individual's mental health problems put him or her at much greater risk of becoming socially marginalised and economically vulnerable. But frequently, the dominant discourse within development does not acknowledge how central mental health – as a focus for both legislation and policy – is to the achievement of social development goals. (Miranda and Patel (2005) have provided a critique regarding the absence of mental health within the Millennium Development Goals (MDGs). There are eight MDGs with a target date of 2015. They range from halving extreme poverty to halting the spread of HIV/AIDS and providing universal primary education. They have been agreed by all the world's countries and form the current framework for development activities worldwide (www.un.org/millenniumgoals).)

There are also significant differences in provisions of mental health care across the world: in many low-income countries, very little money is devoted to mental health care budgets and, as a result, the organisation and provision of formalised mental health care is thinly and fragmentarily distributed. Traditional healers remain for many people with mental health problems the first – and often only – source of treatment. Additionally, attempts to advance the rights and entitlements of people with mental health problems in low-income countries have to contend with competition for limited resources within reform efforts (whether in health or in other sectors), the often limited partnerships between mental health and social development programmes and policies, and the need to build up what is often limited capacity amongst service users and other stakeholders for advocacy on a national stage (Jenkins *et al.*, 2010). And this is to set to one side the multiple difficulties entailed in effectively wielding traditional human rights frameworks and instruments to protect the rights of individual mental health service users. In many countries of the world (for example, in much of southern Africa), there has been little substantive development of legal frameworks within the mental health context and little indication that people with mental health problems have engaged with the legal system as a route either to individual or social justice (Bartlett, 2010).

This implies, at the very least, that there can be no simple 'one-size-fits-all' approach to the use of legislation as a tool to promote human rights and social justice. Legislative approaches to discrimination, injustice and rights violations in low- and middle-income countries will need to work hand in hand with local communities through advocacy and policy programmes that are focused on tackling social, economic and cultural exigencies that have been identified by and have resonance with those communities themselves (Read *et al.*, 2009). Examples of projects and programmes that attempt to do just this are documented in Boxes 2.27 and 2.28 below.

Box 2.27 Project: Ghana, South Africa, Uganda and Zambia

The World Health Organization Mental Health and Poverty Project (MHaPP) is a project that has combined legislative action with multi-sectoral policy, advocacy and poverty reduction programmes to combat the discrimination experienced by people with mental health problems in four sub-Saharan African countries (Ghana, South Africa, Uganda and Zambia).

The MHaPP has produced detailed situational analyses for each of the four countries. These include a review of the current status of mental health policy and legislation, as well as an analysis of existing mental health systems in each country. The country reports are available for download from the MHaPP web site, www.who.int/mental_health/policy/development/mhapp/en

Further discussion of the intersection of legislation and policy in relation to MHaPP, and with particular attention given to the difficulties of policy implementation, is found in Omar *et al.* (2010).

Box 2.28 Project: Movement for Global Mental Health

The Movement for Global Mental Health emerged out of a recent series of articles that were published in *The Lancet* (Horton, 2005).

The Movement for Global Mental Health embeds a focus on human rights within a heterogeneous programme of activities and advocacy to improve the treatment of mental health problems in low-income countries. The movement's goal is to implement the final 'Call for Action' article within *The Lancet* series 'which demands the scaling up of treatments for mental disorders at the same time as close attention to the protection of the human rights of those affected'.

For further information: www.globalmentalhealth.org

Additional details and discussion of the Movement for Global Mental Health are given in Patel *et al.* (2011).

Activists within the Global South have, at the same time, drawn attention to the energy and vigour with which grassroots movements have been developing their own approaches to health and human rights injustices, which are not indebted to expert-driven strategies and models from the Global North. Amita Dhanda and Thelma Nayaran (2007), for example, point to the example of the People's Health Movement (PHM), a grassroots movement that draws together various networks and activists whose work focuses on growing inequities in health (Box 2.29).

Box 2.29 Project: People's Health Movement

The People's Health Movement (PHM) is committed to:

- promoting 'Health for All' through an equitable, participatory and inter-sectoral movement, and as a rights issue;
- encouraging government and other health agencies to ensure universal access to quality health care, education and social services according to people's needs and not their ability to pay;

- promoting the participation of people and people's organisations in the formulation, implementation and evaluation of all health and social policies and programmes;
- promoting health along with equity and sustainable development as top priorities in local, national and international policymaking;
- encouraging people to develop their own solutions to local health problems;
- holding accountable local authorities, national governments, international organisations and corporations.

For further information: www.phmovement.org

2.11 What comes next?

In the following chapters, we provide introductions to some of the most important contexts, arenas and domains that demand consideration when considering how legislation might be used to combat the discrimination, abuse and social injustice experienced by people with mental health problems. Readers should note that these contexts and domains do not cover the entire spectrum that could have been addressed. We have not included, for example, chapters that address family/reproduction/sexuality, or travel/transport/freedom of movement. Both are domains in which people with mental health problems can experience discrimination and abuse. The choice of content was in part guided by the case materials we received from our country informants. We were also driven by our desire to focus on domains and contexts in which a substantial amount of specific legislative and administrative action has already been taken, upon which we can draw for exemplars. We also do not specifically address prisoners with mental health problems. In Chapter 12, we address at some length the question of implementation and enforcement – without which any attempt to use the law to combat discrimination, abuse and social injustice is likely to be ineffective at best and counter-productive at worst.

References

Appelbaum, P (1997) Almost a revolution: an international perspective on the law of involuntary commitment. *J Am Acad Psychiatry Law*, **25**:135–147.

Arboleda-Flórez, J (2002) What causes stigma? *World Psychiatry*, **1**(1):25–26.

Arboleda-Flórez, J (2005) Forensic psychiatry: two masters, one ethics. *Die Psychiatrie*, **2**:153–157.

Arbour, L (2005) Statement by Ms Louise Arbour High Commissioner for Human Rights to the Open-Ended Working Group established by the Commission on Human Rights to consider options regarding the elaboration of an optional protocol to the International Covenant on Economic, Social and Cultural Rights. Second Session, Salle XVII, Palais des Nations, 14 January 2005. (Available online at www.unhchr.ch/huricane/huricane.nsf/0/ECAE2629449C1EBCC1256F8C0035047D?opendocument)

Axelsson, C and Barrett, D (2009) Access to Social Services for Persons with Disabilities in the Middle East – Multi-Stakeholder reflections for policy reform. Disability Rights Monitor Initiative–Middle East, CBM and Handicap International (http://www.makingitwork-crpd.org/fileadmin/user/content/DMI_Documents/DMI_Report_2009_final_version_17-5-2010.pdf).

Bagenstos, SR (2004) The future of disability law. *The Yale Law Journal*, **14**(1): 1–84.

Bartlett, P (2003) Adults, mental illness and incapacity: convergence and overlap in legal regulation. *Journal of Social Welfare and Family Law*, **25**(4):341–353.

Bartlett, P (2010) Thinking about the rest of the world: mental health and rights outside the 'First World'. In: McSherry, B and Weller, P (eds) *Rethinking Rights-Based Mental Health Laws*. Hart, Oxford. pp. 397–418.

Becker, T and Kilian, R (2006) Psychiatric services for people with severe mental illness across western Europe: what can be generalized from current knowledge about differences in provision, costs and outcomes of mental health care? *Acta Psychiatrica Scandinavica*, **429**(Suppl):9–16.

Beresford, P (2002) Thinking about 'mental health': towards a social model. *Journal of Mental Health*, **11**(6):581–584.

Beresford, P, Nettle, M and Perring, R (2010) Towards a social model of madness and distress? Exploring what service users say. Joseph Rowntree Foundation, York.

Bickenbach, JE, Chatterji, S, Badley, EM and Üstün, TB (1999) Models of disablement, universalism and the international classification of impairments, disabilities and handicaps. *Social Science & Medicine*, **48**:1173–1187.

Burns, JK (2009) Mental health and inequity: a human rights approach to inequality, discrimination, and mental disability. *Health and Human Rights*, **11**(2):19–31.

Byrnes, A (2008) The Disability Discrimination Ordinance, the UN Convention on the Rights of Persons with Disabilities, and beyond: achievements and challenges after ten years of Hong Kong anti-discrimination legislation. UN-ESCAP. (http://www.unescap.org/sdd/issues/disability/crpd/files/Paper-III-Andrew-20110121.pdf)

Byrnes, A (2009) Disability discrimination law and the Asia Pacific Region. Expert Group Meeting (EGM) on Harmonization of National Legislation with the Convention on the Rights of Persons with Disabilities in Asia and the Pacific, 8–10 June 2009, Bangkok, ESCAP/OHCHR.

Carson, G (2009) The social model of disability. Scottish Accessible Information Forum. (http://www.ukdpc.net/library/Social%20Model%20of%20Disability2.pdf)

Center for International Rehabilitation (ed.) (2005) International disability rights: an overview and comparative analysis of international and national initiatives to promote and protect the rights of persons with disabilities. The Law Library of Congress, Washington, DC.

Commander, MJ, Odell, SM, Surtees, PG and Sashidharan, SP (2003) Characteristics of patients and patterns of psychiatric service use in ethnic minorities. *International Journal of Social Psychiatry*, **49**(3):216–224.

Constitution Act (1982) Part I of the Constitution Act, 1982 being Schedule B to the Canada Act 1982 (UK), 1982, c. 11.

Council of Europe (2011) *Handbook on European Non-Discrimination Law*. European Union Agency for Fundamental Rights & European Court of Human Rights (Council of Europe), Vienna & Strasbourg.

Crenshaw K (1989) Demarginalizing the intersection of race and sex: a black feminist critique of antidiscrimination doctrine, feminist theory and antiracist politics. University of Chicago Legal Forum, IL. pp. 139–167.

Crocker, J, Major, Band Steele, C (1998) Social stigma. In: Gilbert, D, Fiske, S and Lindzey, G (eds) *Handbook of Social Psychology*, 4th edn. McGraw-Hill, Boston, MA.

Crowley, F (2003) Mental Illness – The Neglected Quarter. Amnesty International (Irish section) Summary Report.

Degener, T (2005) Disability discrimination law: a global comparative approach. In: Lawson, A and Gooding, C (eds) *Disability Rights in Europe: From theory to practice*. Hart, Oxford and Portland, pp. 87–106.

Degener, T (2006) The definition of disability in German and foreign discrimination law. *Disability Studies Quarterly*, **26**(2).

Degener, T and Quinn, G. (2000) A survey of international, comparative and regional disability law reform. International Disability Law and Policy Symposium, sponsored by the US Social Security Administration and organized by the Disability Rights Education and Defense Fund, 22–26 October (2000) Washington, DC. (http://www.nuigalway.ie/law/Common%20Files/Disability%20Research%20Unit/GQ/Degener%20-%20Quinn%20paper.pdf)

De Girolamo, G, Alonso, J and Vilagut, G (2006) The ESEMeD-WMH project: strengthening epidemiological research in Europe through the study of variation in prevalence estimates. *Epidemiol Psichiatr Soc.*, **15**(3):167–173.

Dhanda, A (2007) Legal capacity in the Disability Rights Convention: stranglehold of the past or lodestar for the future. *Syracuse Journal of International Law and Commerce*, **34**(2): 429–462.

Dhanda, A and Narayan, T (2007) Mental health and human rights. *The Lancet*, **370**:1197–1198.

Diekmann, A (2010) *Stellvertretung in Gesundheitsangelegenheiten: Modell eines dreigliedrigen Vertretungssystems*. Universitätsverlag Göttingen.

Ernst, G and Sellmaier, S (eds) (2010) *Universelle Menschenrechte und partikulare Moral*. Kohlhammer, Stuttgart, Germany.

European Commission (2007) *Tackling Multiple Discrimination – Practices, policies and laws*. Office for Offical Publications of the European Communities, Luxembourg.

Expert Group on Mental Health Policy (2006) A Vision for Change. Report of the Expert Group on Mental Health Policy. Department of Health and Children, Dublin.

Farmer, CM (2008) Chile: reforms in national mental health policy. In: Caldas de Almeida, JM and Cohen, A (eds) *Innovative Mental Health Programs in Latin America nad the Caribbean*. Pan American Health Organization, Washington, DC, pp. 44–61.

Fredman, S (2005) Double trouble: multiple discrimination and EU law. *European Anti-Discrimination Law Review*, **2**:13–18.

Friedli, L (2009) Mental health, resilience and inequalities. Mental Health Foundation/World Health Organization, Geneva, Switzerland.

Gostin, LO (2000) Human rights of persons with mental disabilities: the European Convention of Human Rights. *International Journal of Law and Psychiatry*, **23**(2):125–159.

Gostin, L, Bartlett, P, Fennell, P, Fennell, P, McHale, J and Mackay, R (eds) (2010) *Principles of Mental Health Law and Policy*. Oxford University Press, Oxford.

Hannett, S (2003) Equality at the intersections: the legislative and judicial failure to tackle multiple discrimination. *Oxford Journal of Legal Studies*, **23**(1):65–86.

Harpur, P and Bales, R (2010) The positive impact of the Convention on the Rights of Persons with Disabilities: a case study on the South Pacific and lessons from the US experience. *Northern Kentucky Law Review*, **363**:363–388.

Helmchen, H (2010) Informed consent in psychiatric practice. In: Helmchen H and Sartorius N (eds) *Ethics in Psychiatry: European Contributions*. Springer, Dordrecht, pp. 139–146.

Hirschl, R (2000) 'Negative' rights vs. 'positive' entitlements: a comparative study of judicial interpretations of rights in an emerging neo-liberal economic order. *Human Rights Quarterly*, **22**(4):1060–1098.

Horton, R (2007) Launching a new movement for mental health. *The Lancet*, **370**(9590):806.

Human Rights Commission (2010) *Human Rights in New Zealand 2010*. Human Rights Commission, New Zealand.

Isaac, R, Raja, BWD and Ravanan, MP (2010) Integrating people with disabilities: their right – our responsibility. *Disability & Society*, **25**(5):627–630.

Jenkins, R, Baingana, F, Belkin, G, Borowitz, M, Daly, A, Francis P, *et al.* (2010) Mental Health and the Development Agenda in Sub-Saharan Africa. *Psychiatr Serv*, **61**(3):229–334.

Kelly, BD (2005) Structural violence and schizophrenia. *Social Science & Medicine*, **61**:721–730.

Kelly, BD (2006) The power gap: freedom, power and mental illness. *Social Science & Medicine*, **63**:2118–2128.

Kinney, ED (2001) The international human right to health: what does this mean for our nation and our world? *Indiana Law Review*, **34**:1457–1475.

Kock, M (2004) Disability law in Germany: an overview on employment, education and access. *German Law Journal*, **5**:1373–1392.

Krause, C and Scheinin, M (eds) (2009) *International Protection of Human Rights: A Textbook*. Institute for Human Rights, Åbo Akademy University, Turku, Finland.

Lawson, A (2008) People with psychosocial impairments or conditions, reasonable accommodation and the Convention on the Rights of Persons with Disabilities. *Law in Context*, **26**:62–84.

Letelier, LM and Bedregal, P (2006) Health reform in Chile. *The Lancet*, **368**(9554):2197–2198.

Link, BG and Phelan, JC (2001) Conceptualizing stigma. *Annual Review of Sociology*, **27**:363–385.

Lyons, D (2008) New mental health legislation in Scotland. *Adv Psychiatr Treat*, **14**(2):89–97.

Lyons, D and Rush, G (2004) Universal rights and mental illness in Ireland. *Psychiatric Bulletin*, **28**:114–116.

MacGabhann, L, Lakeman, R, McGowan, P, Parkinson, M, Redmond, M, Sibitz, I, *et al.* (2010) Hear my voice: the experience of discrimination of people with mental health problems in Ireland. Dublin City University, Dublin.

McSherry, B and Weller, P (2010) *Rethinking Rights-Based Mental Health Laws*. Hart, Oxford.

Miranda, J and Patel, V (2005) Achieving the Millennium Development Goals: Does mental health play a role? *PLoS Medicine*, **2**(10):e291.

National Centre for Human Rights [of Jordan] (2010) National implementation of the Convention on the Rights of Persons with Disabilities. Response by the National Centre for Human Rights of Jordan. National Centre for Human Rights of Jordan.

Oliver, M (1983) *Social Work with Disabled People*. Macmillan, London.

Oliver, M (1996) *Understanding disability: from theory to practice*. St Martin's, New York.

Oliver, M and Barnes, C (1998) *Disabled People and Social Policy: From exclusion to inclusion*. Longman, London.

Omar, MA, Green, AT, Bird, PK, Mirzoev, T, Flisher, AJ, Kigozi, F, *et al.* (2010) Mental health policy process: a comparative study of Ghana, South Africa, Uganda and Zambia. *Int J Ment Health Syst*, **4**:24.

Parker, C (2007) Developing mental health policy: a human rights perspective. In: Knapp, M, McDaid, D, Mossialos, E and Thornicroft, G (eds) *Mental Health Policy and Practice across Europe: The future direction of mental health care*. Open University Press, Maidenhead, pp. 308–335.

Pascal, E (2008) Welfare rights in state constitutions. *Rutgers Law Journal*, **39**:863–901.

Patel, V, Collins, PY, Copeland, J, Kakuma, R, Katontoka, S, Lamichhane J, *et al.* (2011) The Movement for Global Mental Health. *British Journal of Psychiatry*, **198**:88–90.

Perlin, ML and Szeli E (in press) Mental health and human rights: Evolution and contemporary challenges. In: Dudley, M (ed.) *Mental health and human rights*. Oxford University Press, London.

Read, UM, Adiibokah, E and Nyame, S (2009) Local suffering and the global discourse of mental health and human rights: an ethnographic study of responses to mental illness in rural Ghana. *Global Health*, **5**:13.

Rosenthal, E (2009) MDRI. The rights of children with disabilities in Viet Nam: Bringing Vietnam's laws into compliance with the UN Convention on the Rights of Persons with Disabilities. Prepared for UNICEF.

Rosenthal, E and Sundram, CJ (2004) The role of international human rights in national mental health legislation. Department of Mental Health and Substance Dependence, World Health Organization, Geneva, Switzerland. (http://www.who.int/mental_health/policy/legislation/en/WHO%20chapter%20in%20English_r1.pdf)

Russell, M (2002) What disabilty civil rights cannot do: employment and political economy. *Disability & Society*, **17**(2):117–135.

Russell, H, Quinn, E, O'Riain, RK and McGinnity, F (2008) *The experience of discrimination in Ireland: analysis of the QNHS Equality Module*. The Equality Authority and The Economic and Social Research Institute, Dublin.

SAMH (n.d.) Making Reasonable Adjustments at Work for People with Mental Health Problems: A solutions guide from SAMH. Scottish Association for Mental Health, Glasgow, UK.

Sayce, L (2000) *From Psychiatric Patient to Citizen: Overcoming Discrimination and Social Exclusion*. Palgrave, Basingstoke and New York.

Sayce, L (2003) Beyond good intentions. Making anti-discrimination strategies work. *Disability & Society*, **18**(5):625–642.

Sayce, L and Curran, C (2007) Tackling social exclusion across Europe. In: Knapp, M, McDaid, D, Mossialos, E and Thornicroft, G (eds) *Mental Health Policy and Practice across Europe*. Open University Press, Maidenhead, pp. 34–59.

Schiek, D and Lawson, A (eds) (2011) *European Union Non-Discrimination Law and Intersectionality: Investigating the triangle of racial, gender and disability discrimination*. Ashgate.

Schulze, B (2005) Stigmatisierungserfahrungen von Betroffenen und Angehoerigen: Ergebnisse von Fokusgruppeninterviews. In: Gaebel, W, Moeller, H and Roessler, W (eds) *Stigma – Diskriminierung – Bewaeltigung Der Umgang mit sozialer Ausgrenzung psychisch Kranker*. Kohlhammer, Stuttgart, pp. 122–144.

Scottish Government (2007) With Inclusion in Mind: The local authority's role in promoting wellbeing and social development. Mental Health (Care and Treatment) (Scotland) Act 2003. The Scottish Government, Edinburgh.

Shorter, E 9 1997) *A History of Psychiatry: From the era of the asylum to the age of Prozac*. John Wiley & Sons, Inc., New York.

Stein, MA and Stein, PJS (2007) Beyond disability civil rights. *Hasting Law Journal*, **58**:1203.

Stewart, CL (2004) Chile mental health country profile. *International Review of Psychiatry*, **16**(1–2):73–82.

Stuart, H and Arboleda-Flórez, J (2001) Community attitudes toward people with schizophrenia. *Can J Psychiatry*, **46**(3):55–61.

Syse, A (2006) Equality and accessibility: a proactive approach to strengthen the legal status and protection against discrimination of persons with disabilites. In: Wahlgren, P (ed.) *A Proactive Approach: Law Libraries*. Stockholm Institute for Scandinavian Law, Stockholm.

Szmukler, G (2010) 'Coercive' measures. In: Helmchen, H and Sartorius, N (eds) *Ethics in Psychiatry: European Contributions*. Springer, pp. 321–340.

Terzi, L (2004) The social model of disability: a philosophical critique. *Journal of Applied Philosophy*, **21**(2):141–157.

Thomas, C (2002) Disability theory: key ideas, issues and thinkers. In: Barnes, C, Oliver M and Barton L (eds) *Disability Studies Today*. Polity Press, Cambridge, UK.

Thornicroft, G (2006) *Shunned: discrimination against people with mental illness*. Oxford University Press, Oxford.

Tobin, J (2007) International human rights law and mental illness. *Irish Journal of Psychological Medicine*, **24**(1):31–39.

Weisstub, D and Arboleda-Flórez, J (2005) Les droits en santé mentale au Canada: une perspective internationale. *Santé mentale au Québec*, **30**(2):15–41.

Weller, P (2009) Human rights and social justice: the Convention on the Rights of Persons with Disabilities and the quiet revolution in international law. *Public Space: the Journal of Law and Social Justice*, **4**:74–91.

WHO (1980) *International Classification of Impairments, Disabilities and Handicaps (ICIDH)*. World Health Organization, Geneva, Switzerland.

WHO (1997) *The International Classification of Impairments, Activities and Participation (ICIDH–2)*. World Health Organization, Geneva, Switzerland.

WHO (2001) *ICF: International Classification of Functioning, Disability and Health*. World Health Organization, Geneva, Switzerland.

WHO (2005) *WHO Resource Book on Mental Health, Human Rights and Legislation*. World Health Organization, Geneva, Switzerland;.

WHO (2007) *Mental Health Improvements for Nations' Development. New Legislation to Protect and Promote Human Rights of People with Mental Disorders*. World Health Organization, Geneva, Switzerland.

Yamin, AE (2009) Shades of dignity: exploring the demands of equality in applying human rights frameworks to health. *Health and Human Rights*, **11**(2):1–18.

Yamin, AE and Rosenthal, E (2005) Out of the shadows: using human rights approaches to secure dignity and well-being for people with mental disabilities. *PLoS Medicine*, **2**(4):e71.

CHAPTER 3
Civil and Political Participation

'Civil and political participation' refers to an individual's ability to participate freely and without negative consequences at all levels and in all domains of public and political life and decision-making. Voting is an important example of a political right and is available in democratic nations to all adults with a limited number of exceptions (Klein and Grossman, 1971). Civil and political rights are guaranteed by a government by law – restrictions to such rights both diminish a person's democratic participation and reduce their social status (Thompson and Hall, 1974).

Civil and political rights may be withdrawn from people with mental health problems or people who have a history of psychiatric treatment. Often civil rights are lost as a package. In Lithuania (and in many other countries in central and eastern Europe), many people with a long-term mental illness are placed in residential care homes called 'internats'. About a quarter of such residents have been classified by psychiatrists as being incompetent, and these people lose their right to vote, to stand for elected office, to own property or to sign legal contracts. There are well-substantiated accounts that the designation of 'incompetence' is applied inconsistently, may sometimes be used on behalf of families seeking to take possession of a resident's property, and that once the 'incompetent' label is applied, it is rarely removed. Similarly, in Russia, being 'legally incapacitated' means losing rights to manage property, choose where to live, sign contracts, rent an apartment, be employed, vote in elections, marry, or seek any remedy through the courts (MDAC, 2005). The systematic withdrawal of such fundamental rights can be considered a type of 'civil death' (Burton, 1990).

3.1 Voting

The loss of this vital political right can be seen as an expression of social exclusion (Nash, 2002). As one commentator has put it, 'I vote, I count' (Appelbaum, 2000).

Mental Illness, Discrimination and the Law: Fighting for Social Justice, First Edition.
Felicity Callard, Norman Sartorius, Julio Arboleda-Flórez, Peter Bartlett, Hanfried Helmchen, Heather Stuart, Jose Taborda and Graham Thornicroft.

An important study was carried out by Burton (1990) in 50 of the United States. An initial survey in 1989 described the loss of civil and legal rights for mentally ill and mentally incompetent persons. Interestingly, many states made no distinction between a diagnosis of mental illness and a judicial determination of incompetence. The survey was repeated 10 years later, in 1999, to assess any changes. In most of the states examined, there were restrictions relating to serving on a jury, voting, holding official positions and limitations of parental or marriage rights. The study showed an overall trend towards increasingly curtailed rights over the decade. In 1989, every state restricted at least one of these rights for people with mental illness, while only three states (Alabama, Mississippi and Nevada) restricted all five rights. By 1999, two more states (Georgia and Iowa) had also limited all of these rights. No state had removed any restriction. In 1999, 19 of the states limited voting rights for mentally ill people and 12 restricted voting for those assessed to be incompetent (Burton, 1990; Hemmens *et al.*, 2002). In other words, mentally ill people in the USA are more often deemed to be unsuitable to exercise their basic political right to vote than people who are assessed as being incompetent (Howard and Anthony, 1977).

In November 2010, Kansas, subsequent to significant lobbying by mental health advocates, removed a never-used constitutional provision that allowed the legislature to block people from voting if they have a mental illness (Wichita Eagle, 2010). The Kansas Constitution had stated: 'The legislature may, by law, exclude persons from voting because of mental illness or commitment to a jail or penal institution'.

The United Kingdom has a better record than many of the states of America. In general, detained and informally (voluntarily) admitted psychiatric inpatients are entitled to vote. Complex regulations allow inpatients to vote as long as they have a non-hospital address and they have 'capacity' to vote (Smith and Humphreys, 1997) – established at the polling station by the electoral returning officer, if necessary, who asks the question: 'Are you the person whose name appears on the register of electors?' (Peay, 2004; Dunn, 1999). The general public, however, may not fully support such civil participation: in a survey of psychiatrists and the public, only 1% of the former felt that psychiatric patients should lose their right to vote, compared with 17% of the general population (Zogg *et al.*, 2003).

Even where patients are entitled to vote, their participation in elections may be marginal (Jaychuk and Manchanda, 1991). One study in Germany found that fewer than 10% of inpatients voted in a regional election. A campaign to inform this group of their electoral rights led to a doubling of the number who voted in the next election (Kunze *et al.*, 1982).

The European Court of Human Rights states that people who have lost their legal capacity should not automatically be deprived of their right to political participation, since this contravenes the European Convention on Human Rights (Chapter 14.2.1.1.1). In March 2011, Thomas Hammarberg, the Council of Europe Commissioner for Human Rights, gave added weight to this position, by emphasising, in one of his authoritative 'Human Rights Comments', that people with disabilities – including people with mental health disabilities and intellectual disabilities – should have the right to vote, irrespective of their legal capacity (Hammarberg, 2011). However, a recent comparative law analysis by the European Union Agency for Fundamental Rights (FRA) (Chapter 14.2.1.2.4) has revealed that the majority of Member States in the EU automatically deprive a person who has lost his or her legal capacity from his or her right to political participation (FRA, 2010). The FRA study did, however, reveal a few examples of progressive practice (details from Austria, The Netherlands and the United Kingdom are shown in Box 3.1).

Box 3.1 Legislative Case Studies

Austria

People with mental and problems and people with intellectual disabilities are allowed to vote and to be elected. Article 26(5) of the Austrian Constitution specifies that a person can be deprived of the rights to vote and be elected only because of a criminal conviction.

The Netherlands

The Administrative Jurisdiction Department of the Council of State determined in 2003 that the 1983 Constitutional text – which referred to people under custodial care because of their mental health problems or intellectual disabilities – was in violation of the International Covenant on Civil and Political Rights. The Constitution was amended in 2008, and people with mental health problems and people with intellectual disabilities are now able to exercise their right to vote.

United Kingdom

The Electoral Administration Act 2006 abolished the common law rule that a person lacks legal capacity to vote by reason of mental health problems.

(FRA, 2010)

3.2 Jury service

Another right accorded to most citizens but often withdrawn from people with mental illness is jury service. In the USA in 1999, 42 states restricted this form of social participation (Hemmens *et al.*, 2002).

In England, under the Juries Act 1974, there is a blanket exclusion so that 'mentally disordered persons' are ineligible to serve on a jury. 'Mentally disordered' means 'anyone who suffers or has suffered from mental illness, psychopathic disorder, mental disorder, mental handicap, or severe mental handicap and because of that condition: (a) is resident in hospital or other similar institution, regularly attends for treatment by a medical practitioner, or is under guardianship, or has been determined by a judge to be incapable, by reasons of mental disorder, of managing and administering his/her property and affairs' (Peay, 2004). Since the lifetime prevalence of mental disorders is now understood to be about half of the adult population, such restrictions, consistently applied, might seriously deplete the pool of available jurors! (Kessler *et al.*, 2005). By comparison, for people with physical disabilities, jury service eligibility is considered on a case-by-case basis by the judge concerned.

In March 2010, Ireland's Law Reform Commission launched a consultation paper on jury service, recommending removal of the discriminatory provisions in the Juries Act 1976 (Box 3.2).

Box 3.2 Legislative Case Study: Ireland

Ireland currently excludes people with a mental disorder from undertaking jury service (the Juries Act 1976 specifies that a person with a mental illness is ineligible for jury service if they are resident in a hospital or 'other similar institution' or 'regularly attends for treatment by a medical practitioner'). The Act does not define 'mental illness', and the Law Reform Commission argues that the exclusion is based on status rather than the capacity of the person to undertake jury service. The Law Reform Commission has provisionally recommended that impaired mental health should not automatically exclude a person from jury service (Law Reform Commission, 2010).

For further information: www.lawreform.ie

3.3 Measures intended to optimise civil and political participation

Legislation can introduce specific mechanisms to facilitate the inclusion of people with mental disabilities in policy-making and implementation (Box 3.3).

Box 3.3 Legislative Case Study: Australia, the State of Victoria

The Victorian 2006 Disability Act established the Victorian Disability Advisory Council. This Council was envisaged as a 'way for people with a disability to have a say in decision-making on whole-of-government policy issues' (State Government of Victoria, Australia, Department of Human Services, 2007, Victorian Disability Advisory Council, paragraph 3). Australian disability advisory bodies are mandated to include all the diverse subgroups that comprise 'people with disabilities' (Frawley and Bigby, 2011).

The law can also be used to facilitate the inclusion in decision-making forums of marginalised groups who may face multiple/intersectional discrimination and marginalisation (Box 3.4).

Box 3.4 Legislative Case Study: New Zealand

The Public Health and Disability Act 2000 aims to improve health outcomes for Maori people and provides mechanisms to enable them to contribute to decision-making and the delivery of health and disability services. Measures provided include minimum Maori membership on district health boards; a requirement for health boards to establish and maintain processes to enable Maori people to participate in and contribute to strategies for Maori health improvement; a requirement that health boards continue to foster the development of Maori capacity for participating in the health and disability sector and for providing for their own needs; and an expectation that the health care authorities provide relevant information to Maori people to enable effective participation (Human Rights Commission, 2010).

Many countries aver that they protect the civil and political rights of people with disabilities on an equal basis with others (Box 3.5).

Box 3.5 Legislative Case Studies

Azerbaijan

In terms of civil participation and human rights, mental health legislation assures a set of basic rights guaranteed by the Constitution of the Republic of Azerbaijan and the international documents adopted in the country (including the United Nations Declaration of Human Rights, the International Covenant on Civil and Political Rights, the United Nations General Assembly adopted Resolution 46/119, the European Convention for Protection of Human Rights and Fundamental Freedoms (Chapter 14)). These rights include the right to:

- vote;
- have family, children and to maintain parental rights;
- own property;
- work and employment;
- education;
- freedom of movement and choice of residence;
- health including the right to choose a doctor and health facility;
- a fair trial and due process of law;
- religious freedom and practice.

Greece

Recent explicit anti-discrimination legislation (Law 3304/2005) applies the principle of equal treatment regardless of racial or ethnic origin, religious or other beliefs, disability, age or sexual orientation. It thereby implements the European Union Council Directives 2000/43/EC and 2000/78/EC, which establish a general framework for equal treatment in employment and occupation, and equal treatment between persons irrespective or racial and ethnic origin.

India

Civil participation and human rights are addressed under the relevant provisions of the Constitution of India, which provide a robust framework for the protection of such rights, zealously guarded by India's fiercely independent higher judiciary. Any citizen can approach a state High Court (under Article 226 of the Constitution), or the country's Supreme Court (Article 32: original jurisdiction, exercised under exceptional circumstances), for enforcement of these fundamental liberties/rights.

Lithuania

There is a formal requirement that state and local government institutions and agencies must, within the scope of their competence, ensure that in all the legal Acts drafted and passed by them, equal rights and treatment are laid down. There is also an obligation to draft and implement the programmes and measures designated for ensuring equal treatment, as well as to provide assistance to the programmes, non-governmental organisations, public agencies and charitable and sponsorship foundations which assist in the implementation of equal treatment.

Ukraine

In terms of civil participation and human rights, people with mental disorders formally have the same rights as other people if they are not recognised by the Court as people with incapacity. (In the case of incapacity, the Court appoints a legal representative for that person. There are state regional commissions that monitor the protection of rights of people with incapacity. Beside the commissions, the local public prosecutor monitors the protections of rights of such people.)

The Philippines

Political rights, and the right to assembly and to organise, are specifically included in the Magna Carta for Persons with Disabilities (Chapter 2.3.5).

Overall, it is clear that a number of countries have established formal provisions that intend to offer assurances for full civil, religious and political participation to people with mental health problems (Gostin, 2000, 2001, 2004). Such measures have been described in such differing contexts as Afghanistan (Amowitz *et al.*, 2003), England (Bindman *et al.*, 2003), Australia (McSherry, 2008) and across the Americas (Gable *et al.*, 2005). Yet it needs to be appreciated that there may well be a vital distinction between the enactment of such provisions and their implementation. In Indonesia, for example, despite the adoption in principle of relevant international conventions, it has been found that in practice 'human rights abuses persist, are widespread, and go essentially unremarked and unchallenged' (Irmansyah *et al.*, 2009). Note, too, in the examples of Ukraine and Lithuania that we have referred to or discussed above, these fundamental rights can be withdrawn through the designation of 'incompetence' or of 'legal incapacity' (Chapter 4, Legal capacity, decision-making, discriminatory statutes and practice). Indeed, the relative ease with which 'legal incapacity' can be attached to people with mental disorders in many jurisdictions means that these formal assurances of full civil and political participation ring hollow for many people with mental disabilities. In future, therefore, more investigation is required, not only on how far countries adopt or ratify international 'binding' treaties and conventions, but also on how far these are put into routine practice on the ground.

References

Amowitz, LL, Heisler, M and Iacopino, V (2003) A population-based assessment of women's mental health and attitudes toward women's human rights in Afghanistan. *Journal of Women's Health*, **12**(6):577–587.

Appelbaum, PS (2000) 'I Vote. I Count': Mental Disability and the Right to Vote. *Psychiatr Serv*, **51**(7):849–863.

Bindman, J, Maingay, S and Szmukler, G (2003) The Human Rights Act and mental health legislation. *British Journal of Psychiatry*, **182**:91–94.

Burton, VS (1990) The consequences of official labels: A research note on rights lost by the mentally ill, mentally incompetent, and convicted felons. *Community Mental Health Journal*, **26**(3):267–276.

Dunn, S (1999) Creating Accepting Communities: Report of the MIND inquiry into social exclusion and mental health problems. MIND, London.

FRA (European Union Agency for Fundamental Rights) (2010) The right to political participation of persons with mental health problems and persons with intellectual disabilities. European Union Agency for Fundamental Rights, Vienna, Austria.

Frawley, P and Bigby, C (2011) Inclusion in political and public life: the experiences of people with intellectual disability on government disability advisory bodies in Australia. *Journal of Intellectual & Developmental Disability*, **36**(1):27–38.

Gable, L, Vasquez, J, Gostin, L and Jimenez, H (2005) Mental health and due process in the Americas: protecting the human rights of persons involuntarily admitted to and detained in psychiatric institutions. *Rev Panam Salud Pública*, **4–5**:366–373.

Gostin, LO (2000) Human rights of persons with mental disabilities: the European Convention of Human Rights. *International Journal of Law and Psychiatry*, **23**(2):125–159.

Gostin, LO (2001) Beyond moral claims: a human rights approach in mental health. *Cambridge Quarterly of Healthcare Ethics*, **10**:264–274.

Gostin, LO (2004) International human rights law and mental disability. *Hastings Center Report*. Mar–Apr 2004:11–12.

Hammarberg, T (2011) Persons with disabilities must not be denied the right to vote [updated 22 March 2011]. Available from: http://commissioner.cws.coe.int/tiki-view_blog_post.php?postId=127 (accessed 19 April 2011).

Hemmens, C, Miller, M, Burton, VS and Milner, S (2002) The Consequences of Official Labels: An Examination of the Rights Lost by the Mentally Ill and Mentally Incompetent Ten Years Later. *Community Mental Health Journal*, **38**(2):129–140.

Howard, G and Anthony, R (1977) The right to vote and voting patterns of hospitalized psychiatric patients. *Psychiatric Quarterly*, **49**(2):124–132.

Human Rights Commission (2010) Human Rights in New Zealand 2010. Human Rights Commission, New Zealand.

Irmansyah, I, Prasetyo, Y and Minas, H (2009) Human rights of persons with mental illness in Indonesia: more than legislation is needed. *International Journal of Mental Health Systems*, **3**(1):14.

Jaychuk, G and Manchanda, R (1991) Psychiatric patients and the federal election. *Can J Psychiatry*, **36**(2):124–125.

Kessler, RC, Demler, O, Frank, RG, Olfson, M, Pincus, HA, Walters, EE, *et al.* (2005) Prevalence and Treatment of Mental Disorders, 1990 to 2003. *N Engl J Med,* **352**(24):2515–2523.

Klein, MM and Grossman, SA (1971) Voting Competence and Mental Illness. *Am J Psychiatry,* **127**(11):1562–1565.

Kunze, H, Lutze, P and Stumme, W (1982) [Voting rights of psychiatric patients (author's translation)]. *Psychiatr Prax,* **9**(2):42–50.

Law Reform Commission (2010) Consultation Paper: Jury Service (LRC CP 61–2010). Law Reform Commission, Dublin.

McSherry, B (2008) Mental health and human rights: the role of the law in developing a right to enjoy the highest attainable standard of mental health in Australia. *J Law Med,* **15**(5):773–781.

MDAC (2005) Russia's guardianship system challenged at the European Court of Human Rights. Mental Disability Advocacy Center (MDAC), Budapest.

Nash M (2002) Voting as a means of social inclusion for people with a mental illness. *Journal of Psychiatric and Mental Health Nursing,* **9**:697–703.

Peay, J (2004) Law and stigma: present, future and futuristic solutions. In: Crisp, A (ed.) *Every Family in the Land.* Royal Society of Medicine, London. pp. 367–372.

Smith, H and Humphreys, M (1997) Changes in laws are necessary to allow patients detained under Mental Health Act to vote. *British Medical Journal,* **315**(7105):431.

Thompson, B and Hall, J (1974) Helping psychiatric inpatients exercise their right to vote. *Hosp Community Psychiatry,* **25**(7):441–442.

Wichita Eagle (2010) Kansans approve two amendments. *Wichita Eagle.* 3 November 2010.

Zogg, H, Lauber, C, Ajdacic-Gross, V and Rössler, W (2003) [Expert's and lay attitudes towards restrictions on mentally ill people]. *Psychiatr Prax,* **30**(7):379–383. [in German]

CHAPTER 4
Legal Capacity, Decision-making, Discriminatory Statutes and Practice

General protection of the rights of people with mental health problems and intellectual disabilities in the community is increasingly important, particularly as the focus on service provision moves from institutional to community-based care (Fakhoury and Priebe, 2002; Knapp *et al.*, 2007). A number of other chapters in this book deal with specific instances of that – rights to education, work, and housing, for example – often with programmes directed specifically at people with mental health problems or intellectual disabilities.

This chapter is about more general questions that arise in considering how law addresses mental illness, for example:

- whether an individual can sign contracts on his or her own behalf;
- whether he or she can open a bank account;
- whether he or she can make decisions as to where he or she will live;
- whether he or she can make personal decisions, such as deciding whether or not to consent to medical treatment, in the community.

4.1 Guardianship and the legal right to make decisions

'Guardianship', in this context, refers to a legal relationship established by a court process between an adult who is deemed to lack the requisite capacity to make personal decisions and the person or organisation appointed to make decisions on that adult's behalf. The tradition in many countries has been to allow fierce restrictions on the legal right to make decisions, usually following a court declaration.

In countries in continental Europe, court orders descending from Roman law had the result of removing legal personhood from the individual. As

Mental Illness, Discrimination and the Law: Fighting for Social Justice, First Edition.
Felicity Callard, Norman Sartorius, Julio Arboleda-Flórez, Peter Bartlett, Hanfried Helmchen, Heather Stuart, Jose Taborda and Graham Thornicroft.

a matter of law, individuals ceased to exist: they were no longer a subject with legal rights, and could not litigate, contract or make decisions on their own behalf. (A discussion of the development of this jurisdiction in post-revolutionary France has been given by Robert Castel, 1988.)

In the English common law tradition, although the person never entirely ceased to exist in quite the same way, a largely similar effect resulted historically following an inquiry under the Royal Prerogative powers: the individual could not make contracts on his or her own behalf, and while he or she could litigate to overturn the order, he or she could not commence other litigation before the courts. While a distinction was sometimes made between personal decisions and decisions related to property and finances, this was the only form of partial guardianship. If an individual was found to lack capacity for property and affairs, the law deprived him or her from making all decisions in that realm – thus, for example, a person who could not manage their stocks and bonds also lost the legal authority to manage their daily spending, even if, in fact, they remained quite capable of managing that spending.

These heavily controlling powers have proven remarkably resistant to change. A version of this power as it related to financial decision-making, codified in statute, continued in England until 2007, when the Mental Capacity Act 2005 took effect, and it remains in effect in many former colonies. Much of central and eastern European guardianship law continues to reflect the overarching approach of its Roman law precedents, with only superficial alteration. Even when domestic law in central and eastern Europe allows for more flexible regimes of guardianship, the practice of courts in those jurisdictions seems overwhelmingly to routinely make awards that remove all decision-making authority from individuals, sometimes without the person at issue even being told of the hearing (Shtukaturov v. Russia: ECtHR, application no. 44009/05, judgment of 27 June 2008). (See also Box 4.1.)

Box 4.1 Resource

The Mental Disability Advocacy Center (MDAC) has produced analyses of guardianship in Hungary, Bulgaria, the Czech Republic, Georgia, Kyrgyzstan, Russia and Serbia between 2006 and 2008.

These are available online at: www.mdac.info/reports

Often, it would seem that the jurisdiction is invoked merely upon evidence of mental disorder or intellectual disability, with no meaningful assessment of whether the individual has the mental capacity to make decisions on his or her own behalf. The blanket removal of an individual's rights on this basis can no longer be considered consistent with international law. Within the Council of Europe, such overarching restrictions of rights were coming under challenge by 1999, with the passage of the Recommendation on Principles concerning the Legal Protection of Incapable Adults (Council of Europe, Committee of Ministers, recommendation CM99(4) (1999); Chapter 14.2.1.1.3). This approach, which insists that legal systems be more directly tailored to the actual and specific needs of individuals, is now reflected in Article 12 of the United Nations Convention on the Rights of Persons with Disabilities (CRPD) (Box 4.2).

Box 4.2 UN Convention

UN Convention on the Rights of Persons with Disabilities, Article 12 Equal recognition before the law:

1 States Parties reaffirm that persons with disabilities have the right to recognition everywhere as persons before the law.

2 States Parties shall recognise that persons with disabilities enjoy legal capacity on an equal basis with others in all aspects of life.

3 States Parties shall take appropriate measures to provide access by persons with disabilities to the support they may require in exercising their legal capacity.

4 States Parties shall ensure that all measures that relate to the exercise of legal capacity provide for appropriate and effective safeguards to prevent abuse in accordance with international human rights law. Such safeguards shall ensure that measures relating to the exercise of legal capacity respect the rights, will and preferences of the person, are free of conflict of interest and undue influence, are proportional and tailored to the person's circumstances, apply for the shortest time possible and are subject to regular review by a competent, independent and impartial authority or judicial body. The safeguards shall be proportional to the degree to which such measures affect the person's rights and interests.

5 Subject to the provisions of this Article, States Parties shall take all appropriate and effective measures to ensure the equal right of persons with disabilities to own or inherit property, to control their own financial affairs and to have equal access to bank loans, mortgages and other forms of financial credit, and shall ensure that persons with disabilities are not arbitrarily deprived of their property.

The overarching principle of non-discrimination contained in the CRPD makes it clear that the existence of a mental disorder or learning disability *per se* will not be sufficient to justify a deprivation of legal capacity (Article 5 of the CRPD – Equality and non-discrimination; Chapter 14.4.1). At the very least, there must be evidence that the individual lacks the capacity to make that specific decision. As important, the CRPD requires that practical supports be provided to persons to realise the decisions that they want to take: any restrictions on such choices must be to the most limited degree possible and subject to appropriate safeguards, and may only occur in the clearest cases.

Furthermore, so-called 'plenary' guardianship – legal regimes that removed legal personhood or removed virtually all decision-making power – is no longer acceptable. Guardianship courts must now tailor their judgments to the actual decisions or areas of decision-making where the individual in fact demonstrably lacks capacity. There may be some cases where there will be evidence that the person is incapable of making all decisions, but they will be the rarity. Instead, orders of partial guardianship should now be the norm, acknowledging that the individual retains some or much of his or her decision-making ability in some areas. Further, orders should be time-limited and impose as little as possible on to the life of the individual, and reasonable efforts should be made through mechanisms such as supported decision-making to ensure that legal orders are made only as a last resort (a good example of this is highlighted in Box 4.3).

Box 4.3 Legislative Case Study: Canada, Province of Manitoba

The Manitoba Vulnerable Persons Living with a Mental Disability Act (assented to 1993, came into force 1996):

www.gov.mb.ca/fs/pwd/vpact.html

The Province of Manitoba in Canada promotes and protects via this Act the rights of adults living with a mental disability who need assistance to meet their basic needs. The legislation recognises those Manitobans as 'vulnerable persons'. The Mental Disability Advocacy Center in 2007 cited this as a 'best practice example of legislation' in relationship to guardianship, whereby an adult should not be placed under guardianship unless other less formal arrangements have been exhausted. The Act specifies that a substitute decision-maker not be appointed before it is determined whether the individual has a support network and 'reasonable efforts have been made to involve the support network' (MDAC, 2007).

Due process safeguards must also be observed. This means that proper evidence relating to the alleged incapacity and the need for an order should be provided and the person alleged to be lacking capacity should be seen in person by the court. The person should also be represented by a lawyer or other suitable person and should have an ongoing right to be told of, and to raise objections to, major decisions being made about his or her life or property.

The Mental Capacity Act 2005 in England and Wales provides an interesting example of the new approach (Chapter 2.7), with both strengths and weaknesses (Zigmond, 2009). The Act provides a set of principles in the interpretation of its provisions, including a presumption of capacity, a requirement that reasonable steps be taken to assist a person to make a capable decision, a principle of least restrictive alternative and a requirement that decisions taken under the Act be made in the person's best interests. (A detailed discussion of this legislation is given elsewhere (Bartlett, 2007).) Statutory definitions of incapacity and best interests are provided, to which everyone making decisions involving persons thought to be lacking capacity must refer. Even when a court order appointing a guardian (or 'deputy', to use the English language) is in place, the guardian cannot make a personal decision if the individual has capacity to make that decision at the time it is to be made. This legislation thus incorporates remarkable flexibility into the law, allowing account to be taken of the fact that actual capacity to make some decisions may vary considerably, sometimes in a short space of time.

Where the Mental Capacity Act is strong on substance, it is light on process, however. There are few reporting systems, so it is not clear that meaningful monitoring as to whether the provisions of the Act are in fact being followed can occur, or how its terms are being interpreted by either professional or lay carers on a day-to-day basis. The government has recently commissioned research into these questions.

Many guardianship statutes, including the Mental Capacity Act 2005, create a variety of procedures that allow a person to plan for incapacity. Most frequently, this will be a 'lasting power of attorney' – a document that allows the signatory to appoint someone (the 'attorney') to make decisions for him or her, in the event that the signatory loses capacity. Different legislation will create different restrictions on such documents. Sometimes, legislation will allow the signatory to instruct the attorney on how the power is to be exercised – 'avoid putting me in a nursing home', or 'do not invest in ABC company', for example. Sometimes, legislation will restrict such authority – introducing safeguards prior to the attorney making medical decisions that would terminate the signatory's life, for example.

Other mechanisms for people planning incapacity allow the individual either to refuse specific treatment in advance ('living wills'), or to make expressions of wishes as to their care ('advance directives'), which are to guide, rather than to bind, decision-makers during incapacity (Ambrosini and Crocker, 2007; Sass and May, 2010). In statutes providing for living wills, it is often the case that some form of clause to allow the instrument not to be enforced may be included, usually taking effect when new circumstances have occurred that make it doubtful that the expressed wishes of the individual reflect the choice that the individual would now make, given the new circumstances. While there is much to be said for such limitations, they do provide a 'loophole' and a broad reading of such clauses by a court unsympathetic to a patient's wishes may effectively nullify the advance treatment refusal in inappropriate circumstances.

Guardianship statutes can affect a vast range of possible decisions. Some dispute has occurred as to how they should interact with other legislation relating to mental disorder and mental disability: should, for example, guardianship legislation, which is capacity based, take precedence over civil detention under other mental health legislation? Should an advance refusal of psychiatric treatment be enforceable when an individual has been detained in a psychiatric facility? It is probably too early to say whether there can be fixed good practice here: as in so much of psychiatry, the evidence base on efficacy of law is extremely limited and weak.

It is fair to say that the primacy of mental health legislation over guardianship legislation should not be taken as obviously desirable. Increasingly, human rights bodies and human rights instruments are making it clear that mere detention in a psychiatric facility should not be sufficient to deprive an individual of rights to consent to treatment. (See, for example, Committee for the Prevention of Torture and Inhuman or Degrading Treatment or Punishment (Council of Europe), CPT Standards, (Strasbourg, CPT, 2004), CPT/Inf/E (2002) 1 – rev 2004, Chapter 5, para 41 (Chapter 14.2.1.1.2) and Council of Europe, Committee of Ministers, recommendation CM99(4) (1999), part V (Chapter 14.2.1.1.3).)

In Ontario, Canada, people with capacity detained in psychiatric facilities have been able to refuse psychiatric medication, and have been able to sign advanced decisions refusing psychiatric treatment that are enforceable following psychiatric detention, since the late 1980s (Chapter 2.2). This approach has been controversial, even in Ontario, but results do not appear noticeably worse there than elsewhere in the world. It is therefore difficult to see that mental health legislation should manifestly take precedence over capacity-based legislation in all circumstances. (Regarding issues of potential interface between capacity and mental health legislation, see Dawson and Szmukler (2006) and the discussion in Chapter 2.7).

4.2 Discriminatory statutes and practice

The right to make decisions on one's own behalf is only the first stage in full public participation. Stigma against people with mental health problems and people with intellectual difficulties is still well entrenched internationally (Thornicroft *et al.*, 2009) and this social barrier, often buttressed with discriminatory statutes, may pose a formidable obstacle to full participation in the community.

In some cases, statutes will expressly or effectively preclude an individual's full involvement in society. Some countries, for example, organise benefit systems so that in order for a person with mental disability to take advantage of the benefit, he or she must show that they are incapable of work. The difficulty with such benefits is that many people may be incapable of work at some but not all of the time, or be capable of some work but not full-time work, or be capable of some work, but not the work that they previously had been doing. Inflexible eligibility criteria for benefit systems have the advantage that governments can limit the amount paid out, but it is difficult to see that they work to the advantage of a person with mental disabilities, who for example wishes to try employment to see if it is practicable for him or her, or who wishes to re-integrate slowly into the workforce (Chapter 5, Work and the workplace). Other laws preclude people with mental disabilities from serving on boards of directors, or being members of particular professions, whether or not their disability in fact constitutes a reasonable limitation on their engaging in those activities.

Many of these laws are holdovers from a time when stigma was unchallenged. While it must be acknowledged that some manifestations of mental disability will render a person unable to engage in some sorts of employment or other social participation, the laws restricting access to such participation should be phrased to require a clear demonstration that the mental disability does indeed constitute an appropriate restriction in the case of the individual concerned.

Vignette

A young physician with a relapsing course of schizophrenia did not receive his certificate as a pathologist because his manager and instructor argued that, owing to the lack of pathologists, he would immediately acquire an independent position as a certified pathologist. In such a position, he would be not be monitored for mistakes, which may occur at the start of a relapse, with potentially serious consequences for patients. But under the manager's supervision, the beginning of a relapse in schizophrenia could be detected.

[Vignette provided by one of the authors]

In many of these cases, bringing about change may be a complex affair. Political solutions may be problematic, as there may be few votes in non-discrimination. Further, some corrections may require significant changes to administrative structures of programmes such as disability pensions, which may in turn involve considerable government inconvenience and expense. Litigation may in some circumstances be used to force government's hand, but only if the jurisdiction has an enforceable bill of rights or similar instrument, or has incorporated the relevant international agreements into domestic law.

Other discriminatory actions are not required by law, but are instead part of ingrained practice: people refusing to hire an individual not because law precludes it but because of stigma; people refusing to serve people with mental health problems or intellectual disabilities in shops; travel insurance that does not cover psychiatric disorders; or people otherwise interacting with people with mental disabilities with the expectation that the views or dignity of such people does not matter.

References

Ambrosini, DL and Crocker, AG (2007) Psychiatric advance directives and the right to refuse treatment in Canada. *Canadian Journal of Psychiatry*, **52**:397–402.

Bartlett, P (2007) *Blackstone's Guide to the Mental Capacity Act*, 2nd edn. Oxford University Press, Oxford.

Castel, R (1988) *The Regulation of Madness: the origins of incarceration in France*. Polity, Oxford.

Dawson, J and Szmukler, G (2006) Fusion of mental health and incapacity legislation. *British Journal of Psychiatry*, **188**:504–509.

Fakhoury, W and Priebe, S (2002) The process of deinstitutionalization: an international overview. *Current Opinion in Psychiatry*, **15**(2):187–192.

Knapp, M, McDaid, D, Mossialos, E and Thornicroft, G (eds) (2007) *Mental Health Policy and Practice across Europe: The future direction of mental health care*. Open University Press.

MDAC (2007) Guardianship and Human Rights in Russia: Analysis of Law, Policy and Practice. Mental Disability Advocacy Center (MDAC), Budapest.

Sass, H-M and May, AT (2010) Advance directives: balancing patient's self-determination with professional paternalism. In: Helmchen, H and Sartorius, N (eds), *Ethics in Psychiatry: European Contributions*. Springer, Dordrecht. pp. 147–160.

Thornicroft, G, Brohan, E, Rose, D, Sartorius, N, Leese, M, INDIGO Study Group (2009) Global pattern of experienced and anticipated discrimination against people with schizophrenia: a cross-sectional survey. *The Lancet*, **373**(9661):408–415.

Zigmond, A (2009) Deprivation of liberty safeguards and the Mental Capacity Act. *British Medical Journal*, **338**:1284–1285.

CHAPTER 5

Work and the Workplace

5.1 Mental health problems and labour force participation

Employment discrimination occurs when people are denied a job because of their psychiatric status, without regard to their qualifications or capabilities. Discrimination also occurs when people are 'under-employed' – when the only job they are able to secure is badly paid, inferior to their normal occupation or skill level and does not offer job satisfaction (because they are not in a position to take decisions or have poor relationships with colleagues) (Stuart, 2004). Unemployment and under-employment of people with mental health problems increases the likelihood that they will live in poverty.

Most people with a mental health problem are willing and able to work (Macias *et al.*, 2001; Morgan, 2005). Yet, many studies in a variety of countries have indicated that unemployment is three to five times higher among those with a mental health problem than among their non-disabled counterparts. Of adults with mental disabilities who are of working age 61% are outside of the labour force, compared with 20% of non-disabled adults (Cook *et al.*, 2005). For people with major depression, 40–60% are unemployed, and for those with more serious disorders (such as schizophrenia), 80–90% are unemployed (Crowther *et al.*, 2001), making those with a mental disability one of the largest groups of social security recipients (Sanderson and Andrews, 2006). Between 15 and 30% of employees will experience some form of mental health problem during their working lives, most frequently depression. In any given year, 3% will experience a mental disorder (Harnois and Gabriel, 2000; Liimatainen and Gabriel, 2000). At any given time, 50–60% of those with the most common mental disorders, such as anxiety or depression, will participate in the workforce, though less than one third will be employed full time (Sanderson and Andrews, 2006).

Employers are reluctant to hire someone with a psychiatric history or someone who uses antipsychotic medication (Long and Runch, 1983;

Mental Illness, Discrimination and the Law: Fighting for Social Justice, First Edition.
Felicity Callard, Norman Sartorius, Julio Arboleda-Flórez, Peter Bartlett, Hanfried Helmchen, Heather Stuart, Jose Taborda and Graham Thornicroft.

Manning and White, 1995; Scheid, 1999. People with mental disabilities identify employment discrimination among their most frequent stigma experiences. In a survey of 1150 primary care patients in Minnesota, USA, for example, 67% of those with a history of depression and 58% of those who had consulted a health professional for a psychiatric problem expected to experience employment discrimination that would make it harder for them to find a job. This was twice the proportion of those with medical disabilities such as diabetes or hypertension (Roeloffs *et al.*, 2003).

One in three mental health service users in the United States report being counselled to take jobs below their educational level, intellectual ability or qualifications (Wahl, 1999a). Approximately one in five people with mental disabilities who are in the workforce also report experiencing job-related discrimination, such as being refused a transfer or promotion, having difficulty accessing training, not advancing in a job, or making a lower than average hourly wage (Baldwin and Marcus, 2006). Twice as many mentally disabled workers (almost 40%), compared with non-disabled workers, make close to a minimum wage (Cook, 2006). Mental illnesses are also a leading cause of early retirement. In 2003 in Germany, for example, the average age of people taking early retirement owing to a mental illness was below 48 years, lower than that for all other health conditions listed in the World Health Organization's International Classification of Diseases (10th edition) (Killan and Becker, 2007).

For individuals who have a serious mental illness and who are not in the competitive job market, other work-related activities can provide a feeling of accomplishment and satisfaction with life. These include volunteer work, study, household tasks, self-care and social interaction (Aubin *et al.*, 1999; Leufstadius *et al.*, 2006). Though competitive employment may be more satisfying for many, the provision of meaningful daily occupation has become an important goal of community-based mental health systems. In some countries, such as Sweden, providing satisfactory daily occupations has become a stated reform agenda (Eklund *et al.*, 2004). Nevertheless, research has shown that a significant proportion of people with serious mental illnesses are under-occupied, experience restricted social participation and limited engagement in leisure activities. One in five mental health service users in the United States has been turned down for volunteer jobs and this was true of jobs both inside (20%) and outside (26%) the mental health system (Wahl, 1999a, 1999b).

Mental disorders are among the most frequent causes of occupational disability, accounting for a steadily increasing amount of short- and long-term disability claims (Bilsker, 2006; Dewa *et al.*, 2004; Goldberg and Steury, 2001; Mykletun *et al.*, 2006). In the European Union, the costs of mental disability have been estimated to be 3–4% of the gross domestic product (European Commission, 2005). In Canada, disability claims for mental disorders account for up to 12% of payroll costs and they are the fastest growing claim category (Mercer, 2004). The majority of lost productivity costs associated with mental disability arises from partial disability days that occur when workers reduce their performance (Stewart *et al.*, 2003). A third or more will experience emotional or psychiatric symptoms that will reduce work performance (Wang *et al.*, 2006).

5.2 Intellectual disabilities and labour force participation

Employment integration for people with intellectual disabilities shares many of the same social, organisational and political drivers as employment integration for people with mental health problems. For example, deinstitutionalisation, community-based care and the goal of integration in all spheres of life have influenced where people with intellectual disabilities live, engage in recreational activities and receive education and work. Competitive employment for people with intellectual disabilities improves their quality of life, promotes greater social integration and reduces reliance on welfare-based services (such as sheltered workshops) and disability payments (Eggleton *et al.*, 1999).

Early research on the employability of people with intellectual disabilities, conducted during the 1980s, highlighted severe unemployment, comparable to that of individuals with severe and persistent mental illness (in the range of 90–95%) (Tse, 1994). While employability of people with intellectual disabilities has improved since that time, unemployment still remains inordinately high. For example, Taanila and colleagues (2005) followed a birth cohort of 12 058 live-born infants in northern Finland, which included 129 individuals with an intellectual disability, to assess employment and health outcomes. At the time of follow-up, when the individuals were 34 years old, 85.3% of those with a disability were on some form of disability pension and outside of the competitive workforce. Of those not on pensions, the unemployment rate (between 1993 and 2000) was 56 days out of every 100, compared with 12% for those without an intellectual disability (in this study, those with an IQ of more than 85). People with intellectual disabilities who were employed had jobs that required little training, had few benefits and high turnover.

Negative employer attitudes are a major barrier to successful job placement of people with an intellectual disability. In a study of 50 employers in the United States who had previous experience of hiring someone with an intellectual disability, the jobs considered most appropriate for these workers were low-level, low-pay positions that required minimal training. Also, employers were more willing to hire someone with a physical or mental health disability into these jobs than someone with an intellectual disability, even if the intellectual disability was mild (Gilbride *et al.*, 2000). Employers held lower expectations of workers with an intellectual disability and remained concerned about the ability of intellectually disabled workers to interact appropriately with co-workers, customers and management. Employers who participated in supported employment programmes held more positive views (Hernandez *et al.*, 2000).

5.3 Employment disability legislation

Policy-makers have increasingly viewed employment as an important component of economic security and social inclusion. Thus, disability issues have figured prominently in the international policy agenda and many countries have enacted disability legislation to protect the civil rights of individuals with disabilities and remove barriers to their full employment participation. A weakness of disability legislation is that it has not always provided the hoped-for protections against discrimination and employment inequity.

Disability legislation is often embedded within a broader legislative framework, such as constitutional law or human rights statutes, which are intended to protect the rights and freedoms of citizens. The strength of disability legislation, however, is that it imposes a specific duty on employers to accommodate disabled employees. For example, most disability legislation converges on three key issues. It promotes greater employment for people with physical and mental disabilities. It outlaws occupational discrimination of disabled workers in recruitment, retention and promotion, and it requires employers to make special accommodations for disabled employees (Goss *et al.*, 2000; Lunt and Thornton, 1994). 'Reasonable accommodations' may include physical modifications to the work area, the use of specialised technology, or alterations in work schedules (Banks and Lawrence, 2006; Blanck and Pransky, 1999; European Commission, 2005; Konur, 2007; Liimatainen and Gabriel, 2000; Richardson, 1994).

Affirmative action approaches are less common. In Japan and Brazil, the governments have set specific employment targets and the legislation provides an incentive for employers to incorporate disabled employees into the competitive workforce. In Japan, employers are allowed a trial period followed by an economic incentive if the employee is retained on a regular contract. In Canada, the Canadian Human Rights Act prohibits discrimination on a number of grounds, including physical or mental disability, and this applies to all Canadians. The Employment Equity Act, which is in force alongside the Charter of Rights and Freedoms, requires employers to engage in proactive measures to improve employment opportunities for women, people with disabilities, Aboriginal peoples and visible minorities. The Employment Equity Act is limited to federally regulated industries (such as Crown corporations, banks and railroads) and excludes the vast majority of employers (nearly all retailers and manufacturers). In Israel, the Equal Rights for People with Disabilities Law prohibits discrimination and requires affirmative action to correct present discrimination, develop programmes to integrate people with disabilities into the open work market and provide diagnostic and consulting services. The Rehabilitation of People with Mental Disabilities in the Community Law makes a clear statement that individuals with a mental disability are entitled to live, work and be educated in the community. People who meet eligibility criteria are entitled to rehabilitation services, including employment and training. The law also prohibits workplace discrimination on any grounds and makes it clear that setting irrelevant conditions is also discriminatory.

People with mental health problems are protected only to the extent that their illness falls within the definition of disability under the legislation. Though disability is typically understood in functional terms, as a physical or mental impairment that interferes with, or substantially limits, activity in one or more social or occupational spheres, a significant limitation of much disability legislation is the restrictive or imprecise definition of disability. In other cases, definitions of disability explicitly exclude people with mental health problems. In India, for example, the definition of disability focuses on individuals with learning or developmental disabilities and excludes most mental disorders.

In other countries, mental disorders are not expressly excluded from legislation, but the definition of disability has become so restrictive that people with mental disorders may not meet the disability criteria contained in the statutes. For example, employers in the United States have fought to restrict the definition of disability to exclude mental illnesses (Stuart, 2006) and have otherwise opposed their obligations to make reasonable accommodations on the basis of cost (Verling, 2006). The Americans with Disabilities Act has since been amended (the ADA Amendments Act of 2008, H.R. 3195 (110th)) to restore the original intent of the protections, broaden the definition of mental disability and remove the strict standards that had been applied by Supreme Court decisions that required 'severe' limitations to daily activities and excluded intermittent or episodic illnesses.

Reviews of disability legislation in the United States (Colker, 1999, 2001) (before the amendments to the Act) and in the United Kingdom (Konur, 2007) described the legislation as a 'windfall' for employers. In both countries, the majority of claims (87% in the United States and 63% in the United Kingdom) were resolved in favour of the employer. Countries such as Norway (Box 5.1) have had more success in applying disability legislation, but their reforms have been more recent, sweeping and based on a broad definition of disability.

Box 5.1 Legislative Case Study: Norway

In 2002, the Norwegian government appointed a legal committee to draft a new Bill and amend existing legislation in order to strengthen the legal protections against the discrimination of people with disabilities, following a human rights approach. The Anti-Discrimination and Accessibility Act came into force on 1 January 2009. The Equality and Anti-Discrimination Ombud and Tribunal monitor compliance and help to implement the Act, which offers broad protections to people with mental or physical impairments in all walks of life. The Tribunal has recently used the Working Environment Act – which protects against labour-market-related discrimination – in two cases, one of which involved a person with a mental disability. In this case they found that the employer failed to fulfil the obligations under the Act to adapt the working conditions of an employee with ADHD (attention deficit hyperactivity disorder).

For further information: www.regjeringen.no

The broadest definitions of disability can be found in countries such as Australia, New Zealand, Norway and People's Republic of China (Hong Kong), where anti-discrimination legislation grants protection for the disabled person as well as their friends, relatives and other associates (Chapter 15, Examples of disability legislation from across the world, and Chapter 2.3.4). Several disability Acts also protect disabled people against indirect discrimination. In Sweden, for example, the Prohibition of Discrimination Act (2003) defines indirect discrimination broadly. An employer may not disfavour a job applicant or employee by applying a 'provision, method, or procedure' that appears to be neutral but in practice disadvantages a person with a disability. By comparison, in Azerbaijan a person may be temporarily ineligible (for a period of two years) from entering certain professions if they have a mental disability.

The effectiveness of disability legislation in promoting economic participation of people with mental disabilities is not well understood and its impact on corporate cultures remains the subject of considerable debate. A weakness of disability legislation is that it rests on the assumption that employers will adhere to the various Acts and there is often only a minimal degree of active monitoring and enforcement. In the United States, for example, despite legislation, many companies still do not have corporate disability policies (Schure *et al.*, 2005), or explicit policies for hiring people with a mental disability (Scheid, 2005). In 2003, for example, less than half (42%) of the Fortune 100 companies had workplace diversity policies that expressly included people with disabilities (Ball *et al.*, 2005). Only 3% of 190 employers sampled in the Southern US metropolitan area that had disability policies had developed them following the enactment of the Americans with Disabilities Act (Scheid, 2005).

In cases of wrongdoing, it is generally incumbent upon the wronged individual to call for a redress of their rights. This usually necessitates them putting a claim forward. This requires the individual to know their rights and have the stamina and financial resources to support the investigation. Enforcement through the courts may be slow, as in the case of the Philippines. The Magna Carta for Persons with Disabilities (Chapter 2.3.5 and Chapter 15) provides for the rehabilitation, development and provision of opportunities for disabled people and their integration within society. While this landmark legislation broadly enumerates the rights and privileges of disabled people for employment and access to mainstream society, it has been difficult to implement. The first discussions of a court case came a full decade after the Bill was passed (Ricci *et al.*, 2004).

In countries with active trade unions, such as Ireland and the United Kingdom, an employee may make a charge of discrimination or harassment through their union, which will take legal action on their behalf. Some countries also have legal support services to assist disabled workers in understanding their rights and in making claims. In the Ukraine, the Psychiatric Association has launched an 'Experts Commission' to monitor human rights abuses and provide social and legal assistance to service users and families. People also appeal to the Commission with requests to protect their rights and experts within the Commission can provide legal assistance including representation in court (Gluzman and Kostyuchenko, 2006).

Legal protections for disabled people in the workforce are only one dimension of human rights protection. What the law intends is not always what transpires in day-to-day interactions. Without procedural, organisational, government and cultural change, little progress can be made (Ricci *et al.*, 2004). (The United Kingdom's 'Disability Equality Duty' is an example of a legislative attempt to effect organisational and procedural changes. It places an enforceable obligation on all public authorities to draft a disability action plan, setting out the efforts to be made to provide more accessible services and to include people with disabilities in all aspects of the organisation's work.) Employer attitudes toward people with mental disabilities are central to effective workplace disability management both in terms of the extent to which workplace accommodations are made and whether people with mental disabilities are accepted into the workforce. Employers that hold stigmatising attitudes, such as believing that people with a mental illness are limited in their ability to perform cognitive tasks, can pose a major impediment to employment integration. Many employers are reluctant to hire someone with a mental illness, and some would fire someone with a mental disorder (Manning and White, 1995; Paetzold, 2005; Scheid, 2005). Employer support for anti-discrimination legislation has been poor, not only in countries such as the United States or the United Kingdom (Konur, 2007), but also elsewhere, such as Israel (Vilchinsky and Findler, 2004) and Sweden (Heijbel *et al.*, 2005). Consequently, disability legislation is often limited in its effectiveness.

References

Aubin, G, Hachey, R and Mercier, C (1999) Meaning of daily activities and subjective quality of life in people with severe mental illness. *Scandinavian Journal of Occupational Therapy*, **6**(53–62).

Baldwin, ML and Marcus, SC (2006) Perceived and measured stigma among workers with serious mental illness. *Psychiatr Serv*, **57**(3):388–392.

Ball, P, Monaco, G, Schmeling, J, Schartz, H, Blanck, P (2005) Disability as diversity in Fortune 100 companies. *Behavioral Sciences & the Law*, **23**(1):97–121.

Banks, P and Lawrence, M (2006) The Disability Discrimination Act, a necessary, but not sufficient safeguard for people with progressive conditions in the workplace? The experiences of younger people with Parkinson's disease. *Disability and Rehabilitation*, **28**(1):13–24.

Bilsker, D (2006) Mental healthcare in the workplace. *Can J Psychiatry*, **51**(2):61–62.

Blanck, PD and Pransky, G (1999) Workers with disabilities. *Occupational Medicine – State of the Art Reviews*, **14**(3):581–593.

Colker, R (1999) The Americans with Disabilities Act: A windfall for defendants. *Harvard Civil Rights-Civil Liberties Law Review*, **34**(1):99–162.

Colker, R (2001) Winning and losing under the Americans with Disabilities Act. *Ohio State Law J*, **62**:239–278.

Cook, JA (2006) Employment barriers for persons with psychiatric disabilities: Update of a report for the president's commission. *Psychiatr Serv*, **57**(10):131–405.

Cook, JA, Leff, HS, Blyler, CR, Gold, PB, Goldberg, RW, Mueser, KT, *et al.* (2005) Results of a Multisite Randomized Trial of Supported Employment Interventions for Individuals With Severe Mental Illness. *Arch Gen Psychiatry*, **62**(5):505–512.

Crowther, RE, Marshall, M, Bond, GR and Huxley, P (2001) Helping people with severe mental illness to obtain work: systematic review. *BMJ*, **322**(7280):204–208.

Dewa, C, Lesage, A, Goering, P and Caveen, M (2004) Nature and prevalence of mental illness in the workplace. *HealthCare Papers*, **5**:12–25.

Eggleton, I, Robertson, S, Ryan, Jand Kober, R (1999) The impact of employment on the quality of life of people with an intellectual disability. *Journal of Vocational Rehabilitation*, **13**:95–107.

Eklund, M, Hansson, L and Ahlqvist, C (2004) The importance of work as compared to other forms of daily occupations for wellbeing and functioning among persons with long-term mental illness. *Community Mental Health Journal*, **40**(5):465–477.

European Commission (2005) Green paper. Improving the mental health of the population: towards a strategy for mental health for the European Union. European Commission, Health and Consumer Protectorate Directorate-General, Brussels, Belgium.

Gilbride, D, Stensrud, R, Ehlers, C, Evans, E, Peterson, C (2000) Employers' attitudes toward hiring persons with disabilities and vocational rehabilitation. *Journal of Rehabilitation*, **66**(4):17–23.

Gluzman, S and Kostyuchenko, S (2006) Psychiatry in Ukraine. *International Psychiatry: Bulletin of the Board of International Affairs of the Royal College of Psychiatrists*, **3**(2):38–40.

Goldberg, RJ and Steury, S (2001) Depression in the workplace: Costs and barriers to treatment. *Psychiatr Serv*, **52**(12):1639–1643.

Goss, D, Goss, F and Adam-Smith, D (2000) Disability and employment: a comparative critique of UK legislation. *Int J Hum Resour Manag*, **11**(4):807–821.

Harnois, G and Gabriel, P (2000) Mental health and work: impact, issues and good practices. WHO and the International Labour Organization, Geneva, Switzerland.

Heijbel, B, Josephson, M, Jensen, I and Vingard, E (2005) Employer, insurance, and health system response to long-term sick leave in the public sector: Policy implications. *J Occup Rehabil*, **15**(2):167–176.

Hernandez, B, Keys, C and Balcazar, F (2000) Employer attitudes toward workers with disabilities and their ADA employment rights: a literature review. *Journal of Rehabilitation*, **66**(4):4–16.

Killan, R and Becker, T (2007) Macro-economic indicators and labour force participation of people with schizophrenia. *Journal of Mental Health*, **16**(2):211–222.

Konur, O (2007) A judicial outcome analysis of the *Disability Discrimination Act*: a windfall for employers? *Disability & Society*, **22**(2):187–204.

Leufstadius, C, Erlandsson, L and Eklund, M (2006) Time use and daily activities in people with persistant mental illness. *Occupational Therapy International*, **13**(3):123–141.

Liimatainen, M and Gabriel, P (2000) Mental health in the workplace: situation analysis, United Kingdom. International Labour Office, Geneva, Switzerland.

Long, E and Runch, B (1983) Combating stigma through work for the mentally restored. *Hospital and Community Psychiatry*, **34**(1):19–20.

Lunt, N and Thornton, P (1994) Disability and employment: towards an understanding of discourse and policy. *Disability & Society*, **9**:223–238.

Macias, C, DeCarlo, L, Wang, Q, Frey, J, Barreira and P (2001) Work interest as a predictor of competitive employment: policy implications for psychiatric rehabilitation. *Adm Policy Ment Health*, **28**(4):279–297.

Manning, C and White, P (1995) Attitudes of employers to the mentally ill. *Psychiatr Bull*, **19**:541–543.

Mercer (2004). Few Canadian employers addressing workplace mental health issues. Mercer Human Resource Consulting Group.

Morgan, G (2005) We want to be able to work. *Mental Health Today*. October:32–34.

Mykletun, A, Overland, S, Dahl, AA, Krokstad, S, Bjerkeset, O, Glozier, N *et al.* (2006) A Population-Based Cohort Study of the Effect of Common Mental Disorders on Disability Pension Awards. *Am J Psychiatry*, **163**(8):1412–1418.

Paetzold, RL (2005) Mental illness and reasonable accommodations at work: Definition of a mental disability under the ADA. *Psychiatr Serv*, **56**(10):1188–1190.

Ricci, C, Lee, M-B and Chiu, C-H (2004) A review of the legislative mechanisms available to protect the social participation rights of people with depression in the Asia Pacific region. *Australas Psychiatry*, **12**(Suppl):S16–27.

Richardson, M (1994) The impact of the Americans with Disabilities Act on employment opportunity for people with disabilities. *Annu Rev Public Health.*; **15**(91–105).

Roeloffs, C, Sherbourne, C, Unützer, J, Fink, A, Tang, J and Wells, KB (2003) Stigma and depression among primary care patients. *General Hospital Psychiatry*, **25**:311–315.

Sanderson, K and Andrews, G (2006) Common mental disorders in the workforce: Recent findings from descriptive and social epidemiology. *Can J Psychiat-Rev Can Psychiat.*, **51**(2):63–75.

Scheid, TL (1999) Employment of individuals with mental disabilities: business response to the ADA's challenge. *Behavioral Sciences and the Law*, **17**:73–91.

Scheid, TL (2005) Stigma as a barrier to employment: mental disability and the Americans with Disabilities Act. *International Journal of Law and Psychiatry*, **28**:670–690.

Schur, L, Kruse, D and Blanck, P (2005) Corporate culture and the employment of persons with disabilities. *Behavioral Sciences & the Law*, **23**(1):3–20.

Stewart, WF, Ricci, JA, Chee, E, Hahn, SR and Morganstein, D (2003) Cost of Lost Productive Work Time Among US Workers With Depression. *JAMA*, **289**(23):3135–3144.

Stuart, H (2004) Stigma and work. *HealthCare Papers*, **5**(2):100–111.

Stuart, H (2006) Mental illness and employment discrimination. *Current Opinion in Psychiatry*, **19**:522–526.

Taanila, A, Rantakallio, P, Koiranen, M, Von Wendt, L, and Järvelin, MR (2005) How do persons with intellectual disability manage in the open labour markets? A follow-up of the Northern Finland 1966 Birth Cohort. *Journal of Intellectual Disability Research*, **49**(3), 218–227.

Tse, J (1994) Employers' expectations and evaluation of the job performance of employees with intellectual disability. *Australia and New Zealand Journal of Developmental Disabilities*, **19**(2):139–147.

Verling, L (2006) Resources and case law. *TCM*, March/April **2006**:23–28.

Vilchinsky N and Findler L (2004) Attitudes toward Israel's Equal Rights for People With Disabilities Law: A multiperspective approach. *Rehabil Psychol*, **49**(4):309–316.

Wahl, OF (1999a). Mental health consumers' experiences of stigma. *Schizophrenia Bulletin*, **25**(3):467–478.

Wahl, OF (1999b) *Telling is Risky Business: Mental Health Consumers Confront Stigma*. Rutgers University Press, Piscataway, NJ.

Wang, JL, Adair, CE and Patten, SB (2006) Mental health and related disability among workers: A population-based study. *Am J Ind Med*, **49**(7):514–522.

CHAPTER 6
Education

Because mental illnesses often begin in adolescence, they can cause significant disruptions in education and training, posing a life-long threat to career development and quality of life. Each year, approximately one in five adolescents will experience significant psychosocial impairment owing to a mental illness (Kataoka *et al.*, 2002; Offord *et al.*, 1989) and many more will experience psychosocial problems (such as stress or feelings of depression) that are sufficient to interfere with their daily functioning (Gotlib *et al.*, 1995; Pollock and Martin, 1999; Rushton *et al.*, 2002). Individuals who develop severe mental illness may never complete their education and training and so may never qualify for stable, competitive employment. In both high- and low-income countries, mental illness is associated with an increased probability of termination of education, particularly secondary education (Lee *et al.*, 2009).

In the United States, for example, it has been estimated that the proportion of students failing to complete primary school would drop by 3% and the proportion failing to complete high school would drop by more than 10% in the absence of mental illness. Mental illness also significantly reduces the likelihood that an individual will enter or graduate from college (Breslau *et al.*, 2008).

Non-participation in the labour market is as much a function of lack of education and training due to illness-related disruptions, as it is of stigma and discrimination. Modern labour markets are unforgiving. They demand a mastery of a significant range of cognitive skills and a reasonable level of academic achievement, which increasingly means post-secondary training. In order to improve job tenure among individuals who typically have truncated educational histories, support to complete post-secondary education and training must be provided (Baron and Salzer, 2002; Murphy *et al.*, 2005). Vocational approaches and legal protections that promote the pursuit of education and training by people with psychiatric disabilities are required.

Mental Illness, Discrimination and the Law: Fighting for Social Justice, First Edition.
Felicity Callard, Norman Sartorius, Julio Arboleda-Flórez, Peter Bartlett, Hanfried Helmchen, Heather Stuart, Jose Taborda and Graham Thornicroft.

6.1 United Nations Covenants and examples of country-based legislation

International covenants provide a human rights framework that requires universal access to basic education for all children, and equitable and non-discriminatory access to higher levels of education for all people, including people with disabilities. National and state level legislation provides for specific protections for children and youth with disabilities. In some countries, specific legal provisions also apply, explicitly, to higher learning and vocational retraining.

A human rights-based approach to education seeks to ensure that children have access to quality education that promotes their right to dignity and optimum human development. This right is enshrined in international declarations such as the UN Universal Declaration of Human Rights (1948) (Chapter 14.1.1.8) and UNESCO's (1960) Covenant against Discrimination in Education (www.unesco.org/most/rr4educ.htm), both of which define access to education as a basic human right. Access to education has also been formally recognised as a basic human right in the UN International Covenant on Economic, Social and Cultural Rights (1966) (Chapter 14.1.1.6), the UN Convention on the Elimination of All Forms of Discrimination against Women (1981) (Chapter 14.1.1.4) and the UN Convention on the Rights of the Child (1989) (Chapter 14.1.1.2). Article 24 (Education) of the UN Convention on the Rights of Persons with Disabilities (CRPD) specifies that:

'States Parties shall ensure that:

- Persons with disabilities are not excluded from the general education system on the basis of disability, and that children with disabilities are not excluded from free and compulsory primary education, or from secondary education, on the basis of disability.
- Persons with disabilities can access an inclusive, quality and free primary education and secondary education on an equal basis with others in the communities in which they live.
- Reasonable accommodation of the individual's requirements is provided.
- Persons with disabilities receive the support required, within the general education system, to facilitate their effective education.'

The CRPD clearly establishes the right to inclusive education at all levels. Inclusive education implies giving universal access to education to all children, young people and adults – that is, identifying and addressing barriers that many people encounter in accessing education opportunities and enabling schools and other educational establishments to serve all children, particularly those with special educational needs. It offers a powerful framework to challenge the provision of segregated education (often described under the umbrella term of 'special education') – in which children and young people with mental disabilities are deprived of the opportunity to receive education in mainstream school settings. The CRPD built on previous declarations regarding inclusive education – notably, the UNESCO Salamanca Statement and Framework for Action, which in 1994 specified that:

- schools should accommodate all children regardless of their physical, intellectual, emotional, social, linguistic or other conditions (Article 3); and
- regular schools with this inclusive orientation are the most effective means of combating discriminatory attitudes, creating welcoming communities, building an inclusive society and achieving education for all; moreover, they provide an effective education to the majority of children and improve the efficiency and ultimately the cost-effectiveness of the entire education system (Article 2) (World Conference on Special Needs Education, 1994).

All of these covenants affirm that education is intended to promote personal development, strengthen respect for human rights and freedoms, and enable individuals to participate effectively in a free society. A rights-based approach to education not only reinforces the inherent dignity of people, it engenders a particular focus on discrimination and equity, and establishes an obligation to remove discrimination at all levels of the educational system (Unicef, 2007). There is a continuing and urgent need to address the many discriminatory policies and frameworks within countries that do not uphold children's right to an inclusive education as specified in the UN conventions above, as well as many other charters and declarations. An example of litigation involving Bulgaria is shown in Box 6.1.

Box 6.1 Litigation Case Study: Mental Disability Advocacy Center v. Bulgaria

In 2008, the European Committee of Social Rights for the first time in central and eastern Europe found violations of the right to education (Article 17(2)) and the right to non-discrimination (Article E) of the Revised European Social Charter (Chapter 14.2.1.1.5). The decision in the case of Mental Disability Advocacy Center (MDAC) v. Bulgaria criticised the Bulgarian government for actively depriving children with intellectual disabilities of education.

The Committee found evidence that the Bulgarian government failed to provide education for up to 3000 children with intellectual disabilities living in so-called 'homes for mentally disabled children' across Bulgaria, which highlighted the inadequacy of

Bulgarian standards for inclusive education. Specifically, the European Committee of Social Rights noted that:

- mainstream schools are not accessible nor adaptable to children who live in 'homes for mentally disabled children';
- teacher training is inadequate and educational curricula and teaching resources are not adapted to the special learning needs of children with intellectual disabilities;
- the Bulgarian government failed to implement a 2002 law which provided that children in 'homes for mentally disabled children' could be integrated into schools;
- as a result of the failure to implement the law, only 6.2% of children in 'homes for mentally disabled children' receive an education, whereas primary school attendance for Bulgarian children in general is approximately 94%;
- the disparity between school attendance for children with and without disabilities is so great that it constitutes discrimination against children with intellectual disabilities living in 'homes for mentally disabled children'.

While MDAC chose to bring the case against Bulgaria, the situation remains similar in many European countries (MDAC, 2007). More information is available at: www.mdac.info

Within this broad human rights framework, many countries have enacted educational legislation to govern how agencies and educational institutions will provide education and related services for children, young people and adults with mental disabilities. Examples are given in Boxes 6.2 to 6.5.

Box 6.2 Legislative Case Study: United States

The Individuals with Disabilities Education Act (IDEA) (1975) requires public schools to make available to all eligible children with disabilities (up to age 21) a free appropriate public education in the least restrictive environment appropriate to their individual needs. It further requires public schools to develop appropriate individualised educational programmes for each child, appropriate to their needs.

IDEA is buttressed by other laws that support an inclusive education culture: the Americans with Disabilities Act (ADA), and Section 504 of the Rehabilitation Act of 1973. The Americans with Disabilities Act Amendments Act (ADAAA), which took effect in January 2009, broadens the definition of disability.

For further information: www.ada.gov (www.ada.gov/cguide.htm#anchor65310); see also Smith and Bales (2010).

Box 6.3 Legislative Case Study: Japan

The Fundamental Law of Education of 1947 had specified that children with physical disabilities were to be incorporated in mainstream facilities (it also provided for the establishment of special facilities for children with sensory disabilities).

The Fundamental Law of Education was revised in 2006. The revisions included improvements in special education (and the decision for it to be renamed, in 2007, as special support education) and the inclusion of children with developmental disabilities (including learning disability, Asperger's syndrome, ADHD (attention deficit hyperactivity disorder) and high-functioning autism) in the target population for special support education.

While special support education is provided for children with disabilities both in mainstream schools and classrooms and in special support schools, it appears that most children with severe disabilities are sent to special – not mainstream – support schools (Matsui, 2009).

Box 6.4 Legislative Case Study: Israel

The Special Education Law (1988) is aimed at developing the abilities of children with special needs, including those with mental disabilities, and easing their integration into society. Any child with a disability (aged 3–21) is eligible for free and accessible special education as befitting the child's needs. According to the law, special education pupils are entitled to non-medical therapeutic services, such as physiotherapy, speech therapy and occupational therapy. The law also gives preference to integrated education with a regular classroom setting and provides for special tutorials and aids.

In 2002, the Inclusion Law became the 7th amendment to the Special Education Law. In 2005, the Accessibility Law became the 2nd amendment to the Equality Law: it requires all new schools to be completely accessible and all existing schools to be made accessible in a limited fashion (until an individual student, parent or teacher with disabilities joins the school, at which point the school is upgraded). The Inclusion Law and the Accessibility Law assure inclusive education as the preferred choice.

While Israel has instituted a number of legislative and administrative actions to ensure the social rights of children with disabilities, implementation has been much more difficult: 'Israel still faces the challenges of carrying out the paradigm shift towards the human rights model in practice and ensuring equal opportunities by abolishing the poverty of, and discrimination against, the geographical and social periphery, as well as ensuring inclusive education and accessible public areas and services to all' (Feldman, 2009).

For further information: www.bizchut.org.il

Box 6.5 Legislative Case Study: Vanuatu

The Education Act No. 21 (2001) prohibits discrimination on the grounds of disability so that children with disabilities can access education.

This Act will need certain amendments in order to comply with the provisions of the UN Convention on the Rights of Persons with Disabilities (CRPD) – particularly in relation to inclusive education – and to bring about a shift in perception amongst teachers towards children and young people as rights holders. The National Disability Policy and Plan of Action calls for this shift to be made and the Department of Education is currently drafting an Inclusive Education Policy.

(Harpur and Bales, 2010; Piau-Lynch, 2009)

Several countries (see Boxes 6.6 to 6.10) have also enacted legislation governing educational institutions more broadly, including institutions of higher learning. In Lithuania, for example, the Law on Equal Treatment (2003) makes it unlawful for any educational, science or academic institution to discriminate against people with a disability.

Box 6.6 Legislative Case Study: Republic of Lithuania

The Law on Equal Treatment (2003) No. IX – 1826 was adopted by the Lithuanian Parliament on 18 November 2003, and came into force on 1 January 2005. It prohibits any direct or indirect discrimination based on age, sexual orientation, disability, racial or ethnic origin, religion or beliefs.

Under the law, educational, science and academic institutions must ensure equal conditions: (a) for persons being admitted to schools of general education, vocational institutions, colleges, universities, refresher and retraining and other courses; (b) for persons awarded study grants or loans for study; (c) when drawing up, drafting, approving and selecting curricula; and (d) when assessing knowledge. They must also ensure that there must not be any discrimination or propagation of discrimination in their textbooks and teaching materials. Further details of the law are available from NATLEX, the database of national labour, social security and related human rights legislation maintained by the International Labour Organization's International Labour Standards Department (www.ilo.org).

The Law on Special Education (1998) includes provision for early and pre-school education, general training, vocational, college and university education, adult education and supplementary education of persons with special needs.

(Jonas *et al.*, 2010)

Box 6.7 Legislative Case Study: Australia

The Disability Discrimination Act (1992) makes it unlawful for any educational authority to discriminate against a person on the grounds of disability by refusing or failing to accept the student's application; by creating unreasonable terms or conditions governing admittance of a student; by denying or limiting access to any benefit provided by an educational authority; by expelling a student or subjecting a student to any other detriment. A mental disability is defined as any disorder, illness or disease that affects a person's thought processes, perception of reality, emotions or judgement that results in disturbed behaviour.

The Disability Standards for Education (2005) specify the obligations of education and training service providers and the rights of people with disabilities under the Disability Discrimination Act 1992. The Standards are intended to give students with disability the same rights as other students (including the right to comparable access, services and facilities, and the right to participate in education and training without discrimination). Education providers have a positive obligation to make changes to reasonably accommodate the needs of a student with disability. The Standards are currently under review (October 2011) to consider how effective they have been in assisting in eliminating discrimination (including harassment and victimisation) of people with disability in education and training.

More information is available from The Australian Human Rights Commission (section on Education): www.hreoc.gov.au
(www.hreoc.gov.au/disability_rights/education/education.html#standards)

The Disability Discrimination Act 1992 is available at: www.austlii.edu.au
(www.austlii.edu.au/au/legis/cth/consol_act/dda1992264)

Box 6.8 Vignette: Tunisia

The right to higher education and training was recently illustrated in Tunisia by the case of a young woman who was able to pass her Baccalaureate examination while hospitalised for a manic episode.

[Vignette from one of the book's informants in Tunisia]

Box 6.9 Legislative Case Study: Sri Lanka

The Protection of the Rights of Persons with Disabilities Act (No 28 of 1996) established the National Council for Persons with Disabilities. One of the central functions of the National Council is 'to ensure the promotion, advancement and protection of the rights of persons with disabilities' (s. 12). It states (23 (1)) that: 'No person with a disability shall be discriminated against on the ground of such disability in recruitment for any employment or office or admission to any educational institution.'

Box 6.10 Legislative Case Study: Malta

The Equal Opportunities (Persons with a Disability) Act (2000) made it unlawful to discriminate against disabled people on the basis of their disability and included the areas of education and training. The Act included the principle of reasonable accommodations (Chapter 2.3.2). It also established a legal framework whereby the National Commission of Persons with Disability could take action when there is a case of discrimination in education or training through the Equal Opportunities Compliance Unit.

(v'Dizabilita, 2010)

Some pieces of legislation seemingly work in favour of disabled people, but in effect have adverse effects on their rights. In Thailand, for example, the 1980 Primary Education Act specifies that every child must receive an education (Article 8). But parents who fail to school their disabled children are treated leniently – and many heads of schools attempt to convince parents of children with disabilities to give up schooling their children. This legislative framework has had the effect of not protecting a child's right to education (Namsiripongpun, 2009).

References

Baron, RC and Salzer, MS (2002) Accounting for unemployment among people with mental illness. *Behavioral Sciences & the Law*, **20**(6):585–599.

Breslau, J, Lane, M, Sampson, N and Kessler, RC (2008) Mental disorders and subsequent educational attainment in a US national sample. *Journal of Psychiatric Research*, **42**(9):708–716.

Feldman, D (2009) Human rights of children with disabilities in Israel: the vision and the reality. *Disability Studies Quarterly*, **29**(1).

Gotlib, I, Lewinsohn, P and Seeley, J (1995) Symptoms versus a diagnosis of depression: differences in psychosocial functioning. *J Consulting Clin Psychol*, **63**(1):90–100.

Harpur, P and Bales, R (2010) The positive impact of the Convention on the Rights of Persons with Disabilities: a case study on the South Pacific and lessons from the US experience. *Northern Kentucky Law Review*, **363**:363–388.

Jonas, R, Lcva, E, Rūta, R, Elijošius, E, Melienė, R, Vinikaitytė, J, *et al.* (2010) ANED country report on equality of educational and training opportunities for young disabled people. Academic Network of European Disability Experts (ANED), Lithuania.

Kataoka, SH, Zhang, L and Wells, KB (2002) Unmet need for mental health care among U.S. children: variation by ethnicity and insurance status. *Am J Psychiatry*, **159**(9):1548–1555.

Lee, S, Tsang, A, Breslau, J, Aguilar-Gaxiola, S, Angermeyer, M, Borges, G, *et al.* (2009) Mental disorders and termination of education in high-income and low- and middle-income countries: epidemiological study. *The British Journal of Psychiatry*, **194**(5):411–417.

Matsui, R (2009) Japan. Background paper. In: ESCAP/OHCHR (ed.) Expert Group Meeting (EGM) on Harmonization of National Legislation with the Convention on the Rights of Persons with Disabilities in Asia and the Pacific; 8–10 June 2009, Bangkok. [United Nations Economic and Social Commission for Asia and the Pacific (ESCAP) / Office of the United Nations High Commissioner for Human Rights (OHCHR)]

MDAC (2007) Mental Disability Advocacy Center v. Bulgaria (No 41/2007, European Committee of Social Rights). Analysis and Recommendations. Mental Disability Advocacy Centern, Budapest, Hungary.

Murphy, AA, Mullen, MG and Spagnolo, AB (2005) Enhancing individual placement and support: promoting job tenure by integrating natural supports and supported education. *American Journal of Psychiatric Rehabilitation*, **8**(1):37–61.

Namsiripongpun, W (2009) Thailand. Background Paper. In: ESCAP/OHCHR (ed.) Expert Group Meeting (EGM) on Harmonization of National Legislation with the Convention on the Rights of Persons with Disabilities in Asia and the Pacific; 8–10 June 2009, Bangkok. [United Nations Economic and Social Commission for Asia and the Pacific (ESCAP) / Office of the United Nations High Commissioner for Human Rights (OHCHR)]

Offord, D, Boyle, M, Fleming, J, Blum, H and Grant, N (1989) Ontario child health study. Summary of selected results. *Can J Psychiatry*, **34**(6):483–491.

Piau-Lynch, AS (2009) Vanuatu: Background paper. In: ESCAP/OHCHR (ed.) Expert Group Meeting (EGM) on Harmonization of National Legislation with the Convention on the Rights of Persons with Disabilities in Asia and the Pacific; 8–10 June 2009, Bangkok. [United Nations Economic and Social Commission for Asia and the Pacific (ESCAP) / Office of the United Nations High Commissioner for Human Rights (OHCHR)

Pollock, NK and Martin, CS (1999) Diagnostic Orphans: Adolescents With Alcohol Symptoms Who Do Not Qualify for DSM-IV Abuse or Dependence Diagnoses. *Am J Psychiatry*, **156**(6):897–901.

Rushton, J, Forcier, M and Schectman, R (2002) Epidemiology of depressive symptoms in the National Longitudinal Study of Adolescent Health. *J Am Acad Child Adolesc Psychiatry*, **41**(2):199–205.

Smith, KM and Bales, R (2010) Education for Americans with disabilities: reconciling IDEA with the 2008 ADA amendments. *Northern Kentucky Law Review*, **37**:389–413.

Unicef (2007) A Human Rights-Based Approach to Education for All. United Nations Children's Fund and United Nations Educational, Scientific and Cultural Organization (UNESCO), New York.

v'Dizabilita, KNP (2010) ANED country report on equality of educational and training opportunities for young disabled people. Academic Network of European Disability Experts (ANED), Malta.

World Conference on Special Needs Education (1994) The Salamanca Statement and Framework for Action on Special Needs Education. World Conference on Special Needs Education: Access and Quality; 7–10 June 1994, Salamanca, Spain.

CHAPTER 7
Housing

7.1 Discrimination in housing

There is clear evidence that people with mental health problems living in the community face discrimination in terms of housing (Rubey, 2002). A large survey of almost 2000 service users with severe mental illness across eight of the states in the USA asked about their experiences of discrimination. Almost a quarter (22%) said that they had been homeless and another 32% said that they had experienced housing discrimination (Corrigan *et al.*, 2003). The nature and extent of this form of systematic neglect is evidenced by the consistently high rates of mental illness found among surveys of people who are homeless (Abdul *et al.*, 1993; Herman *et al.*, 1998; Link *et al.*, 1995; Shern *et al.*, 1997).

There is an important difference here between issues that are highlighted from the point of view of service users and those that are identified in research. People who use mental health services frequently mention housing – they describe their lack of choice, the provision of temporary accommodation and the feeling that they receive low-quality provision because of their mental illness. However, there is very little published work about these issues (Dunn, 1999; GLA, 2003; Prior, 1996; Read *et al.*, 1996; Ryan *et al.*, 2001). In part, the geographical segregation of people with severe mental illness into specific neighbourhoods is more closely related to material poverty than to the precise nature of the health problem (Harvey, 1975). Since rates of unemployment are commonly in excess of 90% amongst people with severe mental illness, the choice of residential locations available to people with such disorders is strongly determined by where public housing and low-cost rented accommodation is available (Howard, 2010; Thornicroft *et al.*, 2004). There may, therefore, be discrimination both in access to housing at all – and in access to housing of a reasonable quality (Luhrmann, 2007). Interestingly, data from Chicago suggest that some people with psychotic disorders decide to reject offers of public housing if the quality if very low (Luhrmann, 2008). Notably, many of the women in the Chicago study refused offers of housing help because

Mental Illness, Discrimination and the Law: Fighting for Social Justice, First Edition.
Felicity Callard, Norman Sartorius, Julio Arboleda-Flórez, Peter Bartlett, Hanfried Helmchen, Heather Stuart, Jose Taborda and Graham Thornicroft.

of the way in which the local culture conceptualised acceptance of such help as closely allied to 'being crazy'. The author of the study emphasised that offers of housing help to those who are living on the street with a psychiatric diagnosis might well be more successful when 'explicit psychiatric diagnosis is downplayed' (Luhrmann, 2008).

Perhaps the most visible display of discrimination against people with mental illness in terms of housing is the so-called 'not in my back yard (NIMBY)' phenomenon. This describes the tendency for people to object to proposals to locate a facility for mentally ill people in their own neighbourhood (Herrmann, 1990). For example, *The Star*, a local newspaper in Sheffield (England) featured a large picture of placards held aloft by members of a protesting crowd declaring 'Paranoid Schizophrenic Out!', 'Keep Our Children Safe!' and 'Find Another Community!' The article described a march by local people who opposed plans to create a new nursing home for people with a history of mental illness (Kessen, 2004). Within neighbourhoods, there are clear accounts of the victimisation of people known to have mental illness by neighbours encouraging them to move away. Acts of 'encouragement' include anonymously putting faeces through the letterbox (acts that, if they were related to ethnicity, may in some countries be described as 'hate crimes' (Thornicroft, 2006)).

The Convention for the Rights of Persons with Disabilities (CRPD) Article 19 (Living independently and being included in the community) and Article 28 (Adequate standard of living and social protection) (Chapter 14.1.1.1 and 14.4.1) require: (i) an adequate standard of housing to be provided, (ii) steps to realise and safeguard these provisions, including public housing, and (iii) that these be provided without discrimination in relation to disabilities related to physical or mental disorders. What examples of good practice can be identified in the practical application of these principles?

7.2 Examples of legislation

A number of examples of legislation are shown in Boxes 7.1 to 7.6.

Box 7.1 Legislative Case Study: New Zealand

The Residential Tenancies Act (1996) specifies that discrimination is unlawful and an infringement of the Human Rights Act (1993). It further specifies that:

> 'Discrimination against any person in respect of the grant, continuance, extension, variation, termination, or renewal of a tenancy agreement is in contravention of the Human Rights Act 1993.'

The 'tenancy agreement' referred to includes a prospective tenancy agreement, regardless of whether or not a tenancy is granted.

Box 7.2 Legislative Case Study: United States

The Fair Housing Amendments Act of 1988 (FHAA) prohibits discrimination in the sale or rental of housing on the basis of disability. In enacting this law, Congress recognised the long history of exclusion from the mainstream housing market that many people with disabilities have endured due to 'misperceptions, ignorance and outright prejudice'.

To overcome historical segregation, the FHAA provides protection against discrimination in housing based on one's disability, history of disability or association with a person with a disability. The FHAA provides remedies for discrimination in the application and screening phase, as well as during tenancy or upon eviction proceedings (Petrila, 2002; Petrila and Ayers, 1994; Petrila and Brink, 2001; Schless and Josephs, 1991).

Surveys undertaken some years after the law was introduced show that discrimination in housing remains common, however (Corrigan *et al.*, 2003; Forchuk *et al.*, 2006), and some people needed to change accommodation to improve their living condition (Corrigan *et al.*, 2006).

This law has been used to test the lawfulness of special restrictions applied only to people with mental disabilities and other practices that create barriers to proper housing for people with mental illness.

Box 7.3 Legislative Case Study: Canada, Province of Ontario

In Ontario, the Human Rights Code applies to landlords and tenants. People cannot be refused an apartment, harassed by a housing provider or other tenants, or otherwise treated unfairly on a number of grounds – which include disability. The Ontario Human Rights Commission (OHRC) has produced a policy that is based on its research on discrimination in rental housing; international standards; human rights claims that have come before the OHRC and the Human Rights Tribunal of Ontario; court decisions; and extensive stakeholder consultation (Ontario Human Rights Commission, 2009). Under the Human Rights Code, housing providers have a duty to accommodate the Code-related needs of tenants and to take steps to address barriers that may exist, unless to do so would cause undue hardship. The OHRC policy specifies that the 'duty to accommodate' may require flexibility when enforcing rules and requirements. The policy provides the following example relating to people with mental disabilities:

'Due to unforeseen symptoms arising from a change in medication, a tenant with a mental disability fails to meet the deadline for filing information on a change in income. Before this incident, the tenant had complied fully with the rules and requirements of his social housing program (sic) and had been very proud of his demonstrated ability to live independently. The social housing provider, in this instance, uses his discretion to extend the deadline, thus avoiding much embarrassment for the tenant and a possible revocation of the tenant's subsidy.'

For more information, see the Ontario Human Rights Commission website: www.ohrc.on.ca

(Ontario Human Rights Commission, 2009; www.ohrc.on.ca/en/resources/Policies/housing/pdf)

Box 7.4 Legislative Case Study: Argentina

Law 26.182, Housing for people with disabilities (1 November 2006) allocates 5% of public housing for persons with disabilities or families with at least one member with disabilities who receives funding from FONAVI (the National Housing Fund).

Box 7.5 Legislative Case Study: Finland

The Constitution (Section 19, 'The right to social security') specifies that public authorities shall promote the right of everyone to housing and the opportunity to arrange their own housing.

The Housing Development Act specifies that:

'The goal for developing the quality of housing in Finland is to secure every Finnish citizen's right to adequate housing by:

1 ensuring that every household has access to a dwelling of adequate size, including an adequate number of rooms corresponding to household size and satisfying the basic needs of the members of the household;
2 ensuring that the structure of dwellings is appropriate, that dwellings have basic amenities and are healthy and functional, and that the buildings fit in the environment;
3 ensuring that the housing expenditure is reasonable in relation to the respective size and disposable income and other necessary consumption expenditure of households.

Special attention shall be paid to development of the housing quality of people with inadequate living conditions, people with small or modest incomes, young people and families with children in order to improve their access to housing, to ensure reasonable housing costs and to decrease segregation in different areas and in different population groups.'

The Mental Health Act specifies that:

'In addition to adequate treatment and services, a person suffering from a mental illness or some other mental disorder must be provided with rehabilitative or service housing appropriate to the necessary medical or social rehabilitation as separately decreed. Such housing shall be organised in cooperation with the social welfare department of the municipality in question.'

(Fredriksson and Pätäri, 2006)

Box 7.6 Legislative Case Study: Hong Kong

Under the Disability Discrimination Ordinance 1995, discrimination against people on the ground of 'their or their associates' disability is unlawful in respect of employment, accommodation, education, access to partnerships, membership of trade unions and clubs, access to premises, educational establishments, sporting activities and the provision of goods, services and facilities.'

Disability discrimination legislation often specifies housing as one of the arenas in which discrimination is prohibited (Chapter 2.3 and Chapter 15, Examples of disability legislation from across the world).

7.3 Community living

It should be emphasised that in many countries, the legislative priority for people with mental disabilities in relation to the question of housing is to mandate a move towards deinstitutionalisation, that is, the replacement of institutions for people with disabilities with comprehensive, quality community-based services (ECCL, 2011). We are using the term 'institution' in the sense defined by the European Coalition for Community Living (ECCL):

> 'any place in which people who have been labelled as having a disability are isolated, segregated and/or compelled to live together. An institution is also any place in which people do not have, or are not allowed to exercise control over their lives and their day-to-day decisions. An institution is not defined merely by its size' (ECCL, 2011).

There are a number of examples where legislation has been used in the service of progressive deinstitutionalisation (Boxes 7.7 to 7.12 show examples from Italy, Argentina, Brazil, Azerbaijan, Lithuania and Malta). The most famous of these is almost certainly Italy's Mental Health Law (Law 180) (Box 7.7).

Box 7.7 Legislative Case Study: Italy

The Mental Health Law (Law 180) was one of a set of laws that were part of a reform of Italian mental health law. Law 180 is a national law and there are also 20 regional laws on policies (as the Italian Constitution gives significant autonomy to the regions in planning and administering health services). The national law was first approved in May 1978 and was incorporated in December 1978, with minor modifications, in to the General Health Law (Law 833).

The national law has three main elements:

- a ban on building new mental hospitals and on admitting new patients to the existing ones;
- prevention work, treatment and rehabilitation of people with mental illness should normally be carried out in community services;
- the establishment of Involuntary Health Treatment, on grounds that the patient needs help, not that she or he is dangerous (Giannichedda, 2003).

The national law has not changed in 25 years, but there have been many revisions to all the regional laws.

Reflections on the Italian mental health reforms can be found in Burti (2001), Burti and Benson (1996) and Girolamo and Cozza (2000).

Resources and an archive of texts relating to legislation, policy and mental health care in Italy can be found at: www.triestesalutementale.it

Box 7.8 Legislative Case Study: Argentina

Progressive legislative reform has taken place in particular provincial jurisdictions.

1. Río Negro

Law 2440 – Ley de Promoción Sanitaria y Social de Las Personas que Padecen Sufrimiento Mental (Law for the Promotion of Health Care and Social Services for Persons with Mental Illness) – was presented to the provincial legislature in 1989 and passed in 1991. All mental health service providers – public and private – must conform to its principles. Its first Article specifies that:

> 'The province promotes a health system that, in considering the person as a whole, guarantees the treatment and rehabilitation of people of any age who suffer from a mental disorder.' The law further specifies that: 'The restoration of the identity, dignity and respect of a person with mental disorder, expressed in terms of his or her reintegration into his community, constitute the ultimate goal of this law.'

The law also called for the creation of intermediate or transitional facilities for care and lodging (including halfway houses and hostels for service users who had no home and housing for patients who had committed serious crimes but judged not competent to stand trial). The law banned public or private asylums that did not comply with it. Admission to any psychiatric facility could only be a last therapeutic option (summary taken from Collins (2008), see also Cohen and Natella (1995)).

2. Buenos Aires

The 1996 Constitution of the Autonomous City of Buenos Aires provided the groundwork for reform of the mental health system by redirecting mental health policies away from social control and towards deinstitutionalisation and social protection.

The Ley Básica de Salud, No 153 (Basic Health Law 153) (1999) instructs the city government to implement progressive deinstitutionalisation. Social integration is to be encouraged through the provision of day hospitals, halfway houses and therapeutic communities.

In line with Basic Health Law 153, the Ley de Salud Mental de la Ciudad de Buenos Aires No. 448 (Mental Health Law of the City of Buenos Aires, Law 448) (2000) guarantees the right to mental health and also pushes for deinstitutionalisation, integration and rehabilitation. Article 3 specifies human rights protections for those with mental disabilities. The law reflects many international human rights standards, including the right to informed consent, to community integration and to personalised attention (Cohen and Natella, 1995; Collins, 2008; MDRI, 2007).

3. Province of San Luis

In the Province of San Luis, transformations have taken place in psychiatric provision since the 1990s. They were backed up in 2006 by the province's Ley de Desinstitucionalización (Deinstitutionalisation Law) 2006.

'The 'Institutional Transformation Plan' of the San Luis hospital started in November 1993. It aimed to replace the existing asylum by a new form of psychiatric care. All 120 patients were re-evaluated and institutionalisation was found to be a significant problem. These patients were gradually reintegrated and psychiatric hospitalisation is no longer the main resource available. The hospital now has only 10 beds and a room for care of patients in crisis. The most important feature is outpatient treatment (the annual number of consultations rose from 500 in 1993 to 36 000 in 2008). The participation of family and community (friends and neighbours) in the treatment is encouraged (summary of an unpublished report by Jorge Luis Pelligrini entitled 'Plan de transformación instituticional' 1993–2009, San Luis (Argentina): translation by authors; see also Pellegrini (2009)).

Box 7.9 Legislative Case Study: Brazil

There have been a number of state laws encouraging deinstitutionalisation, such as Law No. 9,716 of Rio Grande do Sul (1992), which outlines the replacement of beds in psychiatric hospitals with community-based health services.

Discussion of deinstitutionalisation in Brazil can be found in Cassis (2008); Csillag (2001); Hazelton (2005); Gastal et al. (2007); Pacheco de Toledo Ferrz and Carlini (2003).

Legislation can also be used to give people with mental health problems access to housing services. It is not necessarily the case, however, that these provisions promote or fully endorse 'independent living' and deinstitutionalisation as defined by the European Coalition for Community Living (ECCL). Box 17.3 comprises a resource that discusses the right to housing within European countries, much of which is of relevance to people with mental health problems.

Box 7.10 Legislative Case Study: Azerbaijan

There is legislative provision for long-stay supported hostels for people with mental disorders who have lost relatives and social ties. This includes the right to freedom of movement and choice of residence.

Box 7.11 Legislative Case Study: Lithuania

In Lithuania, the state supports people with disability through providing social services. The Lithuanian Law on Social Services defines objectives and types of social services, and regulates the management, granting and provision of social services:

'Social services shall be of the following types: (1) social services of general interest provided to a person (family) whose abilities to independently care for his private (family) life and to participate in society may be developed or compensated for by the (2) specific services provided without permanent assistance by specialists. Information, counselling, mediation and representation, social and cultural services, organisation of transportation, organisation of catering, provision of necessary clothes and footwear as well as other services shall be regarded as social services of general interest.'

Box 7.12 Legislative Case Study: Malta

The Equal Opportunities (Persons with A Disability Act) (cap 413) (2000) specifies non-discrimination in relation to disabled people and includes the area of housing. It does refer to 'independent living' but does not focus on establishing how disabled people can have access to independent living (v'Dizabilita, 2010).

A state agency called Agenzija Sapport was established in 2003, and offers supported housing initiatives. This is one of several administrative mechanisms that can assist people with mental health problems in relation to the provision of housing (for example, there are housing subsidies which persons with mental health problems are able to access). Additional context can be found in Galea and Mifsud (2004).

Box 7.13 Resource

A useful discussion of the 'right to housing' in Europe, and an analysis of legislation relating to this 'right to housing' in European countries, is provided in Fredriksson and Pätäri (2006).

References

Abdul, H, Wykes, T and Stansfeld, S (1993) The homeless mentally ill: myths and realities. *Int J Social Psychiatry*, **39**(4):237–254.

Burti, L (2001) Italian psychiatric reform 20 plus years after. *Acta Psychiatr Scand*, **104**(suppl. 410):41–46.

Burti, L and Benson, PR (1996) Psychiatric reform in Italy: developments since 1978. *International Journal of Law and Psychiatry*, **19**(3–4):373–390.

Cassis, H (2008) Brazil – Two experiences with psychiatric deinstitutionalization, Campinas and Sobral. In: Caldas de Almeida, JM and Cohen, A (eds) *Innovative Mental Health Programs in Latin America and the Caribbean*. Pan American Health Organization, Washington, DC. pp. 33–43.

Cohen, H and Natella, G (1995) Trabajar en salud mental, la desmanicomialización en Río Negro. *Lugar* (Editorial), Buenos Aires.

Collins, PY (2008) Argentina – Waving the mental health revolution banner: psychiatric reform and community mental health in the Province of Río Negro. In: Caldas de Almeida, JM and Cohen, A (eds) *Innovative Mental Health Programs in Latin America and the Caribbean*. Pan American Health Organization, Washington, DC. pp. 1–33.

Corrigan, P, Thompson, V, Lambert, D, Sangster, Y, Noel, J and Campbell, J (2003) Perceptions of discrimination among persons with serious mental illness. *Psychiatr Serv*, **54**(8):1105–1110.

Corrigan, P, Larson, J, Watson, A, Boyle, M and Barr, L (2006) Solutions to discrimination in work and housing identified by people with mental illness. *J Nerv Ment Dis*, **194**(9):716–718.

Csillag, C (2001) Psychiatric reform law comes into effect in Brazil. *The Lancet*, **357**(9265):1346.

de Girolamo, G and Cozza, M (2000) The Italian psychiatric reform: a 20-year perspective. *International Journal of Law and Psychiatry*, **23**(3–4):197–214.

Dunn, S (1999) Creating Accepting Communities: Report of the MIND inquiry into social exclusion and mental health problems. MIND, London.

ECCL (2011) (European Coalition for Community Living). Our mission. Available from: http://www.community-living.info/?page=205 [accessed 3 April 2011].

Forchuk, C, Nelson, G and Hall, G (2006) 'It's important to be proud of the place you live in': housing problems and preferences of psychiatric survivors. *Perspectives in Psychiatric Care*, **42**(1):42–52.

Fredriksson, P and Pätäri, J (eds) (2006) Right to Housing in Europe – Need for a Comprehensive Strategy. Housing Rights in Europe Conference, Helsinki.

Galea, S and Mifsud, J (2004) The mental health care system in Malta. *International Psychiatry: Bulletin of the Board of International Affairs of the Royal College of Psychiatrists*, **5**:11–13.

Gastal, FL, Leite, SO, Fernandes, FN, de Borba, AT, Kitamura, CM, Binz, MAR, *et al.* (2007) Psychiatric reform in Rio Grande do Sul: an analysis of history, economy and the impact of 1992 legislation. *Rev psiquiatr Rio Gd Sul* [serial on the Internet], **29**(1): Available from: http://www.scielo.br/scielo.php?script=sci_arttext&pid=S0101-81082007000100020&lng=en.

Giannichedda, MG (2003) The Italian Mental Health Law. Evaluation of the Mental Health Law Reform in Italy – Lessons learned. Presentation for the Second WHO International Training Forum on Mental Health, Human Rights and Legislation, 10–12 November 2003, Geneva, Switzerland. Available from: http://www.triestesalutementale.it/english/doc/psy_reform_act.doc [accessed 3 April 2011].

GLA (Greater London Authority) (2003) Getting a Move On. Addressing the Housing and Support Issues Facing Londoners with Mental Health Needs. Greater London Authority, London.

Harvey, D (1975) *Social Justice and the City*. Edward Arnold, London.

Hazelton, M (2005) Mental health reform, citizenship and human rights in four countries. *Health Sociology Review*, **14**(3):230–241.

Herrmann, J (1990) NIMBY (not-in-my-back-yard) – the lingering stigma of mental illness. *Rev Fed Am Health Syst*, **23**(4):10–11.

Herman, D, Susser, E, Jandorf, L, Lavell, J and Bromet, E (1998) Homelessness among individuals with psychotic disorders hospitalized for the first time: findings from the Suffolk County Mental Health Project. *Am J Psychiatry*, **155**(1):109–113.

Howard, L, Heslin, M, Leese, M, McCrone, P, Rice, C, Jarrett, M, *et al.* (2010) Supported employment: randomised controlled trial. *Br J Psychiatry*, **196**(5):404–411.

Kessen, D (2004) Fury over home for mentally ill. *The Star*, 11 November 2004.

Link, B, Schwartz, S, Moore, R, Phelan, J, Struening, E, Stueve, A, *et al.* (1995) Public knowledge, attitudes, and beliefs about homeless people: evidence for compassion fatigue. *Am J Community Psychol*, **23**(4):533–555.

Luhrmann, T (2007) Social defeat and the culture of chronicity: or, why schizophrenia does so well over there and so badly here. *Cult Med Psychiatry*, **31**(2):135–172.

Luhrmann, T (2008) 'The street will drive you crazy': why homeless psychotic women in the institutional circuit in the United States often say no to offers of help. *Am J Psychiatry*, **165**(1):15–20.

MDRI (Mental Disability Rights International), Center for Legal and Social Studies (CELS) (2007) Ruined Lives: Segregation from society in Argentina's psychiatric asylums. A report on human rights and mental health in Argentina. MDRI, Washington, DC.

Ontario Human Rights Commission (2009) Policy on Human Rights and Rental Housing. Ontario Human Rights Commission, Canada (www.ohrc.on.ca/en/resources/Policies/housing/pdf)

Pacheco de Toledo Ferraz, M and Carlini, EA (2003) Brazilian public mental health policy: education and research. *International Psychiatry: Bulletin of the Board of International Affairs of the Royal College of Psychiatrists*, **1**(1):15–16.

Pellegrini, JL (2009) The process of institutional transformation of San Luis Psychiatric Hospital [in Spanish]. *Vertex*, **20**(88):432–439.

Petrila, J (2002) The US Supreme Court narrows the definition of disability under the Americans with Disabilities Act. *Psychiatr Serv*, **53**(7):797–798, 801.

Petrila, J and Ayers, K (1994) Enforcing the Fair Housing Amendments Act to benefit people with mental disability. *Hosp Community Psychiatry*, **45**(2):156–160.

Petrila, J and Brink, T (2001) Mental illness and changing definition of disability under the Americans with Disabilities Act. *Psychiatr Serv*, **52**(5):626–630.

Prior, C (1996) Housing component of mental health services. In: Thornicroft, G and Strathdee, G (eds) *Commissioning Mental Health Services*. HMSO, London. pp. 177–192.

Read, J and Baker, S (1996) Not Just Sticks and Stones. A Survey of the Stigma, Taboos, and Discrimination Experienced by People with Mental Health Problems. MIND, London.

Rubey, R (2002) There's no place like home: housing for the most vulnerable individuals with severe mental disabilities. *Ohio State Law Journal*, **63**(6), 1729–1753.

Ryan, C, Robinson, D and Hausmann, L (2001) Stereotyping among providers and consumers of public mental health services. The role of perceived group variability. *Behav Modif*, **25**(3):406–442.

Schless, D and Josephs, R (1991) Ins and outs of discrimination. Fair Housing Act triggers sweeping changes. *Contemp Longterm Care*, **14**(9): 58, 98–100, 103.

Shern, D, Felton, C, Hough, R, Lehman, A, Goldfinger, S, Valencia, E, *et al.* (1997) Housing outcomes for homeless adults with mental illness: results from the second-round McKinney program. *Psychiatric Services*, **48**:239–241.

Thornicroft, G (2006) *Shunned: discrimination against people with mental illness*. Oxford University Press, Oxford.

Thornicroft, G, Tansella, M, Becker, T, Knapp, M, Leese, M, Schene, A, *et al.* (2004) The personal impact of schizophrenia in Europe. *Schizophrenia Res*, **69**(2–3):125–132.

v'Dizabilita, KNP (2010) ANED country report on equality of educational and training opportunities for young disabled people. Academic Network of European Disability Experts (ANED), Malta.

CHAPTER 8

Social Security and Social Protection

8.1 What are social security and social protection?

The Universal Declaration of Human Rights (Chapter 14.1.1.8) specifies that 'Everyone . . . has the right to social security' – specifically in the event of 'unemployment, sickness, disability, widowhood, old age or other lack of livelihood in circumstances beyond his control' (Articles 22 and 25). The UN Convention on the Rights of Persons with Disabilities (CRPD) uses the term 'social protection' rather than 'social security'. Article 28 of the CRPD (Adequate standard of living and social protection) specifies that persons with disabilities have the right to:

1 an adequate standard of living for themselves and their families, including adequate food, clothing and housing;
2 social protection and to the enjoyment of that right without discrimination on the basis of disability.

The CRPD specifies, furthermore, that States Parties should:

3 ensure access by persons with disabilities – in particular women, girls and older persons with disabilities – to social protection programmes and poverty reduction programmes;
4 ensure access by persons with disabilities and their families living in situations of poverty to assistance from the State with disability-related expenses (including counselling, training and respite care);
5 ensure equal access by persons with disabilities to retirement benefits and programmes.

There was substantial debate during the drafting of the CRPD over whether to use the term 'social protection' or 'social security', given that the earlier core human rights treaties refer to 'social security' (e.g. Article 9 of the International Covenant on Economic, Social and Cultural Rights (Chapter 14.1.1.6)), and Article 26 of the UN Convention on the Elimination of All Forms of Discrimination Against Women (Chapter 14.1.1.4)).

Mental Illness, Discrimination and the Law: Fighting for Social Justice, First Edition.
Felicity Callard, Norman Sartorius, Julio Arboleda-Flórez, Peter Bartlett, Hanfried Helmchen, Heather Stuart, Jose Taborda and Graham Thornicroft.

The terms 'social security' and 'social protection' are, indeed, used in different ways in different countries, in different contexts and by those with different theoretical and political orientations.

The International Labour Office (ILO) has made the following pragmatic distinction:

> 'Social security: all measures providing benefits, whether in cash or in kind, to secure protection, *inter alia*, from:
>
> **(a)** lack of work-related income (or insufficient income) caused by sickness, disability, maternity, employment injury, unemployment, old age, or death of a family member;
>
> **(b)** lack of access or unaffordable access to health care;
>
> **(c)** insufficient family support, particularly for children and adult dependants;
>
> **(d)** general poverty and social exclusion.

> 'Social protection: This term social protection carries a wider variety of meaning in institutions across the world than social security. It is often interpreted as having a broader character than social security (including, in particular, protection provided between members of the family or members of a local community), but it is also used in some contexts with a narrower meaning (understood as comprising only measures addressed to the poorest, most vulnerable or excluded members of society)' (ILO, 2010).

Social security, then, usually refers to a wide variety of programmes of social protection, which are established by legislation (or other mandatory administrative arrangements) and which aim to give individuals a level of income security when faced with certain contingencies (including unemployment, rearing of children, old age, disability and war trauma). It may also include access to preventative or curative medical care. For people with disabilities, personal support services (including day care services, personal assistants and assistive technologies) are of particular importance.

8.2 Social security and social protection for people with mental health problems

It is clear that the positive right to social protection/social services is far from being realised for a huge proportion of the world's population: 80% of the global population is still without access to social security (ILO, 2008). Indeed, in sub-Saharan Africa and South Asia, it is estimated than fewer than 10% of people have access to even the most basic protection (ILO, 2010). People with disabilities are at a particularly high risk of not having this right met: many social injustices and structural factors contribute to placing many people with physical and mental disabilities in positions of extreme poverty – as well as other forms of social and economic vulnerability (Miranda and Patel, 2005; WHO, 2010; Yeo, 2001, 2005). Many social injustices and structural factors simultaneously contribute to placing many poor people at much greater risk of becoming physically and/or mentally disabled. Additionally, individuals with a disability need more resources to gain access to the support they need to exercise their capabilities.

In many standard models of social security, the contingencies to which social security arrangements are a response are seen as unwelcome 'shocks' – and hence social security programmes are regarded as a 'safety net'. There is a move within the fields of poverty reduction and social development, however, to shift the focus towards conceptualising 'social protection' (which would encompass and extend beyond social security programmes) not as a short-term 'safety net' that responds to 'shocks', but rather as an approach that has long-term socio-political aims as well as short-term functions. These long-term aims would be directed towards helping people to preserve and accumulate assets so that they can begin to transform – and have more control over – the social and economic relationships that characterise their lives (AbiYaghi, 2009; Ball *et al.*, 2006).

Many adherents of this approach emphasise that current socio-economic processes that occur under the umbrella term of neo-liberalism – and which operate in geographically uneven ways (Harvey, 2005) – are fundamental to both understanding and addressing the precarious positions inhabited by many people with mental and physical disabilities. For example, labour relations are being transformed through the growth and intensification of informal and flexible labour practices. The role of the state and of governance practices are also being reshaped, and these changes are reworking the older style of welfare state model in which there was universal social insurance (Destremau, 2008; Larner, 2000). (One exemplar of this older model was the 'Beveridge Plan' in the United Kingdom, which was intended to cover people 'from the cradle to the grave'. Many countries, we should note, have never had this model of citizenship-based social protection.) It is imperative that legislative and policy approaches to social protection for people with mental health problems grapple with these realities. There is the risk of a default to a position in which it is hoped that traditional social protection approaches – which are usually designed in the context of formal, salaried, regular employment – will be enough to transform the lives of people with mental health problems. Given the very significant proportions of people (both with and without mental disabilities) in many countries who are not – or not always – offered formal, salaried employment opportunities, such default reliance on traditional social security/social protection approaches will almost certainly be ineffective. This is particularly likely to be the case in contexts where the role of the state – and/or other formal institutions – is weak or inadequate (Destremau, 2008). (See, for example, issue 1 of The Disability Monitor Initiative (2009), which draws together important conceptual and empirical research on how to address 'social protection' in the Middle East in the context of the CRPD.) The real challenge, as one scholar has put it, in light of the social and economic conditions that characterise the lives of many marginalised people, is how we can effectively move to the legal protection of social rights, so that these social rights are: 'not only virtual entitlements, but claims that individuals can make in the name of their status, gender, position, etc., and that allow them to demand and obtain forms of protection against social and economic disturbances caused by the capitalist market, be they included in it or not' (Destremau, 2008).

Such a formulation indicates that addressing social rights inevitably entails grappling with a country's political and social organisation, as well as with the matter of distributive justice. In this sense, it is important that legislative and administrative attempts to improve the lives of people with mental health problems who are economically marginalised do not simply keep their eyes focused on an 'anti-poverty' agenda. This is because attempts to reduce poverty do not necessarily adhere to a wider commitment towards a just social organisation. (Indeed, some anti-poverty programmes and approaches can end up further exacerbating social inequalities by 'dispensing a neo-liberal market prescription for restructuring societies and economies' (Mittelman, 2008).)

How, then, to proceed with legislative approaches to social protection and social security? The argument presented above is not widely endorsed within substantial sectors of the international development arena, which tends to be dominated by orthodox anti-poverty approaches of the kind we have just criticised. And for people with disabilities – whether mental and/or physical – there is perhaps an additional reason why attempts to develop progressive approaches to social protection have been slow to flourish in certain quarters. This is because for significant sectors of the disability movement, the focus in the last couple of decades has been on anti-discrimination legislation. As a result, many countries have deprioritised the focus on social protection and social welfare legislation. While the former (anti-discrimination legislation) has been regarded as the province of rights-based claims, social protection and social welfare legislation has, for many, been tainted by discourses of 'compensation' or 'charity' (Ellis, 2005). Disability in law, it should be remembered, was traditionally addressed through social security and welfare statutes. This meant that people with disabilities were frequently thought of 'not as subjects of legal rights, but as objects of welfare, health and charity programmes' (Mor, 2011). In the past, social security legislation often had the effect of deepening the social exclusion and segregation of people with mental health problems through the provision of separate services. Progressive use of welfare and social security legislation, therefore, needs to be built around rights and social justice principles: its purpose should be to support people with mental health problems to allow them to participate fully within civil society and to enjoy their capabilities.

There can be fraught political disputes within various sectors within the disability movement over how to respond to policy and legal innovations regarding social/welfare benefits for disabled people. One case study from Israel demonstrates the tension between disability rights advocates – who tend to reject disability allowances as perpetuating the marginalisation of disabled people – and welfare activists, who construe such allowances as a way of responding to economic necessities. The author argues for a model that differs from both these alternatives – stressing that disability allowances should instead be seen as a question of 'social responsibility', whereby a society should be held responsible for 'redressing past wrongs' in relation to those with disabilities (Mor, 2011). The focus within the CRPD on the right to social protection has been one of the factors pointing towards a reappraisal of the importance of progressive social protection/social services legislation. There is increasing realisation that anti-discrimination laws which focus on ensuring that employers make reasonable accommodations for those with disabilities need to be complemented by appropriate government interventions, such as the adequate public funding and provision of benefits (i.e. 'a shift towards a form of non-patronising social welfare law') (Bagenstos, 2004). In such a model, social and welfare law are to be regarded as key elements through which to address the deep structural barriers (to employment, to equal opportunities) that many people with disabilities face. In other words, they form a key plank through which to assist individuals to be ready to apply and to be qualified for jobs in the first place.

8.3 Elements of social protection/social services legislation

There are a number of important elements that need to be in place when planning and developing social protection and social services legislation in order to ensure that such legislation does not fall into the trap of some of the older charity-focused social welfare provisions. Legislation should ensure that:

- It does not exclude people who should be entitled to social services/social protection provisions because of disability being defined too narrowly. Additionally, care needs to be taken in assessing how different laws addressing disability work in tandem with one another. A good anti-discrimination law will need to be broad (e.g. so that it can include people who are perceived to have mental health problems, even if this is not in fact the case, Chapter 2.3.1, 2.3.3, 2.3.4); a social welfare law that provides personal support or assistance benefits might well need to define the target groups to benefit from this law somewhat differently (Degener, 2006).

- It does not embed the common assumption that disabled people (including people with mental health problems) are unable to work. In other words, such legislation should ensure that people are not divided into categories of 'can' and 'cannot' work on the basis of their impairment/or diagnosis (Box 8.1).

Box 8.1 Guidance: An Example from Europe

A recent report by the Academic Network of European Disability Experts emphasised the risk of creating two different groups amongst people with disabilities: those deemed to be able to be helped back into employment, and those assigned to long-term social support. They recommend instead the use of 'flexible approaches to support partial work capacity.' This approach to both employment and social protection legislation is likely to be more inclusive than dividing people into those in receipt of employment-related benefits and those in receipt of non-employment-related social services/'incapacity' benefits (Priestley and Roulstone, 2009).

- Adequate support is given to people with disabilities to gain and retain employment (Chapter 2.3.2 and Chapter 5, Work and the workplace). But legislative and administrative actions should also value the contributions of those people who do not participate in the world of paid work.
- Individuals' self-reliance and independence is supported and promoted (Box 8.2).

Box 8.2 Policy Case Study: The Australian Disability Strategy 2010–2020

The Strategy (Section on Economic Security, Policy Direction 2) specifies that:

- Income support and tax systems should provide an adequate standard of living for people with disability, their families and carers, while fostering personal financial independence and employment.
- Income support payments also need to be geared so that, where possible, they encourage people who choose to seek employment to do so, rather than creating new barriers.

(Commonwealth of Australia, 2011)

For further information: www.fahcsia.gov.au (www.fahcsia.gov.au/sa/disability/progserv/govtint/nds_2010_2020/Documents/National_Disability_Strategy_2010_2020.pdf)

- People's needs for support and care are fairly assessed on an individual basis rather than on an individual's diagnosis and/or disability.
- Particular attention is paid to addressing the rights to social protection/social services of groups who experience higher rates of social and economic marginalisation and exclusion. These include women, children, young people and older adults with mental disabilities, migrants and refugees (the latter are often particularly vulnerable and locked out of many social protection programmes).
- There are no disparities between people with mental disabilities and physical disabilities in terms of entitlements to social protection and social services. (This could occur because the definition of 'disability' excludes certain groups of people with mental health problems, or through discriminatory practices regarding levels of social support; Boxes 8.3 and 8.4.)

Box 8.3 Legislative Case Study: Malta

The Social Security Act (1987) discriminated between mental health diagnoses in that it gave preference to schizophrenia but ignored other psychiatric diagnoses. This applied both to financial benefits as well as to the provision of free drugs.

Box 8.4 Legislative Case Study: Azerbaijan

People with severe mental disorders claiming social security benefits are provided with disability grants at a similar rate as a pension granted to people with a physical disability.

- Carers' and family members' needs are fairly assessed.
- The size of allowances is sufficient. Disability pensions, for example, that are not high enough to cover basic subsistence can unwittingly undermine desinstituionalisation policies by discouraging clinicians from discharging patients from hospitals for fear they will not be able to cope economically (Rezvyy *et al.*, 2007).
- There are effective enforcement mechanisms as well as complaints procedures to ensure that the implementation of social protection and social services legislation is enacted fairly and without discrimination (Chapter 12, Implementation and enforcement; Box 8.5).

Box 8.5 Legislative Case Study: Australia

Under The Commonwealth Disability Discrimination Act 1992, the Commonwealth Ombudsman can investigate complaints about the actions and decisions of all Australian government agencies. This includes decisions related to social security benefits in order to see if they are wrong, unjust, unlawful, discriminatory or just plain unfair.

A powerful set of recommendations regarding social services and social protection has been made by The Disability Rights Monitor – Middle East, which has analysed existing policy and legislation across a number of countries in that region (Alazzeh, 2009; Axelsson and Barrett, 2009; Fakhoury, 2009) (Box 8.6). These recommendations are particularly attentive to the challenges of legislative and policy reform in countries where the state is not necessarily strong – and where there is not the older model of a universal 'welfare state':

Box 8.6 Guidance: The Disability Rights Monitor – Middle East

- Pay close attention to how 'disability' is defined. Access criteria to social protection/social services benefits or programmes are often dependent on how disability has been defined in the national legislation (in specific disability legislation and/or in mainstream legislation). Often, medical diagnostic systems of disability will be used, and this commonly prioritises groups with certain kinds of physical disabilities. Indeed, some Arab disability laws, for example, do not currently recognise mental disabilities, which means that people with mental disabilities would not be able to gain access to existing forms of social protection (Alazzeh, 2009).
- Ensure that responsible bodies are adequately specified and resourced.
- The state should take responsibility in designing and specifying:
  (a) transparent regulatory mechanisms that will govern the relationships between government, service providers, service users;
  (b) appropriate gate-keeping procedures to help regulate the supply of services;
  (c) appropriate standards and funding mechanisms: the general principles governing standards, for example, should be rights-based rather than grounded in charity or compensation;
  (d) appropriate monitoring and evaluation procedures.

(Axelsson and Barrett, 2009)

The Disability Rights Monitor – Middle East identifies Lebanon as an example of good practice in gate-keeping (Box 8.7).

Box 8.7 Legislative Case Study: Lebanon

Lebanon Law No. 243/1993 stipulates general rights for persons with disabilities and constituted the National Committee for the Disabled (NCD). The first National Committee launched the Rights and Access Programme (R&A), designed to ascertain the needs of disabled people in Lebanon and secure access to their rights. This is a semi-public organisation comprising 18 representatives (including government, service providers for the disabled, disabled people's organisations and disabled individuals). Each type of impairment (motor, mental, hearing and visual) is entitled to four representatives each. The focus is on professional work – based on rights and duties, not 'charity work'. Administrative centres are run by trained staff and physicians who are authorised to work with people with disabilities and their families, to create and update personal files, to issue 'Individual Cards' and all other paperwork needed to obtain the rights and services provided by the government according to Law No. 220/2000 (including technical services, special care, exemption from specific taxes, etc.). The R&A Programme uses the World Health Organisation classification of impairments to judge eligibility.

(All details are paraphrased from Fakhoury, 2009.)

8.4 Implementation challenges

The recommendations of Disability Rights Monitor – Middle East indicate how important it is to adequately plan and resource the implementation of social protection and social security legislation. There are number of other challenges and risks associated with implementation that should also be taken into consideration, some of which are itemised in this section. The way in which legislative and policy transformations will actually materialise in practice will often depend on the ways in which service providers and individuals in receipt of social services benefits/programmes are viewed – and view themselves – in the particular context in which those transformations are made.

The complex relationship between mental health problems, poverty, stigma and discrimination can often mean that there is reduced uptake of welfare and other social services and programmes by persons who are legally entitled to them. All too often, the way in which these services and programmes are both rolled out, as well as the stigmatising connotations that become attached to them (e.g. those are for 'crazy people'), make people with mental health problems loathe to avail themselves of what they may rightfully claim (Luhrmann, 2008). Legislative actions ought, therefore, to be buttressed by administrative actions: policies should, for example, encourage the establishment of close links between health service and social services to try to ensure that individuals who might be eligible for benefits do indeed gain access to them. Care should be taken about the language used within advice material to describe those eligible for social services. Stigmatising language, for example, can easily serve to put off people who are legally entitled to those benefits (Boxes 8.8 to 8.10).

Box 8.8 Policy Case Study: United Kingdom

Leaflets describing the old Disability Living Allowance noted that a person, to be eligible for the Allowance, must be 'severely mentally impaired with severe behavioural problems'. Some people who would not have identified themselves with such a description may well have been eligible for the Allowance (Slade *et al.*, 1995).

Box 8.9 Policy Case Study: Russia

The extensive use of the word 'invalid', both within society at large and within the legislative system, has been offered as one of the reasons why relatively few people with neurotic rather than psychotic diagnoses apply for a disability pension (Rezvyy *et al.*, 2007).

Box 8.10 Policy Case Study: Chicago, USA

The study described in Chapter 7.1 indicates how some of the homeless women in Chicago refused offers of social services assistance with housing because of the way in which the local culture conceptualised acceptance of such help as closely allied to 'being crazy' (Luhrmann, 2008).

Where grants or benefits are available on grounds of disability, care needs to be taken in terms of how people are made aware of the existence of the grants, and of how those disbursing them judge eligibility (Box 8.11).

Box 8.11 Policy Case Study: South Africa

The social grants system includes a disability grant that anyone unable to work owing to a disability is entitled to apply for. There is overwhelming demand for the grant, however, in the context of a complex mesh of illnesses, extreme poverty and disabilities. This means that many people apply under the criterion of 'being unable to work owing to a disability'. A recent study in South Africa found that the uptake of the disability grant was between only 35–50% for disabled people in the eight poorest wards of Johannesburg. Nearly half of those interviewed for the study who did not access the grant were denied it through not qualifying because of the nature of their disability. There is apparent confusion around what kind of disability qualifies, with doctors apparently acting cautiously. One interviewee who spoke about his brother said: 'We really did not ask [why he did not qualify]. You know, these social workers treat people in the community badly. They just told us that he must go and work. As I told you, if a person is mentally ill, nobody takes him seriously. I just told myself that I will never go there again' (Graham *et al.*, 2010).

Social protection and social services legislation can, in addition to ensuring access to programmes and benefits, assist in hastening the move towards adequately funded and organised community facilities and services. In other words, such legislation can play a crucial role in encouraging independent living and social inclusion and combating segregation and institutionalisation. Indeed, comprehensive social protection and social services reform can, by ensuring an increase in places as well as an adequate budget for appropriate community support programmes, be one of the most powerful mechanisms through which to bring about change for people with mental health problems.

Often, however, chasms appear between the letter of the law and what is implemented in practice. In Japan, for example, the 1995 revisions to the mental health law (Seishin Hokken oyobi Seishin Shogaisha Fukushi ni Kansuru Horitsu – the Law Related to the Mental Health and Social Welfare of Mentally Ill People) established that local as well as national governments were required to promote the independence of those with mental illness, and additionally created health and welfare benefits comparable for those with physical and developmental disabilities. But community-based services for those with mental illness have been very slow to develop, so the shift towards the creation of comparable health and welfare benefits has actually been of limited effectiveness (Mandiberg, 1996).

8.5 Examples of legislation

There are a variety of ways in which countries can use legislation to support the right to social security/social protection for people with mental health problems. Many laws – including several referred to by the country informants who helped compile information for this book – still operate on the traditional welfare/compensation model rather than a rights-based model. The definition of disability is often flawed, defined in a rigid and biomedical manner, and often installs disparities between people with physical disabilities and people with mental disabilities (de Silva de Alwis, 2010). Our country informants provided a wide range of examples to demonstrate how legislation is being used to provide social protection and social services for people with mental health problems. It was difficult always to ascertain from the details that they provided the extent to which their examples are rights- rather than charity-based. With this proviso, we include them here.

Some countries embed a right to social security/social protection explicitly within their constitution (examples from Thailand and Finland are given in Boxes 8.12 and 8.13).

Box 8.12 Legislative Case Study: Thailand

The Thai Constitution, amended in 2007, enacts anti-discrimination provisions and guarantees accessibility to social welfare and services for persons with disabilities.

Box 8.13 Legislative Case Study: Finland

Section 19 of the Constitution of Finland is about the 'right to social security'. It specifies that:

1 Those who cannot obtain the means necessary for a life of dignity have the right to receive indispensable subsistence and care.

2 Everyone shall be guaranteed by an Act the right to basic subsistence in the event of unemployment, illness, and disability and during old age as well as at the birth of a child or the loss of a provider.
3 The public authorities shall guarantee for everyone, as provided in more detail by an Act, adequate social, health and medical services and promote the health of the population. Moreover, the public authorities shall support families and others responsible for providing for children so that they have the ability to ensure the well-being and personal development of the children.
4 The public authorities shall promote the right of everyone to housing and the opportunity to arrange their own housing.

For further information: www.m.fi/21910.htm

Other country informants provided examples of laws specifically directed to the social services system (examples from Chile and Denmark are given in Boxes 8.14 and 8.15).

Box 8.14 Legislative Case Study: Chile

Law No. 20.255, 17 March 2008, which reformed the Chilean pension system, incorporates into the existing system a basic pension and support system for people with disabilities; benefits for people with disabilities with limited resources; and establishes subsidies for people younger than 18 years of age with mental disabilities.

Box 8.15 Legislative Case Study: Denmark

The Consolidation Act on Social Services of 18 January 2007 specifies that the municipal council shall offer free counselling for people with impaired physical or mental function or with special social problems. Such free counselling shall include fieldwork. These obligations may be discharged in cooperation with other municipalities.

'The objects of this Act are to:

(i) offer counselling and support so as to prevent social problems;
(ii) offer a number of general services designed to serve as preventive measures at the same time; and
(iii) satisfy needs resulting from impaired physical or mental function or special social problems.'

The Act further specifies that the municipal council shall ensure that the users of facilities provided under the Act are given an opportunity to impact on the planning use of the facilities.

The Act is available for download from NATLEX, the database of national labour, social security and related human rights legislation maintained by the International Labour Organizations's International Labour Standards Department at: www.ilo.org

Countries can use national disability policies to support legislative approaches (Box 8.16).

Box 8.16 Policy Case Study: Sri Lanka

In the National Disability Policy, the declared principle in relation to social security is that social protection, including pensions and insurance schemes available to citizens, will be available to people who have disability on an equal basis. Where the disability is too severe for the person to be economically independent, such as in the case of long-term psychiatric disability, profound intellectual disabilities and multiple disabilities, adequate social security measures will be taken to ensure a reasonable quality of living.

There are a number of databases that are useful in accessing details of social security and social protection programmes (see Box 8.17).

Box 8.17 Resources

International Social Security Association (ISSA)

The ISSA includes an Observatory that monitors social security programmes worldwide. Available on its website is an overview of social security systems, information about social security reforms, access to social security legislation, examples of country-based good practice and more than 170 country profiles.

For further information: www.issa.int/Observatory

International Labour Organisation (ILO)

The ILO Social Security Inquiry database provides statistical information on social security, including employment-related social security schemes, public health, welfare and anti-poverty programmes. There is also information about non-public schemes of different types transferring goods, services or cash to poor and vulnerable households. The database is searchable by country and includes details of legislative and administrative frameworks.

For further information: www.ilo.org (www.ilo.org/dyn/ilossi/ssimain.home?p_lang=en)

References

AbiYaghi, M-N (2009) Social protection: a favour or a right? General issues and trends. *Disability Monitor Initiative – Middle East Journal,* 2009 (1):6–9.

Alazzeh, M (2009) Social protection and persons with disabilities in the laws: recognized rights and unframed provisions. *Disability Monitor Initiative – Middle East Journal,* 2009 (1):13–17.

Axelsson, C and Barrett, D (2009) Access to Social Services for Persons with Disabilities in the Middle East – Multi-Stakeholder reflections for policy reform. Disability Rights Monitor Initiative–Middle East, CBM and Handicap International (http://www.makingitwork-crpd.org/fileadmin/user/content/DMI_Documents/DMI_Report_2009_final_version_17-5-2010.pdf).

Bagenstos, SR (2004) The future of disability law. *The Yale Law Journal,* **14**(1):1–84.

Ball, P, Morris, M, Hartnette, J and Blanck, P (2006) Breaking the cycle of poverty: asset accumulation by people with disabilities. *Disability Studies Quarterly,* **26**(1).

Commonwealth of Australia (2011) National Disability Strategy 2010–2020. Commonwealth of Australia, Canberra.

Degener, T (2003) Disability as a subject of international human rights law and comparative discrimination law. In: Herr, SS, Gostin, LO and Koh, HH (eds) *The Human Rights of Persons with Intellectual Disabilities: Different but equal*. Oxford University Press, Oxford. pp. 151–184.

Degener, T (2006) The definition of disability in German and foreign discrimination law. *Disability Studies Quarterly*, **26**(2) (http://dsq-sds.org/article/view/696/87).

de Silva de Alwis, R (2010) The intersections of the CEDAW and CRPD: putting women"s rights and disability rights into action in four Asian Countries. Wellesley Centers for Women, Wellesley, MA.

Destremau, B (2008) Les droits humains, des droits sociaux pour les plus pauvres des pays en développement? In: Domin, J-P (ed.) *Au-delà des droits économiques et des droits politiques, les droits sociaux*? L'Harmattan, Association d'Economie Sociale, Paris, France. pp. 109–124.

The Disability Monitor Initiative – Middle East Journal (2009) Monitoring legislative change, social innovation and public policies (http://www.makingitwork-crpd.org/fileadmin/user/content/Journal-_social_protection.pdf).

Ellis, K (2005) Disability rights in practice: the relationship between human rights and social rights in contemporary social care. *Disability & Society*, **20**(7):691–704.

Fakhoury, H (2009) Initiative for proper gate-keeping: the rights and access programme. Lebanon. *Disability Monitor Initiative – Middle East Journal*, 2009 (1):20–22.

Graham, L, Selipsky, L, Moodley, J, Maina, J and Rowland, W (2010) Understanding poverty and disability in Johannesburg. Centre for Social Development in Africa and University of Johannesburg, Johannesburg, South Africa.

Harvey, D (2005) *A Brief History of Neo-Liberalism*. Oxford University Press, Oxford.

ILO (International Labour Office) (2008) Can low-income countries afford basic social security? Paper 3. International Labour Office, Social Security Department, Geneva, Switzerland.

ILO (International Labour Office) (2010) World Social Security Report 2010/11: Providing coverage in times of crisis and beyond. International Labour Office, Geneva, Switzerland.

Larner, W (2000) Neo-liberalism: policy, ideology, governmentality. *Studies in Political Economy*, **63**: 5–25.

Luhrmann, T (2008) 'The street will drive you crazy': why homeless psychotic women in the institutional circuit in the United States often say no to offers of help. *Am J Psychiatry*, **165**(1):15–20.

Mandiberg, JM (1996) The Japanese mental health system and law: social and structural impediments to reform. *International Journal of Law and Psychiatry*, **19**(3–4): 413–435.

Miranda, J and Patel, V (2005) Achieving the Millennium Development Goals: Does mental health play a role? *PLoS Medicine*, **2**(10):e291.

Mittelman, J (2008) Beyond impoverished anti-poverty paradigms. *Third World Quarterly*, **29**(8):1639–1652.

Mor, S (2011) Disability and the persistence of poverty: reconstructing disability allowances. *Northwestern Journal of Law and Social Policy*, **6**(1):178–214.

Priestley, M and Roulstone, A (2009) Targeting and mainstreaming disability in the 2008–2010 National Reform Programmes for Growth and Jobs. Report prepared for the Academic Network of European Disability experts (ANED), Academic Network of European Disability Experts.

Rezvyy, G, Schonfelder, W, Oiesvold, T, Olstad, R and Midre, G (2007) Between health care and social security – psychiatric patients and the disability pension system in Norway and Russia. *BMC Health Services Research*, **7**(1):128.

Slade, M, McCrone, P and Thornicroft, G (1995) Uptake of welfare benefits by psychiatric patients. *Psychiatric Bulletin*, **19**(7):411–413.

WHO (2010) Mental Health and Development: Targeting people with mental health conditions as a vulnerable group. World Health Organization, Geneva, Switzerland.

Yeo, R (2001) Chronic poverty and disability. Background paper no. 4. Chronic Poverty Research Centre, United Kingdom (http://www.dfid.gov.uk/r4d/PDF/Outputs/ChronicPoverty_RC/04Yeo.pdf.

Yeo, R (2005) Disability, poverty and the new development agenda: A Report to the KaR Programme. Disability Knowledge and Research, London.

CHAPTER 9

Health, Health Care and the Right to Health

9.1 Inferior access to mental health care

One of the consequences of stigma and discrimination is that people with mental health problems commonly avoid seeking help for their problems, often for fear of receiving a mental health related diagnosis (Thornicroft *et al.*, 2009). It is only relatively recently that the full potency of such barriers to finding treatment and care has been recognised (Amaddeo and Jones, 2007; Cooper *et al.*, 2003). Studies from several countries have consistently found that even after a family member has developed clear-cut signs of a psychotic mental health problem, it is, on average, more than a year until the unwell person first receives assessment and treatment. A survey of almost 10 000 adults in 17 countries has added more detail to this picture. The results showed that the majority of people with mental disorders eventually contact treatment services, but they often wait a long time before doing so. There is an average delay before seeking help of eight years for mood disorders and at least nine years for anxiety disorders. People who wait longer than average before receiving care are more likely to be young, old, male, poorly educated or a member of an ethnic or racial minority (Wang *et al.*, 2007).

The following common beliefs are likely to reduce people's likelihood of seeking help: psychiatric treatments are ineffective (Corrigan, 2005); others would react with avoidance; a person should solve his or her own problems (Kessler *et al.*, 2001). At the same time, strong family encouragement to go for mental health assessment and treatment does often work (Link *et al.*, 1989).

9.2 Excess rates of co-morbidity and mortality

People with mental health problems have, on average, far poorer physical health than people without mental health problems. Common serious

Mental Illness, Discrimination and the Law: Fighting for Social Justice, First Edition.
Felicity Callard, Norman Sartorius, Julio Arboleda-Flórez, Peter Bartlett, Hanfried Helmchen, Heather Stuart, Jose Taborda and Graham Thornicroft.

conditions are cardiovascular disease, respiratory disorders, nutritional, metabolic and endocrine disease (Leucht *et al.*, 2007). People with mental health problems are more likely to have one or more of these conditions, and the rates of mortality among people with mental health problems and/or intellectual disabilities are higher than the rates of mortality among the general population (Harris and Barraclough, 1998; Sartorius, 2007). Most notably, there are increased mortality rates among people with mental health problems and/or intellectual disabilities, which are particularly related to higher rates of suicide, accidental or violent death (unnatural causes) and serious physical illnesses, as well as neglect within hospital and social care institutions (Amaddeo *et al.*, 2007), where violations of human rights are relatively common (in relation to the provision of physical and mental health care, for example).

A proportion of such deaths (both for unnatural and natural causes) may be, and should be, avoidable. Only 80% of people with schizophrenia die from natural causes, in comparison with 97% of the general population (Goff *et al.*, 2005; Llorca, 2008), and the higher rates of unnatural deaths are largely attributable to accidents and suicide (which tend to occur more often early in adulthood) (Brown *et al.*, 2000, 2010).

The following types of condition need to be routinely considered when monitoring and assessing the general health care of people with mental health problems and/or intellectual disabilities:

1 respiratory disorders – chronic respiratory problems are more common among these particular groups (Brown *et al.*, 2010);
2 cardiovascular disease – people with several mental disabilities and intellectual disabilities die more frequently from cardiovascular disease and experience sudden death more often (Correll, 2008);
3 nutritional, metabolic and endocrine diseases – the most severe problems are obesity and diabetes associated with the use of antipsychotic medication, both of which in turn contribute to higher rates of cardiovascular disease (Cohen and Correll, 2009). There is also a higher rate of metabolic syndrome in individuals with severe mental health disabilities and intellectual disabilities than in the general population (Newcomer, 2007);
4 cancers – for people with mental disabilities and intellectual disabilities, there are also disparities in screening for cancer and high fatality rates. This is partly owing to the particular challenges when treating these patients – including medical co-morbidity, drug interactions, lack of capacity and difficulties in coping with the treatment as a result of psychiatric symptoms (Catts *et al.*, 2008; Howard *et al.*, 2010; Tran *et al.*, 2009);
5 musculo-skeletal disorders – higher rates of bone mineral density (osteoporosis) have been found among people with schizophrenia, along with less appropriate treatment;

6 dental problems – higher rates of dental decay and tooth loss have been reported among people with mental health disabilities and intellectual disabilities (Gabre, 2000; McCreadie *et al.*, 2004);

7 neurological disorders – the most serious and distressing long-term extra-pyramidal side effect of first generation antipsychotic medication is tardive dyskinesia, while other abnormal motor symptoms (such as akathisia) are also commonly caused by antipsychotic medications (Correll *et al.*, 2004);

8 obstetric complications – there is an extensive literature that demonstrates increased occurrence of obstetric complications among mothers with schizophrenia; this may be associated with high rates of smoking, the use of illicit drugs and alcohol and the use of antipsychotic medication (Howard *et al.*, 2004);

9 hepatitis – an increased prevalence of hepatitis in people with schizophrenia has been reported in many countries, including Jordan, India, the USA, Italy, Turkey and Japan (Rosenberg *et al.*, 2001);

10 HIV/AIDS – higher rates may reflect the frequency of substance misuse, sexual risk behaviours and a reduced knowledge about HIV-related issues (Essock *et al.*, 2003).

In addition, people with intellectual disabilities are also at higher risk of other health problems, including epilepsy (Kerr *et al.*, 2009), cardiovascular abnormalities, spinal deformities and visual and hearing impairments (Bouras and Holt, 2004; Pradhan *et al.*, 2009).

9.3 'Diagnostic overshadowing' and 'treatment overshadowing'

The physical health of people with mental health problems and/or intellectual disabilities needs careful attention – but there is strong evidence that people with mental health disabilities and intellectual disabilities receive worse treatment for physical disorders than the general population. One of the factors contributing to this is 'diagnostic overshadowing'.

This is the process by which people with mental health problems and/or intellectual disabilities receive poorer physical health care because general health care staff misattribute physical symptoms to mental health problems and/or intellectual disabilities.

The concept of diagnostic overshadowing has been explored in the literature on people with intellectual disabilities for more than two decades (Disability Rights Commission, 2006a, 2006b), but it is an area that has received very little attention in the mental health literature, although mental health service users have extensively reported the occurrence of this phenomenon (Jones *et al.*, 2008).

One of the implications of the discrimination and neglect caused by diagnostic overshadowing is a higher mortality rate among people with mental health disabilities and intellectual disabilities for death by cardiac infarctions (Desai *et al.*, 2002; Enger *et al.*, 2004). So, for example, after adjusting for other risk factors such as cardiovascular risk factors and socio-economic status, depression in men has been found to be associated with an increase in cardiovascular-related mortality (Gump *et al.*, 2005).

The stigmatising approaches of physicians and other health care staff reveal negative stereotypes (Filipcic *et al.*, 2003) and contribute to the health care disparities experienced by people with mental health problems and/or intellectual disabilities. More recent studies suggest that another important factor may be that clinicians make different treatment decisions in relation to people with mental illness. 'Treatment overshadowing' is a term that has been proposed to describe possible biases in those treatment decisions. Treatment overshadowing may include a decision against a certain treatment being taken because the clinician assumes that a person's mental illness precludes such an intervention. It has been shown, for example, that people with co-morbid mental disorders were 'substantially less likely to undergo coronary re-vascularisation procedures' than those with no mental disorders (Druss *et al.*, 2000). Similarly, people with co-morbid mental illness and diabetes who presented to an emergency department were less likely to be admitted to hospital for diabetic complications than those with no mental illness (Sullivan *et al.*, 2006).

It is also clear that many physical health care professionals are poorly informed – they are not sufficiently trained to recognise and treat people with mental health and intellectual disabilities and to recognise the many interactions between physical and mental health problems: a toothache, for example, can present as 'challenging behaviour' in a person with limited verbal communication skills.

9.4 The right to health

Which human rights provisions may help to reverse these clear health disparities? The overarching legal framework that is most pertinent to health-related human rights is the United Nations Convention on the Rights of Persons with Disabilities (CRPD) (Chapter 14.1.1.1 and 14.4.1). The CRPD addresses questions of health in a number of Articles, as well as specifically in Article 25 (Health).

Article 25 specifies the right to the enjoyment of the highest attainable standard of health without discrimination on the basis of disability. In those States that have ratified the CRPD, health care providers have legal, professional and ethical obligations to ensure that provisions under

Article 25 are satisfied (Stein *et al.*, 2009). The legislative frameworks used to address health and access to health care need to ensure that there are explicit provisions for people with disabilities to ensure that these rights are affirmed. If they are not made explicit, it is likely that people with mental disabilities and/or intellectual disabilities will not have equal access to necessary health services of the same range, quality and standard as provided to other people.

There is growing interest in 'the right to health' as a way to legislatively protect positive and negative rights (Byrne, 2005; Castellon *et al.*, 2005; Clapham and Robinson, 2009; McSherry, 2008; Yamin, 2005, 2009) (Chapter 2.8.1), as well as for its importance to people with mental health problems (Battams and Henderson, 2010; Gostin and Gable, 2009). Paul Hunt, the former UN Special Rapporteur on the right of everyone to the enjoyment of the highest attainable standard of physical and mental health (2002–2008), has been developing an analytical framework founded upon General Comment 14 of the UN Committee on Economic, Social and Cultural Rights. He has elaborated on what this 'right to health' means – 'in terms of freedoms, entitlements, non-discrimination and equality, participation, international assistance and cooperation, monitoring and accountability' (Hunt and Mesquita, 2006).

Such a model emphasises the importance of understanding the right to health in different contexts – health here is not understood simply as 'the absence of disease'. It certainly includes timely and appropriate health care: of great importance is the need to ensure the establishment of adequate health services that are sufficiently well-equipped to provide care – and do so with no discrimination in access to them (Sartorius, 2009). But, in addition, and crucially, the right to health includes rights in relation to 'the underlying determinants of health'.

The right to health therefore understands health to be anchored within a broad social matrix. It has been argued, therefore, that denial or limitation of basic services – services that would enable people with mental illness to participate actively within their communities – might be considered a possible breach of the right to health and of the International Covenant on Economic, Social and Cultural Rights (Bell, 2005) (Chapter 14.1.1.6). (Article 12 of this Covenant requires governments to recognise 'the right of everyone to the enjoyment of the highest attainable standard of physical and mental health'.)

In relation to the Convention on the Rights of Persons with Disabilities (CRPD), the right to health is not the right to be healthy, but includes the right to the immediate amenities relating to health. This describes safe and effective health care but also a society that provides the best chances for good health for all people, including access to prevention measures, control of diseases and appropriate sanitation. Furthermore, the Council of Europe has issued a Recommendation on 'monitoring the protection of human rights and dignity of persons with mental disorder' (Recommendation CM/Rec (2009)3) (Chapter 14.2.1.1.3) and included the promotion of health care in its eight key principles.

The ITHACA – Institutional Treatment, Human Rights and Care Assessment – study has documented the factors necessary to create and successfully implement policy to promote the human rights, dignity and general health status of residents in psychiatric and social care institutions in Europe, based upon the best available evidence and experience (Box 9.1).

Box 9.1 Resource

The ITHACA study has produced a toolkit (ITHACA Project Group, 2010) that provides information on monitoring practices, explains appropriate human rights literature and conventions and outlines an on-site visit audit. It is significantly shaped by the provisions laid out in the UN Convention on the Rights of Persons with Disabilities.

Audit/monitoring visits will involve a team of monitors to observe the physical conditions and the quality of care received by service users. In addition, monitors will conduct interviews with residents, staff and institution directors and examine relevant documentation. The data collected from these visits will be compiled into reports for people involved at all levels with mental health care – from service users and family members to support/care staff and government officials. The findings from these monitoring visits can be used by local and international advocacy groups as evidence for lobbying and initiating change within the systems which produce human rights violations.

The Toolkit for Monitoring Human Rights and General Health Care in Mental Health and Social Care Institutions is available for download at: www.ithacastudy.eu

Paul Hunt's right to health framework examines issues concerning health care using four constructs: availability, accessibility, acceptability and quality (AAAQ). To implement the right to health framework, Member States should, taking into account available resources, take measures to:

- provide a range of services of appropriate quality to meet the mental health needs of people with mental disorder, taking into account the differing needs of different groups of such persons, and to ensure equitable access to such services;
- make alternatives to involuntary placement and to involuntary treatment as widely available as possible;
- ensure sufficient provision of hospital facilities with appropriate levels of security and of community-based services to meet the health needs of persons with mental disorder involved with the criminal justice system;
- ensure that the physical health care needs of persons with mental disorder are assessed and that they are provided with equitable access to services of appropriate quality to meet such needs.

Details of the reports regarding the 'right to health' are given in Box 9.2. The World Health Organization – Regional Office for South-East Asia has recently surveyed references to the right to health in the Constitutions of Member States of the World Health Organization South-East Region, and emphasises that DPR Korea, Indonesia, Nepal, Thailand and Timor-Leste all specify the right to health or the right to health care as a constitutional right (WHO, 2011).

Box 9.2 Resource

- Report of the Special Rapporteur on the right of everyone to the enjoyment of the highest attainable standard of physical and mental health, UN ESCOR, Commission on Human Rights, 61st session, agenda item 10, UN Doc E/CN.4/2005/51 (2005).
- Report of the Special Rapporteur on the right of everyone to the enjoyment of the highest attainable standard of physical and mental health, UN ESCOR, Commission on Human Rights, 60th Sess, UN Doc E/CN.4/2004/49 (2004).

For further information: www2.ohchr.org/english/issues/health/right

9.5 Examples of legislation

Our country correspondents submitted very few examples of legislation specifically relating to the domain of health. Boxes 9.3 and 9.4 provide examples from New Zealand and the United States.

9.5.1 Legislation addressing the right to health

Box 9.3 Legislative Case Study: New Zealand

The law that most directly addresses the right to health (and health care) is the New Zealand Public Health and Disability Act 2000 (PHDA). This provides a structure for the delivery of personal health, public health and disability support services, and its focus is on:

- improving, promoting and protecting health;
- promoting the inclusion and participation in society and the independence of disabled people;
- ensuring the best care and support of those in need of services;
- reducing health disparities;
- providing a community voice in matters relating to the provision of services by providing for election of members to district health boards, open meetings of these boards and consultation on strategic plans.

The Local Government Act 2002 promotes the general social, cultural and environmental aspects of the right to health. A number of other laws deal with specific issues within the health domain.

The Health and Disability Commissioner Act established a Code of Health and Disability Services Consumers' Rights (this became law on 1 July 1996) which specifies the rights of consumers and the obligations and duties of providers to comply with the Code.

There are 10 rights for consumers: the second is 'the right to freedom from discrimination, coercion, harassment and exploitation.'

(Human Rights Commission, 2010)

9.5.2 Legislation addressing parity in health insurance for people with physical and mental health problems

Box 9.4 Legislative Case Study: United States

In July 2008, the US Senate joined the House in passing the Medicare Improvements for Patients and Providers Act of 2008 (H.R. 6331). This provides new equity between mental health and medical coverage for those receiving outpatient mental health services through Medicare. The previously higher co-payment for mental health services was widely regarded as encouraging the use of inpatient/institutional care rather than outpatient services.

References

Amaddeo, F and Jones, J (2007) What is the impact of socio-economic inequalities on the use of mental health services? *Epidemiol Psichiatr Soc,* **16**(1):16–19.

Amaddeo, F, Barbui, C, Perini, G, Biggeri, A and Tansella, M (2007) Avoidable mortality of psychiatric patients in an area with a community-based system of mental health care. *Acta Psychiatrica Scandinavica,* **115**(4):320–325.

Battams, S and Henderson, J (2010) The physical health of people with mental illness and 'the right to health'. *Advances in Mental Health,* **9**(2):116–129.

Bell, S (2005) What does the 'right to health' have to offer mental health patients? *International Journal of Law and Psychiatry,* **28**:141–153.

Bouras, N and Holt, G (2004) Mental health services for adults with learning disabilities. *British Journal of Psychiatry,* **184**(4):291–292.

Brown, S, Inskip, H and Barraclough, B (2000) Causes of the excess mortality of schizophrenia. *British Journal of Psychiatry,* **177**:212–217.

Brown, S, Kim, M, Mitchell, C and Inskip, H (2010) Twenty-five year mortality of a community cohort with schizophrenia. *British Journal of Psychiatry,* **196**(2):116–121.

Byrne, I (2005) Making the Right to Health a Reality: Legal Strategies for Effective Implementation. Commonwealth Law Conference, London. Available for download at: http://www.escr-net.org/caselaw_more/caselaw_more_show.htm?parent_id = 401236.

Castellon, R and Laplante, LJ (2005) Expanding the definition of the right to mental health: attending to victims of political violence and armed conflict in their communities of origin. *Essex Review of Human Rights,* **2**(1):38–56.

Catts, V, Catts, S, O'Toole, B and Frost, A (2008) Cancer incidence in patients with schizophrenia and their first-degree relatives a meta-analysis. *Acta Psychiatrica Scandinavica*, **117**:323–336.

Clapham, A and Robinson, M (eds) (2009) *Realizing the Right to Health*. Swiss Human Rights Book, Vol. 3. Rüffer & Rub, Zurich, Switzerland.

Cohen, D and Correll, CU (2009) Second-generation antipsychotic-associated diabetes mellitus and diabetic ketoacidosis: mechanisms, predictors, and screening need. *J Clin Psychiatry*, **70**(5):765–766.

Cooper, AE, Corrigan, PW and Watson, AC (2003) Mental illness stigma and care seeking. *Journal of Nervous and Mental Disease*, **191**(5):339–341.

Correll, CU (2008) Elevated cardiovascular risk in patients with bipolar disorder: when does it start and where does it lead? *J Clin Psychiatry*, **69**(12):1948–1952.

Correll, CU, Leucht, S and Kane, JM (2004) Lower Risk for Tardive Dyskinesia Associated With Second-Generation Antipsychotics: A Systematic Review of 1-Year Studies. *Am J Psychiatry*, **161**(3):414–425.

Corrigan, PW (ed.) (2005) On the stigma of mental illness: practical strategies for research and social change. American Psychological Association, Washington, DC.

Desai, MM, Rosenheck, RA, Druss, BG and Perlin, JB (2002) Mental disorders and quality of care among postacute myocardial infarction outpatients. *Journal of Nervous and Mental Disease*, **190**(1):51–53.

Disability Rights Commission (2006a) Formal investigation report. Part 1: Equal Treatment: Closing the Gap. A formal investigation into physical health inequalities experienced by peope with learning disabilities and/or mental health problems. Disability Rights Commission, London.

Disability Rights Commission (2006b) Formal investigation report. Part 2: Report of the DRC Formal Inquiry Panel to the DRC's Formal Investigation. The inequalities in physical health experienced by people with mental health problems and people with learning disabilities. Disability Rights Commission, London.

Druss, BG, Bradford, DW, Rosenheck, RA, Radford, MJ and Krumholz, HM (2000) Mental Disorders and Use of Cardiovascular Procedures After Myocardial Infarction. *The Journal of the American Medical Association*, **283**(4):506–511.

Enger, C, Weatherby, L, Reynolds, RF, Glasser, DB and Walker, AM (2004) Serious Cardiovascular Events and Mortality Among Patients with Schizophrenia. *The Journal of Nervous and Mental Disease*, **192**(1):19–27.

Essock, SM, Dowden, S, Constantine, NT, Katz, L, Swartz, MS, Meador, KG, *et al.* (2003) Blood-Borne Infections and Persons With Mental Illness: Risk Factors for HIV, Hepatitis B, and Hepatitis C Among Persons With Severe Mental Illness. *Psychiatr Serv*, **54**(6):836–841.

Filipcic, I, Pavicic, D, Filipcic, A, Hotujac, L, Begic, D, Grubisin, J, *et al.* (2003) Atttitudes of medical staff towards the psychiatrist label 'schizophrenic patient' tested by an anti-stigma questionnaire. *Coll Antropol*, **27**(1):301–307.

Gabre, P (2000) Studies on oral health in mentally retarded adults. *Swed Dent J Suppl 2000* (142):1–48.

Goff, D, Cather, C, Evins, A, Henderson, D, Freudenreich, O, Copeland, P, *et al.* (2005) Medical morbidity and mortality in schizophrenia: guidelines for psychiatrists. *J Clin Psychiatry*, **66**(2):183–194.

Gostin, LO and Gable, L (2009) Mental health as a human right. In: Clapham, A and Robinson, M (eds) *Realizing the Right to Health*. Swiss Human Rights Book, Vol. 3. Rüffer & Rub, Zurich, Switzerland. pp. 249–261.

Gump, BB, Matthews, KA, Eberly, LE and Chang, Y-f, for the MRFIT Research Group (2005) Depressive Symptoms and Mortality in Men: Results From the Multiple Risk Factor Intervention Trial. *Stroke*, **36**(1):98–102.

Harris, EC and Barraclough, B (1998) Excess mortality of mental disorder. *British Journal of Psychiatry*, **173**:11–53.

Howard, L, Thornicroft, G, Salmon, M and Appleby, L (2004) Predictors of parenting outcome in women with psychotic disorders discharged from mother and baby units. *Acta Psychiatrica Scandinavica*, **110**:347–355.

Howard, LM, Barley, EA, Davies, E, Rigg, A, Lempp, H, Rose, D, *et al.* (2010) Cancer diagnosis in people with severe mental illness: practical and ethical issues. *The Lancet Oncology*, **11**(8):797–804.

Human Rights Commission (2010) Human Rights in New Zealand 2010. Human Rights Commission, New Zealand.

Hunt, P and Mesquita, J (2006) Mental disabilities and the human right to the highest attainable standard of health. *Human Rights Quarterly*, **28**:332–356.

ITHACA Project Group (2010) ITHACA Toolkit for Monitoring Human Rights and General Health Care in Mental Health and Social Care Institutions. Health Service and Population Research Department, Institute of Psychiatry, King's College London, UK.

Jones, S, Howard, L and Thornicroft, G (2008) 'Diagnostic overshadowing': worse physical health care for people with mental illness. *Acta Psychiatrica Scandinavica*, **118**(3):169–171.

Kerr, M, Scheepers, M, Arvio, M, Beavis, J, Brandt, C, Brown, S, *et al.* (2009) Consensus guidelines into the management of epilepsy in adults with an intellectual disability. *Journal of Intellectual Disability Research*, **53**(8):687–694.

Kessler RC, Berglund, PA, Bruce, ML, Koch, JR, Laska, EM, Leaf, PJ, *et al.* (2001) The prevalence and correlates of untreated serious mental illness. *Health Services Research*, **36**(6 Pt 1):987–1007.

Leucht, S, Burkard, T, Henderson, J, Maj, M and Sartorius, N (2007) Physical illness and schizophrenia: a review of the literature. *Acta Psychiatrica Scandinavica*, **116**(5):317–333.

Link, BG, Cullen, FT, Struening, E, Shrout, PE and Dohrenwend, BP (1989) A Modified Labeling Theory Approach to Mental Disorders: An Empirical Assessment. *American Sociological Review*, **54**(3):400–423.

Llorca, PM (2008) Monitoring patients to improve physical health and treatment outcome. *Eur Neuropsychopharmacol*, **18**(Suppl 3):S140–S145.

McCreadie, RG, Stevens, H, Henderson, J, Hall, D, McCaul, R, Filik, R, *et al.* (2004) The dental health of people with schizophrenia. *Acta Psychiatrica Scandinavica*, **110**(4):306–310.

McSherry, B (2008) Mental health and human rights: the role of the law in developing a right to enjoy the highest attainable standard of mental health in Australia. *J Law Med*, **15**(5):773–781.

Newcomer, JW (2007) Metabolic syndrome and mental illness. *Am J Manag Care*, **13**(7 Suppl):S170–S177.

Pradhan, A, Slade, GD and Spencer, AJ (2009) Access to dental care among adults with physical and intellectual disabilities: residence factors. *Australian Dental Journal*, **54**(3):204–211.

Rosenberg, S, Goodman, L, Osher, F, Swartz, M, Essock, S, Butterfield, M, *et al.* (2001) Prevalence of HIV, hepatitis B, and hepatitis C in people with severe mental illness. *Am J Public Health*, **91**(1):31–37.

Sartorius, N (2007) Physical illness in people with mental disorders. *World Psychiatry*, **6**(1):3–4.

Sartorius, N (2009) 'The right to health': a viewpoint. *Mental Health in Family Medicine*, **6**:7–8.

Stein, MA, Stein, PJS, Weiss, D and Lang, R (2009) Health care and the UN Disability Rights Convention. *The Lancet*, **374**(9704):1796–1798.

Sullivan, G, Han, X, Moore, S and Kotrla, K (2006) Disparities in Hospitalization for Diabetes Among Persons With and Without Co-occurring Mental Disorders. *Psychiatr Serv*, **57**(8):1126–1131.

Thornicroft, G, Brohan, E, Rose, D, Sartorius, N, Leese, M, INDIGO Study Group (2009) Global pattern of experienced and anticipated discrimination against people with schizophrenia: a cross-sectional survey. *The Lancet*, **373**(9661):408–415.

Tran, E, Rouillon, F, Loze, J-Y, Casadebaig, F, Philippe, A, Vitry, F, *et al.* (2009) Cancer mortality in patients with schizophrenia. *Cancer*, **115**(15):3555–3562.

Wang, PS, Aguilar-Gaxiola, S, Alonso, J, Angermeyer, MC, Borges, G, Bromet, EJ, *et al.* (2007) Use of mental health services for anxiety, mood, and substance disorders in 17 countries in the WHO world mental health surveys. *The Lancet*, **370**(9590):841–850.

WHO (2011) The Right to Health in the Constitutions of Member States of the World Health Organization South-East Asia Region. World Health Organization, Regional Office for South-East Asia, New Delhi, India.

Yamin, AE (2005) The right to health under international law and its relevance to the United States. *Am J Public Health*, **85**(7):1156–1161.

Yamin, AE (2009) Shades of dignity: exploring the demands of equality in applying human rights frameworks to health. *Health and Human Rights*, **11**(2):1–18.

CHAPTER 10

Protection Against Abuse and Research Involving Vulnerable Populations

More than 60 years ago, in April 1949, the Nuremberg trials came to an end. During these trials, it was disclosed that doctors in the Nazi regime had used the guise of medical science to inflict pain and atrocious suffering on humans (Aziz, 1976). The events still cast a long shadow on how research using human subjects should be conducted.

In addition to bringing the ethics of medical research into public consciousness, the most pronounced effect of Nuremberg was arguably the removal of ethical decision-making from the hands of doctor-researchers. That power has now been vested in multi-disciplinary research ethics committees (in some countries called institutional review boards) that consider the concerns associated with medical research on humans. The aftermath has also included the development of ethical regulations governing research, many of them based on the 'Nuremberg Code' (Box 10.1) issued at the end of the trials. Each of the Code's 10 principles relates to the core elements of social justice.

Box 10.1 Standards: The Nuremberg Code

1 The voluntary consent of the human subject is absolutely essential. This means that the person involved should have legal capacity to give consent; should be so situated as to be able to exercise free power of choice, without the intervention of any element of force, fraud, deceit, duress, over-reaching, or other ulterior form of constraint or coercion; and should have sufficient knowledge and comprehension of the elements of the subject matter involved as to enable him/her to make an understanding and enlightened decision. This latter element requires that before the acceptance of an affirmative decision by the experimental subject there should be

Mental Illness, Discrimination and the Law: Fighting for Social Justice, First Edition.
Felicity Callard, Norman Sartorius, Julio Arboleda-Flórez, Peter Bartlett, Hanfried Helmchen, Heather Stuart, Jose Taborda and Graham Thornicroft.

made known to him the nature, duration, and purpose of the experiment; the method and means by which it is to be conducted; all inconveniences and hazards reasonable to be expected; and the effects upon his health or person which may possibly come from his participation in the experiment. The duty and responsibility for ascertaining the quality of the consent rests upon each individual who initiates, directs or engages in the experiment. It is a personal duty and responsibility which may not be delegated to another with impunity.

2 The experiment should be such as to yield fruitful results for the good of society, unprocurable by other methods or means of study, and not random and unnecessary in nature.

3 The experiment should be so designed and based on the results of animal experimentation and a knowledge of the natural history of the disease or other problem under study that the anticipated results will justify the performance of the experiment.

4 The experiment should be so conducted as to avoid all unnecessary physical and mental suffering and injury.

5 No experiment should be conducted where there is a prior reason to believe that death or disabling injury will occur; except, perhaps, in those experiments where the experimental physicians also serve as subjects.

6 The degree of risk to be taken should never exceed that determined by the humanitarian importance of the problem to be solved by the experiment.

7 Proper preparations should be made and adequate facilities provided to protect the experimental subject against even remote possibilities of injury, disability, or death.

8 The experiment should be conducted only by scientifically qualified persons. The highest degree of skill and care should be required through all stages of the experiment of those who conduct or engage in the experiment.

9 During the course of the experiment the human subject should be at liberty to bring the experiment to an end if he has reached the physical or mental state where continuation of the experiment seems to him to be impossible.

10 During the course of the experiment the scientist in charge must be prepared to terminate the experiment at any stage, if he has probable cause to believe, in the exercise of the good faith, superior skill and careful judgment required of him that a continuation of the experiment is likely to result in injury, disability, or death to the experimental subject (Anon, 1949).

In effect, the Nuremberg Code provides the framework for the conditions under which 'legitimate' medical research should be conducted: 'certain types of experiments on human beings, when kept within reasonably well-defined bounds, conform to the ethics of the medical profession generally . . . as long as basic principles are observed to satisfy moral, ethical, and legal concepts' (Anon, 1949). The common theme of all the codes, guidelines and declarations that have been developed since the Nuremberg trials is: research is allowed but it must be ethical. One of the most influential of these subsequent declarations is the World Medical Association's Declaration of Helsinki (Box 10.2).

Box 10.2 Standards: Declaration of Helsinki

A pivotal element in the Nuremberg Code was the prohibition to use a person as a subject of research if that person had not given, or could not give, a valid informed consent to participate.

This blank prohibition was refined in the World Medical Association Declaration of Helsinki (18th World Assembly, Helsinki, June 1964) (Chapter 14.3.1.1; full text Chapter 14.4.4), which allowed a legal guardian to provide consent for participation in research 'on behalf of incompetent persons incapable of giving consent'.

This relaxation of the prohibition, however, has raised many important points, because individuals incapable of providing consent usually form part of populations considered vulnerable in one or various categories. The prohibition included in the Nuremberg Code was certainly a reaction to the abuses found at the trials, but on further thought, prohibiting research on these populations would also be detrimental to their health interests and, to certain extent, discriminatory, hence several other commissions (Queensland Law Reform Society, 1996) and international bodies have not sustained the blanket prohibition found in the Nuremberg Code.

(CIOMS, 1993)

10.1 General considerations in research

Capacity, competence, age and voluntariness are four factors essential to be considered when assessing the vulnerabilities of potential research participants in decision-making. In this context, capacity in medicine refers to the necessary physiological, mental and emotional integrity required to make decisions, and hence, to be considered legally competent. By comparison, competency is a legal construct referring to a person having the necessary ability to engage in legally defined acts such as entering into contracts, being a witness, being prosecuted, or agreeing to medical interventions (Chapter 4, Legal capacity, decision-making, discriminatory statutes and practice). (In some countries, capacity rather than competency is the legal term used.)

Having capacity and being competent, therefore, are *sine qua non* of legal and ethical decision-making. Diminished capacity may render a person marginally, or totally, incompetent, and incompetent individuals are in need of protection.

Loss of capacity and incompetence may develop at any time in life and therefore put a person in a situation of vulnerability.

Age is also a limiting factor in decision-making. Although there are variations in detail between countries, minors are generally treated as non-persons for the purposes of being capable of carrying out legal obligations, or even committing illegal acts. The legal restrictions on the competency of children lessen as the child matures and becomes more capable. Yet, researchers should not use legal restrictions on consent by minors as an excuse not to consult with the child on decisions that will impact his or her future welfare. A researcher may have to tread carefully if a child refuses to give 'assent' to a medical procedure or to participate in a research project, even if a parent or legal guardian has consented. Similar 'assenting' concerns apply to the elderly and the developmentally disabled (Buchanan, 2004).

Voluntariness may be easily compromised in institutions such as prisons and mental hospitals, where legal or *de facto* compulsion is common. Other situations in which a person could be persuaded to agree to something as a result of coercion, overt or subtle threats or inducements can also vitiate the free exercise of the will – when a researcher-physician recruits his or her own patients to participate in his or her own research projects, for example. The vulnerability is evident as a patient may fear they will be left without support unless they agree (Szmukler and Appelbaum, 2011).

The ethical boundaries may be less clear if the researcher is also motivated by financial or other rewards and has incentives to increase recruitment, or to keep a research subject in a study. Specifically in clinical medical research, the treating physician should not be the same as the physician-researcher. It has been argued that, in this way, 'responsibility for the welfare of the patient is located unequivocally on one identifiable member of the research team', and that, 'if necessary, that person should defend the patient's good against the good of science' (Thomasma and Pellegrino, 1998). It may also be that the patient has to be defended against such less lofty interests of the researcher, such as fraud, bias, or abuse (Anon, 1999a, 1999b, 1999c).

10.2 The nature of vulnerability

Vulnerability is a characteristic ascribed to an individual or group of persons whose judgment and decision-making capacity have been compromised (a definition from the United Kingdom context is shown in Box 10.3). More specifically, vulnerability is 'a substantial incapacity to protect one's own interests owing to such impediments as lack of capability to give informed consent, lack of alternative means of obtaining medical care or other expensive necessities, or being a junior or subordinate member of a hierarchical group' (CIOMS, 1993).

Box 10.3 Legislative Case Study: United Kingdom

The Law Commission in the United Kingdom proposed that a person is vulnerable if he or she 'by reason of old age, infirmity or disability (including mental disorder...) ... is unable to take care of himself or to protect himself from others.'

(Law Commission, 1993)

In the content of research, 'vulnerability' suggests 'an inability to protect oneself from exposure to an unreasonable risk of harm' (Weisstub *et al.*, 1998). People with intellectual disabilities, children, the elderly, people with mental illness and prisoners are traditionally considered vulnerable. Children are of an age when, legally, they cannot consent to any procedures, while older adults may have lost their decision-making capacity. People with more severe forms of intellectual disabilities will usually be considered vulnerable at any age, but both people with episodic conditions or states, such as mental illness and imprisonment, may be vulnerable only for periods.

The fact that a potential research participant belongs to a vulnerable population group, or several such groups at the same time, should not be a bar to participation, but simply a signal to researchers and research committees to raise the expectations for increased ethical awareness and continuing vigilance.

People with mental illness may experience fluctuating periods of incompetence and may not have the capacity during those periods to object to their continuation in a research project, or to withdraw their consent. Arrangements for this eventuality should be made in advance (while the person is competent) and the vulnerability of the patient/participant during those periods of time should be recognised.

Social and legal status may change at any time in the life of a particular individual according to context. A prisoner, for example, who may have been a highly capable and functioning individual free to make decisions while outside prison, may become dependent and subordinate to others in prison (when some rights are suspended and life becomes highly regimented). Prisoners will become doubly vulnerable if they become mentally ill as a result of a worsening of a pre-existing mental condition or because they develop mental health problems while in prison.

10.3 Protection and remedies

The benefits of research should be balanced with the risks the potential research subject will incur, especially those in vulnerable situations. Protections for research subjects include general and specific safeguards to be taken into account at every stage of a research project. Two key set of provisions are the World Psychiatric Association's Declaration of Madrid on Ethical Standards for Psychiatric Practice (Box 10.4) and the International Conference on Harmonisation of Technical Requirements for Registration of Pharmaceuticals for Human Use Good Clinical Practice Guidelines (Box 10.5).

Box 10.4 Standards: The World Psychiatric Association's Declaration of Madrid

(Chapter 14.3.2.3; full text: Chapter 14.4.5)

The Declaration of Madrid indicates that ethical research relies on the qualifications of the researcher and that only those people trained in research methodologies should be involved in conducting independent research. Researchers should also be trained in the ethics of research and should be deeply aware of the vulnerabilities of their potential subjects. Unfortunately, ethics takes a secondary role in medical curricula and researchers tend to just add a perfunctory ethics paragraph at the end of their research protocols without much consideration to the ethical operations of their projects that, when found wanting, cause an erosion of public confidence and lead 'the general public to lose trust in science' (Goffman, 1961). The Declaration of Madrid clearly states that only a deep personal devotion to the tenets of ethical work, in clinics or in research, could guarantee that clinicians or researchers do not transgress.

Box 10.5 Standards: International Conference on Harmonisation of Technical Requirements for Registration of Pharmaceuticals for Human Use Good Clinical Practice (ICH GCP)

In relation to the conduct of clinical trials, the ICH has proposed 13 principles of Good Clinical Practice (GCP). These have become highly influential and are incorporated in many countries' regulations about research.

1 Clinical trials should be conducted in accordance with the ethical principles that have their origin in the Declaration of Helsinki, and that are consistent with GCP and the applicable regulatory requirement(s).

2 Before a trial is initiated, foreseeable risks and inconveniences should be weighed against the anticipated benefit for the individual trial subject and society. A trial should be initiated and continued only if the anticipated benefits justify the risks.

3 The rights, safety, and well-being of the trial subjects are the most important considerations and should prevail over interests of science and society.

4 The available non-clinical and clinical information on an investigational product should be adequate to support the proposed clinical trial.

5 Clinical trials should be scientifically sound, and described in a clear, detailed protocol.

6 A trial should be conducted in compliance with the protocol that has received prior institutional review board/independent ethics committee approval/favourable opinion.

7 The medical care given to, and medical decisions made on behalf of, subjects should always be the responsibility of a qualified physician or, when appropriate, of a qualified dentist.

8 Each individual involved in conducting a trial should be qualified by education, training and experience to perform his or her respective task(s).

9 Freely given informed consent should be obtained from every subject prior to clinical trial participation.

10 All clinical trial information should be recorded, handled, and stored in a way that allows its accurate reporting, interpretation and verification.

11 The confidentiality of records that could identify subjects should be protected, respecting the privacy and confidentiality rules in accordance with the applicable regulatory requirement(s).

12 Investigational products should be manufactured, handled, and stored in accordance with applicable good manufacturing practice. They should be used in accordance with the approved protocol.

13 Systems with procedures that assure the quality of every aspect of the trial should be implemented.

For further information: http://ichgcp.net

Importantly, researchers must now declare – not only to the research ethics committee or institutional review board, but to the research subjects as well – any conflicts of interest they may have, and any financial gains they stand to obtain from the research. Transparency concerning conflicts of interest and financial gain is intended to reduce the risk of fraud and unethical practices in research.

10.4 The nature and quality of the investigation

In medical research, an experiment can fall within a spectrum ranging from 'pure research' with no therapeutic benefit to an individual or group to 'pure therapy'. However, the lines between the different types of experiment may become blurred. For example, untried therapies such as psychological interventions have been used in prisons when the aims or the risks of the intervention are not too well known (Arboleda-Flórez, 1991).

The Stanley case on the use of LSD–25 by the Central Intelligence Agency (CIA) in the United States (US v. Stanley, 107 U.S. 3054 (1987)), and Ewen Cameron's experiments with 'depatterning' or use of large numbers of electroconvulsive therapy treatments in Canada in the early 1960s, are egregious examples of confusion of aims and a lack of care for the effects that an unknown substance or therapeutic intervention might have had on the subjects (Weisstub, 1998). The aims of the intervention as treatment or research, and whether the intervention is generally accepted by the clinical community as a form of therapy, should be matters clearly understood by all those involved and discussed with the research subject.

The scientific quality of a research project is predicated on: (a) that it is conducted by a scientifically qualified person; (b) that it must conform to generally accepted scientific principles; and (c) that it must be based on previous knowledge of the problem to be investigated and of the nature and risks of the intervention. While an experiment must be scientifically sound to be ethical, it can still be scientifically sound and yet completely unethical and even morally reprehensible. As stated in the Declaration of Helsinki, 'the interest of science and society should never take precedence over considerations related to the well-being of the subject' (National Commission for the Protection of Human Subjects of Biomedical and Behavioral Research, 1978).

Where does the primary responsibility lie for the ethical conduct of research? The identification and minimisation of risks rest squarely on the shoulders of the investigator. This is especially important when research is among vulnerable persons.

It is expected that the investigator firstly has to balance potential risks and benefits to the subject, then to the group to which the subject belongs, and finally, to society. The Declaration of Helsinki points out that 'biomedical research involving human subjects cannot legitimately be carried out unless the importance of the objective is in proportion to the inherent risk to the subject'. As risks could materialise any time during an experiment, the investigator must be ready to monitor changes in the subject's consent to continue participating in a study. One approach to how much risk is ethically appropriate is the concept of 'minimal risk' to research subjects.

Although there is controversy about the definition of minimal risk, the one provided by the United States Department of Health and Human Services is commonly followed: 'Minimal risk means that the probability and magnitude of harm or discomfort anticipated in the research are not greater in and of themselves than those ordinarily encountered in daily life or during the performance of routine physical or psychological examinations or tests' (DHHS, 1991).

Having given consent, subjects nevertheless retain the right to withdraw from the study at any time, without any concerns about possible adverse consequences for their future clinical treatment. This is a matter of major concern in clinical trials that provide new medications to subjects, and where availability of treatment is somewhat related to enrolment. The cost of new medications is usually beyond the financial capabilities of many people, especially those belonging to vulnerable populations, such as the mentally ill. In these situations, the researcher should strive to organise the subjects' treatment needs independently from the financial arrangements and free from the drugs inducements encountered in research protocols. Investigators should also be careful not to 'over research' particular groups of patients simply because the population base is not adequate to have a larger pool from which to select potential participants. Multi-site enrolment should be considered in these situations.

Many professional organisations and government commissions have produced guidelines or declarations on the ethical and appropriate management of biomedical research. Such guidelines are necessary because: (a) the discovery of new technologies bring new challenges for ethical consideration and require further regulations because of potential impacts on humans, such as in the case of cloning or the use of stem cells; (b) new political and social realities produce new ethical challenges that should be identified and considered because of their potential impact on, particularly, vulnerable populations – such as euthanasia, torture, or the death penalty; and (c) better and improved guidelines are needed to control the ethical quality of researchers. One such example is the Canadian Tri-Council Policy Statement on Ethical Conduct for Research Involving Humans (Box 10.6).

Box 10.6 Standards Case Study: Canada

The Tri-Council Policy Statement, Ethical Conduct for Research Involving Humans (Canadian Institutes of Health Research, Natural Sciences and Engineering Research Council of Canada, Social Sciences and Humanities Research Council of Canada) (Tri-Council, 2010) states:

1 *Respect for Human Dignity*: The cardinal principle of modern research ethics is respect for human dignity. This principle aspires to protect the multiple and interdependent interests of the person – from bodily to psychological to cultural integrity. This principle forms the basis of the ethical obligations in research that are listed below. It is unacceptable to treat persons solely as means (mere objects or things), because doing so fails to respect their intrinsic human dignity and thus impoverishes all of humanity. Secondly, the welfare and integrity of the individual remain paramount in human research.

2 *Respect for Free and Informed Consent*: Individuals are generally presumed to have the capacity and right to make free and informed decisions. Respect for persons thus means respecting the exercise of individual consent. The principle of respect for persons translates into the process and requirements for free and informed consent by the research subject.

3 *Respect for Vulnerable Persons*: Respect for human dignity entails high ethical obligations towards vulnerable persons – to those whose diminished competence and/or decision-making capacity make them vulnerable. Children, institutionalized (sic) persons or others who are vulnerable are entitled, on grounds of human dignity, caring and fairness, to special protection against abuse, exploitation or discrimination. Ethical obligations to vulnerable individuals in the research enterprise will often translate into special procedures to protect their interests.

4 *Respect for Privacy and Confidentiality*: Respect for human dignity also implies the principles of respect for privacy and confidentiality. Privacy and confidentiality are considered fundamental to human dignity. Thus, standards of privacy and confidentiality protect the access, control and dissemination of personal information. In doing so, such standards help to protect mental or psychological integrity.

5 *Respect for Justice and Inclusiveness*: Justice connotes fairness and equity, and concerns the distribution of benefits and burdens of research. On the one hand, distributive justice means that no segment of the population should be unfairly burdened with the harms of research. It thus imposes particular obligations toward

individuals who are vulnerable and unable to protect their own interests in order to ensure that they are not exploited for the advancement of knowledge. On the other hand, distributive justice also imposes duties neither to neglect nor discriminate against individuals and groups who may benefit from advances in research.

6 *Balancing Harms and Benefits*: The analysis, balance and distribution of harms and benefits are critical to the ethics of human research. Modern research ethics, for instance, require a favourable harms–benefit balance – that is, that the foreseeable harms should not outweigh anticipated benefits.

7 *Minimizing (sic) Harm*: Research subjects must not be subjected to unnecessary risks of harm, and their participation in research must be essential to achieving scientifically and societally important aims that cannot be realized (sic) without the participation of human subjects. In addition, it should be kept in mind that the principle of minimizing (sic) harm requires that the research involve the smallest number of human subjects and the smallest number of tests on these subjects that will ensure scientifically valid data.

Finally, it is important to appreciate that several of the more broad ethical instruments contain sections which are directly related to research, and the reader is particular referred to: (i) the World Medical Association's Statement on Ethical Issues Concerning Patients with Mental Illness Chapter 14.3.1.3); (ii) the Declaration of Hawaii (Chapter 14.3.2.1); (iii) the Convention on Human Rights and Biomedicine (Chapter 14.2.1.1.4); (iv) the Universal Declaration on the Human Genome and Human Rights (Chapter 14.1.2.1); and (v) the Council for International Organizations of Medical Sciences (CIOMS) (Chapter 14.3.4).

References

Anon (1949) The Nuremberg Code (1947). In: Trials of War Criminals before the Nuremberg Military Tribunals under Control Council Law No. 10 (October 1946–April 1949). US Government Printing Office, Washington, DC.

Anon (1999a) Drug-treatment experiments come under fire. *The New Mexican*. Tuesday, 20 April 1999.

Anon (1999b) Research shutdown roils Los Angeles VA. *Science*, **1999**:18–21.

Anon (1999c) Sweden considers more oversight of research. *Science*, **1999**:1829.

Arboleda-Flórez, J (1991) Ethical issues regarding research on prisoners. *International Journal of Offender Therapy and Comparative Criminology*, **35**:1–5.

Aziz, P (1976) Doctors of Death. Ferni Publishers, geneva, Switzerland.

Buchanan, A. (2004) Mental capacity, legal competence and consent to treatment. *Journal of the Royal Society of Medicine*, **97**:415–420.

CIOMS (Council for International Organizations of Medical Sciences) (1993). International Ethical Guidelines for Biomedical Research Involving Human Subjects. World Health Organization (CIOMS), Geneva, Switzerland.

DHHS (US Department of Health & Human Services) (1991) Code of Federal Regulations, Human Subjects Research (45 CFR 46), Para. 46.102 (I). US Department of Health & Human Services, Washington.

Goffman, E (1961) *Asylums*. Doubleday Anchor, New York.

Law Commission (1993) Mentally-incapacitated and other vulnerable adults: public law protection (Consultation paper No. 130). HMSO, London.

National Commission for the Protection of Human Subjects of Biomedical and Behavioral Research (1978) The Belmont Report: Ethical principles for the protection of human subjects in research. US Government Printing Office, Washington, DC.

Queensland Law Reform Society (1996) Assisted and Substituted Decisions: Decision-making by and for People with a Decision-Making Disability, Vol. 3, Summary of Recommendations. Queensland Law Reform Society, Australia.

Szmukler, G. and Appelbaum, P. (2011) Treatment Pressures, Coercion, and Compulsion. In: Thornicroft, G., Drake, RE., Mueser, K. and Szmukler G., *Oxford Textbook of Community Mental Health*. Oxford University Press, Oxford. pp. 238–246.

Thomasma, D and Pellegrino, E (1998) Medicine, science, self-interest: value sets in conflict in human experimentation. In: Weisstub, D (ed.) Research on Human Subjects. Elsevier (Pergamon), Oxford. pp. Preface.

Tri-Council (Medical Research Council, National Sciences and Engineering Research Council, Social Sciences and Humanities Research Council) (2010) Tri-Council Policy Statement: Ethical Conduct for Research Involving Humans. Canadian Institutes of Health Research, Natural Sciences and Engineering Research Council of Canada, Social Sciences and Humanities Research Council of Canada.

Weisstub, D (1998) The ethical parameters of experimentation. In: Weisstub, D (ed.) Research on Human Subjects: Ethics, law, and social policy. Elsevier (Pergamon), Oxford, pp. 1–34.

Weisstub, D, Arboleda-Flórez, J and Tomossy, G. Establishing the boundaries of ethically permissible research with vulnerable populations. In: Weisstub, D (ed.) Research on Human Subjects: Ethics, law, and social policy. Elsevier (Pergamon), Oxford, pp. 355–379.

CHAPTER 11

Promotion of Mental Health and Prevention of Mental Illness

There is a growing body of research that illustrates the impact of social and economic inequalities on the mental health of societies and communities (Friedli, 2009a; Jenkins *et al.*, 2008; Melzer *et al.*, 2004; Wilkinson, 2005; Wilkinson and Pickett, 2010). Effective strategies to promote mental health and prevent mental illness must, therefore, also address social and economic inequalities: mental health promotion can play an important role in combating social injustice. There is growing recognition of the multiple factors that can undermine and enhance people's mental health, and the need for policy and programmes – buttressed by legislation – to work broadly (e.g. across the fields of education, employment, leisure and cultural activities, as well as health) to address these multiple factors. Recent research and policy within the mental health promotion field have demonstrated the importance of these multi-sectoral approaches to mental health promotion/mental illness prevention (Barry and Jenkins, 2007; Herrman *et al.*, 2005; Jané-Llopis and Anderson, 2005, 2007).

The World Health Organization defines a mental disorder as: 'the existence of a clinically recognisable set of symptoms or behaviour associated in most cases with distress and with interference with personal functions' (WHO, 1993). As mental disorders are usually multi-factorial, and the associated mental health problems present extreme diversity, there are equally rich and diverse prevention possibilities for both.

As the Ottawa Charter for Health Promotion (WHO, 1986) states: 'Health promotion is the process of enabling people to increase control over, and to improve, their health. To reach a state of complete physical, mental and social well-being, an individual or group must be able to identify and to realise aspirations, to satisfy needs, and to change or cope with the environment. Health is, therefore, seen as a resource for everyday life, not the objective of living. Health is a positive concept emphasising social and personal resources, as well as physical capacities. Therefore, health

Mental Illness, Discrimination and the Law: Fighting for Social Justice, First Edition.
Felicity Callard, Norman Sartorius, Julio Arboleda-Flórez, Peter Bartlett, Hanfried Helmchen, Heather Stuart, Jose Taborda and Graham Thornicroft.

promotion is not just the responsibility of the health sector, but goes beyond healthy life-styles to well-being.'

In this sense, health promotion demands considering prevention and promotion at all levels – and in particular, focusing on social variables.

11.1 Public health approaches to promotion and prevention

Prevention of mental illness and promotion of mental health are central issues for a public health system. We focus largely in this chapter on the field of public health, since this is the sphere from which most of our country informants' legislative examples derived. We should also note that, traditionally, much of the focus of public health activity has been on physical rather than mental health. It is critical that health policies and programmes – backed up by legislation – ensure that mental health is not de-prioritised in relation to physical health. Namibia is an example of a low-income country whose health policy explicitly includes mental health and disability as one of its 'general public health and social services priorities' (Box 11.1).

Box 11.1 Policy Case Study: Namibia

The Namibia National Health Policy Framework's strategic response directions (for mental health and disability) comprise:

1. emphasis on prevention of mental health problems through a multi-sectoral effort;
2. awareness creation and advocacy for the plight of people with mental health problems;
3. training and deployment of a minimum of specialised human resources;
4. strengthening of specialised referral services for mental health;
5. integration of mental health care at the primary health care level;
6. intensification of community care;
7. support and supervision from specialised doctors and nurses, coordination with social services inside the Ministry of Health and Social Services and in the health system at large.

The Namibia National Health Policy Framework (2010–2020) is available at: www.healthnet.org.na

To understand and analyse how different legislation across the world addresses mental illness prevention and mental health promotion, it is important to summarise some basic concepts from the field of public health.

A comprehensive public health system comprises preventive measures on three different levels: primary, secondary and tertiary (WHO, 1984). In addition, these measures must be taken, if possible, in relation to all variables involved in the process of becoming unwell. Thus, if the traditional bio-psychosocial approach (a model or approach in which biological, psychological and social factors are all considered significant when understanding human functioning in the context of illness) is adopted, it would be possible to find nine distinct kinds of preventive measures, as seen in Figure 11.1.

	Biological variables	Psychological variables	Social variables
Primary prevention			
Secondary prevention			
Tertiary prevention			

Figure 11.1 Levels of prevention and bio-psychosocial variables.

Primary prevention measures comprise all activities with the objective of not letting a disease or illness develop: vaccination is the paradigm of this kind of intervention. Secondary prevention, easily confused with the classical conception of medical practice, encompasses the earliest possible diagnosis and the effective therapy for the case in question. Tertiary prevention occurs when primary and secondary measures have failed, and the patient needs physical or psychosocial recuperation or rehabilitation. A typical example of tertiary intervention would be physiotherapy following a stroke (Jekel *et al.*, 2001).

11.2 UNCRPD in relation to mental health promotion and mental illness prevention

The UN Convention on the Rights of Persons with Disabilities (UNCRPD) includes explicit statements on prevention in Articles 16 (Freedom from exploitation, violence and abuse), 25 (Health) and 26 (Habilitation and rehabilitation). Thus, Article 16, item 4, determines that: 'States Parties shall take all appropriate measures to promote the physical, cognitive and psychological recovery, rehabilitation and social reintegration of persons with disabilities who become victims of any form of exploitation, violence or abuse, including through the provision of protection services. Such recovery and reintegration shall take place in an environment that fosters the health, welfare, self-respect, dignity and autonomy of the person and takes into account gender- and age-specific needs.'

Article 25 establishes that: 'States Parties recognise that persons with disabilities have the right to the enjoyment of the highest attainable standard of health without discrimination on the basis of disability. States Parties shall take all appropriate measures to ensure access for persons with disabilities to health services that are gender-sensitive, including health-related rehabilitation. In particular, States Parties shall: (...) (*b*) Provide those health services needed by persons with disabilities specifically because of their disabilities, including early identification and intervention as appropriate, and services designed to minimise and prevent further disabilities, including among children and older persons; (...) (*e*) Prohibit discrimination against persons with disabilities in the provision of health insurance, and life insurance where such insurance is permitted by national law, which shall be provided in a fair and reasonable manner; (*f*) Prevent discriminatory denial of health care or health services or food and fluids on the basis of disability.'

Article 26 disposes that: 'States Parties shall take effective and appropriate measures, including through peer support, to enable persons with disabilities to attain and maintain maximum independence, full physical, mental, social and vocational ability, and full inclusion and participation in all aspects of life. To that end, States Parties shall organise, strengthen and extend comprehensive habilitation and rehabilitation services and programmes, particularly in the areas of health, employment, education and social services (...)'.

Besides the above-mentioned Articles, which explicitly predict generic and non-specific primary and secondary prevention measures (Article 25) and tertiary prevention measures (Articles 16 and 26), there are other Articles that indirectly refer to prevention measures in relation to mental health problems and mental illnesses. This is the case with: Article 5 (Equality and non-discrimination), which prohibits 'all discrimination on the basis of disability and guarantees to persons with disabilities equal and effective legal protection'; Article 12 (Equal recognition before the law) that reaffirms 'the right to recognition everywhere as persons before the law' and that 'States Parties shall take appropriate measures to provide access by persons with disabilities to the support they may require in exercising their legal capacity'; and Article 19 (Living independently and being included in the community) that recognises the right to live in community and determines State Parties ensure that '(b) persons with disabilities have access to a range of in-home, residential and other community support services, including personal assistance necessary to support living and inclusion in the community, and to prevent isolation or segregation from the community'. Provisions of Articles 5, 12 and 19 can be considered as primary prevention of psychological and social variables and as tertiary prevention of social variables, as they promote the self-esteem of persons with disabilities, reinforce their citizenship and favour their integration within the community.

11.3 Examples of legislation

If we accept that anti-discrimination legislation and access to appropriate health care are central components through which to promote the mental health of both individuals and communities, then it might be said that most of the countries that were reviewed in the course of the research that resulted in this book have legislation in which there are dispositions on prevention (Boxes 11.2 to 11.10). Nevertheless, these dispositions are often closer to a general principle to be observed than to a real, enforceable legal command.

Box 11.2 Legislative Case Study: Argentina

Federal Law 25.421/01 specifies that all individuals are entitled to receive mental health care within primary care services. It also provides for the rehabilitation and social integration of those with mental health problems, which can be considered secondary and tertiary prevention. In the Province of Buenos Aires, Basic Health Law 153/99 encourages social integration through progressive deinstitutionalisation. The same law specifies human rights protections for those with mental disabilities.

Box 11.3 Legislative Case Study: Australia

The 1992 Commonwealth Disability Discrimination Act protects disabled individuals from discrimination, as well as their relatives and friends on grounds of their connection with them. There are also formal appeal mechanisms, such as the Human Rights and Equal Opportunity Commission (HREOC), which can investigate complaints on discrimination. A hotline has been set up for reporting or complaining about the abuse or neglect of a disabled person (Chapter 12.6).

Box 11.4 Legislative Case Study: Brazil

The Federal Constitution forbids discrimination on grounds which include mental disabilities or disorders. Federal Law 10.216/01 (Law on Reform of Psychiatric Care) establishes, in Article 3, that the responsibility of the state is 'the development of the mental health policy; the assistance and promotion of health actions to those suffering from mental disorder' (which is a merely generic disposition). Article 5 mentions that 'the patient who has been in hospital for a long time, or for whom the situation of serious institutional dependence applies resulting from his/her clinical conditions or absence of social support, will be the object of a specific policy of planned hospital release and assisted psychosocial rehabilitation'.

Box 11.5 Legislative Case Study: Denmark

Anti-discrimination legislation covers 'disability' in a broad sense. Disability is defined as a physical, mental or intellectual impairment that causes a need for compensation so that the person can function on equal conditions with other citizens in a comparable situation. Thus, a municipal council shall offer special initiatives for adults with impaired physical or mental function or with special social problems, aimed at preventing a deterioration of the problems facing the individual; to improve the individual's social and personal functions and development potential; and to improve the individual's potential for self-expression through contact, social and other activities, treatment and care.

Box 11.6 Legislative Case Study: Finland

The Constitution of Finland provides an important guarantee that is a kind of primary prevention of mental illness. Section 19 determines that the public authorities shall guarantee for everyone adequate social, health and medical services and promote the health of the population. Moreover, they shall support families and others responsible for providing for children so that they have the ability to ensure the well-being and personal development of the children.

Box 11.7 Legislative Case Study: Israel

There are several laws, which, on the whole, regulate the prevention of mental health problems at all three levels, emphasising psychological and social variables. The Equal Rights for People with Disabilities Law 1998 was enacted in order to promote equality of all people with disabilities, including mental disabilities. There is also a Commission that promotes and monitors the observance of the rights of people with all kinds of disabilities. The Rehabilitation of People with Mental Disabilities in the Community Law 2000 makes clear that individuals with mental disabilities are entitled to live, work and be educated in the community, as well as to have the right to a life of personal dignity. In this way, the Rehabilitation Law recognises the right to professional rehabilitation. Under this law, individual claims regarding infringement of mental health rehabilitation rights may be brought to an appeal committee and general claims are tried under the Labour Courts. The Rights of Patient Law 1996 prohibits any discrimination in the administration of treatment. The National Insurance Law 1995 provides employment diagnostic services to persons with disabilities, as well as vocational guidance and training aimed at enabling them to fulfil their work potential.

Box 11.8 Legislative Case Study: The Netherlands

The Dutch Penal Law was revised in 2006. Since then, incitements to hatred, discrimination or violence against people with disabilities are now a criminal offence, which is a preventive measure of a social variable at a primary level.

Box 11.9 Legislative Case Study: South Africa

The Mental Health Care Act 2002 establishes that a mental health care user may not be unfairly discriminated against on the grounds of his/her mental health status. Moreover, his/her human dignity and privacy must be respected. Health establishments and rehabilitation centres must take steps to ensure that users are protected from exploitation, abusing and/or degrading treatment and that care and treatment and/or rehabilitation services are not used as punishments, or for the convenience of other people. The same law disposes that every mental health care user must receive care, treatment and rehabilitation services according to standards equivalent to those applicable to any other health user. If any kind of discrimination or abuse occurs, the person can apply to the South African Human Rights Commission.

Box 11.10 Legislative Case Study: Tajikistan

The Law on Psychiatric Care 2002 aims at ensuring medical and social aid to people with mental health problems, improving conditions related to their lives and work, as well as preventing mental disorders. Article 16, devoted to psychiatric care and social support, establishes that the state shall guarantee counselling, treatment and rehabilitation at inpatient and outpatient facilities (which can be seen as comprehending the three levels of prevention) and pension, social care and employment support (tertiary prevention on social variables).

The human rights issues raised by the discrimination of people with a mental disorder are now widely recognised, as our book attests. International organisations working in the field of health – such as the World Health Organization, the World Psychiatric Association and the World Association of Social Psychiatry – have all identified mental-health related stigma and discrimination as a key public health issue. In response, a growing number of national governments have included the reduction of stigma and discrimination among their mental health policy aims (Box 11.11).

Box 11.11 Legislative Case Study: United States of America

The Americans with Disabilities Act 1990 (ADA) is designed to integrate people with disabilities fully into the mainstream of American life. It protects people who currently have a disability, people who have a history of a disability and people regarded as having a disability by others, whether or not they actually have one. This Act also protects people who are not themselves disabled, but who are discriminated against on the basis of their relationship with a person who has a disability (parents of children with disabilities, for instance). They cannot be discriminated against in the provision of government programmes, services, benefits and employment. There are many civil procedures that people may pursue if the requirements of the ADA are not met.

Much current legislation addressing health care and treatment prohibits discrimination on the grounds of mental illness. In the same way, many current legislations address the equally relevant issue of rehabilitation as well. Both of them are important preventive measures at primary and tertiary level on social variables, as they seek to prevent new mental health problems in the patient and facilitate his/her integration into the community. Besides, as they diminish the burden of mental illness, they can also benefit the patient's family and caregivers at a primary level.

The problem with the current legislation is the scotoma regarding the biological variables, mainly at a primary level. For instance, of the examples we received, only the response from Tajikistan indicated a law that guarantees counselling to patients, which includes genetic counselling. We received no examples of legislation aimed at protecting pregnant women from viruses, a condition associated with schizophrenia for the infant later in life (Limosin *et al.*, 2003). Notably, we also received no examples aimed at clarifying the role of drugs in relation to mental illness (in the case of marijuana and schizophrenia, for example (Rubino and Parolaro, 2008)).

11.4 Other legislation to promote mental health and prevent mental illness

It is important to emphasise the range of legislation that can have an impact on individuals' and communities' mental health. In addition to health (and anti-discrimination) legislation, there are many other legislative tools that countries can use to promote mental health and prevent mental illness. These include:

- labour regulations;
- health and safety regulations;
- maternity and paternity leave regulations;
- housing law;
- harassment law;
- employment law;
- racial vilification or hate crime legislation designed to combat discrimination and abuse on the basis of race, ethnicity or other protected grounds;
- children's rights and protection legislation, including protection against exploitation in industry or for sex;
- social protection and social security legislation (Chaper 8, Social security and social protection; Friedli, 2009b; Herrman *et al.*, 2005).

One important policy tool, which is increasingly emphasised by mental health promotion experts, is to assess the mental health impact of *any* new policy (and, by implication, of any legislative intervention); this is clear in the World Health Organization's Mental Health Action Plan for Europe (Box 11.12).

Box 11.12 Policy Case Study: World Health Organization Mental Health Action Plan for Europe

The Mental Health Action Plan for Europe states (in its section 'Demonstrating the centrality of mental health'):

'Sound and integrated public policies, such as those on labour, urban planning and socio-economic issues, also have a positive impact on mental health and reduce the risk of mental health problems. The mental health implications of all public policy, and particularly its potential impact on groups at risk, therefore needs to be considered. Mental health policy requires inter-sectoral linkages and should incorporate multi-sectoral and multi-disciplinary approaches' (WHO, 2005; Chapter 16.2.3.4.2).

Mental health promotion and mental illness prevention activities should ensure that policy, legislation, funding and standards are all aligned so as to be able to achieve maximum benefits. Scotland is one example of this approach (Box 11.13). Since 1999, it has established a distinctive and innovative approach to mental health improvement, which has involved pursuing an integrated and multi-sectoral approach combining legislative actions, anti-stigma and discrimination interventions, mental health service redesign, suicide prevention strategies and mental health user involvement.

Box 11.13 Policy and Legislative Case Study: Scotland

Health Scotland – Mental Improvement section (Health Scotland): www.healthscotland.com/mental-health.aspx (Scottish Government, 2009).

The Scottish Government (Mental Health Law): www.scotland.gov.uk (www.scotland.gov.uk/Topics/Health/health/mental-health/mhlaw).

References

Barry, M and Jenkins, R (2007) *Implementing Mental Health Promotion*. Churchill Livingstone.

Friedli, L (2009a) Mental health, resilience and inequalities. Mental Health Foundation/World Health Organization, Geneva, Switzerland 2009.

Friedli, L (2009b) Future directions in mental health promotion and public mental health. In: Norman, I and Ryrie, I (eds) *The Art and Science of Mental Health Nursing*. McGraw-Hill, pp. 43–61.

Herrman, H, Saxena, S and Moodie, R (eds) (2005) Promoting Mental Health: Concepts, emerging evidence, practice. Report of the World Health Organization, Department of Mental Health and Substance Abuse in collaboration with the Victorian Health

Promotion Foundation and the University of Melbourne. World Health Organization, Geneva, Switzerland.

Jané-Llopis, E and Anderson, P (2005) *Mental Health Promotion and Mental Disorder Prevention. A policy for Europe*. Radboud University Nijmegen, Nijmegen, The Netherlands.

Jané-Llopis, E and Anderson, P (2007) A policy framework for the promotion of mental health and the prevention of mental disorders. In: Knapp, M, McDaid, D, Mossialos, E and Thornicroft, G (eds) *Mental Health Policy and Practice across Europe: the future direction of mental health care*. Open University Press, Maidenhead, pp. 188–214.

Jekel, J, Katz, D and Elmore, J (2001) *Epidemiology, Biostatistics, and Preventive Medicine*, 2nd edn. WB Saunders, Philadelphia, PA.

Jenkins, R, Bhugra, D, Bebbington, P, Brugha, T, Farrell, M, Coid, J, *et al.* (2008) Debt, income and mental disorder in the general population. *Psychological Medicine*, **38**(10):1485–1493.

Limosin, F, Rouillon, F, Pavan, C, Cohen, J and Strub, N (2003) Prenatal exposure to influenza as a risk factor for adult schizophrenia. *Acta Psychiatr Scand*, **107**(5):331–335.

Melzer, D, Fryers, T and Jenkins, R (2004) *Social Inequalities and the Distribution of Common Mental Disorders*. Psychology Press, Hove, UK.

Rubino, T and Parolaro, D (2008) Long lasting consequences of cannabis exposure in adolescence. *Mol Cell Endocrinol*, **286**(1–2, Suppl 1):S108–S113.

Scottish Government (2009) Towards a Mentally Flourishing Scotland: Policy and Action Plan 2009–2011. The Scottish Government, Edinburgh. (Available for download at the Health Scotland website: www.healthscotland.com (www.healthscotland.com/mental-health.aspx).)

WHO (1984) Health Promotion: A Discussion Document on the Concept and Principles. WHO Regional Office for Europe, Copenhagen, Denmark.

WHO (1986) The Ottawa Charter for Health Promotion [First International Conference on Health Promotion, Ottawa, 21 November 1986]. World Health Organization, Ottawa.

WHO (1993) The ICD-10 Classification of Mental and Behavioural Disorders: Diagnostic criteria for research. World Health Organization, Geneva, Switzerland.

WHO (2005) Mental Health Action Plan for Europe: Facing the Challenges, Building Solutions. World Health Organization, Copenhagen, Denmark.

Wilkinson, R (2005) *The Impact of Inequality: How to Make Sick Societies Healthier*. Routledge, London.

Wilkinson, R and Pickett, K (2010) *The Spirit Level: Why Equality is Better for Everyone*. Penguin, London.

CHAPTER 12
Implementation and Enforcement

Implementation and enforcement of legal reforms are vital. By far the most frequent comment provided by our country-based informants was that the legislation that existed in their countries, some of which was very good, was not meaningfully or adequately implemented or enforced. One respondent, for example, noted that one of the weaknesses of the legislative framework she had described was that it had no 'legal binding power' consequent upon any 'recognition of discrimination or cruelty'. Another respondent noted that: 'There is no statutory framework for the prevention and detection of abuse of vulnerable adults or for responding to allegations of abuse'. Another said that while the law described provided 'legal safeguards for protection of all basic human rights of a person with mental illness', no 'appeal mechanism ha[d] been established' and hence there was an over-reliance on non-governmental advocacy efforts.

Certainly, the enactment of non-discriminatory legislation may itself have an effect on local conditions, as it may provide an enhanced sense of what it is to behave properly in a society. This is, however, in no way a substitute for proper mechanisms of enforcement and implementation, and there is no shortage of countries in the world where good legislation has made no difference to the condition or lives of people with mental disabilities 'on the ground'.

Proper enforcement and implementation may take a variety of forms, in varying degrees of coerciveness. Almost certainly, a variety will be necessary to ensure a successful result.

12.1 Implementation plans and policies

Legal reform does not exist in a vacuum. For legal reform to be successful, plans for its implementation should be drawn up, considering who needs to be told of the new law, how the information is best conveyed

Mental Illness, Discrimination and the Law: Fighting for Social Justice, First Edition.
Felicity Callard, Norman Sartorius, Julio Arboleda-Flórez, Peter Bartlett, Hanfried Helmchen, Heather Stuart, Jose Taborda and Graham Thornicroft.

to those people and what resources will be required. These plans should be accompanied by sensible costings and a commitment by government to provide the required funding. In this respect, many of our country-based informants commented on the inadequate resourcing of elements of the frameworks they had described, and how these inadequacies weakened the ability of legislative and administrative actions to improve the lives of people with mental health problems. One of our informants, for example, lamented that the introduction of a new mental health law had not been accompanied by any 'comprehensive policy on mental health and no appropriate action plan' and that, additionally, 'the advocacy service was weak and under-financed'.

12.1.1 Mental health policies and national disability policies

Two of the most common ways to help implement and embed legal reform are through the use of comprehensive mental health policies and national disability policies.

A national (and/or regional and/or devolved) policy on mental health that works in tandem with legislative reform or innovation can make a fundamental contribution to securing resources, tackling discrimination and raising awareness. A national mental health policy ought to extend beyond the health sector and ensure that different sectors (education, housing, employment, social care, criminal justice etc.) are adequately involved and communicating appropriately with one another; see the example of the Mental Health and Poverty Project (MHaPP) in Box 12.1.

Box 12.1 Project: The Mental Health and Poverty Project (MHaPP)

The World Health Organization MHaPP has made a number of recommendations in relation to the development of mental health policies and plans in Africa:

1. Strong and clear commitment from government.
2. Involvement of stakeholders.
3. Realism about what can be achieved and how.
4. Elaborated policy areas for action.
5. Internationally recognised best practices.
6. International human rights standards.
7. Formulation of mental health strategic plans to implement policy.

More details regarding these recommendations and specific examples of how the recommendations are, or are not, evident in mental health policy and planning in Ghana, South Africa, Uganda and Zambia are given by Omar *et al.* (2010) and the MHaPP Policy Brief (www.who.int/mental_health/policy/development/MHPB8.pdf) (MHaPP, n.d.).

More details about the MHaPP and its various outputs can be found at: www.who.int/mental_health/policy/development/mhapp/en

Another example of mental health policy development in a low-income, sub-Saharan country is given by Jenkins *et al.* (2011).

Some countries – such as Scotland (Box 12.2) –have been innovative in the ways in which they have married legal reform with policy approaches to mental health that really attempt to work across sectoral boundaries.

Box 12.2 Policy Case Study: Scotland

Scotland has taken a comprehensive approach to mental health in which legislative transformation has taken place alongside policy innovations that have focused on population-level well-being. Government policy on mental health integrates mental health improvement (promotion and prevention) and treatment (implementation of mental health legislation and mental health services). Strategic direction for mental health improvement has involved a number of policy areas: these include public health, social justice and social inclusion, education, enterprise, life-long learning and arts, sports and culture.

Further information can be found on the Health Scotland (Mental Health Improvement) web site: www.healthscotland.com (www.healthscotland.com/mental-health-background.aspx).

See also: The Scottish Government (Mental Health Law): www.scotland.gov.uk (www.scotland.gov.uk/Topics/Health/health/mental-health/mhlaw)

National disability plans can also be critical to advancing and upholding the rights of people with mental health problems. Attention needs to be paid so that physical disabilities are not prioritised at the expense of mental disabilities – frequently, mental health service user organisations have less of a visible presence and 'voice' in the national policy landscape, and so care needs to be taken to ensure that their concerns are addressed just as substantively as those of physical disability organisations.

The Centre for Disability Law and Policy at the National University of Ireland, Galway has been conducting a major comparative study on the implementation and monitoring processes for disability action plans and/or strategies worldwide (Advancing the National Disability Strategy: Building on Comparative and International Innovation, www.nuigalway.ie/cdlp/projects/strategies.html). The Centre has identified success factors based on a comparative analysis of national disability strategies in 11 countries (in the Global North and South), as well as on evidence from literature about strategic and public management. The Centre has also identified a number of examples of good practice taken at a state and community level in relation to implementation and monitoring of disability action plans. Some of those they identified at state level are included below in the list of success factors (more extensive discussion and comparative analysis of national disability plans and strategies is available elsewhere (Flynn, 2011)).

12.1.1.1 Critical success factors for implementing and monitoring national disability strategies

(Taken from: Summary of critical success factors for implementing and monitoring national disability strategies (Centre for Disability Law and Policy, 2010))

1 Leadership: successful implementation of a national disability strategy requires leadership both from community actors (people with disabilities, families, disability organisations etc.) and from state actors (government departments, public bodies etc.).
  See, for example, a best practice from South Africa in Box 12.3.

Box 12.3 Policy Case Study: Example of best practice, South Africa

The South Africa Office on the Status of Persons with Disabilities (OSDP) (now incorporated into the Ministry of Women, Children and Persons with Disabilities) was introduced as part of the Integrated National Disability Strategy. It was first under the Ministry of the Deputy President, but was relocated to the President's Office to provide the OSDP with greater leadership and responsibility.

2 Participation of people with disabilities in implementing and monitoring the national disability strategy: meaningful engagement and participation of people with disabilities throughout the development and delivery of policies affecting them can lead to more effective implementation.
3 Integrating the national disability strategy with domestic implementation of the UN Convention on the Rights of Persons with Disabilities (CRPD).
4 Positive legal obligations and funding programmes to underpin the national disability strategy: for example, obliging actors to take proactive measures to combat discrimination against people with disabilities. These legal obligations should be duties to be proactive in promoting equality (positive action measures, disability equality duties, obligations to include people with disabilities in planning or developing new policies etc.) rather than rights to end product services for people with disabilities (for example, the best practice example from the United Kingdom in Box 12.4). Strategies need to be well-costed: failure to cost implementation has proved a major problem in certain countries.

Box 12.4 Legislative Case Study: Example of best practice, United Kingdom

The Disability Equality Duty (www.dotheduty.org) places an enforceable obligation on all public authorities in the United Kingdom to draft a disability action plan, setting out the efforts to be made to provide more accessible services and to include people with disabilities in all aspects of the organisation's work. The duty applies to all government departments, public authorities and state bodies equally.

5 Transparency and accountability in reporting on progress in delivering the national disability strategy: the state should be open about progress made and barriers encountered.
6 Mainstreaming disability equality – citizenship and the 'life course' approach: disability equality should be 'mainstreamed' across all domains of policy development (e.g. employment, education etc.), since this puts the onus on the particular domain to identify and address barriers encountered by people with disabilities. See Box 12.5 for a tool that assists in mainstreaming disability equality.

Box 12.5 Resource

Leonard Cheshire Disability has developed the EDAMAT (European Disability Action for Mainstreaming Assessment Tool) to assess and promote the effective mainstreaming of disability in general policies, laws and programmes. the EDAMAT emphasises how to practically implement the concept of mainstreaming and ensure that the result has a positive impact on the lives of people with disabilities.

The EDAMAT is available for download at The Leonard Cheshire Disability web site: www.lcint.org (www.lcint.org/?lid=3142).

7 Independent monitoring and review of national disability strategies: reporting on implementation should be done via independent – that is, not government – monitoring to gain an accurate account of progress (Article 33 of the Convention on the Right of Persons with Disabilities; full text: Chapter 14.4.1).
8 Indicators and data – measuring implementation and monitoring: indicators of effectiveness should be developed and data collected in order to determine the effectiveness of the national disability strategy (e.g. how many people with disabilities are employed in the open labour market?).

12.1.1.2 Disability policies, mental health policies and legislative reform at the same time

One powerful way in which countries can proceed is by developing disability policies, mental health policies and legislative reform alongside one another. This is evident in Sri Lanka (Box 12.6).

Box 12.6 Policy Case Study: Sri Lanka

The Ministry of Social Welfare adopted, in 2003, a national disability policy, which provides incentives to employers to hire people with disabilities. The National Policy on Disability for Sri Lanka is available online at:
http://siteresources.worldbank.org/INTSRILANKA/Resources/NatPolicyDisability Sep2003srilanka1.pdf

The government also approved in 2005 a 10-year mental health policy (2005–2015), which prioritised the development of community-based mental health services and the decentralisation of services, including the downsizing of big mental hospitals.

The Mental Health Policy of Sri Lanka, 2005–2015, is available online at:
www.searo.who.int/LinkFiles/On-going_projects_mhp-slr.pdf

A new Mental Health Act has been drafted: www.health.gov.lk/mental_health_act.html

Additional information and analytical discussion can be found in Faunce (2005), Mendis (2004) and Ministry of Health (2001).

It is important that national disability strategies explicitly consider how policy might be used to strengthen rights protections, advocacy and complaints mechanisms. One good example of this is Australia's National Disability Strategy for 2010–2020 (Box 12.7).

Box 12.7 Policy Case Study: Australia

The National Disability Strategy 2010–2020 sets out six priority areas for action to improve the lives of people with disabilities, their families and carers. One priority area is 'rights protection, justice and legislation' – which includes statutory protections such as anti-discrimination measures, complaints mechanisms, advocacy and the electoral and justice systems. Within this area, there are five policy directions:

1. Increase awareness and acceptance of the rights of people with disability.
2. Remove societal barriers preventing people with disability from participating as equal citizens.
3. People with disability have access to justice.
4. People with disability are to be safe from violence, exploitation and neglect.
5. More effective responses from the criminal justice system to people with disability who have complex needs or heightened vulnerabilities.

The National Disability Strategy is available for download at: www.fahcshia.gov.au (www.fahcsia.gov.au/sa/disability/progserv/govtint/Pages/nds.aspx).

In other countries, such as Lesotho (Box 12.8), service development is placed in tandem with mental health law reform. This is a clearly desirable approach, allowing a coherent structure of health and human rights reform.

Box 12.8 Legislative and Policy Case Study: Lesotho

A plan for development of service provision is running in tandem with a reform of mental disability law. Further details on and contextualisation of these developments can be found in Bartlett and Hamzic (2010).

12.1.2 Internal audit and implementation analysis

One way to assess the effectiveness of legislative change is to study the progress of implementation and development through systemic supervision and analysis as the programme is rolled out and beyond (for example, the human rights audit of mental health legislation in Australia; Box 12.9). The precise nature of such study will, of course, depend on the nature of the legal reform. However, the number of people engaging with a programme, or the number of people using a new law, along with outcome measures of what happens to them in the process, is an obvious possible way forward. Social scientists can be very helpful in designing appropriate methodologies specific to the legal reform in question. Mental health service users should also be involved in determining the priorities of what should be measured. Government priorities may be limited to budget reductions rather than the fostering of human rights; involvement of service users and others more removed from government spending priorities may go some way to address these limitations in the design of the audits.

Box 12.9 Resource

Australia: human rights audit of mental health legislation

In the late 1990s, Australia piloted a Rights Analysis Instrument that was envisaged as a quality assurance device to assess whether national legislative practice met international standards. It used benchmarks provided by the UN Mental Illness Principles (Chapter 14.1.2.3). It is a tool that attempts to increase compliance through legal implementation of those measurable UN Principles that focus on civil and political rights, but also with some recognition of economic, social and cultural rights. It has been argued that the audit 'attempts to make the right to mental health operational, rather than merely rhetorical, by measuring its implementation at least in the narrow dimension of law' (Watchirs, 2005). The audit locates best legislative practices (e.g. model mental health tribunal procedures) that might be emulated elsewhere, as well as legal gaps that require remedying.

The pilot's 10 qualitative indicators are, therefore, based on justiciable rights taken from the UN Principles and cover many procedural and substantive issues. Notably, they address not only components of mental health law, but other laws that address questions of discrimination and human rights:

Indicator 1: Legislative objects and framework.

Indicator 2: Safeguards in mental health facilities.

Indicator 3: Determination of disorder and involuntary admission.

Indicator 4: Review body.

Indicator 5: Review process.

Indicator 6: Personal representative.

Indicator 7: Consent to general procedures.

Indicator 8: Consent to special procedures.

Indicator 9: Mental health treatment.

Indicator 10: Other laws.

Further information can be found in Watchirs (2005).

Certainly, the audit should be designed and conducted by people knowledgeable in the field of the audit. Some of our informants noted that in their countries, mental health audit was merely added on, almost as an afterthought, to the duties of people whose primary employment involved other matters and who had no obvious expertise relating to mental disability. Such an approach is unlikely to yield convincing or credible results.

While the actual leg work of conducting the audit may be done by government or contracted out to a consultant or private examiner, it is wise to ensure a reasonable separation between the person conducting the study and performing the analysis and the person or persons who are involved in the administration of the new law. Such a separation goes a considerable distance to ensuring both the actual impartiality of the audit (although there may still be a risk that the person performing the audit will provide results that the funder is perceived to want) and the appearance of impartiality. In much of the world, where services relating to people with mental disability are viewed with suspicion, such transparency and independence may be of considerable importance (Box 12.10).

Box 12.10 Policy Case Study: Georgia

In Georgia, there is a particularly clear example of such independence: audit and monitoring of facilities are performed not by the government at all but by independent non-governmental organisations. While such independent audit may not have as clear a direct effect on government, coming as it does from outside rather than inside the administrative structure, our correspondent in Tbilisi notes that the reports of the non-governmental organisations have been the subject of considerable media attention. In the right circumstances, such visibility may create helpful political pressure on the relevant government officials in a way that internal audits by government do not.

12.2 Participation: professional groups, service user organisations and carer organisations

While government will normally be the key player in ensuring enforcement and implementation of legislative change, it is not the only player.

For implementation to have credibility, it is desirable to include all stakeholders in the process. Certainly, professional bodies (such as medical professional bodies) are likely to be appropriate to involve, particularly where the provision of medical services is at issue (an example case study from Ukraine is shown in Box 12.11).

Box 12.11 Policy Case Study: Ukraine

The Ukrainian Psychiatric Association (UPA) is a non-governmental organisation founded in 1991. It was one of the first NGOs in the area of the former USSR in the period of Gorbachev and was established in order to promote legal and other advocacy for the human and civil rights of people with a mental health disability.

The goal of the UPA is to improve the quality of life for these individuals by advocating public policies that promote community integration, self-determination and support of individuals with mental disabilities and their families. It monitors the political abuse of psychiatry and undertakes advocacy activities. The specialised Expert Committee of the UPA provides social and legal support to Ukrainians making human rights claims to governmental structures. People seeking protection of their rights apply to the Committee. The Committee's team, consisting of psychiatrists, a forensic psychiatrist, a lawyer, a social worker and a forensic psychologist, provides assistance on a daily basis to all those who appeal to the Committee. The experts working in the Committee advocate the interests of people with mental disorders in the courts and provide juridical and social assistance to them.

The UPA also participates in round table discussions, press conferences and so on that are aimed at preventing the abuse of the human rights of psychiatric patients and their families. As the result of work with journalists, the earlier forbidden issue of psychiatry has become open and appeared in many newspapers and journals, TV and radio programmes, many of them including staff of the UPA. In this way they lobby the public opinion of the country.

It is also important that user organisations and carer organisations are involved in substantive – and not merely token – ways (for example, the useful guide from The Hamlet Trust in Box 12.12). Unlike professional bodies, which tend to exist in most of the world, user and carer organisations are much more intermittent in their existence, and it may be necessary to foster these organisations in some countries. This raises difficulties, since while funding of these bodies may of necessity have to come from government, the bodies must also be independent from government to be effective. Practical strategies to ensure such independence must be developed.

Box 12.12 Resource

The Hamlet Trust produced a toolkit, *Pathways to Policy: a toolkit for grassroots involvement in mental health policy* (Bureau and Shears, 2007), that provides a robust framework for establishing policy that allows people with mental health problems to have a real voice in policy-making. It includes training materials that can be applied in a wide variety of contexts and discusses such topics as highlighting deficiencies in legislation and its implementation, as well as building awareness of mental health service users' rights.

The toolkit is available for download at: www.nsue.ie (www.nsue.ie/m/uploads/files/PathwaystoPolicyToolkitfinal.pdf).

The UN Convention on the Rights of Persons with Disabilities (CRPD) provides new impetus for the involvement of civil society (particularly people with disabilities and their representative organisations) in legislative and policy transformation (existing examples – case studies on Cyprus and Denmark – are shown in Boxes 12.13 and 12.14). It specifies that civil society, in particular persons with disabilities and their representative organisations, 'shall be involved and participate fully' in monitoring the implementation of the CRPD (Article 33 – National implementation and monitoring). In other words, any State that has ratified the CRPD must ensure that people with disabilities – through their representative organisations – are closely consulted and actively involved in both the development and the implementation of any law or policy that affects them.

The Mental Disability Advocacy Center has developed practical guidelines (MDAC, 2011) on the implementation and monitoring of Article 33 of the CRPD (Box 12.15).

Box 12.13 Legislative Case Study: Cyprus

The Law regarding the Consultation Procedure between State and other Services on Matters concerning Persons with Disabilities (L143(1)/2006) specifies that each service exercising public authority and examining any subject concerning persons with disabilities is obliged to confer with the Cyprus Confederation of Organisations of the Disabled. This Confederation has been established as the official social partner of the state on matters concerning people with disabilities.

Box 12.14 Legislative Case Study: Denmark

Local government reform in January 2007 has required all municipalities to establish disability councils, where half of the members are from disability organisations and half are municipal politicians or civil servants. The disability councils were set up in order to involve organisations of disabled people in local decisions and to ensure a qualified advisory service be available to decision-makers and administrators in the field of disability. As a result, a large number of local authorities are now formulating a local disability policy. Although there were already local councils for employment of disabled people, this will give an increased attention on disability matters in the municipalities.

(Taken from Priestley, 2010)

Box 12.15 Resource

The Mental Disability Advocacy Center guidelines on the implementation and monitoring of Article 33 of the CRPD also provides recommendations about how to ensure that people with disabilities, and their representative organisations, are meaningfully involved in the development and implementation of any law or policy that affects them.

The guidelines are available for download at: www.mdac.info/reports

12.2.1 Service user organisations and carer organisations

It is worth emphasising that service user organisations and carer organisations represent quite different groups of people. Certainly, some carers will also be service users and vice versa, but this is often not the case. While the same legislation can be used to combat the discrimination that family and friends of people with mental health problems can experience by virtue of their association with people with mental health problems (Chapter 2.3.4), often legislative approaches to improving the lives of mental health service users and the lives of carers/family members of mental health service users will need to diverge (Berzins, 2003; Venkatarman and McSherry, 2010). It is important to acknowledge that the needs and interests of the groups are often substantially different (Box 12.16), and this should be recognised in the fostering of service user and carer/family organisations.

Box 12.16 Legislative Case Study: Scotland

When revising its mental health legislation in 2003, Scotland removed the role of family members in compulsory admittance to mental health care, since it believed that this had the potential to cause conflict between the relative and the person with the mental health problem.

12.2.2 Service user leadership and involvement

Involving users of mental health services is, then, a matter of social justice. Such involvement brings additional benefits: it can reduce social exclusion, provide new perspectives on how services can be organised and developed and produce new knowledge about mental health and disability. One important development that has taken place in the last quarter century is in mental health service user-led research (i.e. research in which service users take the lead in defining the research question, the methods and the analysis of data). Service user leadership in research can make an important contribution to the empowerment of all people with mental health problems by contributing to the development of innovative methods of addressing important issues in mental health service users' lives – thereby advancing conceptual debates regarding the rights and entitlements of people with mental health problems (Sweeney *et al.*,2009; Wallcraft *et al.*, 2009).

There are a number of ways in which policy-makers and legislators can assist in strengthening service user empowerment and leadership in research and related activities (some suggestions are given in Callard and Rose, in press; also in Box 12.17). Building the capacity of service users in research can also allow service users to have a greater voice in legislative and policy transformation.

Box 12.17 Resource

England

The Department of Health set up and funds INVOLVE, a national advisory group which supports greater public involvement in NHS, public health and social care research – so as to improve the way that research is prioritised, commissioned, undertaken, communicated and used. It has significantly strengthened service user and carer involvement in research.

http://www.invo.org.uk

12.3 Inspections and visitation

While administrative audit is important, it does not take the place of visitation and inspection of institutional environments to find out what is happening on the ground. Inspection should be by individuals who receive appropriate training and are sufficiently removed from the governance structures of the institution to ensure objectivity. The involvement of professional groups, user groups and carer groups in providing personnel for these inspections may well be appropriate.

Sometimes these inspections are the function of government-related organisations, as is the case in Great Britain as well as the Republic of Ireland (Boxes 12.18 and 12.19).

Box 12.18 Legislative Case Study: Great Britain

England and Wales

Inspections were performed until 2009 by the Mental Health Act Commission (MHAC), which published biennial reports about the situation of people in psychiatric institutions. More recently, the MHAC has been absorbed into the Care Quality Commission (CQC), a larger government-related body that looks at care provision more broadly than in the psychiatric inpatient sphere. Certainly, there will be advantages to this, as the newer body will not be as constrained by arbitrary lines as to how an individual is classified in the institution in which he or she is located, but the placement of these investigations into this broader framework makes the mental health concerns a smaller fish in a bigger pond. It remains to be seen whether the benefits outweigh the disadvantages.

The biennial reports of the MHAC are available on the CQC web site, www.cqc.org.uk The reports demonstrate how service users were embedded within all activities of the MHAC. They are, therefore, a rich resource for others planning how to ensure that service users have a substantive role in monitoring and inspection activities.

Scotland

By comparison, Scotland has kept its Mental Health Commission separate. It is probably safe to say that the appropriate arrangement of the monitoring services will depend on the local circumstances. In all cases, however, a reasonable independence from the institutions and institutional structures under investigation is vital if the process is to have credibility.

Box 12.19 Legislative Case Study: Republic of Ireland

The Inspectorate of Mental Health Services is required by law (Mental Health Act, 2001, s.51(1)(a)) to visit and inspect every approved centre annually and, as the Inspectorate think appropriate, to visit and inspect any other premises where mental health services are being provided. As part of its inspections, the Inspectorate meets with service users, who are given the opportunity to report any allegations of abuse with the mental health services.

Further details on the Inspectorate and to access a copy of the Mental Health Act 2001 and relevant guidance notes and regulations are available via the Mental Health Commission web site: www.mhcirl.ie

Inspections do not need to be the work of government or government-related agencies, however. Increasingly, organisations established under international law are engaging in visitation and monitoring work. A particularly good example is the Committee for the Prevention of Torture and Inhuman or Degrading Treatment or Punishment (CPT), established in the Council of Europe (COE) (www.cpt/coe/int/en; Chapter 14.2.1.1.2). This body makes routine visits to places where people are, or are believed to be, detained in COE member countries, and makes reports to the relevant governments. These reports are posted on the Committee's website in due course. The Committee reports on standards and the provision of rights in psychiatric institutions, and indeed has a published set of standards regarding such institutions (Chapter 14.2.1.1.2). It also reports on the situation of people with psychiatric difficulties detained in non-psychiatric facilities.

Another powerful mechanism is the Optional Protocol to the UN Convention against Torture (OPCAT) (Chapter 14.1.1.3; Box 12.20), since those countries that have ratified OPCAT are under a legal duty to develop inspectorates of institutions. One priority for those committed to the use of UN conventions to improve the lives of people with mental illness is to encourage more countries to ratify OPCAT.

Box 12.20 Resource

The Association for the Prevention of Torture has developed The Optional Protocol to the UN Convention against Torture: Implementation Manual (APT/IIHR, 2010). The manual aims to support and strengthen the work of international, regional and national actors involved in OPCAT ratification and implementation. It emphasises the process and challenges of implementing the OPCAT and provides concrete examples of good practice drawn from around the world.

The Manual can be downloaded at: www.apt.ch (www.apt.ch/index.php?option=com_docman&task=cat_view&gid=239&Itemid=256&lang=en).

Non-governmental organisations and similar organisations can also organise visits and monitoring (Boxes 12.21 and 12.22). Again, this will be particularly helpful in countries where no other organised system of inspections exists, or where a government-based system does not enjoy public confidence.

Box 12.21 Resource

A useful handbook for inspections is published by the Mental Disability Advocacy Center (MDAC, 2006). It presents a checklist of eight requirements that MDAC has developed for establishing inspectorates of mental health and social care institutions. These requirements will help to ensure that inspectorates are able to function effectively so that 'people with disabilities and detained in insituations will become less vulnerable to abuse and neglect; they will become more visible to the protective gaze of society, their voices will be heard, services consequently improved and abuses remedied' (MDAC, 2006). The requirements are:

1 Ratify the Optional Protocol to the UN Convention against Torture (OPCAT).
2 Establish inspectorates with a legal mandate.
3 Ensure inspectorates are independent.
4 Recruit qualified and experienced inspectors.
5 Ensure that visits are effective.
6 Publish comprehensive reports.
7 Ensure maximum impact.
8 Coordinate activities.

The handbook (Inspect! Inspectorates of Mental Health and Social Care Institutions in the European Union) is available via http://mdac.info (http://mdac.info/documents/122_Inspect.pdf).

Box 12.22 Resource

The ITHACA study – Institutional Treatment, Human Rights and Care Assessment – has produced a toolkit (ITHACA Project Group, 2010) that provides information on monitoring practices, explains appropriate human rights literature and conventions and outlines an on-site visit audit. It is significantly shaped by the provisions laid out in the UN Convention on the Rights of Persons with Disabilities.

Audit/monitoring visits will involve a team of monitors to observe the physical conditions and the quality of care received by service users. In addition, monitors will conduct interviews with residents, staff and institution directors and examine relevant documentation. The data collected from these visits will be compiled into reports for people involved at all levels with mental health care – from service users and family members to support/care staff and government officials. Local and international advocacy groups can use the findings as evidence for lobbying and initiating change within systems that produce human rights violations.

The Toolkit for Monitoring Human Rights and General Health Care in Mental Health and Social Care Institutions is available for download at: www.ithacastudy.eu

Most mental health commissions are established to carry out inspectorial and regulatory functions. However, there is growing interest in how mental health commissions can take on a 'wider, more systemic mandate', so as to focus 'on a more positive agenda of encouraging service users and providers in their aspirations for service development, and persuading governments to commit to sorely needed enhancements' (Rosen *et al.*, 2010). The Mental Health Commission in New Zealand (Box 12.23), which began work in 1996 with this wider mandate, has been credited with bringing real momentum and focus to the process of mental health reform in that country. Crucially, it remains independent of government, though it works productively with government, as well as with providers and mental health service users.

Box 12.23 Legislative Case Study: New Zealand

The function of the Mental Health Commission, as specified in the Mental Health Commission Act 1998, no. 5, includes:

- reporting to the Minster on the implementation of the National Mental Health Strategy;
- working with all those involved in the care and treatment of people with mental illness and their families and caregivers:
  - **(i)** to promote better understanding, by the community, of mental illness; and
  - **(ii)** to reduce the stigma associated with mental illness and the prejudice shown to people with mental illness and their families and caregivers; and
  - **(iii)** to eliminate discrimination on the ground of mental illness against people with mental illness and their families and caregivers; and
  - **(iv)** to promote employment in the mental health field as a desirable career choice; and
  - **(v)** to work with all those involved in training for employment in the mental health field (a) to promote the provision of training opportunities of an appropriate range and quality; and (b) to promote the obtaining and maintaining, by people employed in the mental health field, of skills of an appropriate range and quality.

Some of its central achievements have been characterised (Saville-Smith, 2002) as:

- significant increases in the funding directed to mental health services;
- new mechanisms in the health sector to prioritise and plan for improved access to mental health services;
- a new paradigm for an integrated mental health service;
- promotion of and mechanisms for developing the mental health workforce;
- anti-discrimination initiatives via implementation of local community and mass media campaigns;
- an active recognition of the need for service models that address the special needs of diverse communities, particularly Maori and Pacific peoples;
- the importance of service users and their families in the planning, specification and delivery of mental health services;
- the development and promulgation of the recovery paradigm;
- identification of gaps in service provision, costing of the gaps and encouragement of government to bridge gaps in provision;
- undertaking independent reviews on behalf of the Minister and vertical reviews to identify systemic performance issues;
- engaging with mental health services through its programme of visits;
- promoting the service user voice and the skills of service users in the context of mental health service development.

Further discussion of the Mental Health Commission is given by Rosen *et al.* (2004, 2010). Two examples of the Commission's work in addressing discrimination are: Mental Health Commission (2004, 2005). The Commission's website is: www.mhc.govt.nz

12.4 Hearings

It is often appropriate to provide individuals with a forum to press their own cases. Indeed, for much anti-discrimination law, the provision of such a forum is a significant part of the legal reform itself. If a person believes himself or herself to be the subject of unfair discrimination, he or she can bring a legal case and demand satisfaction – generally the payment of money, or sometimes to be placed in the situation he or she would have been in but for the unfair discrimination.

The most traditional mechanism to provide such redress is a court. While virtually all countries use courts for some purposes, in many contexts review tribunals are also used. This is often the case where a detailed knowledge of a specific area of law will be at issue. Thus, it is frequent for employment-related matters to go, at least initially, to an employment tribunal, not to the courts directly. Similarly, matters relating to anti-discrimination law often go to tribunals that specialise in – and are restricted to – this area. The advantages of this approach are that the specialist tribunal becomes more expert in specific areas of law and members of the tribunal can be selected because of their specific expertise. Frequently, membership is not restricted to judges, but may include lay people, lawyers, or other professionals (although usually they are chaired by a lawyer or judge). Tribunals are often less formal than courts, and often less expensive. The disadvantage is that it is often thought appropriate to restrict the redress they can give. Their mandate will also usually be restricted to enforcement of specific legislation, creating problems if a complaint raises issues both inside and outside that legislation. In that case, a tribunal hearing and a court hearing may both be necessary, which is wasteful and gives rise to potentially inconsistent results.

The choice between courts and tribunals, and how to frame the mandate of a tribunal if that option is chosen, varies between countries and between legislative contexts. It is important to remember, however, that even if a specialist tribunal is chosen to implement specific legislation, the members may require training on issues related to mental disability. Just because an individual is appointed to an employment tribunal, for example, it does not follow that he or she understands the issues particularly relevant to mental disability in employment.

How successful the court or tribunal will be in furthering the rights of people with mental disabilities will depend on many factors. Certainly, the legal culture of the jurisdiction will be relevant. Thus, in countries with traditions of judicial activism, courts may be of more assistance. Many of the significant rights breakthroughs in the United States, for example, have been through litigation, but our country-based informants have also provided encouraging examples from, for example, India (Box 12.24) and Sri Lanka.

Box 12.24 Legislative Case Study: India

The National Human Rights Commission (NHRC) has a member (usually a retired Supreme Court judge) specifically designated for matters relating to mental health. The NHRC has played a critical role in addressing the problems of people with mental health problems in India, particularly in the area of mental hospital reform.

The mainstream judicial system in India has also played a crucial role in combating the discrimination and abuse experienced by individuals with mental disorders. The higher judiciary is invested with a potent and comprehensive writ jurisdiction. The Indian courts have been very proactive in this regard, particularly through public interest litigation, which can be initiated by any concerned citizen or non-governmental organisation.

Historical and legal contextualisation regarding India can be found in Dhanda (2000, 2005) and Kala and Kala (2007).

Some of the possibilities for success may flow from more specific aspects of legal culture. It would seem that common law jurisdictions such as the United States, Canada and England are particularly hesitant about making findings that would require the spending of government money to improve the situation of people with mental health problems and other mental disabilities. It would seem that this is not a reticence necessarily found in some South American countries – countries with lower GDPs than the common law examples, and where the money to fund the improvements is presumably, therefore, tighter.

Courts and tribunals often constitute a vast administrative system and their effectiveness raises many of the same questions as are raised in this chapter about the effectiveness of enforcement of litigation. Thus, it may well make sense for many of the mechanisms discussed in this chapter to be applied equally to courts and tribunals – audit, the use of user pressure groups, visitation and monitoring, for example. Sadly, this does not generally happen. There are admirable exceptions in unusual circumstances – the role of the Black Sash at recording the role of the courts in apartheid South Africa for example – but too frequently, courts are viewed as above criticism. This is unfortunate, as there is evidence that courts do not necessarily do an adequate job at defending and promoting the rights of people with mental disabilities (for example, see the reports (2006–2008) of the Mental Disability Advocacy Center (MDAC) into guardianship, as well as *Liberty Denied*, the report of MDAC into trial proceedings in Hungary – all available at www.mdac.info).

12.5 National Human Rights Institutions (NHRIs)

National Human Rights Institutions (NHRIs) are bodies to promote and protect human rights, established by countries under their national legislation or under their constitutions. NHRIs are responsible for promoting and monitoring the effective implementation of international human rights standards at the national level. The United Nations Paris Principles (Box 12.25), which are internationally recognised standards that have been adopted by the United Nations General Assembly, specify that NHRIs should be independent from government and representative of civil society. While the specific mandate of NHRIs differs from country to country, their activities include: providing guidance on human rights issues to government; conducting inquiries; receiving individual complaints; launching investigations; intervening in court cases; advising on legislation; and developing strategies and policies to strength human rights. NHRIs include human rights commissions, ombudsman institutions, and a hybrid form (single-office holder human rights ombudsman/commissioners).

Box 12.25 Standards

Principles relating to the Status of National Institutions (The Paris Principles), adopted by General Assembly resolution 48/134 of 20 December 1993:
www2.ohchr.org/english/law/parisprinciples.htm

12.5.1 Ombudsmen

In some countries, ombudsmen are charged with the authority to consider issues related to alleged unfair treatment at the hands of government, including unfair treatment based on an individual's mental disability. In these systems, usually the ombudsman will have the legal authority to examine the facts of the case. This can be a considerable advantage, as the ombudsman may have more extensive access to records than the complainant, and may have specialised skills in this sort of examination. Such complaints are also generally free, and since there is not necessarily a need to hire a lawyer to pursue these complaints, they may be a practical and effective way forward for people who believe their rights have been violated. Denmark (Box 12.26), Ireland and Lithuania, for example, allow complaints against public bodies in this way.

Box 12.26 Legislative Case Study: Denmark

The Danish Administrative Law contains a principle of equality that prohibits identical cases to be treated differently. A person can lodge a complaint with the Danish Parliamentary Ombudsman if he/she feels that he/she has been treated differently from a person in a similar situation. The Ombudsman's jurisdiction extends to all parts of the public administration except the court system.

The Ombudsman also considers cases on his or her own initiative, for instance about matters that have been mentioned in the media.

For further information: http://en.ombudsmanden.dk

There may, nonetheless, be problems. An ombudsman will be subject to the legislation that creates the post. Frequently, their jurisdiction is limited to complaints against government or government officials: they may not have jurisdiction to consider discrimination or unfair treatment that occurs in the private sector. Some statutes also limit the remedies that ombudsmen may give. Sometimes monetary damages may not be given, for example, and sometimes the report of an ombudsman is merely a recommendation to the government, rather than an enforceable order. Even 'successful' complainants may thus come out with nothing. Finally, ombudsmen's offices are often understaffed, with long waiting times before complaints are dealt with. The ombudsman may further have considerable discretion as to what cases he or she wishes to investigate, and if the ombudsman refuses a case, there may be little a complainant may do about it.

Ombudsmen are a particularly formalised type of complaint mechanism. Many other organisations (both in government and in the private sector) have complaints mechanisms and these will vary considerably in their format. It is not always the case, for example, that the organisation complained to will view it as its job to investigate the complaint: often, it is up to the complainant to provide the evidence in support of his or her complaint. This raises difficulties if the complainant does not have access to key documents. The legal structure of these complaint mechanisms may also vary considerably in their formality: some mechanisms have strong legal foundations in statute law; others are informal arrangements that have grown up by practice over time. This will, of course, affect the enforceability of any result obtained. A mechanism that is backed by statute may be able to give enforceable decisions, where an informal complaint mechanism may be merely advisory.

12.5.2 Human Rights Commissions

Other countries and jurisdictions will have human rights commissions (Boxes 12.27 and 12.28 show examples from Canada and Indonesia), which like ombudsmen, vary significantly in their ability to protect and advance the human rights of people with mental health problems.

Box 12.27 Legislative and Policy Case Study: Canada, Province of Ontario.

Ontario's Human Rights Code – the first in Canada – was enacted in 1962. The Code protects people in Ontario against discrimination, including on grounds of disability. The Ontario Human Rights Commission (OHRC) is an independent statutory body, which was established in 1961 to administer the Code and to provide leadership for the promotion, protection and advancement of human rights.

The OHRC is currently developing a human rights mental health strategy that will address systemic areas of discrimination affecting people with mental health disabilities. See the section on 'mental health' on the web site: www.ohrc.on.ca

Box 12.28 Legislative Case Study: Indonesia

The National Human Rights Commission in Indonesia did not focus its attention on the rights of people with mental health problems when it was first founded in 1993. However, in the last few years, it has taken greater interest in the intersection of human rights and health – in large part because of the efforts of the Advocacy and Human Rights Working Group of the National Taskforce on Mental Health System Development in Indonesia (Irmansyah *et al.*, 2009).

12.6 Other complaints mechanisms

There are a variety of other complaints mechanisms (such as national hotlines, Box 12.29, as well as legislative provisions ensuring the right to complain, Box 12.30) to address experiences of discrimination and abuse, as well as unacceptable experiences of health and social care.

Box 12.29 Policy Case Study: Australia

A national hotline exists (the National Disability Abuse and Neglect Hotline) for reporting or complaining about the abuse or neglect of a person with disability using government-funded services (for example, open or supported employment, accommodation, community and respite care services). If a caller reports abuse or neglect in a government-funded service, the Hotline staff will refer the report to the government body that funds the service. The funding body will investigate the report.

For further information: www.disabilityhotline.org

Box 12.30 Legislative Case Study: Denmark

Patients have the right to complain in relation to psychiatric care.

Order No. 1303 of 14 December 2004, on the rules applicable to complaints boards for psychiatric patients, includes the right of complaint and guidance with respect to complaints.

Order No. 1337 of 15 December 2004, on patient influence on psychiatric hospitals and wards, requires persons in charge of psychiatric hospitals and wards to provide opportunities for patients to express their views on matters affecting their stay in hospital (general care, leisure facilities, accommodation, equipment etc.).

12.7 Advocacy

The law discussed in this book, like so much law, can be complex. Just as people without disabilities may need assistance in navigating legal channels, so people with mental disabilities may require advice and assistance. Advocacy is likely to be a part of any serious legislative reform related to anti-discrimination.

Advocacy can take many forms. Sometimes, it is built into the tribunal structure, as part of the legislative reform. Thus, the Ontario Human Rights Code provides that the Ontario Human Rights Commission (established by the Code) will have staff to investigate complaints, including complaints related to discrimination based on mental disability. Where such complaints are found to be potentially warranted, the Commission provides a lawyer to represent the complainant before a review tribunal. While this has obvious benefits for the complainant – he or she gets the required legal representation without charge and has the advantage of professional investigation of his or her complaint – there are also disadvantages. Waiting times for complaints to be dealt with have been excessive in the past, for example. Furthermore, the complainant may lose control of the complaints process: the progress of a potentially meritorious complaint may well be affected by the initial views of the investigator, or by whether the organisation views the particular complaint as being of a sort that is of priority to the organisation at a given time.

Some countries, including Canada, The Netherlands, England and Wales, have developed institutional advocates. These may be professional or lay advocates (an innovative example from Sweden is shown in Box 12.31), often with a history of mental disability themselves, who work in institutional settings in which people with mental disabilities may be housed. Their role is defined by their country's specific legislation, but it will generally include the provision of rights advice, advocacy on the individual's behalf within the institutional context and, where appropriate, referral to a lawyer outside the institution in the event that litigation is needed. As with the other enforcement mechanisms discussed in this chapter, it is likely to be of pivotal importance that the advocates be subject to an administrative structure that is insulated from the organisation to which representations will be made. Hospital advocates should not be employed by the hospital and subject to its medical director, for example, as this creates a clear conflict of interest, and the robustness with which the advocate makes representations risks being affected.

Box 12.31 Policy Case Study: Sweden

Sweden has developed a service user-run 'Personal Ombud' service for psychiatric patients. This service emerged in the context of wider psychiatric reform in the mid-1990s. The Personal Ombud (PO) has no tie to psychiatry, social services or to any other authority, including the patient's family members or anyone else in the patient's network. The PO usually works with his/her client for several years in order to develop a trusting, one-to-one relationship. The PO system has a particular focus on supporting psychiatric patients who are usually deemed the 'hardest to reach' and the most marginalised and excluded (e.g. homeless people who have received psychotic diagnoses). The PO service in the city of Skåne is of particular interest: most of the POs there are employed by PO-Skåne, an independent non-governmental organisation that is run by a service user-led organisation (RSMH – the Swedish National Association for Social and Mental Health) and the family organisation IFS (Schizophrenia Fellowship Association). All POs at PO-Skåne are highly trained – many are social workers, some are lawyers – and they are able to argue effectively for their clients' rights in court or in front of authorities. The PO-Skåne service is financed two-thirds by the state and one-third by the community.

For further information: www.po-skane.org (www.po-skane.org/ombudsman-for-psychiatric-patients-30.php)

Statistically, people with mental disabilities may often be of very limited economic means, so that when a lawyer is necessary, the provision of legal aid is often vital. Legal aid will often be conditional on the resources of the client to pay for representation ('means tested'). Some jurisdictions, however (such as England and Wales, and Tajikistan), provide legal aid for civil detention hearings as a matter of right: whatever the client's assets, the state pays the lawyer's fees. This has the advantage of not delaying the confinement hearing pending determination of means-tested legal aid eligibility. Either way, there is a serious issue about how the person with mental disability will know to exercise their right to a lawyer, particularly in situations where more grass-roots level advocacy is not provided (one innovative example from New Zealand is given in Box 12.32).

Box 12.32 Policy Case Study: New Zealand

One response to regular reports from disabled people about the challenges of being expected to represent themselves has been the establishment of a pilot 'Special Circumstances Court', set up in 2010 in Auckland. It is a special solution-focused court that is designed to 'aid in the reduction of chronic public space offending in Auckland's inner city by those who are homeless . . . and have ongoing mental illness and/or addictions, or who are mentally impaired through either injury or disability' (Human Rights Commission, 2010).

Sometimes, a specialist lawyer service is provided as a mechanism in itself to address discrimination (Box 12.33).

Box 12.33 Policy Case Study: Canada, province of Ontario

As part of Ontario's response to the UN International Year of the Handicapped (1976), the government created a legal clinic, ARCH (the Advocacy Resource Centre for the Handicapped). This is composed of lawyers and paralegals and has been engaged primarily in targeted litigation to further the rights of people with disabilities since that time. It has been responsible for much of the important litigation concerning the rights of people with mental disabilities in Ontario for more than thirty years.

For further information: www.archdisabilitylaw.ca

References

APT/IIHR (Association for the Prevention of Torture/Inter-American Institute of Human Rights) (2010) Optional Protocol to the UN Convention against Torture: Implementation Manual. Association for the Prevention of Torture (APT) and Inter-American Institute for Human Rights (IIHR), Geneva, Switzerland and San José, Costa Rica.

Bartlett, P and Hamzic, V (2010) Reforming mental disability law in Africa: practical tips and suggestions. Human Rights Centre, Nottingham, UK.

Berzins, K (2003) Legislation affecting carers of people with mental health problems. EU-FAMI (European Federation of Associations of Families of People with Mental Illness), Leuven, Belgium.

Bureau, J and Shears, J (2007) Pathways to Policy: A toolkit for grassroots involvement in mental health policy. Hamlet Trust, London.

Callard, F and Rose, D (in press) The mental health strategy for Europe: why service user leadership in research is indispensable. *Journal of Mental Health.*

Centre for Disability Law & Policy (2010) Summary of critical success factors for implementing and monitoring national disability strategies. National University of Ireland, Galway.

Dhanda, A (2000) *Legal Order and Mental Disorder*. Sage, New Delhi and London.

Dhanda, A (2005) The right to treatment of persons with psychosocial disabilities and the role of the courts. *International Journal of Law and Psychiatry,* **28**:155–170.

Faunce, TA (2005) Collaborative research trials: a strategy for fostering mental health protections in developing nations. *International Journal of Law and Psychiatry,* **28**: 171–181.

Flynn, E (2011) *From Rhetoric to Action: Implementing the UN Convention on the Rights of Persons with Disabilities*. Cambridge University Press, Cambridge.

Human Rights Commission (2010) *Human Rights in New Zealand 2010*. Human Rights Commission, New Zealand.

Irmansyah, I, Prasetyo, Y and Minas, H (2009) Human rights of persons with mental illness in Indonesia: more than legislation is needed. *International Journal of Mental Health Systems,* **3**(1):14.

ITHACA Project Group (2010) ITHACA Toolkit for Monitoring Human Rights and General Health Care in Mental Health and Social Care Institutions. Health Service and Population Research Department, Institute of Psychiatry, King's College London, UK.

Jenkins, R, Mussa, M, Haji, S, Haji, MS, Salim, A, Suleiman, S, *et al.* (2011) Developing and implementing mental health policy in Zanzibar, a low income country off the coast of East Africa. *Int J Ment Health Syst,* **5**(6).

Kala, K and Kala, AK (2007) Mental health legislation in contemporary India: a critical review. *International Psychiatry: Bulletin of the Board of International Affairs of the Royal College of Psychiatrists,* **4**(3):69–71.

MDAC (Mental Disability Advocacy Center) (2006) Inspect! Inspectorates of Mental Health and Social Care Institutions in the European Union. Mental Disability Advocacy Center, Hungary.

MDAC (Mental Disability Advocacy Center) (2011) Building the Architecture for Change: Guidelines on Article 33 of the UN Convention on the rights of Persons with Disabilities. Mental Disability Advocacy Center, Hungary .

Mendis, N (2004) Mental health services in Sri Lanka. *International Psychiatry: Bulletin of the Board of International Affairs of the Royal College of Psychiatrists,* **3**:10–12.

Mental Health Commission (2004) Journeys towards equality: taking stock of New Zealand's efforts to reduce discrimination against people with experience of mental illness. Mental Health Commission, Wellington, New Zealand.

Mental Health Commission (2005) Reducing discrimination against people with mental illness / Te Hekenga: Whakamana i te Tangata Whaiora: Multi-Agency Plan 2005–2007. Mental Health Commission, Wellington, New Zealand.

MHaPP (Mental Health and Policy Project) (n.d.) Policy Brief: Developing effective mental health policies and plans in Africa. 7 key lessons. Available from: http://www.who.int/mental_health/policy/development/MHPB8.pdf [accessed 19 April 2011].

Ministry of Health (2001) National Mental Health Plan, Strategy to Strengthen Mental Health Care in Sri Lanka. Ministry of Health, Colombo, Sri Lanka.

Omar, MA, Green, AT, Bird, PK, Mirzoev, T, Flisher, AJ, Kigozi, F, *et al.* (2010) Mental health policy process: a comparative study of Ghana, South Africa, Uganda and Zambia. *Int J Ment Health Syst*, **4**:24.

Priestley, M (2010) Synthesis report on disability mainstreaming in the 2008–2010 National Strategy Reports for Social Protection and Social Inclusion (NSRs): Academic Network of European Disability experts (ANED).

Rosen, A, McGorry, P, Groom, G, Hickie, I, Gurr, R, Hocking, B, *et al.* (2004) Australia needs a mental health commission. *Australasian Psychiatry*, **12**(3):213–219.

Rosen, A, Goldbloom, D and McGeorge, P (2010) Mental Health Commissions: making the critical difference to the development and reform of mental health services. *Current Opinion in Psychiatry*, **23**(6):593–603.

Saville-Smith, K (2002) A Strategic Analysis of the Role, Functions and Focus of the Mental Health Commission. Mental Health Commission, Wellington, New Zealand.

Sweeney, A, Beresford, P, Faulkner, A, Nettle, M and Rose, D (eds) (2009) *This is Survivor Research*. PCCS Books, Ross-on-Wye, UK.

Venkatarman, P and McSherry, B (2010) Incorporating carers' rights in mental health legislation. *J Law Med*, **17**(4):481–486.

Wallcraft, J, Schrank, B and Amering, M (2009) (eds) *Handbook of Service User Involvement in Mental Health Research*. John Wiley & Sons Ltd, Chichester.

Watchirs, H (2005) Human rights audit of mental health legislation–results of an Australian pilot. *International Journal of Law and Psychiatry*, **28**:99–125.

CHAPTER 13
Summary and Conclusions

> 'In the complicated setting of mental health care, it is clearly essential that involuntary detention is appropriately regulated and monitored, so as to preserve the individual's right to liberty. An exclusive focus on this right alone, however, fails to address or even acknowledge a range of broader social injustices and denials of human rights commonly experienced by individuals with enduring mental illness.'
>
> (Kelly, 2007)

The quotation from Brendan Kelly, a psychiatrist who has written extensively about social justice in relation to mental health, emphasises that if we focus exclusively on the critical protection of human rights in situations of involuntary psychiatric detention, we shall find it impossible fully to recognise – let alone to address – those 'broader social injustices and denials of human rights' that are commonly experienced by people with mental health problems. Kelly borrows the phrase 'structural violence' from the anthropologist Paul Farmer (2004) and applies it in the context of mental health. Such 'structural violence' means that people with severe mental illness are, because of 'overarching social and economic circumstances, . . . systematically excluded from full participation in civic and social life, and are constrained to live lives that are shaped, in large part, by stigma, isolation, homelessness and the denial of basic human rights' (Kelly, 2005). He presents us with a harsh vision of the lives of many people with severe mental illness. He also presents us with a seemingly difficult scenario – 'overarching social and economic circumstances' – in which it might be possible to intervene.

In this book, we have provided numerous examples of the 'systematic exclusion' and 'structural violence' that many people with mental health problems experience. They (as well as their families and friends) can often be victims of negative discrimination, harassment, violence and abuse. Discrimination and abuse can occur in all walks of life: in seeking and keeping jobs, in housing, in education, in health care, in political

---

Mental Illness, Discrimination and the Law: Fighting for Social Justice, First Edition.
Felicity Callard, Norman Sartorius, Julio Arboleda-Flórez, Peter Bartlett, Hanfried Helmchen, Heather Stuart, Jose Taborda and Graham Thornicroft.

participation, and in undertaking legally-binding actions within the law. If people, as well as having mental health problems, are also from minority ethnic groups, are migrants or refugees, are women, are children, or are from sexual minorities, this discrimination can be compounded. Through a complex mix of legislative, social and economic processes, the capabilities (in Amartya Sen's (2009) sense of this term) that many people with mental health problems across the globe are able to enjoy are undoubtedly constrained and reduced.

In a number of chapters in this book, we have given specific examples of how the civil, political and social rights of people with mental health problems can be withheld, undermined and not recognised. These rights violations can take place through designations of legal incapacity that result in plenary guardianship and hence 'civil death' (Chapter 4), through discriminatory access to healthcare (Chapter 9) and housing (Chapter 7) and through inadequate social services and social protection (Chapter 8). They can also take place – though many still refuse to acknowledge this as a rights violation – through the use of charity-focused, social welfare programmes that frequently result in the provision of separate, segregated services (e.g. sheltered workshops, education in separate settings). In the course of the book, we have also argued that significant social and economic inequalities – both within and across countries – can have serious impacts on the mental health of groups, communities and individuals. It is only relatively recently that policy-makers, researchers and advocacy organisations have begun seriously to grapple with the complex two-way relationship between poverty and mental disability in both low- and high-income countries.

The high prevalence of mental illnesses and poor mental health are, then, major issues – for the whole of society as well as in relation to public health. Mental illnesses can not only bring with them untold suffering for the people experiencing them, as well as for those close to them, but also carry significant social, economic and legal losses. If people do not have adequate access to appropriate health care, as well as to other sources of (formal and informal) support, mental illnesses can result in lasting impairments and disability.

We have, then, indicated some formidable obstacles to social justice for people with mental health problems. But our book is not intended to be a sombre one. Rather, we write with optimism, for our key aim within the book has been to demonstrate the role that legislative reform can play, and is playing, in combating some of these human rights violations and social injustices.

Much of the this new international and country-based law has come into the world in large part owing to the struggle, advocacy and perseverance of people with mental health problems, their families and advocates (both within and outside of the mental health field). The United Nations Convention on the Rights of Persons with Disabilities has given significant added energy and authority to the diverse groups who are advocating – in countries across the world – for legislative and policy change. But while in certain communities there is growing knowledge of and mobilisation around these new legislative tools, it is undoubtedly the case that much more capacity building needs to be done.

Many more people – not least mental health service users and all those who work within mental health and allied fields – need to become aware of these new legislative tools and this shift in focus to the positive rights of social participation. Many people remain stuck in the older model, in which they regard people receiving psychiatric treatment simply as 'mental patients'. The necessary shift that was indicated in the title of Liz Sayce's (2000) influential book, *From Psychiatric Patient to Citizen* – which was, we should note, written over a decade ago – has for many not yet taken place. There is often little awareness on the part of mental health staff – and indeed of mental health service users – of the rich array of legislative structures outside of the health sphere that can be used to protect and ensure the rights of people with mental health problems in a number of different domains.

We see this book, then, as a call to wake up and to mobilise. Most of us who have written this book work directly within the mental health field, where it is abundantly clear that there is need for much more engagement with and knowledge of legislation as a tool to push for social justice. We wrote this book intending for it to be a practical – and indeed policy-oriented – tool. We hope that both the conceptual arguments and the country-based and international examples can be taken up by readers in order to put pressure on their own governments, service providers, and other public, as well as private, bodies. For even if the legislative framework in any particular country is available and a good one, it is too often the case that implementation is inadequate or lacking. There are, of course, many countries in the world where legislative transformation of the kinds we have been describing in this book has been slower to take place or has not – in certain domains – even got off the ground. We hope, in these contexts, that the examples we have been provided here might act as a catalyst and inspiration, so as to engender new ideas for action.

Before closing, some of the main arguments that we have made in the course of this book are very briefly summarised. This is done by laying out 10 central principles that should be kept in mind when planning and implementing legislative action to combat the discrimination, abuse and social injustice experienced by people with mental health problems. We regard this list as a way to sharpen the conceptual tools that we might have at our disposal when responding to the 'call to action' that we hope that the content of this volume comprises.

1. The purview of potential legislative transformation should encompass multiple domains and should certainly not be confined to reforms in health law. If the main route to be taken is that of a disability anti-discrimination law, this law should be buttressed by additional laws in a number of sectors – such as housing, education – so as to provide a strong lattice of legislative mechanisms through which to move towards substantive equality for people with mental health problems.
2. Legislation must be accompanied by provisions and mechanisms that will enforce its implementation and application. There should, additionally, be policies across multiple sectors that will help not only to embed within society the legislative changes, but the principles of equality and non-discrimination that underpin them. Provisions to enforce the application of legislation should ensure that there is not an over-reliance on mechanisms that require individuals who have been wronged to seek redress. Instead, thought should be given to establishing enforceable duties upon sectors and bodies to protect and promote the rights of people with mental health problems to participate (in educational establishments, in the workplace etc.) on an equal basis with others.
3. Legislative reform needs to go hand in hand with enhancing direct political participation by people with mental health problems. Powerful mechanisms include upholding the right of people with mental health problems to vote and ensuring that people with mental health problems are actively involved in developing, implementing and monitoring legislation and policy relating to them. Any legislative and policy reforms should ensure that mental health service users (and their representative organisations) can be meaningfully involved in these reforms – and not merely 'consulted' in a tokenistic way. Such meaningful involvement should be seen both as a matter of social justice and as a pragmatic tool through which to increase the likelihood that transformations will be beneficial, effective and welcomed by those affected by them.
4. All legislative reform should recognise the capacity of people with mental health problems and should seek to support and encourage the exercise of people's capacity.
5. Legislative action requires the support of a number of key stakeholders for it to be successful. While government will usually be the key player in ensuring the successful implementation and enforcement of legislation, it is important to build constituencies of support in a number of spheres. Advocates within the sphere of mental health, for example, will need to make alliances in a number of other sectors –

such as housing, social protection/social services and employment. Networks that bring together service user organisations, progressive clinicians and mental health staff, sympathetic parliamentarians and people working within government can contribute to building up the impetus for sustained action.

6. Legislative clarity is paramount. Particular care should be taken with how disability, mental illness and discrimination are defined within legislative provisions. This is critical in order to ensure protections for all those who experience discrimination on grounds of mental health, as well as to enable just access to social protection/social services.
7. Legislative reform should go hand in hand with strengthening the role and sustainability of mental health service user organisations. While it is also important to enhance the contributions of other advocacy organisations (including carer/family organisations, professional-led organisations, human rights organisations), the empowerment and self-advocacy of people with mental health problems, as well as of their representative organisations, should be a priority.
8. Legislative and policy reform should ensure that it reduces rather than exacerbates social inequalities. Reforms should be particularly attentive to multiple/intersectional discrimination – and should therefore ensure that they are attentive to disparities and inequalities that exist on grounds of gender, ethnicity, sexuality, religion and age (as well as in relation to mental health). Parliamentarians and people working in government would do well to consider the mental health impact of any legislative change (no matter what its explicit focus), as well as the impact on socio-economic inequalities. Legislative reform should, then, ideally retain a dual focus. The law should be used to protect, promote and ensure the rights of people with mental health problems. At the same time, the law – in combination with policy – should be seen as a tool that can be used to address mental health inequalities within the population as a whole.
9. Legislation in all domains should establish people with mental health problems as rights bearers rather than the recipients of compensation or charity. In so doing, legislation should serve to facilitate the full participation of people with mental health problems within society.
10. Legislative action should give significant attention to deepening governance, accountability, transparency and quality procedures and standards. This is relevant, for example, in terms of planning entitlements not only to health, but to housing and social protection/social services.

Rights-based legislative and administrative actions – whether in the form of conventions, statutes, monitoring standards or mental health/disability policies – cannot, of course, by themselves usher in social justice. But creative and animated human rights thinking and practice can push us all towards formulating new ways in which we can use the law to plot a pathway towards social justice. What we have hoped to do in this volume is both to draw attention to, and to further, the utopian promise of legislation in relation to the everyday lives of people with mental health problems.

References

Farmer, P (2004) An anthropology of structural violence. *Current Anthropology*, **45**(3):305–324.

Kelly, BD (2005) Structural violence and schizophrenia. *Social Science & Medicine*, **61**:721–730.

Kelly, BD (2007) Social justice, human rights and mental illness. *Irish Journal of Psychological Medicine*, **24**(1):3–4.

Sayce, L (2000) *From Psychiatric Patient to Citizen: overcoming discrimination and social exclusion*. Palgrave, Basingstoke and New York.

Sen, A (2009) *The Idea of Justice*. Allen Lane, London.

CHAPTER 14

International and Regional Instruments, Standards, Guidelines and Declarations

In the course of this book, we have referred frequently to a number of international and regional instruments, declarations, principles, standards and technical guidelines. There is now a significant body of such instruments, standards and guidelines that have particular relevance to people with mental health problems. Those who work to combat the discrimination and abuse experienced by people with mental health problems are, therefore, becoming increasingly interested in how such instruments and standards can be used both to enforce and to cajole (Parker, 2007; WHO, 2005). While use of the recently adopted UN Convention on the Rights of Persons with Disabilities (CRPD) arguably characterises many of the most progressive activities that are currently focused around disability, it is only one of many instruments that can be used both as enforcement and advocacy tools. These instruments and guidelines can be used, for example:

- to promote social inclusion through addressing the various factors that exacerbate social exclusion and inequalities and produce segregation;
- to provide adequate community care as well as access to adequate housing and employment opportunities;
- to protect people's rights to political participation;
- to redress past discrimination (in employment, housing etc.) as well as attempt to prevent future discrimination;
- to safeguard the rights of people receiving psychiatric care as well as those people who participate in research.

Because the international array of instruments and guidelines is at this point both extensive and complex, we consider it helpful to enumerate and summarise the most relevant of them in this chapter. Not all relevant instruments, standards and guidelines have been included, not least because some of those developed a number of years ago have now been

---

Mental Illness, Discrimination and the Law: Fighting for Social Justice, First Edition.
Felicity Callard, Norman Sartorius, Julio Arboleda-Flórez, Peter Bartlett, Hanfried Helmchen, Heather Stuart, Jose Taborda and Graham Thornicroft.

superseded. We have chosen to reproduce in full certain of these instruments, standards and guidelines (Section 14.4) because of their significance and authority in relation to the topic of this book. That should not dissuade readers from using and referring to other instruments where appropriate.

One important distinction is that between binding and non-binding international and regional human rights instruments:

- *Binding instruments* – often known as 'hard law' – confer legal obligations on those States Parties that ratify them. They include charters, treaties and conventions including, for example, the UN Convention on the Rights of the Child and, perhaps most important for our purposes, the UN Convention on the Rights of Persons with Disabilities. They also include regional conventions such as the European Convention on Human Rights and Fundamental Freedoms and the African Charter on Human and Peoples' Rights.
- *Non-binding instruments* – often known as 'soft law' – include declarations, standards, resolutions and recommendations issued by the United Nations General Assembly or Council of Human Rights and by other specialised UN and regional agencies. They confer moral obligations on States through the issuing of principles, guidelines, standards or rules and are considered to be authoritative interpretations of international convention requirements. Over time, 'soft law' can in effect become binding if it becomes broadly accepted as customary law (e.g. as with the UN Universal Declaration of Human Rights, Section 14.1.1.8). It can also be used as an aid to interpret 'hard' law, such as provisions of conventions. States are also often invited to implement recommendations, though these are not formally binding.

Other organisations (e.g. the World Medical Association) also issue declarations, standards, principles and guidelines. Some of these declarations, for example the World Medical Association's Declaration of Helsinki (Section 14.3.1.1), while not legally binding in international law, draw extensive authority from the fact that they become codified in, and exert significant influence on, national or regional legislation and regulations, and on judges and policy-makers.

Literature

Parker, C (2007) Developing mental health policy: a human rights perspective. In: Knapp, M, McDaid, D, Mossialos, E and Thornicroft, G (eds) *Mental Health Policy and Practice across Europe: The future direction of mental health care*. Open University Press, Maidenhead. pp. 308–335.

WHO (2005) *WHO Resource Book on Mental Health, Human Rights and Legislation*. World Health Organization, Geneva, Switzerland.

14.1 International instruments and standards

14.1.1 United Nations Treaties

The following are key United Nations treaties that can be used to protect people with mental health problems from discrimination and abuse, and to promote and ensure their human rights and freedoms. The United Nations Office of the High Commissioner for Human Rights (www.ohchr.org) tracks which Member States have ratified these treaties.

14.1.1.1 UN Convention on the Rights of Persons with Disabilities (CRPD)

www.un.org/disabilities

Adopted 13 December 2006. The Convention and its Optional Protocol entered into force on 12 May 2008.

This Convention is arguably the most powerful binding instrument of use in protecting those with mental health problems from discrimination and abuse. It is a groundbreaking human rights instrument with an explicit social development dimension and was created with extensive involvement from civil society. States who ratify the Convention and its Optional Protocol commit to enact laws and measures to improve disability rights and to abolish discriminatory legislation, customs, and practices. It might be considered to be an 'iron fist within a velvet glove', since it has strong mechanisms to secure its implementation.

The Convention endorses a social model of disability (Chapter 2.6), defining persons with disabilities as: 'those who have long-term physical, mental, intellectual or sensory impairments which in interaction with various barriers may hinder their full and effective participation in society on an equal basis with others'.

Notably, it emphasises that discrimination includes 'denial of reasonable accommodation', stating that 'discrimination on the basis of disability' means 'any distinction, exclusion or restriction on the basis of disability which has the purpose or effect of impairing or nullifying the recognition, enjoyment or exercise, on an equal basis with others, of all human rights and fundamental freedoms in the political, economic, social, cultural, civil or any other field. It includes all forms of discrimination, including denial of reasonable accommodation.'

The obligations of States Parties include:

- adopting all appropriate legislative, administrative and other measures for the implementation of the rights recognised in the present Convention;
- taking all appropriate measures, including legislation, to modify or abolish existing laws, regulations, customs and practices that constitute discrimination against persons with disabilities;

- taking into account the protection and promotion of the human rights of persons with disabilities in all policies and programmes;
- taking all appropriate and effective measures to ensure the equal right of persons with disabilities to own or inherit property, to control their own financial affairs and to have equal access to bank loans, mortgages and other forms of financial credit; and additionally to ensure that persons with disabilities are not arbitrarily deprived of their property.

The Optional Protocol to the CRPD is a separate treaty, which sets up a complaints and inquiry procedure. The Optional Protocol is intended to supplement the CRPD and strengthen and promote its implementation and monitoring. Complaints can be lodged with the CRPD Committee from or on behalf of individuals or groups of individuals who claim to be victims of a violation under the CRPD. The Committee can also investigate, report on and make recommendations on 'grave or systematic violations' of the Convention. The right to petition before the CRPD Committee is important not only in protecting and promoting the rights of people with disabilities, but in helping to advance progressive jurisprudence in this field. It is hoped that the availability of remedies at the international level will encourage the development of domestic and regional systems for remedy and redress. In December 2011, there were 90 signatories and 63 ratifications of the Optional Protocol.

Literature

Arnardóttir, OM and Quinn, G (eds) (2009) *The United Nations Convention on the Rights of Persons with Disabilities: European and Scandinavian perspectives.* Martin Nijhoff, Leiden, The Netherlands.

Byrnes, A, Conte, A, Gonnot, J-P, Larsson, L, Schindlmayr, T, Shepherd, N, *et al.* (2007) *From Exclusion to Equality. Realising the Rights of Persons with Disabilities: Handbook for Parliamentarians on the Convention on the Rights of Persons with Disabilities and its Optional Protocol.* United Nations, Geneva, Switzerland.

Dhanda, A (2007) Legal capacity in the Disability Rights Convention: stranglehold of the past or lodestar for the future. *Syracuse Journal of International Law and Commerce*, **34**(2):429–462.

Jones, M (2005) Can international law improve mental health? Some thoughts on the proposed convention on the rights of people with disabilities. *International Journal of Law and Psychiatry*, **28**:183–205.

Kayess, R and French, P (2008) Out of darkness into light? Introducing the Convention on the Rights of Persons with Disabilities. *Human Rights Law Review*, **8**(1):1–34.

Lawson, A (2007) The United Nations Convention on the Rights of Persons with Disabilities: new era or false dawn? *Syracuse Journal of International Law and Commerce*, **34**(2):563–619.

Lawson, A (2008) People with psychosocial impairments or conditions, reasonable accommodation and the Convention on the Rights of Persons with Disabilities. *Law in Context*, **26**:62–84.

Lewis O (2010) The expressive, educational and proactive role of human rights: an analysis of the United Nations Convention on the Rights of Persons with Disabilities. In McSherry B, Weller, P (eds) *Rethinking Rights-Based Mental Health Laws.* Oxford: Hart, pp. 97–128.

MDAC (Mental Disability Advocacy Center) (2011) Building the Architecture for Change: Guidelines on Article 33 of the UN Convention on the rights of Persons with Disabilities. Mental Disability Advocacy Center, Hungary .

The full text of the CRPD is given in Section 14.4.1.

14.1.1.2 UN Convention on the Rights of the Child

www2.ohchr.org/english/law/crc.htm

Adopted and opened for signature and ratification 20 November 1989. Entered into force 2 September 1990.

This Convention explicitly recognised disability as a ground for discrimination for the first time. (Earlier UN conventions had, of course, included people with disabilities by implication. The Universal Declaration of Human Rights, for example, applies as much to people with disabilities as to anyone else, and open-ended non-discrimination provisions in other treaties and conventions may be interpreted to include people with disabilities within their protection. The explicit mention of disability within a UN convention was, nonetheless, a new and important departure, indicating a coming of age of the disability movement in international law). Many articles within this Convention are relevant to children and young people with mental health problems, for example:

- Article 23: this specifies that a mentally or physically disabled child should enjoy a full and decent life in conditions that ensure dignity and promote self-reliance and active participation in the community. The disabled child has the right to special care. Assistance shall be provided free-of-charge, whenever possible.
- Article 24: this specifies the right of the child to the enjoyment of the highest attainable standard of health, and States Parties shall endeavour to ensure that no child is deprived of his/her right to access health care services.
- Article 25: a child who has been placed by competent authorities for the purposes of care, protection or treatment of his or her physical or mental health has the right to a periodic review of the treatment provided and all other relevant circumstances.

- Article 27: this specifies the right of the child to a standard of living adequate for his/her physical, mental, spiritual, moral and social development.
- Article 32: this concerns the right of the child to be protected from economic exploitation and work likely to be harmful to the child's health or to his/her mental, spiritual, moral or social development.
- Article 39: this specifies the duty of States Parties to promote physical and psychological recovery and social reintegration of a child victim of neglect, exploitation, or abuse; torture or any other form of cruel, inhuman or degrading treatment or punishment; or armed conflicts. Such recovery and reintegration shall take place in an environment that fosters the health, self-respect and dignity of the child.

14.1.1.3 UN Convention against Torture and Other Cruel, Inhuman or Degrading Treatment or Punishment

www2.ohchr.org/english/law/cat.htm

Adopted 10 December 1984. Entered into force 26 June 1987.

This Convention gives powerful protections to people with both mental and physical health problems within public institutions. Article 16 is of particular relevance to individuals receiving treatment in mental health care facilities and to prisoners. It specifies that States Parties to the Convention are responsible for preventing acts of cruel inhuman or degrading treatment or punishment when such acts are committed by, or at the instigation of, or with the consent or acquiescence of, a public official or other person acting in an official capacity.

There is also an Optional Protocol to the UN Convention against Torture (OPCAT). Those countries that ratify OPCAT are under a legal duty to develop inspectorates of institutions (Chapter 12.3 and Section 14.2.1.1.2).

Literature

APT/IIHR (Association for the Prevention of Torture/Inter-American Institute of Human Rights) (2010) Optional Protocol to the UN Convention against Torture: Implementation Manual. Association for the Prevention of Torture (APT) and Inter-American Institute for Human Rights (IIHR), Geneva, Switzerland and San José, Costa Rica.

14.1.1.4 UN Convention on the Elimination of All Forms of Discrimination Against Women (CEDAW)

www2.ohchr.org/english/law/cedaw.htm

Adopted 18 December 1979. Entered into force as an international treaty on 3 September 1981.

Articles 11 and 12 are of particular relevance to mental health.

- Article 11: specifies that States Parties shall take all appropriate measures to eliminate discrimination against women in the field of employment in order to ensure, on a basis of equality of men and women, the same rights. These include the right to equal remuneration; the right to social security (particularly in cases of retirement, unemployment, sickness, invalidity and old age and other incapacity to work); and the right to protection of health and to safety in working conditions.
- Article 12: specifies that States Parties shall take all appropriate measures to eliminate discrimination against women in the field of health care in order to ensure, on a basis of equality of men and women, access to health care services, including those related to family planning.

14.1.1.5 International Covenant on Civil and Political Rights (ICCPR)

www2.ohchr.org/english/law/ccpr.htm

Adopted and opened for signature by General Assembly resolution 2200A (XXI) of 16 December 1966. Entered into force 23 March 1976.

This powerful Covenant protects civil and political rights, including those of persons with disabilities. It recognises that all people are equal before the law, and entitled to equal protection from the law, without any discrimination. The following rights are of particularly profound importance in international law, and should be interpreted particularly strictly:

- Article 6: the right to life.
- Article 7: freedom from torture and from cruel, inhuman, or degrading treatment or punishment.
- Article 9: the right to liberty and security of the person, and the prohibition of state action that arbitrarily restricts the liberty of the person.
- Article 16: the right to recognition as a person before the law.
- Article 18: freedom of thought, conscience and religion.

Some rights may be limited under certain conditions.

The rights enshrined in the ICCPR are promoted and protected by the UN Human Rights Committee. In 1989, the Committee issued General Comment 18 about non-discrimination. The First Optional Protocol to the ICCPR empowers individuals to seek redress for Covenant violations from the Human Rights Committee, but is only available against States that have ratified the First Optional Protocol (approximately half of those that are parties to the Covenant).

14.1.1.6 International Covenant on Economic, Social and Cultural Rights (ICESR)

http://www2.ohchr.org/english/law/cescr.htm

Adopted and opened for signature by General Assembly resolution 2200A (XXI) of 16 December 1966. Entered into force 3 January 1976.

The ICESR focuses largely on providing the foundation for 'positive rights' (including family protection, an adequate standard of living and education and the right to participate in cultural life and to benefit from scientific progress). In 1987, States Parties to the ICESR articulated their understanding of the ICESR rights in the Limburg Principles. These Principles provide guidance to States Parties on the practical scope of their responsibilities under the ICESR, and the expectations on those States Parties as to how the ICESR will be implemented.

Article 12 of the ICESR requires governments to recognise 'the right of everyone to the highest attainable standard of physical and mental health'. This article has been the recent focus of extensive attention by those seeking to promote and ensure the rights of people with mental health problems. Two General Comments that have been issued to assist with interpretation of ICESR rights are of particular relevance to individuals with mental health problems. They are General Comment 5 and General Comment 14.

- The Committee on Economic, Social and Cultural Rights adopted General Comment 5: 'Persons with disabilities' in 1996. It details how the ICESR would apply to people with mental and physical disabilities and specifies that the right to health includes the right to access rehabilitation services.
- General Comment 14: 'The right to the highest attainable standard of health' was adopted in 2000. The right to health is a right to facilities, goods, services and conditions that are conducive to the realisation of the highest attainable standard of physical and mental health. The General Comment formulates a framework of norms and obligations making up this right (Chapter 9.4 gives further discussion of this important right in relation to people with mental health problems).

Maastricht guidelines on violations of economic, social and cultural rights

www1.umn.edu/humanrts/instree/Maastrichtguidelines_.html

Maastricht, 22–26 January 1997

Discrimination, under international law, need not be deliberate nor *de jure* to violate relevant treaties. On the 10th anniversary of the Limburg Principles on the Implementation of the International Covenant on Economic, Social and Cultural Rights, more than 30 experts met at the invitation of the International Commission of Jurists (Geneva, Switzerland), the Urban Morgan Institute on Human Rights (Cincinnati, Ohio, USA) and the Centre for Human Rights of the Faculty of Law of Maastricht University (The Netherlands). They elaborated on the Limburg Principles through agreeing a set of guidelines of use in understanding the nature and scope of violations of economic, social and cultural rights and in responding to and remedying these violations.

The guidelines are designed to be of use to all who are concerned with understanding and determining violations of economic, social and cultural rights and in providing remedies thereto, in particular monitoring and adjudicating bodies at the national, regional and international levels.

Paragraph 11, for example, specifies that:

> 'A violation of economic, social and cultural rights occurs when a State pursues, by action or omission, a policy or practice which deliberately contravenes or ignores obligations of the Covenant, or fails to achieve the required standard of conduct or result. Furthermore, any discrimination on grounds of race, colour, sex, language, religion, political or other opinion, national or social origin, property, birth or other status with the purpose or effect of nullifying or impairing the equal enjoyment or exercise of economic, social and cultural rights constitutes a violation of the Covenant.'

14.1.1.7 International Convention on the Elimination of All Forms of Racial Discrimination (CERD)

www2.ohchr.org/english/law/cerd.htm

Adopted and opened for signature and ratification 21 December 1965. Entered into force 4 January 1969.

Of particular relevance to mental health is Article 5, which specifies that States Parties will undertake to prohibit and to eliminate racial discrimination in all its forms and to guarantee the right of everyone, without distinction as to race, colour, or national or ethnic origin, to equality before the law.

Rights include:

- the right to equal treatment before the tribunals and all other organs administering justice;
- the right to security of person and protection by the State against violence or bodily harm;
- political rights, including: the right to participate in elections, right to nationality, right to inherit and so on;
- economic, social and cultural rights, including: the rights to work, to free choice of employment, to just and favourable conditions of work, the right to housing, the right to public health, medical care, social security and social services, the right to education and training, the right to equal participation in cultural activities, the right of access to any place or service intended for use by the general public.

14.1.1.8 Universal Declaration of Human Rights (UDHR)

www.un.org/en/documents/udhr

Adopted by the UN General Assembly on 10 December 1948.

The UDHR sets out 30 Articles which emphasise principles of dignity, liberty, equality and brotherhood. It recognises civil and political rights, as well as economic, social and cultural rights. Of particular relevance to people with mental health problems are Articles 1, Article 5 and 25.

- Article 1: All human beings are born free and equal in dignity and rights.
- Article 5: No one shall be subjected to torture or to cruel, inhuman or degrading treatment or punishment.
- Article 25: Everyone has the right to a standard of living adequate for the health and well-being of himself and his family, including food, clothing, housing and medical care and necessary social services, and the right to security in the event of unemployment, sickness, disability, widowhood, old age or other lack of livelihood in circumstances beyond his control.

While the UDHR is a declaration and not a binding convention, it is widely regarded as carrying authoritative interpretative powers. It is in many ways thought of as part of customary – and enforceable – international law, and hence has been included in this section on binding United Nations treaties.

14.1.2 Non-binding international instruments

14.1.2.1 Universal Declaration on the Human Genome and Human Rights

www.unesco.org/new/en/social-and-human-sciences/themes/bioethics/human-genome-and-human-rights

The Declaration was adopted at UNESCO's 29th General Conference on 11 November 1997. The following year, the United Nations General Assembly endorsed the Declaration.

The Declaration is concerned with the rights of persons in relation to human genome research. Articles 2 and 6 are of particular relevance in protecting the rights of persons with mental health problems.

- Article 2: (a) everyone has a right to respect for their dignity and for their rights regardless of their genetic characteristics; (b) that dignity makes it imperative not to reduce individuals to their genetic characteristics and to respect their uniqueness and diversity.
- Article 6: No one shall be subjected to discrimination based on genetic characteristics that is intended to infringe or has the effect of infringing human rights, fundamental freedoms and human dignity.

14.1.2.2 The Standard Rules on the Equalisation of Opportunities for Persons with Disabilities (Standard Rules)

www.un.org/esa/socdev/enable/dissre00.htm

Adopted by the United Nations General Assembly, 48th session, resolution 48/96, annex, of 20 December 1993.

These 22 rules relate to responsibility, action and cooperation as regards health care, rehabilitation, support services, awareness raising, education, employment, family life, policy-making and legislation. The rules emphasise that people with disabilities should participate in society as citizens. The Standard Rules had a Special Rapporteur (who had relevant and extensive experience of disability issues) and a panel of experts which monitored and promoted their implementation. The panel of experts included representatives from the World Federation of Psychiatric Survivors and Users.

The Standard Rules followed from the United Nations Decade of Disabled Persons from 1983 to 1992, which was in turn initiated by the 1982 World Programme of Action Concerning Disabled Persons (Section 14.1.2.4). The Standard Rules have been superseded by the UN Convention on the Rights of Persons with Disabilities (Section 14.1.1.1). However, when they were adopted, they played a significant role in encouraging governments to take action to attain equalisation of opportunities for persons with disabilities.

The full text of the Standard Rules is given in Section 14.4.2.

14.1.2.3 Principles for the Protection of Persons with Mental Illness and the Improvement of Mental Health Care ('MI Principles')

http://www2.ohchr.org/english/law/principles.htm

Adopted by the UN General Assembly on 17 December 1991.

The 25 Principles (commonly termed the 'MI Principles') are applicable to those with mental illness and anyone else in a mental health care facility. They outline the minimum human rights standards concerning mental health care and are primarily concerned with protection against abuses (rather than on positive obligations of care).

- Principles 1 and 8 specify access to high quality care. (Principle 1.1 states that '[a]ll persons have the right to the best available mental health care, which shall be part of the health and social care system'. This does indicate recognition of the importance of positive rights.)
- Principles 3 and 7 specify a human rights preference for community care.
- Principle 9 specifies less restrictive environments to preserve and enhance autonomy.
- Principle 16 specifies standards and procedures for involuntary admission to hospital.
- Principles 17 and 18 specify procedural safeguards (a fair hearing by a judicial or other independent review with representation, rights to information and attendance).

Some of the Principles have been contested on the ground that they offer inadequate protections. This is particularly the case as regards informed consent, the limitation on the right to consent to treatment and the absence of a right to refuse treatment (Gendreau, 1997; United Nations, 2003). It has been argued that the rights of those with capacity who refuse treatment are violated because they are prevented from exercising their right to self-determination (Gendreau, 1997). In addition, there is no requirement for a guardian not to have a conflict of interest and for children's guardians to be chosen in accordance with their best interests and their express wishes or preferences (in contrast to the Convention on the Rights of the Child, Section 14.1.1.2) (Watchirs, 2005).

The 'MI Principles' are still considered by many to be the most complete and extensive international standards for persons with mental illness within the mental health context. There is currently vigorous debate over the extent to which the 'MI Principles' have been superseded by the Convention on the Rights of Persons with Disabilities (Section 14.1.1.1).

Literature

Gendreau, C (1997) The rights of psychiatric patients in the light of the principles announced by the United Nations: a recognition of the right to consent to treatment? *International Journal of Law and Psychiatry*, **20**(2):259–278.

Harding, TW (2000) Human rights law in the field of mental health: a critical review. *Acta Psychiatr Scand*, **399**:24–30.

Maingay, S, Thornicroft, G, Huxley, P, Jenkins, R and Szmukler, G (2002) Mental health and human rights: the MI Principles – turning rhetoric into action. *International Review of Psychiatry*, **14**:19–25.

Rees, N (2003) International human rights obligations and mental health review tribunals. *Psychiatry, Psychology and Law*, **10**(1):33–43.

United Nations (2003) Progress of Efforts to Ensure the Full Recognition and Enjoyment of the Human Rights of Persons with Disabilities – Report of the Secretary-General [A/58/181].

Watchirs, H (2005) Human rights audit of mental health legislation – results of an Australian pilot. *International Journal of Law and Psychiatry*, **28**:99–125.

Zifcak, S (1996) The United Nations Principles for the Protection of People with Mental Illness: applications and limitations. *Psychiatry, Psychology and Law*, **3**(1):1–9.

The full text of the MI Principles is given in Section 14.4.3.

14.1.2.4 World Programme of Action concerning Disabled Persons

www.un.org/disabilities/default.asp?id=23

Adopted by the UN General Assembly on 3 December 1982.

The World Programme of Action concerning Disabled Persons was important in shifting the emphasis towards human rights and away from an overreliance on rehabilitation measures. It recommended actions at a variety of scales (national, regional and international) through which to improve the lives of persons with disabilities and ensure their access to equal opportunities. The Standard Rules (Section 14.1.2.2) was one of the major outcomes of the World Programme of Action.

14.2 Regional human rights systems, treaties, conventions, charters and standards

14.2.1 European Region

14.2.1.1 Council of Europe (COE)

14.2.1.1.1 European Convention on Human Rights

Available for download from the European Court of Human Rights website: www.echr.coe.int

The Convention for the Protection of Human Rights and Fundamental Freedoms is better known as the European Convention on Human Rights. It was opened for signature in 1950 and entered into force in 1953.

It is the largest and most developed regional human rights protection mechanism and is binding on all those countries that have ratified it.

The full-time European Court of Human Rights (based in Strasbourg) rules on applications from individuals and States alleging violation of the civil and political rights set out in the Convention. Individuals can apply directly to the Court.

Decisions made by the European Court of Human Rights regarding a particular case are then applicable to all countries that have ratified the Convention – 47 Member States at 2011 (all European Union Member States and some others). This is hard law that is directly enforceable in domestic courts, though dependent on the specifics of the domestic legal system. 13 Protocols have been adopted to strengthen and clarify the original agreement. The Court is much more frequently used by individuals than by States, and its decisions can lead to reform of national legislations (Niveau and Materi, 2006). Central to the Convention is the duty of government to avoid arbitrary confinement and the reliable finding of 'mental disability' through objective medical evidence. Patients have a right to a speedy review of detention by an independent authority, and this authority must have the power to release unlawfully detained patients.

There have been some particularly important, precedent-setting judgements in relation to the human rights of people with mental health problems.

Winterwerp v. The Netherlands, 33 Eur. Ct. H.R. (ser. A) (1979) was the first mental disability case to reach the Strasbourg Court. Judgement was made that civil commitment must follow a 'procedure prescribed by law' and cannot be arbitrary. Mental disorder needs to be validated by objective medical expertise; furthermore, 'the mental disorder must be of a kind or degree warranting compulsory confinement'; and 'the validity of continued confinement depends upon the persistence of such a disorder.' The person confined has the right to require reconsideration of the detention at periodic intervals.

X v. United Kingdom, 46 Eur. Ct. H.R. (ser. A) (1981) begins the long line of cases establishing the requirements of the Winterwerp hearings. It mandated that anyone being committed to confinement must be provided with speedy periodic legal review with the essential elements of due process.

Aerts v. Belgium, App No 25357/94, Eur Ct HR (1998). The Court held that there must be some relationship between the reason for detention and the objectives of treatment. In principle, the 'detention' of a person as a mental health patient will only be 'lawful' if effected in a hospital, clinic or other appropriate institution.

Shtukaturov v. Russia, 44009/05, judgment 27 March 2008 establishes procedural and substantive requirements for determinations of incapacity, and the appointment and conduct of guardians for those found incapable.

There is an extensive body of case law from the European Court of Human Rights, much of it of relevant to mental disability (further details of this case law are given in Resources in Boxes 14.1 and 14.2). (We do not discuss this case law here, but rather refer readers to the book by Bartlett, Lewis and Thorold (2007).) Several cases have led to the modification of national legislation pertaining to psychiatric commitment (e.g. in The Netherlands, in the United Kingdom and in Austria).

Box 14.1 Resource

The HUDOC database on the European Court of Human Rights website provides free online access to the case law of the Court, of the European Commission of Human Rights and of the Committee of Ministers. There is a sophisticated search facility.

www.echr.coe.int/ECHR/EN/hudoc

Box 14.2 Resource

The Mental Disability Advocacy Center (MDAC) has published a summary of mental disability cases decided by the European Court of Human Rights. The publication is designed to help lawyers and judges across Europe apply the Convention and the case law of the Court in domestic proceedings. It is also intended as an advocacy document for people with intellectual or psychosocial disabilities.

MDAC (2007) Summaries of Mental Disability Cases Decided by the European Court of Human Rights. MDAC, Budapest, available from the MDAC website: http://mdac.info

Literature

Bartlett, P, Lewis, O and Thorold, O (2007) *Mental Disability and the European Convention on Human Rights*. Brill/Martinus Nijhoff, Leiden, The Netherlands.

Gostin, LO (2000) Human rights of persons with mental disabilities: the European Convention of (sic) Human Rights. *International Journal of Law and Psychiatry*, **23**(2):125–159.

Hale, B (2007) Justice and quality in mental health law: the European experience. *International Journal of Law and Psychiatry*, **30**:18–28.

Lewis, O (2002) Mental disability law in central and eastern Europe: paper, practice, promise. *Journal of Mental Health Law*, **8**(December):293–303.

Lewis, O (2002) Protecting the rights of people with mental disabilities: the European Convention on Human Rights. *European Journal of Health Law*, **9**:293–320.

Niveau, G and Materi, J (2006) Psychiatric commitment: over 50 years of case law from the European Court of Human Rights. *European Psychiatry*, **21**:427–435.

Prior, PM (2007) Mentally disordered offenders and the European Court of Human Rights. *International Journal of Law and Psychiatry*, **30**:546–557.

Richardson, G (2005) The European convention and mental health law in England and Wales: moving beyond process? *International Journal of Law and Psychiatry*, **28**:127–139.

14.2.1.1.2 Committee for the Prevention of Torture and Inhuman or Degrading Treatment or Punishment (CPT)

www.cpt.coe.int/en

The European Convention on the Prevention of Torture and Inhuman or Degrading Treatment or Punishment in 1987 established the European Committee for the Prevention of Torture and Inhuman or Degrading Treatment or Punishment (CPT).

The CPT visits places of detention within any of the States that are signatories to the Convention to examine 'the treatment of all categories of person deprived of their liberty by a public authority, including persons with mental health problems' (CPT Standards, Paragraph 25).

The CPT outlines a general right to consent to or refuse treatment except in clearly and strictly defined exceptional circumstances: 'Regarding Article 3 of the European Convention on Human Rights: Patients should, as a matter of principle, be placed in a position to give their free and informed consent to treatment. The admission of a person to a psychiatric establishment on a voluntary basis should not be construed as authorising treatment without his consent. It follows that every competent patient, whether voluntary or involuntary, should be given the opportunity to refuse treatment or other medical intervention. Any derogation from this fundamental principle should be based upon law and only relate to clearly and strictly defined exceptional circumstances.'

The CPT's eighth report discussed the prevention of ill treatment during involuntary committal to a psychiatric unit, and proposed the following minimal basic standards for non-voluntary psychiatric hospitalisation (Box 14.3):

- mandatory separation of adults and minors;
- respect of patients' dignity and intimacy;
- individualisation of treatment protocols;
- prohibition of electroconvulsive therapy (ECT) in its unmodified form;
- qualitative and quantitative requirements for staff;
- strict regulation of the use of restraint methods;
- safeguards in the committal procedure, particularly in respect of the principle of the right to take legal action.

These principles ought to apply in any environment where people are deprived of liberty on psychiatric grounds (i.e. in prison environments and high security facilities as well as hospitals).

Box 14.3 Standards

The CPT Standards

www.cpt.coe.int/EN/docsstandards.htm

Strasbourg, CPT, 2004, CPT/Inf/E (2002) 1 – rev 2004

The CPT Standards allow the CPT to clearly outline to national authorities – in advance of visits – its views on how persons deprived of their liberty ought to be treated. The Standards bring together some of the substantive issues which the CPT pursues when carrying out visits. The substantive sections currently drawn up include: police custody, imprisonment, training of law enforcement personnel, health care services in prisons, foreign nationals detained under aliens legislation, involuntary placement in psychiatric establishments and juveniles and women deprived of their liberty (Chapter 12.3).

Literature

MDAC (Mental Disability Advocacy Center) (2006) Inspect! Inspectorates of Mental Health and Social Care Institutions in the European Union. Mental Disability Advocacy Center, Hungary.

Niveau, G (2004) Preventing human rights abuses in psychiatric establishments: the work of the CPT. *European Psychiatry*, **19**(3):146–154.

14.2.1.1.3 Council of Europe Recommendations

The Committee of Ministers of the Council of Europe (COE) issues Recommendations to Member States on matters for which the Committee has agreed a common policy. Recommendations are not binding on Member

States. Several Recommendations made within the last decade are of direct relevance to combating the discrimination and abuse experienced by people with mental health problems.

COE Recommendation Rec (2004) 10 concerning the protection of the human rights and dignity of persons with mental disorder

Adopted 22 September 2004.

This Recommendation provides detailed guidance in relation to the protection of the human rights of service users, involuntary psychiatric hospital admissions, conditions of hospitalisation and circumstances in which treatment without consent can be justified. The provisions of the Recommendation also uphold the principle of non-discrimination, civil and political rights and the promotion of mental health.

Recommendation 1235 (1994) of the Parliamentary Assembly of the Council of Europe on psychiatry and human rights

Text adopted by the Assembly 12 April 1994.

The Recommendation outlined rules regarding:

- admission procedures and conditions;
- treatment;
- problems and abuses in psychiatry;
- situation of detained persons (in penal institutions).

Recommendation Rec (98) 7 concerning the ethical and organisational aspects of health care in prison

Adopted 8 April 1998.

The appendix to this Recommendation outlines the main characteristics of the right to health in prison. Its section on the management of certain common problems in prisons includes psychiatric symptoms, mental disturbance, major personality disorders and risk of suicide. Paragraph 55 of the appendix specifies that:

> 'Prisoners suffering from serious mental disturbance should be kept and cared for in a hospital facility which is adequately equipped and possesses appropriately trained staff. The decision to admit an inmate to a public hospital should be made by a psychiatrist, subject to authorisation by the competent authorities.'

Recommendation No R(99)4 of the Committee of Ministers to Member States on Principles concerning the Legal Protection of Incapable Adults

Adopted 23 February 1999.

The Recommendation emphasises maximum preservation of capacity, and recommends in Principle 3 that:

> 'The legislative framework should, so far as possible, recognise that different degrees of incapacity may exist and that incapacity may vary from time to time. Accordingly a measure of protection should not result automatically in a complete removal of legal capacity. However, a restriction of legal capacity should be possible where it is shown to be necessary for the protection of the person concerned.'

Recommendation CM/Rec (2009)3 on monitoring the protection of human rights and dignity of persons with mental disorder

Adopted 20 May 2009

This Recommendation issues a checklist that it recommends as the basis for the development of monitoring tools to assist in determining States' level of compliance with Recommendation Rec (2004)10 (above) in order to protect the dignity and human rights of persons with mental disorder and ensure appropriate care for them.

The checklist presents the series of principles from Rec (2004)10 – for example, non-discrimination, civil and political rights, promotion of physical and mental health – alongside questions and measures that might help to assess these principles. The checklist is a useful and practical tool that outlines how both legislative and administrative actions might be taken to uphold the rights of individuals with mental health problems.

Literature

Kingdon, D, Jones, R and Lonnqvist, J (2004) Protecting the human rights of people with mental disorder: new recommendations emerging from the Council of Europe. *British Journal of Psychiatry*, **185**:277–279.

14.2.1.1.4 Convention on Human Rights and Biomedicine

(Convention for the Protection of Human Rights and Dignity of the Human Being with regard to the Application of Biology and Medicine) (the 'Oviedo Convention')

http://conventions.coe.int/Treaty/EN/Treaties/Html/164.htm

Opened for signature 4 April 1997, entered into force 1 December 1999.

The Convention imposes both negative obligations and positive duties on States Parties and provides a set of minimum standards for the protection of the patient during research participation. To use the colloquial language, this Convention (like all others) is a floor not a ceiling. States Parties are of course at liberty to adopt standards in excess of those required by the Oviedo Convention, and a number have done so regarding patient protection in research. The Oviedo Convention does not, however, contain a monitoring mechanism, so it is not clear how extensively it has been implemented.

Literature

Adorno, R (2005) The Oviedo Convention: A European legal framework at the intersection of human rights and health law. *Journal of International Biotechnology Law*, **2**:113–143.

Callard, F (2010) Between legislation and bioethics: the European Convention on Human Rights and Biomedicine. In: Helmchen, H and Sartorius, N (eds) *Ethics in Psychiatry: European contributions*. Springer, Dordrecht, pp. 73–96.

de Wachter, MA (1997) The European Convention on bioethics. *Hastings Center Report*, **27**(1):13–23.

14.2.1.1.5 European Social Charter

www.coe.int/t/dghl/monitoring/socialcharter

Adopted in 1961, revised in 1996. The Revised Social Charter opened for signature 3 May 1996 and entered into force 1 July 1999.

Revisions to the Charter included the right to housing. States must submit annual reports to the European Committee of Social Rights to demonstrate how they are implementing the Charter. Through the monitoring system, States alter their legislation and/or practice to bring these into line with the Charter. Complaints about violations of the Charter may be lodged with the European Committee of Social Rights. The case that the Mental Disability Advocacy Center successfully brought against Bulgaria in relation to rights to education for children with disabilities is outlined in Chapter 6.1.

14.2.1.2 European Union

14.2.1.2.1 Treaty of Amsterdam (Article 13)

Signed 2 October 1997, entered into force 1 May 1999.

Article 13 makes all discrimination in the workplace illegal – this includes discrimination on grounds of disability. Institutions must be set up to enforce the law.

14.2.1.2.2 European Charter of Fundamental Rights

www.europarl.europa.eu/charter/default_en.htm

The European Parliament gave its agreement to the Charter on 14 November 2000 and the European Commission on 6 December 2000. It was signed by the Presidents of the European Parliament, the Council and the Commission on 7 December 2000.

The Charter sets out the whole range of civil, political, economic and social rights of European citizens and all persons resident in the European Union. These rights are divided into six sections:

- dignity;
- freedoms;
- equality;
- solidarity;
- citizens' rights;
- justice.

Article 26, 'Integration of persons with disabilities' states that: 'The Union recognises and respects the right of persons with disabilities to benefit from measures designed to ensure their independence, social and occupational integration and participation in the life of the community.'

14.2.1.2.3 Lisbon Treaty

The Lisbon Treaty establishes the EU Charter of Fundamental Rights 2000 as a European Union law: it makes the Charter enforceable in the European Court. It also allows the European Union to become a party to the European Convention on Human Rights (ECHR). While all Member States of the European Union have long been parties to the ECHR, the European Union itself has not been. This will allow the European Union to sign and ratify the ECHR, so that all European Union administration will be bound by it.

14.2.1.2.4 European Union Agency for Fundamental Rights (FRA)

http://fra.europa.eu

The FRA provides the relevant institutions and authorities of the European Union and its Member States with assistance and expertise when they are implementing Community law relating to fundamental rights.

It also carries out data collection, research and analysis and cooperates with civil society and awareness raising. From 2009–2011, the FRA was conducting a project to better understand how the fundamental rights of people with intellectual disabilities and people with mental health problems are safeguarded in the European Union and where violations of rights occur (FRA, 2010).

Literature

FRA (European Union Agency for Fundamental Rights) (2010) The right to political participation of persons with mental health problems and persons with intellectual disabilities. European Union Agency for Fundamental Rights, Vienna, Austria.

14.2.1.2.5 European Policy Regarding Mental Health

http://ec.europa.eu/health/mental_health/policy/index_en.htm

In November 2005, the European Commission published the Green Paper, *Improving the mental health of the population: Towards a mental health strategy for the European Union,* in response to the World Health Organization Mental Health Declaration for Europe (Chapter 16.2.3.4.1). It subsequently launched the European Pact for Mental Health and Well-being

(Chapter 16.2.3.4.3) at a mental health conference in Brussels on 13 June 2008. The Pact is now being implemented through a series of conferences on five priorities, one of which is combating stigma and exclusion. The Pact invited policy-makers and stakeholders to take action, including:

- promoting active inclusion of people with mental health problems in society, including improvement of their access to appropriate employment, training and educational opportunities;
- involving people with mental health problems and their families and carers in relevant policy and decision-making processes.

Literature

Duquette, ES (2001–2002) The human rights of the mentally disabled: can European Union law help? *New York Law School Journal of International and Comparative Law*, **21**:573–591.

European Commission (2005) Green Paper *Improving the mental health of the population: Towards a strategy on mental health for the European Union* (http://ec.europa.eu/health/ph_determinants/life_style/mental/green_paper/mental_gp_en.pdf).

European Pact for Mental Health and Well-being (http://ec.europa.eu/health/archive/ph_determinants/life_style/mental/docs/pact_en.pdf).

14.2.2 Region of the Americas

14.2.2.1 American Convention on Human Rights (Pact of San José)

Adopted at the Inter-American Specialised Conference on Human Rights, San José, Costa Rica, 22 November 1969. Entered into force 18 July 1978.

The American Convention on Human Rights (also known as the Pact of San José) is an international human rights instrument. Compliance with the Convention is overseen by the Inter-American Commission on Human Rights and the Inter-American Court of Human Rights (www.cidh.oas.org), both of which are organs of the Organization of American States (OAS).

There is an Additional Protocol to the American Convention on Human Rights in the area of Economic, Social and Cultural Rights (frequently known as the 'Protocol of San Salvador'). It was opened for signature in the city of San Salvador, El Salvador, on 17 November 1988. It aims to ensure the protection of economic, social and cultural rights (it refers, for example, to the right to work, the right to health, the right to education, and the right to food). (See: www.oas.org/juridico/english/treaties/a-52.html)

There are been some particularly important cases of relevance to mental disability considered by the Inter-American Commission and Court on/of Human Rights (IACHR).

In Victoria Rosario Congo v. Ecuador, Report 63/99, Case 11.427, April 13, 1999, a mentally ill prisoner at a rehabilitation centre had been denied psychiatric care, struck on the head, denied medical treatment and left in isolation for 40 days. He subsequently died. The IACHR found violations of the rights to physical integrity, life, and judicial protection under the American Convention on Human Rights.

In December 2003, the IACHR approved 'precautionary measures' to protect the lives, liberty and personal security of 460 people detained in a psychiatric institution in Paraguay. 'Precautionary measures' mean that advocates can avoid the time-consuming process of 'exhausting domestic remedies' before gaining access to the IACHR. The Commission has also facilitated a settlement between applicants and the government of Paraguay guaranteeing the rights of patients to live and receive mental health care in the community.

In the Case of Damião Ximenes Lopes (4 July 2006), the Inter-American Court of Human Rights condemned the state of Brazil to pay indemnity to relatives (mother, sister and brothers) of the late Damião Ximenes Lopes. He had been a long-term patient who had received many psychiatric inpatient treatments. On 1 October 1999, Damião Ximenes Lopes was admitted to Casa de Repouso Guararapes, a psychiatric hospital, located in Sobral, State of Ceará, Brazil. Three days later, on 4 October, his mother found him bleeding and in agony when she visited. A few hours later, he died. The investigation disclosed that he had become aggressive and was beaten to death by nurses. The relatives sued the Brazilian state – via the Inter-American Court of Human Rights – for human rights violations, as the patient was a SUS patient (SUS stands for Sistema Único de Saúde – a universal health/public health system.) This decision is a landmark because it is the first Court decision related to abuse of the human rights of a person with a mental disorder.

Literature

Gostin, LO (2004) International human rights law and mental disability. *Hastings Center Report*. Mar–Apr 2004:11–12.

Gable, L, Vásquez, J, Gostin, L and Jiménez, H (2005) Mental health and due process in the Americas: protecting the human rights of persons involuntarily admitted to and detained in psychiatric institutions. *Rev Panam Salud Pública*, **4-5**:366–373.

Hillman, A (2005) Protecting mental disability rights: a success story in the Inter-American Human Rights System. *Human Rights Brief*, **12**:25–28.

Levav, I and González Uzcátegui, R (2000) Rights of persons with mental illness in Central America. *Acta Psychiatrica Scandinavica*, **101**: 83–86.

Vásquez, J and Caldas de Almeida, JM (2004) Salud mental y derechos humanos. *Atopos*, **2**:45–56.

14.2.2.2 Inter-American Convention on the Elimination of All Forms of Discrimination Against Persons with Disabilities (IACPWD)

www.oas.org/Juridico/english/sigs/a-65.html

This Convention was adopted by the Organization of American States in 1999, making it the first intergovernmental organisation to have a binding human rights treaty on disability. It does not contain individual rights, but is the first regional treaty to define disability-based discrimination:

1 'The term "disability" means a physical, mental, or sensory impairment, whether permanent or temporary, that limits the capacity to perform one or more essential activities of daily life, and which can be caused or aggravated by the economic and social environment.'
2 'The term "discrimination against persons with disabilities" means any distinction, exclusion, or restriction based on a disability, record of disability, condition resulting from a previous disability, or perception of disability, whether present or past, which has the effect or objective of impairing or nullifying the recognition, enjoyment, or exercise by a person with a disability of his or her human rights and fundamental freedoms.'

14.2.3 African Region

14.2.3.1 African (Banjul) Charter on Human and Peoples' Rights (ACHPR)

www.achpr.org/english/_info/charter_en.html

Adopted by the Organization of African Unity, 27 June 1981. Entered into force 21 October 1986.

The Charter is supervised by the African Commission on Human and Peoples' Rights. Particularly relevant clauses are Articles 4, 5, 16 and 18(4):

- Article 4: 'Human beings are inviolable. Every human being shall be entitled to respect for his life and the integrity of his person. No one may be arbitrarily deprived of this right'.
- Article 5: 'Every individual shall have the right to the respect of the dignity inherent in a human being and to the recognition of his legal status. All forms of exploitation and degradation of man, particularly slavery, slave trade, torture, cruel, inhuman or degrading punishment and treatment shall be prohibited'.
- Article 16:

'1. Every individual shall have the right to enjoy the best attainable state of physical and mental health.

2. State Parties to the present Charter shall take the necessary measures to protect the health of their people and to ensure that they receive medical attention when they are sick'.

- Article 18:

'4. The aged and the disabled shall also have the right to special measures of protection in keeping with their physical or moral needs.'

The case of Purohit and Moore v. Gambia (241/2001) is widely regarded as 'a landmark case in the jurisprudence of the African Commission' (Baderin, 2005). Paul Moore, a mental health advocate, observed inhuman treatment of mental health patients in the psychiatric unit of the Royal Victoria Hospital, Gambia. Purohit and Moore alleged violations of Articles 2, 3, 5, 7(1)(a), 13(1), 16 and 18(4) of the ACHPR. The African Commission specified the obligation on States Parties 'to take concrete and targeted steps, while taking full advantage of their available resources, to ensure that the right to health is fully realised in all its aspects without discrimination of any kind'. The African Commission therefore found the Republic of Gambia in violation of certain articles of the African Charter, and strongly urged the government to develop new mental health legislation, as well as to provide adequate medical and material care for people with mental health problems in The Gambia.

Originally, the ACHPR provided only for a Commission, not a Court. More recently, like other regional human rights systems such as the European Convention on Human Rights and the American Convention on Human Rights, a Court has been established. It has not yet had occasion to rule on matters relating to mental disability.

Literature

Alem, A (2000) Human rights and psychiatric care in Africa with particular reference to the Ethiopian situation. *Acta Psychiatrica Scandinavica*, **101**:93–96.

Anyidoho, M (2004) The right to health for mental health patients: African Commission. *Housing and ESC Rights Law Quarterly*, **1**(1):4–5.

Baderin, MA (2005) Recent developments in the African Regional Human Rights System. *Human Rights Law Review*, **5**(1):117–149.

Bartlett, P and Hamzic, V (2010) Reforming mental disability law in Africa: practical tips and suggestions. Human Rights Centre, Nottingham, UK.

Murray, R (2006) International human rights: neglect of perspectives from African institutions. *International and Comparative Law Quarterly*, **55**(1):193–204.

Wachira, G (2008) African Court on Human and Peoples' Rights: Ten years on and still no justice. Minority Rights Group International, London.

14.2.4 Arab States

14.2.4.1 Arab Charter on Human Rights

An English translation of the original charter in Arabic is available at: www1.umn.edu/humanrts/instree/arabhrcharter.html#%231

The Arab Charter on Human Rights entered into force on 15 March 2008, two months after receiving seven ratifications from individual States (in accordance with Article 45 of the Charter).

Literature

Rishmawi, M (2010) The Arab Charter on Human Rights and the League of Arab States: An Update. *Human Rights Law Review*, **10**(1):169–178.

14.3 Non-binding standards, guidelines and declarations

14.3.1 World Medical Association (WMA)

www.wma.net

The World Medical Association is an international organisation representing physicians. It was created to ensure the independence of physicians and to work for the highest possible standards of ethical behaviour and care by physicians, at all times. The WMA has made both declarations and statements that address the protection of patients from abuse and unethical treatment.

14.3.1.1 WMA Declaration of Helsinki – Ethical Principles for Medical Research Involving Human Subjects

www.wma.net/en/30publications/10policies/b3/index.html

The Declaration of Helsinki sets out the ethical principles for medical research involving human subjects, and was adopted by the 18th WMA General Assembly in Helsinki, Finland, in 1964. It has been amended and clarified eight times since then. The current WMA Declaration of Helsinki – Ethical Principles for Medical Research Involving Human Subjects is that adopted at the 59th WMA General Assembly, held in Seoul in October 2008.

The full text of the Declaration of Helsinki is given in Section 14.4.4.

14.3.1.2 WMA Declaration of Tokyo – Guidelines for Physicians Concerning Torture and other Cruel, Inhuman or Degrading Treatment or Punishment in Relation to Detention and Imprisonment

www.wma.net/en/30publications/10policies/c18/index.html

Adopted by the 29th World Medical Assembly, Tokyo, Japan, October 1975. Editorially revised May 2005 and May 2006.

This Declaration notably includes a statement regarding the capacity of prisoners:

> 'Where a prisoner refuses nourishment and is considered by the physician as capable of forming an unimpaired and rational judgment concerning the consequences of such a voluntary refusal of nourishment, he or she shall not be fed artificially. The decision as to the capacity of the prisoner to form such a judgment should be confirmed by at least one other independent physician. The consequences of the refusal of nourishment shall be explained by the physician to the prisoner.'

14.3.1.3 WMA Statement on Ethical Issues Concerning Patients with Mental Illness

www.wma.net/en/30publications/10policies/e11/index.html

Adopted by the 47th General Assembly, Bali, Indonesia, September 1995 and revised by the WMA General Assembly, Pilanesberg, South Africa, October 2006.

The Statement itemises a number of ethical principles. These include:

- the need to eliminate the discrimination associated with psychiatry and the mentally ill;
- the requirement that psychiatric patients, in the absence of legally adjudicated incompetence, must be dealt with as though they are legally competent.

14.3.2 World Psychiatric Association (WPA)

www.wpanet.org

The World Psychiatric Association promotes the advancement of psychiatry and mental health for all peoples of the world. It aims to:

- promote mental health;
- preserve the rights of the mentally ill;
- promote the development and observance of the highest ethical standards in psychiatric care, teaching and research;
- promote non-discrimination (parity) in the provision of care of the mentally ill;
- protect the rights of psychiatrists.

The WPA has issued several declarations and charters on ethical standards with psychiatry, the most relevant of which are briefly outlined here.

14.3.2.1 Declaration of Hawaii

http://www.wpanet.org/detail.php?section_id=5&content_id=27

Approved by the General Assembly of the World Psychiatric Association in 1977 and updated by the General Assembly in Vienna, Austria, on 10 July 1983.

The Declaration of Hawaii was the first time that the psychiatric profession had issued a position statement on ethical matters. It was preoccupied with the political misuse of psychiatric concepts, knowledge and terminology.

14.3.2.2 World Psychiatric Association Statement and Viewpoints on the Rights and Legal Safeguards of the Mentally Ill

www.wpanet.org/detail.php?section_id=5&content_id=29

Adopted by the World Psychiatric Association General Assembly in Athens, 17 October 1989.

This focuses on the rights of mental patients and extends and complements the Declaration of Hawaii.

14.3.2.3 Declaration of Madrid

www.wpanet.org/detail.php?section_id=5&content_id=48

Approved by the General Assembly of the World Psychiatric Association on August 25, 1996, and amended by the General Assembly in Yokohama, Japan in August 2002.

The Declaration of Madrid updates the Declaration of Hawaii. Most notably, Ethical Standard 4 states that: 'When the patient is gravely disabled, incapacitated and/or incompetent to exercise proper judgment because of a mental disorder, the psychiatrists should consult with the family and, if appropriate, seek legal counsel, to safeguard the human dignity and the legal rights of the patient. No treatment should be provided against the patient's will, unless withholding treatment would endanger the life of the patient and/or the life of others. Treatment must always be in the best interest of the patient.'

The full text of the Declaration of Madrid is given in Section 14.4.5.

Literature

Helmchen, H and Okasha, A (2000) From the Hawaii Declaration to the Declaration of Madrid. *Acta Psychiatrica Scandinavica*, **101**:20–23.

Steenfeldt-Foss, OW (2010) Ethical principles in psychiatry: the Declarations of Hawaii and Madrid. In Helmchen, H and Sartorius, N (eds) *Ethics in Psychiatry: European Contributions*. Springer. pp. 129–138.

World Psychiatric Association (1989) Statements and Viewpoints on the Rights and Legal Safeguards of the Mentally Ill. World Congress. World Psychiatric Association, Athens & New York.

14.3.3 World Federation for Mental Health (WFMH)

www.wfmh.org

WFMH is an international membership organization founded in 1948 to advance, among all peoples and nations, the prevention of mental and emotional disorders, the proper treatment and care of those with such disorders, and the promotion of mental health.

14.3.3.1 Declaration of Luxor: Declaration of Human Rights and Mental Health

http://www.wfmh.org/PDF/DeclarationHR&MH.pdf

Adopted January 17, 1989 by the Niles Congress, Luxor, celebrating the 40th Anniversary of the World Federation for Mental Health.

The Declaration of Luxor comprises eight Articles that include:

- Article 4: The fundamental rights of persons who are labelled, or diagnosed, treated or defined as mentally or emotionally ill or distressed, shall be the same as those of all other citizens. (Article 4 outlines the right to coercion-free treatment, freedom from discrimination, protection from physical or psychological abuse; it also outlines the right to treatment.)
- Article 5: All mentally ill persons have the right to be treated under the same professional and ethical standards as other ill persons. This must include efforts to promote the greatest degree of self-determination and personal responsibility on their part.

14.3.4 Council for International Organizations of Medical Sciences (CIOMS)

www.cioms.ch

CIOMS is an international, non-governmental, non-profit organisation established jointly by the World Health Organization and UNESCO (United Nations Educational, Scientific and Cultural Organisation) in 1949. It has a significant focus on bioethics and has issued a number of guidelines in this area, most notably the International Ethical Guidelines for Biomedical Research Involving Human Subjects (revised and updated in 2002) (Box 14.4). These Guidelines address: biomedical research involving human subjects, including ethical justification and scientific validity of research; ethical review; informed consent; the vulnerability of individuals, groups, communities and populations; and confidentiality. They are designed to be of use to countries when defining national policies on the ethics of biomedical research involving human subjects, applying ethical standards in local circumstances and establishing or improving ethical review mechanisms. A particular aim is to reflect the conditions and the needs of low resource countries and the implications for multinational or transnational research in which they may be partners.

CIOMS has also recently revised its guidelines for epidemiological research (Box 14.4). These are designed to provide ethical guidance for epidemiologists as well as for those sponsoring, reviewing or participating in epidemiological studies.

Box 14.4 Resources

CIOMS (Council for International Organisations of Medical Sciences) (2002) International Ethical Guidelines for Biomedical Research Involving Human Subjects. CIOMS, Geneva, Switzerland. Available online at: www.cioms.ch/publications/layout_guide2002.pdf

CIOMS (Council for International Organizations of Medical Sciences) (2009) International Ethical Guidelines for Epidemiological Research. CIOMS, Geneva, Switzerland.

14.3.5 Pan American Health Organization (PAHO)

www.paho.org

Refer to Chapter 16 (Section 16.2.3.2) for details on PAHO.

14.3.5.1 Declaration of Caracas on the Restructuring of Psychiatric Care in Latin America

This Declaration on the restructuring of psychiatric care in Latin America was made at a regional conference, convened by PAHO and the World Health Organization on 11–14 November 1990. The Declaration promoted respect for the human and civil rights of the mentally ill, and called for revisions of mental health legislation so as to guarantee the fulfilment of the human and civil rights of people with mental illness.

Literature

Caldas de Almeida, JM and Horvitz-Lennon, MC (2010) Mental health care reforms in Latin America: an overview of mental health care reforms in Latin America and the Caribbean. *Psychiatric Services*, **61**:218–221.

Bolis, M (2002) The impact of the Caracas Declaration on the modernisation of mental health leglislation in Latin America and the English-speaking Caribbean. XXVII International Congress on Law and Mental Health, 9–12 July 2002, Amsterdam, The Netherlands, Organización Panamericana de la Salud.

Lolas, F (2010) Psychiatry and human rights in Latin America: ethical dilemmas and the future. *International Review of Psychiatry*, **22**(4):325–329.

14.3.5.2 PAHO/World Health Organization Resolution CD47.R1. Disability: Prevention and Rehabilitation in the Context of the Right to the Enjoyment of the Highest Attainable Standard of Physical and Mental Health and Other Related Rights

http://www.paho.org/english/gov/cd/CD47.r1-e.pdf

Adopted at the 47th Directing Council, 58th Session of the Regional Committee, Washington, DC, 25–29 September 2006.

This instrument provides recommendations to PAHO Member States about the promotion and protection of the human rights and fundamental freedoms of people with disabilities, particularly as regards the right to the enjoyment of the highest attainable standard of physical and mental health. The resolution refers to specific measures that can be undertaken to improve the well-being of people with mental disabilities.

14.3.5.3 Montreal Declaration on Intellectual Disability

www.declaracionmontreal.com/english/declaration.htm

Adopted in Montreal, Canada, 6 October 2004 (at the Pan American Health Organization/World Health Organization Conference on Intellectual Disability).

The Montreal Declaration recognises the human rights of people with intellectual disabilities, including the right to health, and the interconnections between this and other rights:

> '4. ... the right to the highest possible level of physical and mental health and well-being is inter-connected with other civil, political, economic, social, and cultural rights and fundamental freedoms. For persons with intellectual disabilities, as for other persons, the exercise of the right to health requires full social inclusion, an adequate standard of living, access to inclusive education, access to work justly compensated and access to community services.'

The Montreal Declaration is considered a breakthrough in terms of the fundamental rights of people with an intellectual disability. It effected a paradigm shift – moving to a model in which people with a disability are entitled to rights inherent to their condition as humans, rather than entitled to rights as a result of having a disability.

14.4 Full texts

14.4.1 Full text of the United Nations Convention on the Rights of Persons with Disabilities (CRPD)

Preamble

The States Parties to the present Convention,

(a) Recalling the principles proclaimed in the Charter of the United Nations which recognize the inherent dignity and worth and the equal and inalienable rights of all members of the human family as the foundation of freedom, justice and peace in the world,

(b) Recognizing that the United Nations, in the Universal Declaration of Human Rights and in the International Covenants on Human Rights, has proclaimed and agreed that everyone is entitled to all the rights and freedoms set forth therein, without distinction of any kind,

(c) Reaffirming the universality, indivisibility, interdependence and interrelatedness of all human rights and fundamental freedoms and the need for persons with disabilities to be guaranteed their full enjoyment without discrimination,

(d) Recalling the International Covenant on Economic, Social and Cultural Rights, the International Covenant on Civil and Political Rights, the International Convention on the Elimination of All Forms of Racial Discrimination, the Convention on the Elimination of All Forms of Discrimination against Women, the Convention against Torture and Other Cruel, Inhuman or Degrading Treatment or Punishment, the Convention on the Rights of the Child, and the International Convention on the Protection of the Rights of All Migrant Workers and Members of Their Families,

(e) Recognizing that disability is an evolving concept and that disability results from the interaction between persons with impairments and attitudinal and environmental barriers that hinders their full and effective participation in society on an equal basis with others,

(f) Recognizing the importance of the principles and policy guidelines contained in the World Programme of Action concerning Disabled Persons and in the Standard Rules on the Equalization of Opportunities for Persons with Disabilities in influencing the promotion, formulation and evaluation of the policies, plans, programmes and actions at the national, regional and international levels to further equalize opportunities for persons with disabilities,

(g) Emphasizing the importance of mainstreaming disability issues as an integral part of relevant strategies of sustainable development,

(h) Recognizing also that discrimination against any person on the basis of disability is a violation of the inherent dignity and worth of the human person,

(i) Recognizing further the diversity of persons with disabilities,

(j) Recognizing the need to promote and protect the human rights of all persons with disabilities, including those who require more intensive support,

(k) Concerned that, despite these various instruments and undertakings, persons with disabilities continue to face barriers in their participation as equal members of society and violations of their human rights in all parts of the world,

(l) Recognizing the importance of international cooperation for improving the living conditions of persons with disabilities in every country, particularly in developing countries,

(m) Recognizing the valued existing and potential contributions made by persons with disabilities to the overall well-being and diversity of their communities, and that the promotion of the full enjoyment by persons with disabilities of their human rights and fundamental freedoms and of full participation by persons with disabilities will result in their enhanced sense of belonging and in significant advances in the human, social and economic development of society and the eradication of poverty,

(n) Recognizing the importance for persons with disabilities of their individual autonomy and independence, including the freedom to make their own choices,

(o) Considering that persons with disabilities should have the opportunity to be actively involved in decision-making processes about policies and programmes, including those directly concerning them,

(p) Concerned about the difficult conditions faced by persons with disabilities who are subject to multiple or aggravated forms of discrimination on the basis of race, colour, sex, language, religion, political or other opinion, national, ethnic, indigenous or social origin, property, birth, age or other status,

(q) Recognizing that women and girls with disabilities are often at greater risk, both within and outside the home, of violence, injury or abuse, neglect or negligent treatment, maltreatment or exploitation,

(r) Recognizing that children with disabilities should have full enjoyment of all human rights and fundamental freedoms on an equal basis with other children, and recalling obligations to that end undertaken by States Parties to the Convention on the Rights of the Child,

(s) Emphasizing the need to incorporate a gender perspective in all efforts to promote the full enjoyment of human rights and fundamental freedoms by persons with disabilities,

(t) Highlighting the fact that the majority of persons with disabilities live in conditions of poverty, and in this regard recognizing the critical need to address the negative impact of poverty on persons with disabilities,

(u) Bearing in mind that conditions of peace and security based on full respect for the purposes and principles contained in the Charter of the United Nations and observance of applicable human rights instruments are indispensable for the full protection of persons with disabilities, in particular during armed conflicts and foreign occupation,

(v) Recognizing the importance of accessibility to the physical, social, economic and cultural environment, to health and education and to information and communication, in enabling persons with disabilities to fully enjoy all human rights and fundamental freedoms,

(w) Realizing that the individual, having duties to other individuals and to the community to which he or she belongs, is under a responsibility to strive for the promotion and observance of the rights recognized in the International Bill of Human Rights,

(x) Convinced that the family is the natural and fundamental group unit of society and is entitled to protection by society and the State, and that persons with disabilities and their family members should receive the necessary protection and assistance to enable families to contribute towards the full and equal enjoyment of the rights of persons with disabilities,

(y) Convinced that a comprehensive and integral international convention to promote and protect the rights and dignity of persons with disabilities will make a significant contribution to redressing the profound social disadvantage of persons with disabilities and promote their participation in the civil, political, economic, social and cultural spheres with equal opportunities, in both developing and developed countries,

Have agreed as follows:

Article 1 Purpose

The purpose of the present Convention is to promote, protect and ensure the full and equal enjoyment of all human rights and fundamental freedoms by all persons with disabilities, and to promote respect for their inherent dignity.

Persons with disabilities include those who have long-term physical, mental, intellectual or sensory impairments, which in interaction with various barriers may hinder their full and effective participation in society on an equal basis with others.

Article 2 Definitions

For the purposes of the present Convention:

"Communication" includes languages, display of text, Braille, tactile communication, large print, accessible multimedia as well as written, audio, plain-language, human-reader and augmentative and alternative modes, means and formats of communication, including accessible information and communication technology;

"Language" includes spoken and signed languages and other forms of non-spoken languages;

"Discrimination on the basis of disability" means any distinction, exclusion or restriction on the basis of disability which has the purpose or effect of impairing or nullifying the recognition, enjoyment or exercise, on an equal basis with others, of all human rights and fundamental freedoms in the political, economic, social, cultural, civil or any other field. It includes all forms of discrimination, including denial of reasonable accommodation;

"Reasonable accommodation" means necessary and appropriate modification and adjustments not imposing a disproportionate or undue burden, where needed in a particular case, to ensure to persons with disabilities the enjoyment or exercise on an equal basis with others of all human rights and fundamental freedoms;

"Universal design" means the design of products, environments, programmes and services to be usable by all people, to the greatest extent possible, without the need for adaptation or specialized design. "Universal design" shall not exclude assistive devices for particular groups of persons with disabilities where this is needed.

Article 3 General principles

The principles of the present Convention shall be:

(a) Respect for inherent dignity, individual autonomy including the freedom to make one's own choices, and independence of persons;
(b) Non-discrimination;
(c) Full and effective participation and inclusion in society;
(d) Respect for difference and acceptance of persons with disabilities as part of human diversity and humanity;
(e) Equality of opportunity;
(f) Accessibility;
(g) Equality between men and women;
(h) Respect for the evolving capacities of children with disabilities and respect for the right of children with disabilities to preserve their identities.

Article 4 General obligations

1 States Parties undertake to ensure and promote the full realization of all human rights and fundamental freedoms for all persons with disabilities without discrimination of any kind on the basis of disability. To this end, States Parties undertake:

(a) To adopt all appropriate legislative, administrative and other measures for the implementation of the rights recognized in the present Convention;
(b) To take all appropriate measures, including legislation, to modify or abolish existing laws, regulations, customs and practices that constitute discrimination against persons with disabilities;
(c) To take into account the protection and promotion of the human rights of persons with disabilities in all policies and programmes;
(d) To refrain from engaging in any act or practice that is inconsistent with the present Convention and to ensure that public authorities and institutions act in conformity with the present Convention;
(e) To take all appropriate measures to eliminate discrimination on the basis of disability by any person, organization or private enterprise;
(f) To undertake or promote research and development of universally designed goods, services, equipment and facilities, as defined in article 2 of the present Convention, which should require the minimum possible adaptation and the least cost to meet the specific needs of a person with disabilities, to promote their availability and

use, and to promote universal design in the development of standards and guidelines;

(g) To undertake or promote research and development of, and to promote the availability and use of new technologies, including information and communications technologies, mobility aids, devices and assistive technologies, suitable for persons with disabilities, giving priority to technologies at an affordable cost;

(h) To provide accessible information to persons with disabilities about mobility aids, devices and assistive technologies, including new technologies, as well as other forms of assistance, support services and facilities;

(i) To promote the training of professionals and staff working with persons with disabilities in the rights recognized in this Convention so as to better provide the assistance and services guaranteed by those rights.

2 With regard to economic, social and cultural rights, each State Party undertakes to take measures to the maximum of its available resources and, where needed, within the framework of international cooperation, with a view to achieving progressively the full realization of these rights, without prejudice to those obligations contained in the present Convention that are immediately applicable according to international law.

3 In the development and implementation of legislation and policies to implement the present Convention, and in other decision-making processes concerning issues relating to persons with disabilities, States Parties shall closely consult with and actively involve persons with disabilities, including children with disabilities, through their representative organizations.

4 Nothing in the present Convention shall affect any provisions which are more conducive to the realization of the rights of persons with disabilities and which may be contained in the law of a State Party or international law in force for that State. There shall be no restriction upon or derogation from any of the human rights and fundamental freedoms recognized or existing in any State Party to the present Convention pursuant to law, conventions, regulation or custom on the pretext that the present Convention does not recognize such rights or freedoms or that it recognizes them to a lesser extent.

5 The provisions of the present Convention shall extend to all parts of federal states without any limitations or exceptions.

Article 5 Equality and non-discrimination

1 States Parties recognize that all persons are equal before and under the law and are entitled without any discrimination to the equal protection and equal benefit of the law.

2 States Parties shall prohibit all discrimination on the basis of disability and guarantee to persons with disabilities equal and effective legal protection against discrimination on all grounds.
3 In order to promote equality and eliminate discrimination, States Parties shall take all appropriate steps to ensure that reasonable accommodation is provided.
4 Specific measures which are necessary to accelerate or achieve de facto equality of persons with disabilities shall not be considered discrimination under the terms of the present Convention.

Article 6 Women with disabilities

1 States Parties recognize that women and girls with disabilities are subject to multiple discrimination, and in this regard shall take measures to ensure the full and equal enjoyment by them of all human rights and fundamental freedoms.
2 States Parties shall take all appropriate measures to ensure the full development, advancement and empowerment of women, for the purpose of guaranteeing them the exercise and enjoyment of the human rights and fundamental freedoms set out in the present Convention.

Article 7 Children with disabilities

1 States Parties shall take all necessary measures to ensure the full enjoyment by children with disabilities of all human rights and fundamental freedoms on an equal basis with other children.
2 In all actions concerning children with disabilities, the best interests of the child shall be a primary consideration.
3 States Parties shall ensure that children with disabilities have the right to express their views freely on all matters affecting them, their views being given due weight in accordance with their age and maturity, on an equal basis with other children, and to be provided with disability and age-appropriate assistance to realize that right.

Article 8 Awareness-raising

1 States Parties undertake to adopt immediate, effective and appropriate measures:
  (a) To raise awareness throughout society, including at the family level, regarding persons with disabilities, and to foster respect for the rights and dignity of persons with disabilities;
  (b) To combat stereotypes, prejudices and harmful practices relating to persons with disabilities, including those based on sex and age, in all areas of life;
  (c) To promote awareness of the capabilities and contributions of persons with disabilities.

2 Measures to this end include:

(a) Initiating and maintaining effective public awareness campaigns designed:

(i) To nurture receptiveness to the rights of persons with disabilities;

(ii) To promote positive perceptions and greater social awareness towards persons with disabilities;

(iii) To promote recognition of the skills, merits and abilities of persons with disabilities, and of their contributions to the workplace and the labour market;

(b) Fostering at all levels of the education system, including in all children from an early age, an attitude of respect for the rights of persons with disabilities;

(c) Encouraging all organs of the media to portray persons with disabilities in a manner consistent with the purpose of the present Convention;

(d) Promoting awareness-training programmes regarding persons with disabilities and the rights of persons with disabilities.

Article 9 Accessibility

1 To enable persons with disabilities to live independently and participate fully in all aspects of life, States Parties shall take appropriate measures to ensure to persons with disabilities access, on an equal basis with others, to the physical environment, to transportation, to information and communications, including information and communications technologies and systems, and to other facilities and services open or provided to the public, both in urban and in rural areas. These measures, which shall include the identification and elimination of obstacles and barriers to accessibility, shall apply to, inter alia:

(a) Buildings, roads, transportation and other indoor and outdoor facilities, including schools, housing, medical facilities and workplaces;

(b) Information, communications and other services, including electronic services and emergency services.

2 States Parties shall also take appropriate measures to:

(a) Develop, promulgate and monitor the implementation of minimum standards and guidelines for the accessibility of facilities and services open or provided to the public;

(b) Ensure that private entities that offer facilities and services which are open or provided to the public take into account all aspects of accessibility for persons with disabilities;

(c) Provide training for stakeholders on accessibility issues facing persons with disabilities;

(d) Provide in buildings and other facilities open to the public signage in Braille and in easy to read and understand forms;

(e) Provide forms of live assistance and intermediaries, including guides, readers and professional sign language interpreters, to facilitate accessibility to buildings and other facilities open to the public;

(f) Promote other appropriate forms of assistance and support to persons with disabilities to ensure their access to information;

(g) Promote access for persons with disabilities to new information and communications technologies and systems, including the Internet;

(h) Promote the design, development, production and distribution of accessible information and communications technologies and systems at an early stage, so that these technologies and systems become accessible at minimum cost.

Article 10 Right to life

States Parties reaffirm that every human being has the inherent right to life and shall take all necessary measures to ensure its effective enjoyment by persons with disabilities on an equal basis with others.

Article 11 Situations of risk and humanitarian emergencies

States Parties shall take, in accordance with their obligations under international law, including international humanitarian law and international human rights law, all necessary measures to ensure the protection and safety of persons with disabilities in situations of risk, including situations of armed conflict, humanitarian emergencies and the occurrence of natural disasters.

Article 12 Equal recognition before the law

1 States Parties reaffirm that persons with disabilities have the right to recognition everywhere as persons before the law.

2 States Parties shall recognize that persons with disabilities enjoy legal capacity on an equal basis with others in all aspects of life.

3 States Parties shall take appropriate measures to provide access by persons with disabilities to the support they may require in exercising their legal capacity.

4 States Parties shall ensure that all measures that relate to the exercise of legal capacity provide for appropriate and effective safeguards to prevent abuse in accordance with international human rights law. Such safeguards shall ensure that measures relating to the exercise of legal capacity respect the rights, will and preferences of the person, are free of conflict of interest and undue influence, are proportional and tailored to the person's circumstances, apply for the shortest time possible and are subject to regular review by a competent, independent and impartial authority or judicial body. The safeguards shall be proportional to the degree to which such measures affect the person's rights and interests.

5 Subject to the provisions of this article, States Parties shall take all appropriate and effective measures to ensure the equal right of persons with disabilities to own or inherit property, to control their own financial affairs and to have equal access to bank loans, mortgages and other forms of financial credit, and shall ensure that persons with disabilities are not arbitrarily deprived of their property.

Article 13 Access to justice

1 States Parties shall ensure effective access to justice for persons with disabilities on an equal basis with others, including through the provision of procedural and age-appropriate accommodations, in order to facilitate their effective role as direct and indirect participants, including as witnesses, in all legal proceedings, including at investigative and other preliminary stages.

2 In order to help to ensure effective access to justice for persons with disabilities, States Parties shall promote appropriate training for those working in the field of administration of justice, including police and prison staff.

Article 14 Liberty and security of the person

1 States Parties shall ensure that persons with disabilities, on an equal basis with others:

- **(a)** Enjoy the right to liberty and security of person;
- **(b)** Are not deprived of their liberty unlawfully or arbitrarily, and that any deprivation of liberty is in conformity with the law, and that the existence of a disability shall in no case justify a deprivation of liberty.

2 States Parties shall ensure that if persons with disabilities are deprived of their liberty through any process, they are, on an equal basis with others, entitled to guarantees in accordance with international human rights law and shall be treated in compliance with the objectives and principles of this Convention, including by provision of reasonable accommodation.

Article 15 Freedom from torture or cruel, inhuman or degrading treatment or punishment

1 No one shall be subjected to torture or to cruel, inhuman or degrading treatment or punishment. In particular, no one shall be subjected without his or her free consent to medical or scientific experimentation.

2 States Parties shall take all effective legislative, administrative, judicial or other measures to prevent persons with disabilities, on an equal basis with others, from being subjected to torture or cruel, inhuman or degrading treatment or punishment.

Article 16 Freedom from exploitation, violence and abuse

1 States Parties shall take all appropriate legislative, administrative, social, educational and other measures to protect persons with disabilities, both within and outside the home, from all forms of exploitation, violence and abuse, including their gender-based aspects.
2 States Parties shall also take all appropriate measures to prevent all forms of exploitation, violence and abuse by ensuring, inter alia, appropriate forms of gender- and age-sensitive assistance and support for persons with disabilities and their families and caregivers, including through the provision of information and education on how to avoid, recognize and report instances of exploitation, violence and abuse. States Parties shall ensure that protection services are age-, gender- and disability-sensitive.
3 In order to prevent the occurrence of all forms of exploitation, violence and abuse, States Parties shall ensure that all facilities and programmes designed to serve persons with disabilities are effectively monitored by independent authorities.
4 States Parties shall take all appropriate measures to promote the physical, cognitive and psychological recovery, rehabilitation and social reintegration of persons with disabilities who become victims of any form of exploitation, violence or abuse, including through the provision of protection services. Such recovery and reintegration shall take place in an environment that fosters the health, welfare, self-respect, dignity and autonomy of the person and takes into account gender- and age-specific needs.
5 States Parties shall put in place effective legislation and policies, including women- and child-focused legislation and policies, to ensure that instances of exploitation, violence and abuse against persons with disabilities are identified, investigated and, where appropriate, prosecuted.

Article 17 Protecting the integrity of the person

Every person with disabilities has a right to respect for his or her physical and mental integrity on an equal basis with others.

Article 18 Liberty of movement and nationality

1 States Parties shall recognize the rights of persons with disabilities to liberty of movement, to freedom to choose their residence and to a

nationality, on an equal basis with others, including by ensuring that persons with disabilities:

(a) Have the right to acquire and change a nationality and are not deprived of their nationality arbitrarily or on the basis of disability;

(b) Are not deprived, on the basis of disability, of their ability to obtain, possess and utilize documentation of their nationality or other documentation of identification, or to utilize relevant processes such as immigration proceedings, that may be needed to facilitate exercise of the right to liberty of movement;

(c) Are free to leave any country, including their own;

(d) Are not deprived, arbitrarily or on the basis of disability, of the right to enter their own country.

2 Children with disabilities shall be registered immediately after birth and shall have the right from birth to a name, the right to acquire a nationality and, as far as possible, the right to know and be cared for by their parents.

Article 19 Living independently and being included in the community

States Parties to this Convention recognize the equal right of all persons with disabilities to live in the community, with choices equal to others, and shall take effective and appropriate measures to facilitate full enjoyment by persons with disabilities of this right and their full inclusion and participation in the community, including by ensuring that:

(a) Persons with disabilities have the opportunity to choose their place of residence and where and with whom they live on an equal basis with others and are not obliged to live in a particular living arrangement;

(b) Persons with disabilities have access to a range of in-, residential and other community support services, including personal assistance necessary to support living and inclusion in the community, and to prevent isolation or segregation from the community;

(c) Community services and facilities for the general population are available on an equal basis to persons with disabilities and are responsive to their needs.

Article 20 Personal mobility

States Parties shall take effective measures to ensure personal mobility with the greatest possible independence for persons with disabilities, including by:

(a) Facilitating the personal mobility of persons with disabilities in the manner and at the time of their choice, and at affordable cost;

(b) Facilitating access by persons with disabilities to quality mobility aids, devices, assistive technologies and forms of live assistance and intermediaries, including by making them available at affordable cost;
(c) Providing training in mobility skills to persons with disabilities and to specialist staff working with persons with disabilities;
(d) Encouraging entities that produce mobility aids, devices and assistive technologies to take into account all aspects of mobility for persons with disabilities.

Article 21 Freedom of expression and opinion, and access to information

States Parties shall take all appropriate measures to ensure that persons with disabilities can exercise the right to freedom of expression and opinion, including the freedom to seek, receive and impart information and ideas on an equal basis with others and through all forms of communication of their choice, as defined in article 2 of the present Convention, including by:
(a) Providing information intended for the general public to persons with disabilities in accessible formats and technologies appropriate to different kinds of disabilities in a timely manner and without additional cost;
(b) Accepting and facilitating the use of sign languages, Braille, augmentative and alternative communication, and all other accessible means, modes and formats of communication of their choice by persons with disabilities in official interactions;
(c) Urging private entities that provide services to the general public, including through the Internet, to provide information and services in accessible and usable formats for persons with disabilities;
(d) Encouraging the mass media, including providers of information through the Internet, to make their services accessible to persons with disabilities;
(e) Recognizing and promoting the use of sign languages.

Article 22 Respect for privacy

1 No person with disabilities, regardless of place of residence or living arrangements, shall be subjected to arbitrary or unlawful interference with his or her privacy, family, or correspondence or other types of communication or to unlawful attacks on his or her honour and reputation. Persons with disabilities have the right to the protection of the law against such interference or attacks.
2 States Parties shall protect the privacy of personal, health and rehabilitation information of persons with disabilities on an equal basis with others.

Article 23 Respect for and the family

1 States Parties shall take effective and appropriate measures to eliminate discrimination against persons with disabilities in all matters relating to marriage, family, parenthood and relationships, on an equal basis with others, so as to ensure that:

(a) The right of all persons with disabilities who are of marriageable age to marry and to found a family on the basis of free and full consent of the intending spouses is recognized;

(b) The rights of persons with disabilities to decide freely and responsibly on the number and spacing of their children and to have access to age-appropriate information, reproductive and family planning education are recognized, and the means necessary to enable them to exercise these rights are provided;

(c) Persons with disabilities, including children, retain their fertility on an equal basis with others.

2 States Parties shall ensure the rights and responsibilities of persons with disabilities, with regard to guardianship, wardship, trusteeship, adoption of children or similar institutions, where these concepts exist in national legislation; in all cases the best interests of the child shall be paramount. States Parties shall render appropriate assistance to persons with disabilities in the performance of their child-rearing responsibilities.

3 States Parties shall ensure that children with disabilities have equal rights with respect to family life. With a view to realizing these rights, and to prevent concealment, abandonment, neglect and segregation of children with disabilities, States Parties shall undertake to provide early and comprehensive information, services and support to children with disabilities and their families.

4 States Parties shall ensure that a child shall not be separated from his or her parents against their will, except when competent authorities subject to judicial review determine, in accordance with applicable law and procedures, that such separation is necessary for the best interests of the child. In no case shall a child be separated from parents on the basis of a disability of either the child or one or both of the parents.

5 States Parties shall, where the immediate family is unable to care for a child with disabilities, undertake every effort to provide alternative care within the wider family, and failing that, within the community in a family setting.

Article 24 Education

1 States Parties recognize the right of persons with disabilities to education. With a view to realizing this right without discrimination and on the basis of equal opportunity, States Parties shall ensure an inclusive education system at all levels and lifelong learning directed to:

- **(a)** The full development of human potential and sense of dignity and self-worth, and the strengthening of respect for human rights, fundamental freedoms and human diversity;
- **(b)** The development by persons with disabilities of their personality, talents and creativity, as well as their mental and physical abilities, to their fullest potential;
- **(c)** Enabling persons with disabilities to participate effectively in a free society.

2 In realizing this right, States Parties shall ensure that:

- **(a)** Persons with disabilities are not excluded from the general education system on the basis of disability, and that children with disabilities are not excluded from free and compulsory primary education, or from secondary education, on the basis of disability;
- **(b)** Persons with disabilities can access an inclusive, quality and free primary education and secondary education on an equal basis with others in the communities in which they live;
- **(c)** Reasonable accommodation of the individual's requirements is provided;
- **(d)** Persons with disabilities receive the support required, within the general education system, to facilitate their effective education;
- **(e)** Effective individualized support measures are provided in environments that maximize academic and social development, consistent with the goal of full inclusion.

3 States Parties shall enable persons with disabilities to learn life and social development skills to facilitate their full and equal participation in education and as members of the community. To this end, States Parties shall take appropriate measures, including:

- **(a)** Facilitating the learning of Braille, alternative script, augmentative and alternative modes, means and formats of communication and orientation and mobility skills, and facilitating peer support and mentoring;
- **(b)** Facilitating the learning of sign language and the promotion of the linguistic identity of the deaf community;
- **(c)** Ensuring that the education of persons, and in particular children, who are blind, deaf or deaf-blind, is delivered in the most appropriate languages and modes and means of communication for the individual, and in environments which maximize academic and social development.

4 In order to help ensure the realization of this right, States Parties shall take appropriate measures to employ teachers, including teachers with disabilities, who are qualified in sign language and/or Braille, and to train professionals and staff who work at all levels of education. Such training shall incorporate disability awareness and the use of appropriate augmentative and alternative modes, means and formats of communication, educational techniques and materials to support persons with disabilities.

5 States Parties shall ensure that persons with disabilities are able to access general tertiary education, vocational training, adult education and lifelong learning without discrimination and on an equal basis with others. To this end, States Parties shall ensure that reasonable accommodation is provided to persons with disabilities.

Article 25 Health

States Parties recognize that persons with disabilities have the right to the enjoyment of the highest attainable standard of health without discrimination on the basis of disability. States Parties shall take all appropriate measures to ensure access for persons with disabilities to health services that are gender-sensitive, including health-related rehabilitation. In particular, States Parties shall:

(a) Provide persons with disabilities with the same range, quality and standard of free or affordable health care and programmes as provided to other persons, including in the area of sexual and reproductive health and population-based public health programmes;

(b) Provide those health services needed by persons with disabilities specifically because of their disabilities, including early identification and intervention as appropriate, and services designed to minimize and prevent further disabilities, including among children and older persons;

(c) Provide these health services as close as possible to people's own communities, including in rural areas;

(d) Require health professionals to provide care of the same quality to persons with disabilities as to others, including on the basis of free and informed consent by, inter alia, raising awareness of the human rights, dignity, autonomy and needs of persons with disabilities through training and the promulgation of ethical standards for public and private health care;

(e) Prohibit discrimination against persons with disabilities in the provision of health insurance, and life insurance where such insurance is permitted by national law, which shall be provided in a fair and reasonable manner;

(f) Prevent discriminatory denial of health care or health services or food and fluids on the basis of disability.

Article 26 Habilitation and rehabilitation

1 States Parties shall take effective and appropriate measures, including through peer support, to enable persons with disabilities to attain and maintain maximum independence, full physical, mental, social and vocational ability, and full inclusion and participation in all aspects of life. To that end, States Parties shall organize, strengthen and extend comprehensive habilitation and rehabilitation services and programmes, particularly in the areas of health, employment, education and social services, in such a way that these services and programmes:

(a) Begin at the earliest possible stage, and are based on the multidisciplinary assessment of individual needs and strengths;

(b) Support participation and inclusion in the community and all aspects of society, are voluntary, and are available to persons with disabilities as close as possible to their own communities, including in rural areas.

2 States Parties shall promote the development of initial and continuing training for professionals and staff working in habilitation and rehabilitation services.

3 States Parties shall promote the availability, knowledge and use of assistive devices and technologies, designed for persons with disabilities, as they relate to habilitation and rehabilitation.

Article 27 Work and employment

1 States Parties recognize the right of persons with disabilities to work, on an equal basis with others; this includes the right to the opportunity to gain a living by work freely chosen or accepted in a labour market and work environment that is open, inclusive and accessible to persons with disabilities. States Parties shall safeguard and promote the realization of the right to work, including for those who acquire a disability during the course of employment, by taking appropriate steps, including through legislation, to, inter alia:

(a) Prohibit discrimination on the basis of disability with regard to all matters concerning all forms of employment, including conditions of recruitment, hiring and employment, continuance of employment, career advancement and safe and healthy working conditions;

(b) Protect the rights of persons with disabilities, on an equal basis with others, to just and favourable conditions of work, including equal opportunities and equal remuneration for work of equal value, safe and healthy working conditions, including protection from harassment, and the redress of grievances;

(c) Ensure that persons with disabilities are able to exercise their labour and trade union rights on an equal basis with others;

(d) Enable persons with disabilities to have effective access to general technical and vocational guidance programmes, placement services and vocational and continuing training;

(e) Promote employment opportunities and career advancement for persons with disabilities in the labour market, as well as assistance in finding, obtaining, maintaining and returning to employment;
(f) Promote opportunities for self-employment, entrepreneurship, the development of cooperatives and starting one's own business;
(g) Employ persons with disabilities in the public sector;
(h) Promote the employment of persons with disabilities in the private sector through appropriate policies and measures, which may include affirmative action programmes, incentives and other measures;
(i) Ensure that reasonable accommodation is provided to persons with disabilities in the workplace;
(j) Promote the acquisition by persons with disabilities of work experience in the open labour market;
(k) Promote vocational and professional rehabilitation, job retention and return-to-work programmes for persons with disabilities.

2 States Parties shall ensure that persons with disabilities are not held in slavery or in servitude, and are protected, on an equal basis with others, from forced or compulsory labour.

Article 28 Adequate standard of living and social protection

1 States Parties recognize the right of persons with disabilities to an adequate standard of living for themselves and their families, including adequate food, clothing and housing, and to the continuous improvement of living conditions, and shall take appropriate steps to safeguard and promote the realization of this right without discrimination on the basis of disability.

2 States Parties recognize the right of persons with disabilities to social protection and to the enjoyment of that right without discrimination on the basis of disability, and shall take appropriate steps to safeguard and promote the realization of this right, including measures:

(a) To ensure equal access by persons with disabilities to clean water services, and to ensure access to appropriate and affordable services, devices and other assistance for disability-related needs;
(b) To ensure access by persons with disabilities, in particular women and girls with disabilities and older persons with disabilities, to social protection programmes and poverty reduction programmes;
(c) To ensure access by persons with disabilities and their families living in situations of poverty to assistance from the State with disability-related expenses, including adequate training, counselling, financial assistance and respite care;

(d) To ensure access by persons with disabilities to public housing programmes;

(e) To ensure equal access by persons with disabilities to retirement benefits and programmes.

Article 29 Participation in political and public life

States Parties shall guarantee to persons with disabilities political rights and the opportunity to enjoy them on an equal basis with others, and shall undertake to:

(a) Ensure that persons with disabilities can effectively and fully participate in political and public life on an equal basis with others, directly or through freely chosen representatives, including the right and opportunity for persons with disabilities to vote and be elected, inter alia, by:

  (i) Ensuring that voting procedures, facilities and materials are appropriate, accessible and easy to understand and use;

  (ii) Protecting the right of persons with disabilities to vote by secret ballot in elections and public referendums without intimidation, and to stand for elections, to effectively hold office and perform all public functions at all levels of government, facilitating the use of assistive and new technologies where appropriate;

  (iii) Guaranteeing the free expression of the will of persons with disabilities as electors and to this end, where necessary, at their request, allowing assistance in voting by a person of their own choice;

(b) Promote actively an environment in which persons with disabilities can effectively and fully participate in the conduct of public affairs, without discrimination and on an equal basis with others, and encourage their participation in public affairs, including:

  (i) Participation in non-governmental organizations and associations concerned with the public and political life of the country, and in the activities and administration of political parties;

  (ii) Forming and joining organizations of persons with disabilities to represent persons with disabilities at international, national, regional and local levels.

Article 30 Participation in cultural life, recreation, leisure and sport

1 States Parties recognize the right of persons with disabilities to take part on an equal basis with others in cultural life, and shall take all appropriate measures to ensure that persons with disabilities:

  (a) Enjoy access to cultural materials in accessible formats;

(b) Enjoy access to television programmes, films, theatre and other cultural activities, in accessible formats;
(c) Enjoy access to places for cultural performances or services, such as theatres, museums, cinemas, libraries and tourism services, and, as far as possible, enjoy access to monuments and sites of national cultural importance.

2 States Parties shall take appropriate measures to enable persons with disabilities to have the opportunity to develop and utilize their creative, artistic and intellectual potential, not only for their own benefit, but also for the enrichment of society.

3 States Parties shall take all appropriate steps, in accordance with international law, to ensure that laws protecting intellectual property rights do not constitute an unreasonable or discriminatory barrier to access by persons with disabilities to cultural materials.

4 Persons with disabilities shall be entitled, on an equal basis with others, to recognition and support of their specific cultural and linguistic identity, including sign languages and deaf culture.

5 With a view to enabling persons with disabilities to participate on an equal basis with others in recreational, leisure and sporting activities, States Parties shall take appropriate measures:
(a) To encourage and promote the participation, to the fullest extent possible, of persons with disabilities in mainstream sporting activities at all levels;
(b) To ensure that persons with disabilities have an opportunity to organize, develop and participate in disability-specific sporting and recreational activities and, to this end, encourage the provision, on an equal basis with others, of appropriate instruction, training and resources;
(c) To ensure that persons with disabilities have access to sporting, recreational and tourism venues;
(d) To ensure that children with disabilities have equal access with other children to participation in play, recreation and leisure and sporting activities, including those activities in the school system;
(e) To ensure that persons with disabilities have access to services from those involved in the organization of recreational, tourism, leisure and sporting activities.

Article 31 Statistics and data collection

1 States Parties undertake to collect appropriate information, including statistical and research data, to enable them to formulate and implement policies to give effect to the present Convention. The process of collecting and maintaining this information shall:

(a) Comply with legally established safeguards, including legislation on data protection, to ensure confidentiality and respect for the privacy of persons with disabilities;
(b) Comply with internationally accepted norms to protect human rights and fundamental freedoms and ethical principles in the collection and use of statistics.

2 The information collected in accordance with this article shall be disaggregated, as appropriate, and used to help assess the implementation of States Parties' obligations under the present Convention and to identify and address the barriers faced by persons with disabilities in exercising their rights.

3 States Parties shall assume responsibility for the dissemination of these statistics and ensure their accessibility to persons with disabilities and others.

Article 32 International cooperation

1 States Parties recognize the importance of international cooperation and its promotion, in support of national efforts for the realization of the purpose and objectives of the present Convention, and will undertake appropriate and effective measures in this regard, between and among States and, as appropriate, in partnership with relevant international and regional organizations and civil society, in particular organizations of persons with disabilities. Such measures could include, inter alia:
(a) Ensuring that international cooperation, including international development programmes, is inclusive of and accessible to persons with disabilities;
(b) Facilitating and supporting capacity-building, including through the exchange and sharing of information, experiences, training programmes and best practices;
(c) Facilitating cooperation in research and access to scientific and technical knowledge;
(d) Providing, as appropriate, technical and economic assistance, including by facilitating access to and sharing of accessible and assistive technologies, and through the transfer of technologies.

2 The provisions of this article are without prejudice to the obligations of each State Party to fulfil its obligations under the present Convention.

Article 33 National implementation and monitoring

1 States Parties, in accordance with their system of organization, shall designate one or more focal points within government for matters relating to the implementation of the present Convention, and shall give due consideration to the establishment or designation of a coordination

mechanism within government to facilitate related action in different sectors and at different levels.

2 States Parties shall, in accordance with their legal and administrative systems, maintain, strengthen, designate or establish within the State Party, a framework, including one or more independent mechanisms, as appropriate, to promote, protect and monitor implementation of the present Convention. When designating or establishing such a mechanism, States Parties shall take into account the principles relating to the status and functioning of national institutions for protection and promotion of human rights.

3 Civil society, in particular persons with disabilities and their representative organizations, shall be involved and participate fully in the monitoring process.

Article 34 Committee on the Rights of Persons with Disabilities

1 There shall be established a Committee on the Rights of Persons with Disabilities (hereafter referred to as 'the Committee'), which shall carry out the functions hereinafter provided.

2 The Committee shall consist, at the time of entry into force of the present Convention, of twelve experts. After an additional sixty ratifications or accessions to the Convention, the membership of the Committee shall increase by six members, attaining a maximum number of eighteen members.

3 The members of the Committee shall serve in their personal capacity and shall be of high moral standing and recognized competence and experience in the field covered by the present Convention. When nominating their candidates, States Parties are invited to give due consideration to the provision set out in article 4.3 of the present Convention.

4 The members of the Committee shall be elected by States Parties, consideration being given to equitable geographical distribution, representation of the different forms of civilization and of the principal legal systems, balanced gender representation and participation of experts with disabilities.

5 The members of the Committee shall be elected by secret ballot from a list of persons nominated by the States Parties from among their nationals at meetings of the Conference of States Parties. At those meetings, for which two thirds of States Parties shall constitute a quorum, the persons elected to the Committee shall be those who obtain the largest number of votes and an absolute majority of the votes of the representatives of States Parties present and voting.

6 The initial election shall be held no later than six months after the date of entry into force of the present Convention. At least four months before the date of each election, the Secretary-General of the United Nations shall address a letter to the States Parties inviting them to submit the nominations within two months. The Secretary-General shall subsequently prepare a list in alphabetical order of all persons thus nominated, indicating the State Parties which have nominated them, and shall submit it to the States Parties to the present Convention.

7 The members of the Committee shall be elected for a term of four years. They shall be eligible for re-election once. However, the term of six of the members elected at the first election shall expire at the end of two years; immediately after the first election, the names of these six members shall be chosen by lot by the chairperson of the meeting referred to in paragraph 5 of this article.

8 The election of the six additional members of the Committee shall be held on the occasion of regular elections, in accordance with the relevant provisions of this article.

9 If a member of the Committee dies or resigns or declares that for any other cause she or he can no longer perform her or his duties, the State Party which nominated the member shall appoint another expert possessing the qualifications and meeting the requirements set out in the relevant provisions of this article, to serve for the remainder of the term.

10 The Committee shall establish its own rules of procedure.

11 The Secretary-General of the United Nations shall provide the necessary staff and facilities for the effective performance of the functions of the Committee under the present Convention, and shall convene its initial meeting.

12 With the approval of the General Assembly, the members of the Committee established under the present Convention shall receive emoluments from United Nations resources on such terms and conditions as the Assembly may decide, having regard to the importance of the Committee's responsibilities.

13 The members of the Committee shall be entitled to the facilities, privileges and immunities of experts on mission for the United Nations as laid down in the relevant sections of the Convention on the Privileges and Immunities of the United Nations.

Article 35 Reports by States Parties

1 Each State Party shall submit to the Committee, through the Secretary-General of the United Nations, a comprehensive report on measures taken to give effect to its obligations under the present Convention and on the progress made in that regard, within two years after the entry into force of the present Convention for the State Party concerned.

2 Thereafter, States Parties shall submit subsequent reports at least every four years and further whenever the Committee so requests.

3 The Committee shall decide any guidelines applicable to the content of the reports.

4 A State Party which has submitted a comprehensive initial report to the Committee need not, in its subsequent reports, repeat information previously provided. When preparing reports to the Committee, States Parties are invited to consider doing so in an open and transparent process and to give due consideration to the provision set out in article 4.3 of the present Convention.

5 Reports may indicate factors and difficulties affecting the degree of fulfilment of obligations under the present Convention.

Article 36 Consideration of reports

1 Each report shall be considered by the Committee, which shall make such suggestions and general recommendations on the report as it may consider appropriate and shall forward these to the State Party concerned. The State Party may respond with any information it chooses to the Committee. The Committee may request further information from States Parties relevant to the implementation of the present Convention.

2 If a State Party is significantly overdue in the submission of a report, the Committee may notify the State Party concerned of the need to examine the implementation of the present Convention in that State Party, on the basis of reliable information available to the Committee, if the relevant report is not submitted within three months following the notification. The Committee shall invite the State Party concerned to participate in such examination. Should the State Party respond by submitting the relevant report, the provisions of paragraph 1 of this article will apply.

3 The Secretary-General of the United Nations shall make available the reports to all States Parties.

4 States Parties shall make their reports widely available to the public in their own countries and facilitate access to the suggestions and general recommendations relating to these reports.

5 The Committee shall transmit, as it may consider appropriate, to the specialized agencies, funds and programmes of the United Nations, and other competent bodies, reports from States Parties in order to address a request or indication of a need for technical advice or assistance contained therein, along with the Committee's observations and recommendations, if any, on these requests or indications.

Article 37 Cooperation between States Parties and the Committee

1 Each State Party shall cooperate with the Committee and assist its members in the fulfilment of their mandate.

2 In its relationship with States Parties, the Committee shall give due consideration to ways and means of enhancing national capacities for the implementation of the present Convention, including through international cooperation.

Article 38 Relationship of the Committee with other bodies

In order to foster the effective implementation of the present Convention and to encourage international cooperation in the field covered by the present Convention:

(a) The specialized agencies and other United Nations organs shall be entitled to be represented at the consideration of the implementation of such provisions of the present Convention as fall within the scope of their mandate. The Committee may invite the specialized agencies and other competent bodies as it may consider appropriate to provide expert advice on the implementation of the Convention in areas falling within the scope of their respective mandates. The Committee may invite specialized agencies and other United Nations organs to submit reports on the implementation of the Convention in areas falling within the scope of their activities;

(b) The Committee, as it discharges its mandate, shall consult, as appropriate, other relevant bodies instituted by international human rights treaties, with a view to ensuring the consistency of their respective reporting guidelines, suggestions and general recommendations, and avoiding duplication and overlap in the performance of their functions.

Article 39 Report of the Committee

The Committee shall report every two years to the General Assembly and to the Economic and Social Council on its activities, and may make suggestions and general recommendations based on the examination of reports and information received from the States Parties. Such suggestions and general recommendations shall be included in the report of the Committee together with comments, if any, from States Parties.

Article 40 Conference of States Parties

1 The States Parties shall meet regularly in a Conference of States Parties in order to consider any matter with regard to the implementation of the present Convention.

2 No later than six months after the entry into force of the present Convention, the Conference of the States Parties shall be convened by the Secretary-General of the United Nations. The subsequent meetings shall be convened by the Secretary-General of the United Nations biennially or upon the decision of the Conference of States Parties.

Article 41 Depositary

The Secretary-General of the United Nations shall be the depositary of the present Convention.

Article 42 Signature

The present Convention shall be open for signature by all States and by regional integration organizations at United Nations Headquarters in New York as of 30 March 2007.

Article 43 Consent to be bound

The present Convention shall be subject to ratification by signatory States and to formal confirmation by signatory regional integration organizations. It shall be open for accession by any State or regional integration organization which has not signed the Convention.

Article 44 Regional integration organizations

1 'Regional integration organization' shall mean an organization constituted by sovereign States of a given region, to which its member States have transferred competence in respect of matters governed by this Convention. Such organizations shall declare, in their instruments of formal confirmation or accession, the extent of their competence with respect to matters governed by this Convention. Subsequently, they shall inform the depositary of any substantial modification in the extent of their competence.

2 References to "States Parties" in the present Convention shall apply to such organizations within the limits of their competence.

3 For the purposes of article 45, paragraph 1, and article 47, paragraphs 2 and 3, any instrument deposited by a regional integration organization shall not be counted.

4 Regional integration organizations, in matters within their competence, may exercise their right to vote in the Conference of States Parties, with a number of votes equal to the number of their member States that are Parties to this Convention. Such an organization shall not exercise its right to vote if any of its member States exercises its right, and vice versa.

Article 45 Entry into force

1 The present Convention shall enter into force on the thirtieth day after the deposit of the twentieth instrument of ratification or accession.
2 For each State or regional integration organization ratifying, formally confirming or acceding to the Convention after the deposit of the twentieth such instrument, the Convention shall enter into force on the thirtieth day after the deposit of its own such instrument.

Article 46 Reservations

1 Reservations incompatible with the object and purpose of the present Convention shall not be permitted.
2 Reservations may be withdrawn at any time.

Article 47 Amendments

1 Any State Party may propose an amendment to the present Convention and submit it to the Secretary-General of the United Nations. The Secretary-General shall communicate any proposed amendments to States Parties, with a request to be notified whether they favour a conference of States Parties for the purpose of considering and deciding upon the proposals. In the event that, within four months from the date of such communication, at least one third of the States Parties favour such a conference, the Secretary-General shall convene the conference under the auspices of the United Nations. Any amendment adopted by a majority of two thirds of the States Parties present and voting shall be submitted by the Secretary-General to the General Assembly for approval and thereafter to all States Parties for acceptance.
2 An amendment adopted and approved in accordance with paragraph 1 of this article shall enter into force on the thirtieth day after the number of instruments of acceptance deposited reaches two thirds of the number of States Parties at the date of adoption of the amendment. Thereafter, the amendment shall enter into force for any State Party on the thirtieth day following the deposit of its own instrument of acceptance. An amendment shall be binding only on those States Parties which have accepted it.
3 If so decided by the Conference of States Parties by consensus, an amendment adopted and approved in accordance with paragraph 1 of this article which relates exclusively to articles 34, 38, 39 and 40 shall enter into force for all States Parties on the thirtieth day after the number of instruments of acceptance deposited reaches two thirds of the number of States Parties at the date of adoption of the amendment.

Article 48 Denunciation

A State Party may denounce the present Convention by written notification to the Secretary-General of the United Nations. The denunciation shall become effective one year after the date of receipt of the notification by the Secretary-General.

Article 49 Accessible format

The text of the present Convention shall be made available in accessible formats.

Article 50 Authentic texts

The Arabic, Chinese, English, French, Russian and Spanish texts of the present Convention shall be equally authentic.

In witness thereof the undersigned plenipotentiaries, being duly authorized thereto by their respective Governments, have signed the present Convention.

14.4.2 Full text of the Standard Rules on the Equalization of Opportunities for Persons with Disabilities

INTRODUCTION

Background and current needs

1 There are persons with disabilities in all parts of the world and at all levels in every society. The number of persons with disabilities in the world is large and is growing.

2 Both the causes and the consequences of disability vary throughout the world. Those variations are the result of different socio-economic circumstances and of the different provisions that States make for the well-being of their citizens.

3 Present disability policy is the result of developments over the past 200 years. In many ways it reflects the general living conditions and social and economic policies of different times. In the disability field, however, there are also many specific circumstances that have influenced the living conditions of persons with disabilities. Ignorance, neglect, superstition and fear are social factors that throughout the history of disability have isolated persons with disabilities and delayed their development.

4 Over the years disability policy developed from elementary care at institutions to education for children with disabilities and rehabilitation for persons who became disabled during adult life. Through education and rehabilitation, persons with disabilities became more active and a driving force in the further development of disability policy. Organizations of persons with disabilities, their families and advocates were formed,

which advocated better conditions for persons with disabilities. After the Second World War the concepts of integration and normalization were introduced, which reflected a growing awareness of the capabilities of persons with disabilities.

5 Towards the end of the 1960s organizations of persons with disabilities in some countries started to formulate a new concept of disability. That new concept indicated the close connection between the limitation experienced by individuals with disabilities, the design and structure of their environments and the attitude of the general population. At the same time the problems of disability in developing countries were more and more highlighted. In some of those countries the percentage of the population with disabilities was estimated to be very high and, for the most part, persons with disabilities were extremely poor.

Previous international action

6 The rights of persons with disabilities have been the subject of much attention in the United Nations and other international organizations over a long period of time. The most important outcome of the International Year of Disabled Persons, 1981, was the World Programme of Action concerning Disabled Persons, adopted by the General Assembly by its resolution 37/52 of 3 December 1982. The Year and the World Programme of Action provided a strong impetus for progress in the field. They both emphasized the right of persons with disabilities to the same opportunities as other citizens and to an equal share in the improvements in living conditions resulting from economic and social development. There also, for the first time, handicap was defined as a function of the relationship between persons with disabilities and their environment.

7 The Global Meeting of Experts to Review the Implementation of the World Programme of Action concerning Disabled Persons at the Mid-Point of the United Nations Decade of Disabled Persons was held at Stockholm in 1987. It was suggested at the Meeting that a guiding philosophy should be developed to indicate the priorities for action in the years ahead. The basis of that philosophy should be the recognition of the rights of persons with disabilities.

8 Consequently, the Meeting recommended that the General Assembly convene a special conference to draft an international convention on the elimination of all forms of discrimination against persons with disabilities, to be ratified by States by the end of the Decade.

9 A draft outline of the convention was prepared by Italy and presented to the General Assembly at its forty-second session. Further presentations concerning a draft convention were made by Sweden at the forty-fourth session of the Assembly. However, on both occasions, no consensus could be reached on the suitability of such a convention. In the opinion of many representatives, existing human rights documents seemed to guarantee persons with disabilities the same rights as other persons.

Towards standard rules

10 Guided by the deliberations in the General Assembly, the Economic and Social Council, at its first regular session of 1990, finally agreed to concentrate on the elaboration of an international instrument of a different kind. By its resolution 1990/26 of 24 May 1990, the Council authorized the Commission for Social Development to consider, at its thirty-second session, the establishment of an ad hoc open-ended working group of government experts, funded by voluntary contributions, to elaborate standard rules on the equalization of opportunities for disabled children, youth and adults, in close collaboration with the specialized agencies, other intergovernmental bodies and non-governmental organizations, especially organizations of disabled persons. The Council also requested the Commission to finalize the text of those rules for consideration in 1993 and for submission to the General Assembly at its forty-eighth session.

11 The subsequent discussions in the Third Committee of the General Assembly at the forty-fifth session showed that there was wide support for the new initiative to elaborate standard rules on the equalization of opportunities for persons with disabilities.

12 At the thirty-second session of the Commission for Social Development, the initiative for standard rules received the support of a large number of representatives and discussions led to the adoption of resolution 32/2 of 20 February 1991, in which the Commission decided to establish an ad hoc open-ended working group in accordance with Economic and Social Council resolution 1990/26.

Purpose and content of the Standard Rules on the Equalization of Opportunities for Persons with Disabilities

13 The Standard Rules on the Equalization of Opportunities for Persons with Disabilities have been developed on the basis of the experience gained during the United Nations Decade of Disabled Persons (1983–1992). The International Bill of Human Rights, comprising the Universal Declaration of Human Rights, the International Covenant on Economic, Social and Cultural Rights and the International Covenant on Civil and Political Rights, the Convention on the Rights of the Child and the Convention on the Elimination of All Forms of Discrimination against Women, as well as the World Programme of Action concerning

Disabled Persons, constitute the political and moral foundation for the Rules.

14 Although the Rules are not compulsory, they can become international customary rules when they are applied by a great number of States with the intention of respecting a rule in international law. They imply a strong moral and political commitment on behalf of States to take action for the equalization of opportunities for persons with disabilities. Important principles for responsibility, action and cooperation are indicated. Areas of decisive importance for the quality of life and for the achievement of full participation and equality are pointed out. The Rules offer an instrument for policy-making and action to persons with disabilities and their organizations. They provide a basis for technical and economic cooperation among States, the United Nations and other international organizations.

15 The purpose of the Rules is to ensure that girls, boys, women and men with disabilities, as members of their societies, may exercise the same rights and obligations as others. In all societies of the world there are still obstacles preventing persons with disabilities from exercising their rights and freedoms and making it difficult for them to participate fully in the activities of their societies. It is the responsibility of States to take appropriate action to remove such obstacles. Persons with disabilities and their organizations should play an active role as partners in this process. The equalization of opportunities for persons with disabilities is an essential contribution in the general and worldwide effort to mobilize human resources. Special attention may need to be directed towards groups such as women, children, the elderly, the poor, migrant workers, persons with dual or multiple disabilities, indigenous people and ethnic minorities. In addition, there are a large number of refugees with disabilities who have special needs requiring attention.

Fundamental concepts in disability policy

16 The concepts set out below appear throughout the Rules. They are essentially built on the concepts in the World Programme of Action concerning Disabled Persons. In some cases they reflect the development that has taken place during the United Nations Decade of Disabled Persons.

Disability and handicap

17 The term 'disability' summarizes a great number of different functional limitations occurring in any population in any country of the world. People may be disabled by physical, intellectual or sensory impairment, medical conditions or mental illness. Such impairments, conditions or illnesses may be permanent or transitory in nature.

18 The term 'handicap' means the loss or limitation of opportunities to take part in the life of the community on an equal level with others. It describes the encounter between the person with a disability and the environment. The purpose of this term is to emphasize the focus on the shortcomings in the environment and in many organized activities in society, for example, information, communication and education, which prevent persons with disabilities from participating on equal terms.

19 The use of the two terms 'disability' and 'handicap', as defined in paragraphs 17 and 18 above, should be seen in the light of modern disability history. During the 1970s there was a strong reaction among representatives of organizations of persons with disabilities and professionals in the field of disability against the terminology of the time. The terms 'disability' and 'handicap' were often used in an unclear and confusing way, which gave poor guidance for policy-making and for political action. The terminology reflected a medical and diagnostic approach, which ignored the imperfections and deficiencies of the surrounding society.

20 In 1980, the World Health Organization adopted an international classification of impairments, disabilities and handicaps, which suggested a more precise and at the same time relativistic approach. The International Classification of Impairments, Disabilities, and Handicaps [World Health Organization, International Classification of Impairments, Disabilities, and Handicaps: A manual of classification relating to the consequences of disease (Geneva, 1980)] makes a clear distinction between 'impairment', 'disability' and 'handicap'. It has been extensively used in areas such as rehabilitation, education, statistics, policy, legislation, demography, sociology, economics and anthropology. Some users have expressed concern that the Classification, in its definition of the term 'handicap', may still be considered too medical and too centred on the individual, and may not adequately clarify the interaction between societal conditions or expectations and the abilities of the individual. Those concerns, and others expressed by users during the 12 years since its publication, will be addressed in forthcoming revisions of the Classification.

21 As a result of experience gained in the implementation of the World Programme of Action and of the general discussion that took place during the United Nations Decade of Disabled Persons, there was a deepening of knowledge and extension of understanding concerning disability issues and the terminology used. Current terminology recognizes the necessity of addressing both the individual needs (such as rehabilitation and technical aids) and the shortcomings of the society (various obstacles for participation).

Prevention

22 The term 'prevention' means action aimed at preventing the occurrence of physical, intellectual, psychiatric or sensory impairments (primary prevention) or at preventing impairments from causing a permanent functional limitation or disability (secondary prevention). Prevention may include many different types of action, such as primary health care, prenatal and postnatal care, education in nutrition, immunization campaigns against communicable diseases, measures to control endemic diseases, safety regulations, programmes for the prevention of accidents in different environments, including adaptation of workplaces to prevent occupational disabilities and diseases, and prevention of disability resulting from pollution of the environment or armed conflict.

Rehabilitation

23 The term 'rehabilitation' refers to a process aimed at enabling persons with disabilities to reach and maintain their optimal physical, sensory, intellectual, psychiatric and/or social functional levels, thus providing them with the tools to change their lives towards a higher level of independence. Rehabilitation may include measures to provide and/or restore functions, or compensate for the loss or absence of a function or for a functional limitation. The rehabilitation process does not involve initial medical care. It includes a wide range of measures and activities from more basic and general rehabilitation to goal-oriented activities, for instance vocational rehabilitation.

Equalization of opportunities

24 The term 'equalization of opportunities' means the process through which the various systems of society and the environment, such as services, activities, information and documentation, are made available to all, particularly to persons with disabilities.

25 The principle of equal rights implies that the needs of each and every individual are of equal importance, that those needs must be made the basis for the planning of societies and that all resources must be employed in such a way as to ensure that every individual has equal opportunity for participation.

26 Persons with disabilities are members of society and have the right to remain within their local communities. They should receive the support they need within the ordinary structures of education, health, employment and social services.

27 As persons with disabilities achieve equal rights, they should also have equal obligations. As those rights are being achieved, societies should raise their expectations of persons with disabilities. As part of the process of equal opportunities, provision should be made to assist persons with disabilities to assume their full responsibility as members of society.

I. PRECONDITIONS FOR EQUAL PARTICIPATION

Rule 1 Awareness-raising

States should take action to raise awareness in society about persons with disabilities, their rights, their needs, their potential and their contribution.

1 States should ensure that responsible authorities distribute up-to-date information on available programmes and services to persons with disabilities, their families, professionals in the field and the general public. Information to persons with disabilities should be presented in accessible form.

2 States should initiate and support information campaigns concerning persons with disabilities and disability policies, conveying the message that persons with disabilities are citizens with the same rights and obligations as others, thus justifying measures to remove all obstacles to full participation.

3 States should encourage the portrayal of persons with disabilities by the mass media in a positive way; organizations of persons with disabilities should be consulted on this matter.

4 States should ensure that public education programmes reflect in all their aspects the principle of full participation and equality.

5 States should invite persons with disabilities and their families and organizations to participate in public education programmes concerning disability matters.

6 States should encourage enterprises in the private sector to include disability issues in all aspects of their activity.

7 States should initiate and promote programmes aimed at raising the level of awareness of persons with disabilities concerning their rights and potential. Increased self-reliance and empowerment will assist persons with disabilities to take advantage of the opportunities available to them.

8 Awareness-raising should be an important part of the education of children with disabilities and in rehabilitation programmes. Persons with disabilities could also assist one another in awareness-raising through the activities of their own organizations.

9 Awareness-raising should be part of the education of all children and should be a component of teacher-training courses and training of all professionals.

Rule 2 Medical care

States should ensure the provision of effective medical care to persons with disabilities.

1 States should work towards the provision of programmes run by multidisciplinary teams of professionals for early detection, assessment and treatment of impairment. This could prevent, reduce or eliminate disabling effects. Such programmes should ensure the full participation of persons with disabilities and their families at the individual level, and of organizations of persons with disabilities at the planning and evaluation level.
2 Local community workers should be trained to participate in areas such as early detection of impairments, the provision of primary assistance and referral to appropriate services.
3 States should ensure that persons with disabilities, particularly infants and children, are provided with the same level of medical care within the same system as other members of society.
4 States should ensure that all medical and paramedical personnel are adequately trained and equipped to give medical care to persons with disabilities and that they have access to relevant treatment methods and technology.
5 States should ensure that medical, paramedical and related personnel are adequately trained so that they do not give inappropriate advice to parents, thus restricting options for their children. This training should be an ongoing process and should be based on the latest information available.
6 States should ensure that persons with disabilities are provided with any regular treatment and medicines they may need to preserve or improve their level of functioning.

Rule 3 Rehabilitation

States should ensure the provision of rehabilitation services to persons with disabilities in order for them to reach and sustain their optimum level of independence and functioning.

1 States should develop national rehabilitation programmes for all groups of persons with disabilities. Such programmes should be based on the actual individual needs of persons with disabilities and on the principles of full participation and equality.

2 Such programmes should include a wide range of activities, such as basic skills training to improve or compensate for an affected function, counselling of persons with disabilities and their families, developing self-reliance, and occasional services such as assessment and guidance.
3 All persons with disabilities, including persons with severe and/or multiple disabilities, who require rehabilitation should have access to it.
4 Persons with disabilities and their families should be able to participate in the design and organization of rehabilitation services concerning themselves.
5 All rehabilitation services should be available in the local community where the person with disabilities lives. However, in some instances, in order to attain a certain training objective, special time-limited rehabilitation courses may be organized, where appropriate, in residential form.
6 Persons with disabilities and their families should be encouraged to involve themselves in rehabilitation, for instance as trained teachers, instructors or counsellors.
7 States should draw upon the expertise of organizations of persons with disabilities when formulating or evaluating rehabilitation programmes.

Rule 4 Support services

States should ensure the development and supply of support services, including assistive devices for persons with disabilities, to assist them to increase their level of independence in their daily living and to exercise their rights.

1 States should ensure the provision of assistive devices and equipment, personal assistance and interpreter services, according to the needs of persons with disabilities, as important measures to achieve the equalization of opportunities.
2 States should support the development, production, distribution and servicing of assistive devices and equipment and the dissemination of knowledge about them.
3 To achieve this, generally available technical know-how should be utilized. In States where high-technology industry is available, it should be fully utilized to improve the standard and effectiveness of assistive devices and equipment. It is important to stimulate the development and production of simple and inexpensive devices, using local material and local production facilities when possible. Persons with disabilities themselves could be involved in the production of those devices.
4 States should recognize that all persons with disabilities who need assistive devices should have access to them as appropriate, including financial accessibility. This may mean that assistive devices and equipment

should be provided free of charge or at such a low price that persons with disabilities or their families can afford to buy them.

5 In rehabilitation programmes for the provision of assistive devices and equipment, States should consider the special requirements of girls and boys with disabilities concerning the design, durability and age-appropriateness of assistive devices and equipment.

6 States should support the development and provision of personal assistance programmes and interpretation services, especially for persons with severe and/or multiple disabilities. Such programmes would increase the level of participation of persons with disabilities in everyday life at home, at work, in school and during leisure-time activities.

7 Personal assistance programmes should be designed in such a way that the persons with disabilities using the programmes have a decisive influence on the way in which the programmes are delivered.

II. TARGET AREAS FOR EQUAL PARTICIPATION

Rule 5 Accessibility

States should recognize the overall importance of accessibility in the process of the equalization of opportunities in all spheres of society. For persons with disabilities of any kind, States should (a) introduce programmes of action to make the physical environment accessible; and (b) undertake measures to provide access to information and communication.

(a) Access to the physical environment

1 States should initiate measures to remove the obstacles to participation in the physical environment. Such measures should be to develop standards and guidelines and to consider enacting legislation to ensure accessibility to various areas in society, such as housing, buildings, public transport services and other means of transportation, streets and other outdoor environments.

2 States should ensure that architects, construction engineers and others who are professionally involved in the design and construction of the physical environment have access to adequate information on disability policy and measures to achieve accessibility.

3 Accessibility requirements should be included in the design and construction of the physical environment from the beginning of the designing process.

4 Organizations of persons with disabilities should be consulted when standards and norms for accessibility are being developed. They should also be involved locally from the initial planning stage when public construction projects are being designed, thus ensuring maximum accessibility.

(b) Access to information and communication

5 Persons with disabilities and, where appropriate, their families and advocates should have access to full information on diagnosis, rights and available services and programmes, at all stages. Such information should be presented in forms accessible to persons with disabilities.

6 States should develop strategies to make information services and documentation accessible for different groups of persons with disabilities. Braille, tape services, large print and other appropriate technologies should be used to provide access to written information and documentation for persons with visual impairments. Similarly, appropriate technologies should be used to provide access to spoken information for persons with auditory impairments or comprehension difficulties.

7 Consideration should be given to the use of sign language in the education of deaf children, in their families and communities. Sign language interpretation services should also be provided to facilitate the communication between deaf persons and others.

8 Consideration should also be given to the needs of people with other communication disabilities.

9 States should encourage the media, especially television, radio and newspapers, to make their services accessible.

10 States should ensure that new computerized information and service systems offered to the general public are either made initially accessible or are adapted to be made accessible to persons with disabilities.

11 Organizations of persons with disabilities should be consulted when measures to make information services accessible are being developed.

Rule 6 Education

States should recognize the principle of equal primary, secondary and tertiary educational opportunities for children, youth and adults with disabilities, in integrated settings. They should ensure that the education of persons with disabilities is an integral part of the educational system.

1 General educational authorities are responsible for the education of persons with disabilities in integrated settings. Education for persons with disabilities should form an integral part of national educational planning, curriculum development and school organization.

2 Education in mainstream schools presupposes the provision of interpreter and other appropriate support services. Adequate accessibility and support services, designed to meet the needs of persons with different disabilities, should be provided.

3 Parent groups and organizations of persons with disabilities should be involved in the education process at all levels.

4 In States where education is compulsory it should be provided to girls and boys with all kinds and all levels of disabilities, including the most severe.

5 Special attention should be given in the following areas:
  - **(a)** Very young children with disabilities;
  - **(b)** Pre-school children with disabilities;
  - **(c)** Adults with disabilities, particularly women.

6 To accommodate educational provisions for persons with disabilities in the mainstream, States should:
  - **(a)** Have a clearly stated policy, understood and accepted at the school level and by the wider community;
  - **(b)** Allow for curriculum flexibility, addition and adaptation;
  - **(c)** Provide for quality materials, ongoing teacher training and support teachers.

7 Integrated education and community-based programmes should be seen as complementary approaches in providing cost-effective education and training for persons with disabilities. National community-based programmes should encourage communities to use and develop their resources to provide local education to persons with disabilities.

8 In situations where the general school system does not yet adequately meet the needs of all persons with disabilities, special education may be considered. It should be aimed at preparing students for education in the general school system. The quality of such education should reflect the same standards and ambitions as general education and should be closely linked to it. At a minimum, students with disabilities should be afforded the same portion of educational resources as students without disabilities. States should aim for the gradual integration of special education services into mainstream education. It is acknowledged that in some instances special education may currently be considered to be the most appropriate form of education for some students with disabilities.

9 Owing to the particular communication needs of deaf and deaf/blind persons, their education may be more suitably provided in schools for such persons or special classes and units in mainstream schools. At the initial stage, in particular, special attention needs to be focused on culturally sensitive instruction that will result in effective communication skills and maximum independence for people who are deaf or deaf/blind.

Rule 7 Employment

States should recognize the principle that persons with disabilities must be empowered to exercise their human rights, particularly in the field of employment. In both rural and urban areas they must have equal opportunities for productive and gainful employment in the labour market.

1 Laws and regulations in the employment field must not discriminate against persons with disabilities and must not raise obstacles to their employment.
2 States should actively support the integration of persons with disabilities into open employment. This active support could occur through a variety of measures, such as vocational training, incentive-oriented quota schemes, reserved or designated employment, loans or grants for small business, exclusive contracts or priority production rights, tax concessions, contract compliance or other technical or financial assistance to enterprises employing workers with disabilities. States should also encourage employers to make reasonable adjustments to accommodate persons with disabilities.
3 States' action programmes should include:
   (a) Measures to design and adapt workplaces and work premises in such a way that they become accessible to persons with different disabilities;
   (b) Support for the use of new technologies and the development and production of assistive devices, tools and equipment and measures to facilitate access to such devices and equipment for persons with disabilities to enable them to gain and maintain employment;
   (c) Provision of appropriate training and placement and ongoing support such as personal assistance and interpreter services.
4 States should initiate and support public awareness-raising campaigns designed to overcome negative attitudes and prejudices concerning workers with disabilities.
5 In their capacity as employers, States should create favourable conditions for the employment of persons with disabilities in the public sector.
6 States, workers' organizations and employers should cooperate to ensure equitable recruitment and promotion policies, employment conditions, rates of pay, measures to improve the work environment in order to prevent injuries and impairments and measures for the rehabilitation of employees who have sustained employment-related injuries.
7 The aim should always be for persons with disabilities to obtain employment in the open labour market. For persons with disabilities whose needs cannot be met in open employment, small units of sheltered or supported employment may be an alternative. It is important that the quality of such programmes be assessed in terms of their relevance and sufficiency in providing opportunities for persons with disabilities to gain employment in the labour market.
8 Measures should be taken to include persons with disabilities in training and employment programmes in the private and informal sectors.

9 States, workers' organizations and employers should cooperate with organizations of persons with disabilities concerning all measures to create training and employment opportunities, including flexible hours, part-time work, job-sharing, self-employment and attendant care for persons with disabilities.

Rule 8 Income maintenance and social security

States are responsible for the provision of social security and income maintenance for persons with disabilities.

1 States should ensure the provision of adequate income support to persons with disabilities who, owing to disability or disability-related factors, have temporarily lost or received a reduction in their income or have been denied employment opportunities. States should ensure that the provision of support takes into account the costs frequently incurred by persons with disabilities and their families as a result of the disability.
2 In countries where social security, social insurance or other social welfare schemes exist or are being developed for the general population, States should ensure that such systems do not exclude or discriminate against persons with disabilities.
3 States should also ensure the provision of income support and social security protection to individuals who undertake the care of a person with a disability.
4 Social security systems should include incentives to restore the income-earning capacity of persons with disabilities. Such systems should provide or contribute to the organization, development and financing of vocational training. They should also assist with placement services.
5 Social security programmes should also provide incentives for persons with disabilities to seek employment in order to establish or re-establish their income-earning capacity.
6 Income support should be maintained as long as the disabling conditions remain in a manner that does not discourage persons with disabilities from seeking employment. It should only be reduced or terminated when persons with disabilities achieve adequate and secure income.
7 States, in countries where social security is to a large extent provided by the private sector, should encourage local communities, welfare organizations and families to develop self-help measures and incentives for employment or employment-related activities for persons with disabilities.

Rule 9 Family life and personal integrity

States should promote the full participation of persons with disabilities in family life. They should promote their right to personal integrity and ensure that laws do not discriminate against persons with disabilities with respect to sexual relationships, marriage and parenthood.

1 Persons with disabilities should be enabled to live with their families. States should encourage the inclusion in family counselling of appropriate modules regarding disability and its effects on family life. Respite-care and attendant-care services should be made available to families which include a person with disabilities. States should remove all unnecessary obstacles to persons who want to foster or adopt a child or adult with disabilities.
2 Persons with disabilities must not be denied the opportunity to experience their sexuality, have sexual relationships and experience parenthood. Taking into account that persons with disabilities may experience difficulties in getting married and setting up a family, States should encourage the availability of appropriate counselling. Persons with disabilities must have the same access as others to family-planning methods, as well as to information in accessible form on the sexual functioning of their bodies.
3 States should promote measures to change negative attitudes towards marriage, sexuality and parenthood of persons with disabilities, especially of girls and women with disabilities, which still prevail in society. The media should be encouraged to play an important role in removing such negative attitudes.
4 Persons with disabilities and their families need to be fully informed about taking precautions against sexual and other forms of abuse. Persons with disabilities are particularly vulnerable to abuse in the family, community or institutions and need to be educated on how to avoid the occurrence of abuse, recognize when abuse has occurred and report on such acts.

Rule 10 Culture

States will ensure that persons with disabilities are integrated into and can participate in cultural activities on an equal basis.

1 States should ensure that persons with disabilities have the opportunity to utilize their creative, artistic and intellectual potential, not only for their own benefit, but also for the enrichment of their community, be they in urban or rural areas. Examples of such activities are dance, music, literature, theatre, plastic arts, painting and sculpture. Particularly in developing countries, emphasis should be placed on traditional and contemporary art forms, such as puppetry, recitation and story-telling.
2 States should promote the accessibility to and availability of places for cultural performances and services, such as theatres, museums, cinemas and libraries, to persons with disabilities.

3 States should initiate the development and use of special technical arrangements to make literature, films and theatre accessible to persons with disabilities.

Rule 11 Recreation and sports

States will take measures to ensure that persons with disabilities have equal opportunities for recreation and sports.

1 States should initiate measures to make places for recreation and sports, hotels, beaches, sports arenas, gym halls, etc., accessible to persons with disabilities. Such measures should encompass support for staff in recreation and sports programmes, including projects to develop methods of accessibility, and participation, information and training programmes.
2 Tourist authorities, travel agencies, hotels, voluntary organizations and others involved in organizing recreational activities or travel opportunities should offer their services to all, taking into account the special needs of persons with disabilities. Suitable training should be provided to assist that process.
3 Sports organizations should be encouraged to develop opportunities for participation by persons with disabilities in sports activities. In some cases, accessibility measures could be enough to open up opportunities for participation. In other cases, special arrangements or special games would be needed. States should support the participation of persons with disabilities in national and international events.
4 Persons with disabilities participating in sports activities should have access to instruction and training of the same quality as other participants.
5 Organizers of sports and recreation should consult with organizations of persons with disabilities when developing their services for persons with disabilities.

Rule 12 Religion

States will encourage measures for equal participation by persons with disabilities in the religious life of their communities.

1 States should encourage, in consultation with religious authorities, measures to eliminate discrimination and make religious activities accessible to persons with disabilities.
2 States should encourage the distribution of information on disability matters to religious institutions and organizations. States should also encourage religious authorities to include information on disability policies in the training for religious professions, as well as in religious education programmes.
3 They should also encourage the accessibility of religious literature to persons with sensory impairments.

4 States and/or religious organizations should consult with organizations of persons with disabilities when developing measures for equal participation in religious activities.

III. IMPLEMENTATION MEASURES

Rule 13 Information and research

States assume the ultimate responsibility for the collection and dissemination of information on the living conditions of persons with disabilities and promote comprehensive research on all aspects, including obstacles that affect the lives of persons with disabilities.

1 States should, at regular intervals, collect gender-specific statistics and other information concerning the living conditions of persons with disabilities. Such data collection could be conducted in conjunction with national censuses and household surveys and could be undertaken in close collaboration, inter alia, with universities, research institutes and organizations of persons with disabilities. The data collection should include questions on programmes and services and their use.
2 States should consider establishing a data bank on disability, which would include statistics on available services and programmes as well as on the different groups of persons with disabilities. They should bear in mind the need to protect individual privacy and personal integrity.
3 States should initiate and support programmes of research on social, economic and participation issues that affect the lives of persons with disabilities and their families. Such research should include studies on the causes, types and frequencies of disabilities, the availability and efficacy of existing programmes and the need for development and evaluation of services and support measures.
4 States should develop and adopt terminology and criteria for the conduct of national surveys, in cooperation with organizations of persons with disabilities.
5 States should facilitate the participation of persons with disabilities in data collection and research. To undertake such research States should particularly encourage the recruitment of qualified persons with disabilities.
6 States should support the exchange of research findings and experiences.
7 States should take measures to disseminate information and knowledge on disability to all political and administration levels within national, regional and local spheres.

Rule 14 Policy-making and planning

States will ensure that disability aspects are included in all relevant policy-making and national planning.

1 States should initiate and plan adequate policies for persons with disabilities at the national level, and stimulate and support action at regional and local levels.
2 States should involve organizations of persons with disabilities in all decision-making relating to plans and programmes concerning persons with disabilities or affecting their economic and social status.
3 The needs and concerns of persons with disabilities should be incorporated into general development plans and not be treated separately.
4 The ultimate responsibility of States for the situation of persons with disabilities does not relieve others of their responsibility. Anyone in charge of services, activities or the provision of information in society should be encouraged to accept responsibility for making such programmes available to persons with disabilities.
5 States should facilitate the development by local communities of programmes and measures for persons with disabilities. One way of doing this could be to develop manuals or check-lists and provide training programmes for local staff.

Rule 15 Legislation

States have a responsibility to create the legal bases for measures to achieve the objectives of full participation and equality for persons with disabilities.
1 National legislation, embodying the rights and obligations of citizens, should include the rights and obligations of persons with disabilities. States are under an obligation to enable persons with disabilities to exercise their rights, including their human, civil and political rights, on an equal basis with other citizens. States must ensure that organizations of persons with disabilities are involved in the development of national legislation concerning the rights of persons with disabilities, as well as in the ongoing evaluation of that legislation.
2 Legislative action may be needed to remove conditions that may adversely affect the lives of persons with disabilities, including harassment and victimization. Any discriminatory provisions against persons with disabilities must be eliminated. National legislation should provide for appropriate sanctions in case of violations of the principles of non-discrimination.
3 National legislation concerning persons with disabilities may appear in two different forms. The rights and obligations may be incorporated in general legislation or contained in special legislation. Special legislation for persons with disabilities may be established in several ways:
   (a) By enacting separate legislation, dealing exclusively with disability matters;

(b) By including disability matters within legislation on particular topics;

(c) By mentioning persons with disabilities specifically in the texts that serve to interpret existing legislation.

A combination of those different approaches might be desirable. Affirmative action provisions may also be considered.

4 States may consider establishing formal statutory complaints mechanisms in order to protect the interests of persons with disabilities.

Rule 16 Economic policies

States have the financial responsibility for national programmes and measures to create equal opportunities for persons with disabilities.

1 States should include disability matters in the regular budgets of all national, regional and local government bodies.

2 States, non-governmental organizations and other interested bodies should interact to determine the most effective ways of supporting projects and measures relevant to persons with disabilities.

3 States should consider the use of economic measures (loans, tax exemptions, earmarked grants, special funds, and so on) to stimulate and support equal participation by persons with disabilities in society.

4 In many States it may be advisable to establish a disability development fund, which could support various pilot projects and self-help programmes at the grass-roots level.

Rule 17 Coordination of work

States are responsible for the establishment and strengthening of national coordinating committees, or similar bodies, to serve as a national focal point on disability matters.

1 The national coordinating committee or similar bodies should be permanent and based on legal as well as appropriate administrative regulation.

2 A combination of representatives of private and public organizations is most likely to achieve an intersectoral and multidisciplinary composition. Representatives could be drawn from concerned government ministries, organizations of persons with disabilities and non-governmental organizations.

3 Organizations of persons with disabilities should have considerable influence in the national coordinating committee in order to ensure proper feedback of their concerns.

4 The national coordinating committee should be provided with sufficient autonomy and resources to fulfil its responsibilities in relation to its decision-making capacities. It should report to the highest governmental level.

Rule 18 Organizations of persons with disabilities

States should recognize the right of the organizations of persons with disabilities to represent persons with disabilities at national, regional and local levels. States should also recognize the advisory role of organizations of persons with disabilities in decision-making on disability matters.

1 States should encourage and support economically and in other ways the formation and strengthening of organizations of persons with disabilities, family members and/or advocates. States should recognize that those organizations have a role to play in the development of disability policy.
2 States should establish ongoing communication with organizations of persons with disabilities and ensure their participation in the development of government policies.
3 The role of organizations of persons with disabilities could be to identify needs and priorities, to participate in the planning, implementation and evaluation of services and measures concerning the lives of persons with disabilities, and to contribute to public awareness and to advocate change.
4 As instruments of self-help, organizations of persons with disabilities provide and promote opportunities for the development of skills in various fields, mutual support among members and information sharing.
5 Organizations of persons with disabilities could perform their advisory role in many different ways such as having permanent representation on boards of government-funded agencies, serving on public commissions and providing expert knowledge on different projects.
6 The advisory role of organizations of persons with disabilities should be ongoing in order to develop and deepen the exchange of views and information between the State and the organizations.
7 Organizations should be permanently represented on the national coordinating committee or similar bodies.
8 The role of local organizations of persons with disabilities should be developed and strengthened to ensure that they influence matters at the community level.

Rule 19 Personnel training

States are responsible for ensuring the adequate training of personnel, at all levels, involved in the planning and provision of programmes and services concerning persons with disabilities.

1 States should ensure that all authorities providing services in the disability field give adequate training to their personnel.
2 In the training of professionals in the disability field, as well as in the provision of information on disability in general training programmes,

the principle of full participation and equality should be appropriately reflected.

3 States should develop training programmes in consultation with organizations of persons with disabilities, and persons with disabilities should be involved as teachers, instructors or advisers in staff training programmes.

4 The training of community workers is of great strategic importance, particularly in developing countries. It should involve persons with disabilities and include the development of appropriate values, competence and technologies as well as skills which can be practised by persons with disabilities, their parents, families and members of the community.

Rule 20 National monitoring and evaluation of disability programmes in the implementation of the Rules

States are responsible for the continuous monitoring and evaluation of the implementation of national programmes and services concerning the equalization of opportunities for persons with disabilities.

1 States should periodically and systematically evaluate national disability programmes and disseminate both the bases and the results of the evaluations.

2 States should develop and adopt terminology and criteria for the evaluation of disability-related programmes and services.

3 Such criteria and terminology should be developed in close cooperation with organizations of persons with disabilities from the earliest conceptual and planning stages.

4 States should participate in international cooperation in order to develop common standards for national evaluation in the disability field. States should encourage national coordinating committees to participate also.

5 The evaluation of various programmes in the disability field should be built in at the planning stage, so that the overall efficacy in fulfilling their policy objectives can be evaluated.

Rule 21 Technical and economic cooperation

States, both industrialized and developing, have the responsibility to cooperate in and take measures for the improvement of the living conditions of persons with disabilities in developing countries.

1 Measures to achieve the equalization of opportunities of persons with disabilities, including refugees with disabilities, should be integrated into general development programmes.

2 Such measures must be integrated into all forms of technical and economic cooperation, bilateral and multilateral, governmental and

non-governmental. States should bring up disability issues in discussions on such cooperation with their counterparts.

3 When planning and reviewing programmes of technical and economic cooperation, special attention should be given to the effects of such programmes on the situation of persons with disabilities. It is of the utmost importance that persons with disabilities and their organizations are consulted on any development projects designed for persons with disabilities. They should be directly involved in the development, implementation and evaluation of such projects.

4 Priority areas for technical and economic cooperation should include:

(a) The development of human resources through the development of skills, abilities and potentials of persons with disabilities and the initiation of employment-generating activities for and of persons with disabilities;

(b) The development and dissemination of appropriate disability-related technologies and know-how.

5 States are also encouraged to support the formation and strengthening of organizations of persons with disabilities.

6 States should take measures to improve the knowledge of disability issues among staff involved at all levels in the administration of technical and economic cooperation programmes.

Rule 22 International cooperation

States will participate actively in international cooperation concerning policies for the equalization of opportunities for persons with disabilities.

1 Within the United Nations, the specialized agencies and other concerned intergovernmental organizations, States should participate in the development of disability policy.

2 Whenever appropriate, States should introduce disability aspects in general negotiations concerning standards, information exchange, development programmes, etc.

3 States should encourage and support the exchange of knowledge and experience among:

(a) Non-governmental organizations concerned with disability issues;

(b) Research institutions and individual researchers involved in disability issues;

(c) Representatives of field programmes and of professional groups in the disability field;

(d) Organizations of persons with disabilities;

(e) National coordinating committees.

4 States should ensure that the United Nations and the specialized agencies, as well as all intergovernmental and interparliamentary bodies, at global and regional levels, include in their work the global and regional organizations of persons with disabilities.

IV. MONITORING MECHANISM

1 The purpose of a monitoring mechanism is to further the effective implementation of the Rules. It will assist each State in assessing its level of implementation of the Rules and in measuring its progress. The monitoring should identify obstacles and suggest suitable measures that would contribute to the successful implementation of the Rules. The monitoring mechanism will recognize the economic, social and cultural features existing in individual States. An important element should also be the provision of advisory services and the exchange of experience and information between States.

2 The Rules shall be monitored within the framework of the sessions of the Commission for Social Development. A Special Rapporteur with relevant and extensive experience in disability issues and international organizations shall be appointed, if necessary, funded by extrabudgetary resources, for three years to monitor the implementation of the Rules.

3 International organizations of persons with disabilities having consultative status with the Economic and Social Council and organizations representing persons with disabilities who have not yet formed their own organizations should be invited to create among themselves a panel of experts, on which organizations of persons with disabilities shall have a majority, taking into account the different kinds of disabilities and necessary equitable geographical distribution, to be consulted by the Special Rapporteur and, when appropriate, by the Secretariat.

4 The panel of experts will be encouraged by the Special Rapporteur to review, advise and provide feedback and suggestions on the promotion, implementation and monitoring of the Rules.

5 The Special Rapporteur shall send a set of questions to States, entities within the United Nations system, and intergovernmental and nongovernmental organizations, including organizations of persons with disabilities. The set of questions should address implementation plans for the Rules in States. The questions should be selective in nature and cover a number of specific rules for in-depth evaluation. In preparing the questions the Special Rapporteur should consult with the panel of experts and the Secretariat.

6 The Special Rapporteur shall seek to establish a direct dialogue not only with States but also with local non-governmental organizations, seeking their views and comments on any information intended to be included in the reports. The Special Rapporteur shall provide advisory

services on the implementation and monitoring of the Rules and assistance in the preparation of replies to the sets of questions.

7 The Department for Policy Coordination and Sustainable Development of the Secretariat, as the United Nations focal point on disability issues, the United Nations Development Programme and other entities and mechanisms within the United Nations system, such as the regional commissions and specialized agencies and inter-agency meetings, shall cooperate with the Special Rapporteur in the implementation and monitoring of the Rules at the national level.

8 The Special Rapporteur, assisted by the Secretariat, shall prepare reports for submission to the Commission for Social Development at its thirty-fourth and thirty-fifth sessions. In preparing such reports, the Rapporteur should consult with the panel of experts.

9 States should encourage national coordinating committees or similar bodies to participate in implementation and monitoring. As the focal points on disability matters at the national level, they should be encouraged to establish procedures to coordinate the monitoring of the Rules. Organizations of persons with disabilities should be encouraged to be actively involved in the monitoring of the process at all levels.

10 Should extrabudgetary resources be identified, one or more positions of interregional adviser on the Rules should be created to provide direct services to States, including:

- **(a)** The organization of national and regional training seminars on the content of the Rules;
- **(b)** The development of guidelines to assist in strategies for implementation of the Rules;
- **(c)** Dissemination of information about best practices concerning implementation of the Rules.

11 At its thirty-fourth session, the Commission for Social Development should establish an open-ended working group to examine the Special Rapporteur's report and make recommendations on how to improve the application of the Rules. In examining the Special Rapporteur's report, the Commission, through its open-ended working group, shall consult international organizations of persons with disabilities and specialized agencies, in accordance with rules 71 and 76 of the rules of procedure of the functional commissions of the Economic and Social Council.

12 At its session following the end of the Special Rapporteur's mandate, the Commission should examine the possibility of either renewing that mandate, appointing a new Special Rapporteur or considering another monitoring mechanism, and should make appropriate recommendations to the Economic and Social Council.

13 States should be encouraged to contribute to the United Nations Voluntary Fund on Disability in order to further the implementation of the Rules.

14.4.3 Full text of the Principles for the Protection of Persons with Mental Illness and the Improvement of Mental Health Care (MI Principles)

The General Assembly,

Mindful of the provisions of the Universal Declaration of Human Rights, the International Covenant on Civil and Political Rights, the International Covenant on Economic, Social and Cultural Rights and other relevant instruments, such as the Declaration on the Rights of Disabled Persons and the Body of Principles for the Protection of All Persons under Any Form of Detention or Imprisonment,

Recalling its resolution 33/53 of 14 December 1978, in which it requested the Commission on Human Rights to urge the Subcommission on Prevention of Discrimination and Protection of Minorities to undertake, as a matter of priority, a study of the question of the protection of those detained on the grounds of mental ill-health, with a view to formulating guidelines,

Recalling also its resolution 45/92 of 14 December 1990, in which it welcomed the progress made by the working group of the Commission on Human Rights in elaborating a draft body of principles for the protection of persons with mental illness and for the improvement of mental health care on the basis of a draft submitted to the Commission by the Subcommission on Prevention of Discrimination and Protection of Minorities,

Taking note of Commission on Human Rights resolution 1991/46 of 5 March 1991, in which the Commission endorsed the draft body of principles that had been submitted to it by the working group and decided to transmit it, as well as the report of the working group, to the General Assembly, through the Economic and Social Council,

Taking note also of Economic and Social Council resolution 1991/29 of 31 May 1991, in which the Council decided to submit the draft body of principles and the report of the working group to the General Assembly,

Taking note further of the recommendations of the Commission on Human Rights in its resolution 1991/46 and of the Economic and Social Council in its resolution 1991/29 that, on the adoption by the General Assembly of the draft body of principles, the full text thereof should be given the widest possible dissemination and that the introduction to the body of principles should at the same time be published as an accompanying document for the benefit of Governments and the public at large,

Taking note of the note by the Secretary-General, the annex to which contains the draft body of principles and the introduction to the body of principles,

1 Adopts the Principles for the Protection of Persons with Mental Illness and for the Improvement of Mental Health Care, the text of which is contained in the annex to the present resolution;

2 Requests the Secretary-General to include the text of the Principles, together with the introduction, in the next edition of the publication entitled 'Human Rights: A Compilation of International Instruments';

3 Requests the Secretary-General to give the Principles the widest possible dissemination and to ensure that the introduction is published at the same time as an accompanying document for the benefit of Governments and the public at large.

ANNEX

Principles for the protection of persons with mental illness and for the improvement of mental health care.

Application

The present Principles shall be applied without discrimination on any grounds, such as disability, race, colour, sex, language, religion, political or other opinion, national, ethnic or social origin, legal or social status, age, property or birth.

Definitions

In the present Principles:

(a) 'Counsel' means a legal or other qualified representative;

(b) 'Independent authority' means a competent and independent authority prescribed by domestic law;

(c) 'Mental health care' includes analysis and diagnosis of a person's mental condition, and treatment, care and rehabilitation for a mental illness or suspected mental illness;

(d) 'Mental health facility' means any establishment, or any unit of an establishment, which as its primary function provides mental health care;

(e) 'Mental health practitioner' means a medical doctor, clinical psychologist, nurse, social worker or other appropriately trained and qualified person with specific skills relevant to mental health care;

(f) 'Patient' means a person receiving mental health care and includes all persons who are admitted to a mental health facility;

(g) 'Personal representative' means a person charged by law with the duty of representing a patient's interests in any specified respect or of exercising specified rights on the patient's behalf, and includes the parent or legal guardian of a minor unless otherwise provided by domestic law;

(h) 'The review body' means the body established in accordance with principle 17 to review the involuntary admission or retention of a patient in a mental health facility.

General limitation clause

The exercise of the rights set forth in the present Principles may be subject only to such limitations as are prescribed by law and are necessary to protect the health or safety of the person concerned or of others, or otherwise to protect public safety, order, health or morals or the fundamental rights and freedoms of others.

Principle 1: Fundamental freedoms and basic rights

1 All persons have the right to the best available mental health care, which shall be part of the health and social care system.

2 All persons with a mental illness, or who are being treated as such persons, shall be treated with humanity and respect for the inherent dignity of the human person.

3 All persons with a mental illness, or who are being treated as such persons, have the right to protection from economic, sexual and other forms of exploitation, physical or other abuse and degrading treatment.

4 There shall be no discrimination on the grounds of mental illness. 'Discrimination' means any distinction, exclusion or preference that has the effect of nullifying or impairing equal enjoyment of rights. Special measures solely to protect the rights, or secure the advancement, of persons with mental illness shall not be deemed to be discriminatory. Discrimination does not include any distinction, exclusion or preference undertaken in accordance with the provisions of the present Principles and necessary to protect the human rights of a person with a mental illness or of other individuals.

5 Every person with a mental illness shall have the right to exercise all civil, political, economic, social and cultural rights as recognized in the Universal Declaration of Human Rights, the International Covenant on Economic, Social and Cultural Rights, the International Covenant on Civil and Political Rights and in other relevant instruments, such as the Declaration on the Rights of Disabled Persons and the Body of Principles for the Protection of All Persons under Any Form of Detention or Imprisonment.

6 Any decision that, by reason of his or her mental illness, a person lacks legal capacity, and any decision that, in consequence of such incapacity, a personal representative shall be appointed, shall be made only after a fair hearing by an independent and impartial tribunal established by domestic law. The person whose capacity is at issue shall be entitled to be represented by a counsel. If the person whose capacity is at issue does not himself or herself secure such representation, it shall be made available without payment by that person to the extent that he or she does not have sufficient means to pay for it. The counsel shall not in the same proceedings represent a mental health facility or its personnel and shall not also represent a member of the family of the person whose capacity is at issue unless the tribunal is satisfied that there is no conflict of interest. Decisions regarding capacity and the need for a personal representative shall be reviewed at reasonable intervals prescribed by domestic law. The person whose capacity is at issue, his or her personal representative, if any, and any other interested person shall have the right to appeal to a higher court against any such decision.

7 Where a court or other competent tribunal finds that a person with mental illness is unable to manage his or her own affairs, measures shall be taken, so far as is necessary and appropriate to that person's condition, to ensure the protection of his or her interests.

Principle 2: Protection of minors

Special care should be given within the purposes of the Principles and within the context of domestic law relating to the protection of minors to protect the rights of minors, including, if necessary, the appointment of a personal representative other than a family member.

Principle 3: Life in the community

Every person with a mental illness shall have the right to live and work, to the extent possible, in the community.

Principle 4: Determination of mental illness

1 A determination that a person has a mental illness shall be made in accordance with internationally accepted medical standards.

2 A determination of mental illness shall never be made on the basis of political, economic or social status, or membership in a cultural, racial or religious group, or for any other reason not directly relevant to mental health status.

3 Family or professional conflict, or non-conformity with moral, social, cultural or political values or religious beliefs prevailing in a person's community, shall never be a determining factor in the diagnosis of mental illness.

4 A background of past treatment or hospitalization as a patient shall not of itself justify any present or future determination of mental illness.

5 No person or authority shall classify a person as having, or otherwise indicate that a person has, a mental illness except for purposes directly relating to mental illness or the consequences of mental illness.

Principle 5: Medical examination

No person shall be compelled to undergo medical examination with a view to determining whether or not he or she has a mental illness except in accordance with a procedure authorized by domestic law.

Principle 6: Confidentiality

The right of confidentiality of information concerning all persons to whom the present Principles apply shall be respected.

Principle 7: Role of community and culture

1 Every patient shall have the right to be treated and cared for, as far as possible, in the community in which he or she lives.
2 Where treatment takes place in a mental health facility, a patient shall have the right, whenever possible, to be treated near his or her home or the home of his or her relatives or friends and shall have the right to return to the community as soon as possible.
3 Every patient shall have the right to treatment suited to his or her cultural background.

Principle 8: Standards of care

1 Every patient shall have the right to receive such health and social care as is appropriate to his or her health needs, and is entitled to care and treatment in accordance with the same standards as other ill persons.
2 Every patient shall be protected from harm, including unjustified medication, abuse by other patients, staff or others or other acts causing mental distress or physical discomfort.

Principle 9: Treatment

1 Every patient shall have the right to be treated in the least restrictive environment and with the least restrictive or intrusive treatment appropriate to the patient's health needs and the need to protect the physical safety of others.
2 The treatment and care of every patient shall be based on an individually prescribed plan, discussed with the patient, reviewed regularly, revised as necessary and provided by qualified professional staff.
3 Mental health care shall always be provided in accordance with applicable standards of ethics for mental health practitioners, including internationally accepted standards such as the Principles of Medical Ethics relevant to the role of health personnel, particularly physicians, in the

protection of prisoners and detainees against torture and other cruel, inhuman or degrading treatment or punishment, adopted by the United Nations General Assembly. Mental health knowledge and skills shall never be abused.

4 The treatment of every patient shall be directed towards preserving and enhancing personal autonomy.

Principle 10: Medication

1 Medication shall meet the best health needs of the patient, shall be given to a patient only for therapeutic or diagnostic purposes and shall never be administered as a punishment or for the convenience of others. Subject to the provisions of paragraph 15 of principle 11 below, mental health practitioners shall only administer medication of known or demonstrated efficacy.

2 All medication shall be prescribed by a mental health practitioner authorized by law and shall be recorded in the patient's records.

Principle 11: Consent to treatment

1 No treatment shall be given to a patient without his or her informed consent, except as provided for in paragraphs 6, 7, 8, 13 and 15 of the present principle.

2 Informed consent is consent obtained freely, without threats or improper inducements, after appropriate disclosure to the patient of adequate and understandable information in a form and language understood by the patient on:

(a) The diagnostic assessment;

(b) The purpose, method, likely duration and expected benefit of the proposed treatment;

(c) Alternative modes of treatment, including those less intrusive;

(d) Possible pain or discomfort, risks and side-effects of the proposed treatment.

3 A patient may request the presence of a person or persons of the patient's choosing during the procedure for granting consent.

4 A patient has the right to refuse or stop treatment, except as provided for in paragraphs 6, 7, 8, 13 and 15 of the present principle. The consequences of refusing or stopping treatment must be explained to the patient.

5 A patient shall never be invited or induced to waive the right to informed consent. If the patient should seek to do so, it shall be explained to the patient that the treatment cannot be given without informed consent.

6 Except as provided in paragraphs 7, 8, 12, 13, 14 and 15 of the present principle, a proposed plan of treatment may be given to a patient without a patient's informed consent if the following conditions are satisfied:

(a) The patient is, at the relevant time, held as an involuntary patient;

(b) An independent authority, having in its possession all relevant information, including the information specified in paragraph 2 of the present principle, is satisfied that, at the relevant time, the patient lacks the capacity to give or withhold informed consent to the proposed plan of treatment or, if domestic legislation so provides, that, having regard to the patient's own safety or the safety of others, the patient unreasonably withholds such consent;

(c) The independent authority is satisfied that the proposed plan of treatment is in the best interest of the patient's health needs.

7 Paragraph 6 above does not apply to a patient with a personal representative empowered by law to consent to treatment for the patient; but, except as provided in paragraphs 12, 13, 14 and 15 of the present principle, treatment may be given to such a patient without his or her informed consent if the personal representative, having been given the information described in paragraph 2 of the present principle, consents on the patient's behalf.

8 Except as provided in paragraphs 12, 13, 14 and 15 of the present principle, treatment may also be given to any patient without the patient's informed consent if a qualified mental health practitioner authorized by law determines that it is urgently necessary in order to prevent immediate or imminent harm to the patient or to other persons. Such treatment shall not be prolonged beyond the period that is strictly necessary for this purpose.

9 Where any treatment is authorized without the patient's informed consent, every effort shall nevertheless be made to inform the patient about the nature of the treatment and any possible alternatives and to involve the patient as far as practicable in the development of the treatment plan.

10 All treatment shall be immediately recorded in the patient's medical records, with an indication of whether involuntary or voluntary.

11 Physical restraint or involuntary seclusion of a patient shall not be employed except in accordance with the officially approved procedures of the mental health facility and only when it is the only means available to prevent immediate or imminent harm to the patient or others. It shall not be prolonged beyond the period which is strictly necessary for this purpose. All instances of physical restraint or involuntary seclusion, the reasons for them and their nature and extent shall be recorded in the patient's medical record. A patient who is restrained or secluded shall be kept under humane conditions and be under the care and close and regular supervision of qualified members of the staff. A personal representative, if any and if relevant, shall be given prompt notice of any physical restraint or involuntary seclusion of the patient.

12 Sterilization shall never be carried out as a treatment for mental illness.

13 A major medical or surgical procedure may be carried out on a person with mental illness only where it is permitted by domestic law, where it is considered that it would best serve the health needs of the patient and where the patient gives informed consent, except that, where the patient is unable to give informed consent, the procedure shall be authorized only after independent review.

14 Psychosurgery and other intrusive and irreversible treatments for mental illness shall never be carried out on a patient who is an involuntary patient in a mental health facility and, to the extent that domestic law permits them to be carried out, they may be carried out on any other patient only where the patient has given informed consent and an independent external body has satisfied itself that there is genuine informed consent and that the treatment best serves the health needs of the patient.

15 Clinical trials and experimental treatment shall never be carried out on any patient without informed consent, except that a patient who is unable to give informed consent may be admitted to a clinical trial or given experimental treatment, but only with the approval of a competent, independent review body specifically constituted for this purpose.

16 In the cases specified in paragraphs 6, 7, 8, 13, 14 and 15 of the present principle, the patient or his or her personal representative, or any interested person, shall have the right to appeal to a judicial or other independent authority concerning any treatment given to him or her.

Principle 12: Notice of rights

1 A patient in a mental health facility shall be informed as soon as possible after admission, in a form and a language which the patient understands, of all his or her rights in accordance with the present Principles and under domestic law, and the information shall include an explanation of those rights and how to exercise them.

2 If and for so long as a patient is unable to understand such information, the rights of the patient shall be communicated to the personal representative, if any and if appropriate, and to the person or persons be stable to represent the patient's interests and willing to do so.

3 A patient who has the necessary capacity has the right to nominate a person who should be informed on his or her behalf, as well as a person to represent his or her interests to the authorities of the facility.

Principle 13: Rights and conditions in mental health facilities

1 Every patient in a mental health facility shall, in particular, have the right to full respect for his or her:

(a) Recognition everywhere as a person before the law;

(b) Privacy;

(c) Freedom of communication, which includes freedom to communicate with other persons in the facility; freedom to send and receive uncensored private communications; freedom to receive, in private, visits from a counsellor personal representative and, at all reasonable times, from other visitors; and freedom of access to postal and telephone services and to newspapers, radio and television;

(d) Freedom of religion or belief.

2 The environment and living conditions in mental health facilities shall be as close as possible to those of the normal life of persons of similar age and in particular shall include:

(a) Facilities for recreational and leisure activities;

(b) Facilities for education;

(c) Facilities to purchase or receive items for daily living, recreation and communication;

(d) Facilities, and encouragement to use such facilities, for a patient's engagement in active occupation suited to his or her social and cultural background, and for appropriate vocational rehabilitation measures to promote reintegration in the community. These measures should include vocational guidance, vocational training and placement services to enable patients to secure or retain employment in the community.

3 In no circumstances shall a patient be subject to forced labour. Within the limits compatible with the needs of the patient and with the requirements of institutional administration, a patient shall be able to choose the type of work he or she wishes to perform.

4 The labour of a patient in a mental health facility shall not be exploited. Every such patient shall have the right to receive the same remuneration for any work which he or she does as would, according to domestic law or custom, be paid for such work to a non-patient. Every such patient shall, in any event, have the right to receive a fair share of any remuneration which is paid to the mental health facility for his or her work.

Principle 14: Resources for mental health facilities

1 A mental health facility shall have access to the same level of resources as any other health establishment, and in particular:

(a) Qualified medical and other appropriate professional staff insufficient numbers and with adequate space to provide each patient with privacy and a programme of appropriate and active therapy;
(b) Diagnostic and therapeutic equipment for the patient;
(c) Appropriate professional care;
(d) Adequate, regular and comprehensive treatment, including supplies of medication.

2 Every mental health facility shall be inspected by the competent authorities with sufficient frequency to ensure that the conditions, treatment and care of patients comply with the present Principles.

Principle 15: Admission principles

1 Where a person needs treatment in a mental health facility, every effort shall be made to avoid involuntary admission.
2 Access to a mental health facility shall be administered in the same way as access to any other facility for any other illness.
3 Every patient not admitted involuntarily shall have the right to leave the mental health facility at any time unless the criteria for his or her retention as an involuntary patient, as set forth in principle 16 below, apply, and he or she shall be informed of that right.

Principle 16: Involuntary admission

1 A person may (a) be admitted involuntarily to a mental health facility as a patient or, (b) having already been admitted voluntarily as a patient, be retained as an involuntary patient in the mental health facility if, and only if, a qualified mental health practitioner authorized by law for that purpose determines, in accordance with principle 4 above, that that person has a mental illness and considers:

(a) That, because of that mental illness, there is a serious likelihood of immediate or imminent harm to that person or to other persons; or
(b) That, in the case of a person whose mental illness is severe and whose judgement is impaired, failure to admit or retain that person is likely to lead to a serious deterioration in his or her condition or will prevent the giving of appropriate treatment that can only be given by admission to a mental health facility in accordance with the principle of the least restrictive alternative.

In the case referred to in subparagraph (b), a second such mental health practitioner, independent of the first, should be consulted where possible. If such consultation takes place, the involuntary admission or retention may not take place unless the second mental health practitioner concurs.

2 Involuntary admission or retention shall initially be for a short period as specified by domestic law for observation and preliminary treatment pending review of the admission or retention by the review body. The grounds of the admission shall be communicated to the patient without delay and the fact of the admission and the grounds for it shall also be communicated promptly and in detail to the review body, to the patient's personal representative, if any, and, unless the patient objects, to the patient's family.
3 A mental health facility may receive involuntarily admitted patients only if the facility has been designated to do so by a competent authority prescribed by domestic law.

Principle 17: Review body

1 The review body shall be a judicial or other independent and impartial body established by domestic law and functioning in accordance with procedures laid down by domestic law. It shall, in formulating its decisions, have the assistance of one or more qualified and independent mental health practitioners and take their advice into account.
2 The initial review of the review body, as required by paragraph 2 of principle 16 above, of a decision to admit or retain a person as an involuntary patient shall take place as soon as possible after that decision and shall be conducted in accordance with simple and expeditious procedures as specified by domestic law.
3 The review body shall periodically review the cases of involuntary patients at reasonable intervals as specified by domestic law.
4 An involuntary patient may apply to the review body for release or voluntary status, at reasonable intervals as specified by domestic law.
5 At each review, the review body shall consider whether the criteria for involuntary admission set out in paragraph 1 of principle 16 above are still satisfied, and, if not, the patient shall be discharged as an involuntary patient.
6 If at any time the mental health practitioner responsible for the case is satisfied that the conditions for the retention of a person as an involuntary patient are no longer satisfied, he or she shall order the discharge of that person as such a patient.
7 A patient or his personal representative or any interested person shall have the right to appeal to a higher court against a decision that the patient be admitted to, or be retained in, a mental health facility.

Principle 18: Procedural safeguards

1 The patient shall be entitled to choose and appoint a counsel to represent the patient as such, including representation in any complaint procedure or appeal. If the patient does not secure such services, a

counsel shall be made available without payment by the patient to the extent that the patient lacks sufficient means to pay.

2 The patient shall also be entitled to the assistance, if necessary, of the services of an interpreter. Where such services are necessary and the patient does not secure them, they shall be made available without payment by the patient to the extent that the patient lacks sufficient means to pay.

3 The patient and the patient's counsel may request and produce at any hearing an independent mental health report and any other reports and oral, written and other evidence that are relevant and admissible.

4 Copies of the patient's records and any reports and documents to be submitted shall be given to the patient and to the patient's counsel, except in special cases where it is determined that a specific disclosure to the patient would cause serious harm to the patient's health or put at risk the safety of others. As domestic law may provide, any document not given to the patient should, when this can be done in confidence, be given to the patient's personal representative and counsel. When any part of a document is withheld from a patient, the patient or the patient's counsel, if any, shall receive notice of the withholding and the reasons for it and it shall be subject to judicial review.

5 The patient and the patient's personal representative and counsel shall be entitled to attend, participate and be heard personally in any hearing.

6 If the patient or the patient's personal representative or counsel requests that a particular person be present at a hearing, that person shall be admitted unless it is determined that the person's presence could cause serious harm to the patient's health or put at risk the safety of others.

7 Any decision on whether the hearing or any part of it shall be in public or in private and may be publicly reported shall give full consideration to the patient's own wishes, to the need to respect the privacy of the patient and of other persons and to the need to prevent serious harm to the patient's health or to avoid putting at risk the safety of others.

8 The decision arising out of the hearing and the reasons for it shall be expressed in writing. Copies shall be given to the patient and his or her personal representative and counsel. In deciding whether the decision shall be published in whole or in part, full consideration shall be given to the patient's own wishes, to the need to respect his or her privacy and that of other persons, to the public interest in the open administration of justice and to the need to prevent serious harm to the patient's health or to avoid putting at risk the safety of others.

Principle 19: Access to information

1 A patient (which term in the present Principle includes a former patient) shall be entitled to have access to the information concerning the

patient in his or her health and personal records maintained by a mental health facility. This right may be subject to restrictions in order to prevent serious harm to the patient's health and avoid putting at risk the safety of others. As domestic law may provide, any such information not given to the patient should, when this can be done in confidence, be given to the patient's personal representative and counsel. When any of the information is withheld from a patient, the patient or the patient's counsel, if any, shall receive notice of the withholding and the reasons for it and it shall be subject to judicial review.

2 Any written comments by the patient or the patient's personal representative or counsel shall, on request, be inserted in the patient's file.

Principle 20: Criminal offenders

1 The present Principle applies to persons serving sentences of imprisonment for criminal offences, or who are otherwise detained in the course of criminal proceedings or investigations against them, and who are determined to have a mental illness or who it is believed may have such an illness.

2 All such persons should receive the best available mental health care as provided in principle 1 above. The present Principles shall apply to them to the fullest extent possible, with only such limited modifications and exceptions as are necessary in the circumstances. No such modifications and exceptions shall prejudice the persons' rights under the instruments noted in paragraph 5 of principle 1 above.

3 Domestic law may authorize a court or other competent authority, acting on the basis of competent and independent medical advice, to order that such persons be admitted to a mental health facility.

4 Treatment of persons determined to have a mental illness shall in all circumstances be consistent with principle 11 above.

Principle 21: Complaints

Every patient and former patient shall have the right to make a complaint through procedures as specified by domestic law.

Principle 22: Monitoring and remedies

States shall ensure that appropriate mechanisms are in force to promote compliance with the present Principles, for the inspection of mental health facilities, for the submission, investigation and resolution of complaints and for the institution of appropriate disciplinary or judicial proceedings for professional misconduct or violation of the rights of a patient.

Principle 23: Implementation

1 States should implement the present Principles through appropriate legislative, judicial, administrative, educational and other measures, which they shall review periodically.
2 States shall make the present Principles widely known by appropriate and active means.

Principle 24: Scope of principles relating to mental health facilities

The present Principles apply to all persons who are admitted to a mental health facility.

Principle 25: Saving of existing rights

There shall be no restriction upon or derogation from any existing rights of patients, including rights recognized in applicable international or domestic law, on the pretext that the present Principles do not recognize such rights or that they recognize them to a lesser extent.

14.4.4 Full text of the World Medical Association's Declaration of Helsinki

A. INTRODUCTION

1 The World Medical Association (WMA) has developed the Declaration of Helsinki as a statement of ethical principles for medical research involving human subjects, including research on identifiable human material and data.

   The Declaration is intended to be read as a whole and each of its constituent paragraphs should not be applied without consideration of all other relevant paragraphs.
2 Although the Declaration is addressed primarily to physicians, the WMA encourages other participants in medical research involving human subjects to adopt these principles.
3 It is the duty of the physician to promote and safeguard the health of patients, including those who are involved in medical research. The physician's knowledge and conscience are dedicated to the fulfilment of this duty.
4 The Declaration of Geneva of the WMA binds the physician with the words, 'The health of my patient will be my first consideration', and the International Code of Medical Ethics declares that, 'A physician shall act in the patient's best interest when providing medical care'.
5 Medical progress is based on research that ultimately must include studies involving human subjects. Populations that are underrepresented in medical research should be provided appropriate access to participation in research.

6 In medical research involving human subjects, the well-being of the individual research subject must take precedence over all other interests.

7 The primary purpose of medical research involving human subjects is to understand the causes, development and effects of diseases and improve preventive, diagnostic and therapeutic interventions (methods, procedures and treatments). Even the best current interventions must be evaluated continually through research for their safety, effectiveness, efficiency, accessibility and quality.

8 In medical practice and in medical research, most interventions involve risks and burdens.

9 Medical research is subject to ethical standards that promote respect for all human subjects and protect their health and rights. Some research populations are particularly vulnerable and need special protection. These include those who cannot give or refuse consent for themselves and those who may be vulnerable to coercion or undue influence.

10 Physicians should consider the ethical, legal and regulatory norms and standards for research involving human subjects in their own countries as well as applicable international norms and standards. No national or international ethical, legal or regulatory requirement should reduce or eliminate any of the protections for research subjects set forth in this Declaration.

B. BASIC PRINCIPLES FOR ALL MEDICAL RESEARCH

11 It is the duty of physicians who participate in medical research to protect the life, health, dignity, integrity, right to self-determination, privacy, and confidentiality of personal information of research subjects.

12 Medical research involving human subjects must conform to generally accepted scientific principles, be based on a thorough knowledge of the scientific literature, other relevant sources of information, and adequate laboratory and, as appropriate, animal experimentation. The welfare of animals used for research must be respected.

13 Appropriate caution must be exercised in the conduct of medical research that may harm the environment.

14 The design and performance of each research study involving human subjects must be clearly described in a research protocol. The protocol should contain a statement of the ethical considerations involved and should indicate how the principles in this Declaration have been addressed. The protocol should include information regarding funding, sponsors, institutional affiliations, other potential conflicts of interest, incentives for subjects and provisions for treating and/or

compensating subjects who are harmed as a consequence of participation in the research study. The protocol should describe arrangements for post-study access by study subjects to interventions identified as beneficial in the study or access to other appropriate care or benefits.

15 The research protocol must be submitted for consideration, comment, guidance and approval to a research ethics committee before the study begins. This committee must be independent of the researcher, the sponsor and any other undue influence. It must take into consideration the laws and regulations of the country or countries in which the research is to be performed as well as applicable international norms and standards but these must not be allowed to reduce or eliminate any of the protections for research subjects set forth in this Declaration. The committee must have the right to monitor ongoing studies. The researcher must provide monitoring information to the committee, especially information about any serious adverse events. No change to the protocol may be made without consideration and approval by the committee.

16 Medical research involving human subjects must be conducted only by individuals with the appropriate scientific training and qualifications. Research on patients or healthy volunteers requires the supervision of a competent and appropriately qualified physician or other health care professional. The responsibility for the protection of research subjects must always rest with the physician or other health care professional and never the research subjects, even though they have given consent.

17 Medical research involving a disadvantaged or vulnerable population or community is only justified if the research is responsive to the health needs and priorities of this population or community and if there is a reasonable likelihood that this population or community stands to benefit from the results of the research.

18 Every medical research study involving human subjects must be preceded by careful assessment of predictable risks and burdens to the individuals and communities involved in the research in comparison with foreseeable benefits to them and to other individuals or communities affected by the condition under investigation.

19 Every clinical trial must be registered in a publicly accessible database before recruitment of the first subject.

20 Physicians may not participate in a research study involving human subjects unless they are confident that the risks involved have been adequately assessed and can be satisfactorily managed. Physicians must immediately stop a study when the risks are found to outweigh the potential benefits or when there is conclusive proof of positive and beneficial results.

21 Medical research involving human subjects may only be conducted if the importance of the objective outweighs the inherent risks and burdens to the research subjects.

22 Participation by competent individuals as subjects in medical research must be voluntary. Although it may be appropriate to consult family members or community leaders, no competent individual may be enrolled in a research study unless he or she freely agrees.

23 Every precaution must be taken to protect the privacy of research subjects and the confidentiality of their personal information and to minimize the impact of the study on their physical, mental and social integrity.

24 In medical research involving competent human subjects, each potential subject must be adequately informed of the aims, methods, sources of funding, any possible conflicts of interest, institutional affiliations of the researcher, the anticipated benefits and potential risks of the study and the discomfort it may entail, and any other relevant aspects of the study. The potential subject must be informed of the right to refuse to participate in the study or to withdraw consent to participate at any time without reprisal. Special attention should be given to the specific information needs of individual potential subjects as well as to the methods used to deliver the information. After ensuring that the potential subject has understood the information, the physician or another appropriately qualified individual must then seek the potential subject's freely-given informed consent, preferably in writing. If the consent cannot be expressed in writing, the non-written consent must be formally documented and witnessed.

25 For medical research using identifiable human material or data, physicians must normally seek consent for the collection, analysis, storage and/or reuse. There may be situations where consent would be impossible or impractical to obtain for such research or would pose a threat to the validity of the research. In such situations the research may be done only after consideration and approval of a research ethics committee.

26 When seeking informed consent for participation in a research study the physician should be particularly cautious if the potential subject is in a dependent relationship with the physician or may consent under duress. In such situations the informed consent should be sought by an appropriately qualified individual who is completely independent of this relationship.

27 For a potential research subject who is incompetent, the physician must seek informed consent from the legally authorized representative. These individuals must not be included in a research study that has no likelihood of benefit for them unless it is intended to promote

the health of the population represented by the potential subject, the research cannot instead be performed with competent persons, and the research entails only minimal risk and minimal burden.

28 When a potential research subject who is deemed incompetent is able to give assent to decisions about participation in research, the physician must seek that assent in addition to the consent of the legally authorized representative. The potential subject's dissent should be respected.

29 Research involving subjects who are physically or mentally incapable of giving consent, for example, unconscious patients, may be done only if the physical or mental condition that prevents giving informed consent is a necessary characteristic of the research population. In such circumstances the physician should seek informed consent from the legally authorized representative. If no such representative is available and if the research cannot be delayed, the study may proceed without informed consent provided that the specific reasons for involving subjects with a condition that renders them unable to give informed consent have been stated in the research protocol and the study has been approved by a research ethics committee. Consent to remain in the research should be obtained as soon as possible from the subject or a legally authorized representative.

30 Authors, editors and publishers all have ethical obligations with regard to the publication of the results of research. Authors have a duty to make publicly available the results of their research on human subjects and are accountable for the completeness and accuracy of their reports. They should adhere to accepted guidelines for ethical reporting. Negative and inconclusive as well as positive results should be published or otherwise made publicly available. Sources of funding, institutional affiliations and conflicts of interest should be declared in the publication. Reports of research not in accordance with the principles of this Declaration should not be accepted for publication.

C. ADDITIONAL PRINCIPLES FOR MEDICAL RESEARCH COMBINED WITH MEDICAL CARE

31 The physician may combine medical research with medical care only to the extent that the research is justified by its potential preventive, diagnostic or therapeutic value and if the physician has good reason to believe that participation in the research study will not adversely affect the health of the patients who serve as research subjects.

32 The benefits, risks, burdens and effectiveness of a new intervention must be tested against those of the best current proven intervention, except in the following circumstances:

5 The use of placebo, or no treatment, is acceptable in studies where no current proven intervention exists; or

6 Where for compelling and scientifically sound methodological reasons the use of placebo is necessary to determine the efficacy or safety of an intervention and the patients who receive placebo or no treatment will not be subject to any risk of serious or irreversible harm. Extreme care must be taken to avoid abuse of this option.

33 At the conclusion of the study, patients entered into the study are entitled to be informed about the outcome of the study and to share any benefits that result from it, for example, access to interventions identified as beneficial in the study or to other appropriate care or benefits.

34 The physician must fully inform the patient which aspects of the care are related to the research. The refusal of a patient to participate in a study or the patient's decision to withdraw from the study must never interfere with the patient-physician relationship.

35 In the treatment of a patient, where proven interventions do not exist or have been ineffective, the physician, after seeking expert advice, with informed consent from the patient or a legally authorized representative, may use an unproven intervention if in the physician's judgement it offers hope of saving life, reestablishing health or alleviating suffering. Where possible, this intervention should be made the object of research, designed to evaluate its safety and efficacy. In all cases, new information should be recorded and, where appropriate, made publicly available.

14.4.5 Full text of the Madrid Declaration on Ethical Standards for Psychiatric Practice

In 1977, the World Psychiatric Association approved the Declaration of Hawaii, which set out ethical guidelines for the practice of psychiatry. The Declaration was updated in Vienna in 1983. To reflect the impact of changing social attitudes and new medical developments on the psychiatric profession, the World Psychiatric Association has once again undertaken a review of ethical standards that should be abided to by all its members and all persons practicing psychiatry.

Medicine is both a healing art and a science. The dynamics of this combination are best reflected in psychiatry, the branch of medicine that specializes in the care and protection of those who are ill or infirm, because of a mental disorder or impairment. Although there may be cultural, social and national differences, the need for ethical conduct and continual review of ethical standards is universal.

As practitioners of medicine, psychiatrists must be aware of the ethical implications of being a physician, and of the specific ethical demands of the specialty of psychiatry. As members of society, psychiatrists must advocate for fair and equal treatment of the mentally ill, for social justice and equity for all.

Ethical practice is based on the psychiatrist's individual sense of responsibility to the patient and judgment in determining what is correct and appropriate conduct. External standards and influences such as professional codes of conduct, the study of ethics, or the rule of law by themselves will not guarantee the ethical practice of medicine.

Psychiatrists should keep in mind at all times the boundaries of the psychiatrist-patient relationship, and be guided primarily by the respect for patients and concern for their welfare and integrity.

It is in this spirit that the World Psychiatric Association approved at the General Assembly on 25 August 1996, amended on 8 August 1999 and on 26 August 2002 the following ethical standards that should govern the practice of psychiatrists universally.

1 Psychiatry is a medical discipline concerned with the prevention of mental disorders in the population, the provision of the best possible treatment for mental disorders, the rehabilitation of individuals suffering from mental illness and the promotion of mental health. Psychiatrists serve patients by providing the best therapy available consistent with accepted scientific knowledge and ethical principles. Psychiatrists should devise therapeutic interventions that are least restrictive to the freedom of the patient and seek advice in areas of their work about which they do not have primary expertise. While doing so, psychiatrists should be aware of and concerned with the equitable allocation of health resources.

2 It is the duty of psychiatrists to keep abreast of scientific developments of the specialty and to convey updated knowledge to others. Psychiatrists trained in research should seek to advance the scientific frontiers of psychiatry.

3 The patient should be accepted as a partner by right in the therapeutic process. The psychiatrist-patient relationship must be based on mutual trust and respect to allow the patient to make free and informed decisions. It is the duty of psychiatrists to provide the patient with all relevant information so as to empower the patient to come to a rational decision according to personal values and preferences.

4 When the patient is gravely disabled, incapacitated and/or incompetent to exercise proper judgment because of a mental disorder, the psychiatrists should consult with the family and, if appropriate, seek legal counsel, to safeguard the human dignity and the legal rights of the patient. No treatment should be provided against the patient's will, unless withholding treatment would endanger the life of the patient and/or the life of others. Treatment must always be in the best interest of the patient.

5 When psychiatrists are requested to assess a person, it is their duty first to inform and advise the person being assessed about the purpose of the intervention, the use of the findings, and the possible repercussions of the assessment. This is particularly important when psychiatrists are involved in third party situations.

6 Information obtained in the therapeutic relationship is private to the patient and should be kept in confidence and used, only and exclusively, for the purpose of improving the mental health of the patient. Psychiatrists are prohibited from making use of such information for personal reasons, or personal benefit. Breach of confidentiality may only be appropriate when required by law (as in obligatory reporting of child abuse) or when serious physical or mental harm to the patient or to a third person would ensue if confidentiality were maintained; whenever possible, psychiatrists should first advise the patient about the action to be taken.

7 Research that is not conducted in accordance with the canons of science and that is not scientifically valid is unethical. Research activities should be approved by an appropriately constituted ethics committee. Psychiatrists should follow national and international rules for the conduct of research. Only individuals properly trained for research should undertake or direct it. Because psychiatric patients constitute a particularly vulnerable research population, extra caution should be taken to assess their competence to participate as research subjects and to safeguard their autonomy and their mental and physical integrity. Ethical standards should also be applied in the selection of population groups, in all types of research including epidemiological and sociological studies and in collaborative research involving other disciplines or several investigating centres.

GUIDELINES CONCERNING SPECIFIC SITUATIONS

The World Psychiatric Association Ethics Committee recognizes the need to develop a number of specific guidelines on a number of specific situations. The first five were approved by the General Assembly in Madrid, Spain, on 25 August 1996, the 6 through 8 by the General Assembly in Hamburg, Germany, on 8 August 1999, the 9 through 12 by the General Assembly in Yokohama, Japan, on 26 August 2002, and the 13 through 15 at the General Assembly in Cairo, Egypt, on 12 September 2005.

1 **Euthanasia:** A physician's duty, first and foremost, is the promotion of health, the reduction of suffering, and the protection of life.

The psychiatrist, among whose patients are some who are severely incapacitated and incompetent to reach an informed decision, should be particularly careful of actions that could lead to the death of those who cannot protect themselves because of their disability. The psychiatrist should be aware that the views of a patient may be distorted by mental illness such as depression. In such situations, the psychiatrist's role is to treat the illness.

2 **Torture:** Psychiatrists shall not take part in any process of mental or physical torture, even when authorities attempt to force their involvement in such acts.

3 **Death Penalty:** Under no circumstances should psychiatrists participate in legally authorized executions nor participate in assessments of competency to be executed.

4 **Selection of Sex:** Under no circumstances should a psychiatrist participate in decisions to terminate pregnancy for the purpose of sex selection.

5 **Organ Transplantation:** The role of the psychiatrist is to clarify the issues surrounding organ donations and to advise on religious, cultural, social and family factors to ensure that informed and proper decisions be made by all concerned. The psychiatrists should not act as a proxy decision maker for patients nor use psychotherapeutic skills to influence the decision of a patient in these matters. Psychiatrists should seek to protect their patients and help them exercise self-determination to the fullest extent possible in situations of organ transplantation.

6 **Psychiatrists addressing the media.** In all contacts with the media psychiatrists shall ensure that people with mental illness are presented in a manner which preserves their dignity and pride, and which reduces stigma and discrimination against them.

An important role of psychiatrists is to advocate for those people who suffer from mental disorders. As the public perception of psychiatrists and psychiatry reflects on patients, psychiatrists shall ensure that in their contact with the media they represent the profession of psychiatry with dignity.

Psychiatrists shall not make announcements to the media about presumed psychopathology on any individuals.

In presenting research findings to the media, psychiatrists shall ensure the scientific integrity of the information given and be mindful of the potential impact of their statements on the public perception of mental illness and on the welfare of people with mental disorders.

7 **Psychiatrists and discrimination on ethnic or cultural grounds.** Discrimination by psychiatrists on the basis of ethnicity or culture, whether directly or by aiding others is unethical. Psychiatrists shall

never be involved or endorse, directly or indirectly, any activity related to ethnic cleansing.

8 **Psychiatrists and genetic research and counselling:** Research on the genetic bases of mental disorders is rapidly increasing and more people suffering from mental illness are participating in such research. Psychiatrists involved in genetic research or counselling shall be mindful of the fact that the implication of genetic information is not limited to the individual from whom it was obtained and that its disclosure can have negative and disruptive effects on the families and communities of the individuals concerned.

  Psychiatrist shall therefore ensure that:

  7 People and families who participate in genetic research do so with a fully informed consent;
  8 Any genetic information in their possession is adequately protected against unauthorized access, misinterpretation or misuse;
  9 Care is taken in communication with patients and families to make clear that current genetic knowledge is incomplete and may be altered by future findings.

    Psychiatrists shall only refer people to facilities for diagnostic genetic testing if that facility has:

  10 Demonstrated satisfactory quality assurance, procedures for such testing;
  11 Adequate and easily accessible resources for genetic counselling.

    Genetic counselling with regard to family planning or abortion shall be respectful of the patients' value system, while providing sufficient medical and psychiatric information to aid patients make decisions they consider best for them.

9 **Ethics of Psychotherapy in Medicine:** Medical treatments of any nature should be administered under the provisions of good practice guidelines regarding their indications, effectiveness, safety, and quality control. Psychotherapy, in its broadest sense, is an accepted component of many medical interactions. In a more specific and restricted sense, psychotherapy utilizes techniques involving verbal and nonverbal communication and interaction to achieve specified treatment goals in the care of specific disorders. Psychiatrists providing specific forms of psychotherapy must have appropriate training in such techniques. The general guidelines that apply to any medical treatment also apply to specific forms of psychotherapy in regard to its indications and outcomes, positive or negative. The effectiveness of psychotherapy and its place in a treatment plan are important subjects for both researchers and clinicians.

  Psychotherapy by psychiatrists is a form of treatment for mental and other illnesses and emotional problems. The treatment approach utilized is determined in concert by the doctor and patient and/or the patient's family and/or guardians following a careful history and examination employing all relevant clinical and laboratory studies. The approach employed should be specific to the disease and patient's needs and sensitive to personal, familial, religious and cultural factors. It should be based on sound research and clinical wisdom and have the purpose of removing, modifying or retarding symptoms or disturbed patterns of behaviour. It should promote positive adaptations including personal growth and development.

Psychiatrists and other clinicians responsible for a patient have to ensure that these guidelines are fully applied. Therefore, the psychiatrist or other delegated qualified clinician should determine the indications for psychotherapy and follow its development. In this context the essential notion is that the treatment is the consequence of a diagnosis and both are medical acts performed to take care of an ill person. These two levels of decisions, interventions and responsibilities are similar to other situations in clinical medicine; however, this does not exclude other interventions such as rehabilitation, which can be administered by non-medical personnel.

1 Like any other treatment in medicine, the prescription of psychotherapy should follow accepted guidelines for obtaining informed consent prior to the initiation of treatment as well as updating it in the course of treatment if goals and objectives of treatment are modified in a significant way.
2 If clinical wisdom, long standing and well-established practice patterns (this takes into consideration cultural and religious issues) and scientific evidence suggest potential clinical benefits to combining medication treatment with psychotherapy this should be brought to the patient's attention and fully discussed.
3 Psychotherapy explores intimate thoughts, emotions and fantasies, and as such may engender intense transference and countertransference. In a psychotherapy relationship the power is unequally shared between the therapist and patient, and under no circumstances shall the psychotherapist use this relationship to personal advantage or transgress the boundaries established by the professional relationship.
4 At the initiation of psychotherapy, the patient shall be advised that information shared and health records will be kept in confidence except where the patient gives specific informed consent for release of information to third parties, or where a court order may require the production of records. The other exception is where there is a legal requirement to report certain information as in the case of child abuse.

10 **Conflict of Interest in Relationship with Industry:** Although most organizations and institutions, including the WPA, have rules and regulations governing their relationship with industry and donors, individual physicians are often involved in interactions with the pharmaceutical industry, or other granting agencies that could lead to ethical conflict In these situations psychiatrists should be mindful of and apply the following guidelines.

1 The practitioner must diligently guard against accepting gifts that could have an undue influence on professional work.
2 Psychiatrists conducting clinical trials are under an obligation to disclose to the Ethics Review Board and their research subjects their financial and contractual obligations and benefits related to the sponsor of the study. Every effort should be made to set up review boards composed of researchers, ethicists and community representatives to assure the rights of research subjects are protected.
3 Psychiatrists conducting clinical trials have to ensure that their patients have understood all aspects of the informed consent. The level of education or sophistication of the patient is no excuse for bypassing this commitment. If the patient is deemed incompetent the same rules would apply in obtaining informed consent from the substitute decision maker. Psychiatrists must be cognizant that covert commercial influence on the trial design, promotion of drugs trials without scientific value, breach of confidentiality, and restrictive contractual clauses regarding publication of results may each in different ways encroach upon the freedom of science and scientific information.

11 **Conflicts Arising with Third Party Players:** The obligations of organizations toward shareholders or the administrator regarding maximization of profits and minimization of costs can be in conflict with the principles of good practice Psychiatrists working in such potentially conflicting environments, should uphold the rights of the patients to receive the best treatment possible.

1 In agreement with the UN Resolution 46/119 of the 'Principles for the Protection of Persons with Mental Illness', psychiatrists should oppose discriminatory practices which limit their benefits and entitlements, deny parity curb the scope of treatment, or limit their access to proper medications for patients with a mental disorder.
2 Professional independence to apply best practice guidelines and clinical wisdom in upholding the welfare of the patient should be the primary considerations for the psychiatrist. It is also the duty of the psychiatrist to protect the patient privacy and confidentiality as part of preserving the sanctity and healing potential of the doctor-patient relationship.

12 **Violating the Clinical Boundaries and Trust Between Psychiatrists and Patients:** The psychiatrist-patient relationship may be the only relationship that permits an exploration of the deeply personal and emotional space, as granted by the patient. Within this relationship, the psychiatrist's respect for the humanity and dignity of the patient builds a foundation of trust that is essential for a comprehensive treatment plan. The relationship encourages the patient to explore deeply held strengths, weaknesses, fears, and desires, and many of these might be related to sexuality. Knowledge of these characteristics of the patient places the psychiatrist in a position of advantage that the patient allows on the expectation of trust and respect. Taking advantage of that knowledge by manipulating the patient's sexual fears and desires in order to obtain sexual access is a breach of the trust, regardless of consent. In the therapeutic relationship, consent on the part of the patient is considered vitiated by the knowledge the psychiatrists possesses about the patient and by the power differential that vests the psychiatrist with special authority over the patient. Consent under these circumstances will be tantamount to exploitation of the patient.

The latent sexual dynamics inherent in all relationships can become manifest in the course of the therapeutic relationship and if they are not properly handled by the therapist can produce anguish to the patient. This anguish is likely to become more pronounced if seductive statements and inappropriate non-verbal behaviour are used by the therapist. Under no circumstances, therefore, should a psychiatrist get involved with a patient in any form of sexual behaviour, irrespective of whether this behaviour is initiated by the patient or the therapist.

13 **Protection of the Rights of Psychiatrists:**

1 Psychiatrists need to protect their right to live up to the obligations of their profession and to the expectations the public has of them to treat and to advocate for the welfare of their patients.

2 Psychiatrists ought to have the right to practice their specialty at the highest level of excellence by providing independent assessments of a persons' mental condition and by instituting effective treatment and management protocols in accordance to best practices and evidence-based medicine.

3 There are aspects in the history of psychiatry and in present working expectations in some totalitarian political regimes and profit driven economical systems that increase psychiatrists' vulnerabilities to be abused in the sense of having to acquiesce to inappropriate demands to provide inaccurate psychiatric reports that help the system, but damage the interests of the person being assessed.

4 Psychiatrists also share the stigma of their patients and, similarly, can become victims of discriminatory practices. It should be the right and the obligation of psychiatrists to practice their profession and to advocate for the medical needs and the social and political rights of their patients without suffering being outcast by the profession, being ridiculed in the media or persecuted.

14 **Disclosing the Diagnosis of Alzheimer's Disease (AD) and Other Dementias:** AD patient's right to know is now a well established priority, recognised by healthcare professionals. Most patients want all information available and to be actively involved in making decision about treatments. At the same time, patients have the right also not to know if that is their wish. All must be given the opportunity to learn as much or as little as they want to know.

The alteration of patient's cognition makes the ability to make judgements and insight more difficult. Patients with dementia are also often brought by family members which introduces into the doctor-patient relationship a third partner.

Doctors, patients and families who share the responsibilities for fighting and coping with Alzheimer's disease for years all require access to information on the disease, including the diagnosis.

In addition to the 'patient's right to know', telling the patient has many benefits. Patients and/or families should be told the diagnosis as early as possible in the disease process. Having family (or informal carer) involved in the discussion of the disclosure process is highly beneficial.

The physician should give accurate and reliable information, using simple language. He also should assess the patient's and the family's understanding of the situation. As usual, the bad news should be accompanied by information on a treatment and management plan. Information on physical or speech therapy, support groups, day care centres, and other interventions should be provided. It should also be emphasised that a reorganised family network can alleviate the carer's burden and maintain quality of life as far as possible.

There are some exceptions, some of them transitory, to the disclosure of the diagnosis to a patient with dementia:

1 severe dementia where understanding the diagnosis is unlikely,
2 when a phobia about the condition is likely, or
3 when a patient is severely depressed;

15 **Dual Responsibilities of Psychiatrists:** These situations may arise as part of legal proceedings (i.e. fitness to stand trial, criminal responsibility, dangerousness, testamentary capacity) or other competency related needs, such as for insurance purposes when evaluating claims

for benefits, or for employment purposes when evaluating fitness to work or suitability for a particular employment or specific task.

During therapeutic interactions conflicting situations may arise if the physician's knowledge of the patient's condition cannot be kept private or when clinical notes or medical records are part of a larger employment dossier, hence not confidential to the clinical personnel in charge of the case (i.e. the military, correctional systems, medical services for employees of large corporations, treatment protocols paid by third parties).

It is the duty of a psychiatrist confronted with dual obligations and responsibilities at assessment time to disclose to the person being assessed the nature of the triangular relationship and the absence of a therapeutic doctor-patient relationship, besides the obligation to report to a third party even if the findings are negative and potentially damaging to the interests of the person under assessment. Under these circumstances, the person may choose not to proceed with the assessment.

Additionally, psychiatrists should advocate for separation of records and for limits to exposure of information such that only elements of information that are essential for purposes of the agency can be revealed.

CHAPTER 15

Examples of Disability Legislation from Across the World

In this chapter, we give examples of ways countries have addressed the protection of the rights of people with disabilities. It has been composed from submissions received from country informants who helped us compile this book.

The guide does not necessarily include all relevant legislation within each country that is itemised. It is intended, rather, to give a range of examples of ways in which countries have addressed the protection of the rights of people with disabilities. Also note that these are *not* necessarily best practice examples.

Country	Legislation	Description
Australia	Disability Discrimination Act (1992)	Protects against direct and indirect discrimination in many parts of life, including employment and education. The Act makes harassment on the basis of disability against the law. It also protects friends and relatives and others from discrimination because of their connection to someone with a disability. Legal centres exist across the country that may assist people with mental illnesses in relation to complaints.
Azerbaijan	Employment legislation	Includes provisions for employment against discrimination and allows for special conditions (including sheltered workplaces) for people with psychiatric disorders. At the same time, a person may be temporarily ineligible (for a period of two years) from entering certain professions.

(Continued)

Mental Illness, Discrimination and the Law: Fighting for Social Justice, First Edition.
Felicity Callard, Norman Sartorius, Julio Arboleda-Flórez, Peter Bartlett, Hanfried Helmchen, Heather Stuart, Jose Taborda and Graham Thornicroft.

Country	Legislation	Description
Brazil	Federal Constitution	Forbids discrimination on any grounds.
	Federal Decree nb 3298 (1999)	Requires companies to set aside a quota for disabled people (referring to all disability groups), ranging from 2 to 5%, depending on the size of the company and forbids discrimination in employment and salaries.
Canada	Canadian Charter of Rights and Freedoms (1982)	Prohibits discrimination on a number of grounds, including physical or mental disability. Legislation and government actions may be challenged through a constitutional review in the courts.
	Canadian Human Rights Act (1977)	Federal statute that ensures equal opportunity to individuals who may be victims of discrimination based on prohibited grounds such as gender, disability or religion. It applies throughout Canada but is limited to federally regulated activities. Provinces and Territories have their own anti-discrimination laws for non-federally regulated activities.
	Employment Equity Act (1995)	Federal legislation that is limited to federally regulated activities. It encourages preferential treatment in employment practices for designated groups: women, people with disabilities, Aboriginal peoples and visible minorities. Employment equity goes beyond non-discrimination and requires these groups to be targeted for proactive treatment.
Denmark	The Act on Prohibition Against Differential Treatment in the Labour Market	Contains a prohibition against differential treatment due to disability and obliges employers to take appropriate measures to enable a person with a disability to access employment. People who are part of trade unions may receive help and unions may take legal steps on behalf of the complainant. No legislation protects people with disabilities outside of the labour market.
	Consolidation Act on Social Services (2007)	Municipal councils are required to provide sheltered employment for persons under the age of 65 who are physically or mentally disabled and are unable to find or maintain employment and who are not provided for under any other legislation. Municipal councils may provide special employment opportunities.

Country	Legislation	Description
Finland	The Constitution of Finland	Guarantees the right to basic subsistence in the event of unemployment, illness and disability.
Germany	General Equalisation Law (BGG) (2002)	Protection in several areas of public life (e.g. the workplace) against discrimination for several reasons, among others: disability (mental illness not specifically mentioned).
	Social Law Book IX (2001)	Rehabilitation and participation of disabled persons.
	Social Law Book V Section 2a (2005)	Regulation of contributions, benefits, payments to disabled persons and those with chronic illness.
Greece	Law 3304 (2005)	Anti-discrimination legislation that applies the principle of equal treatment and prohibits discrimination on a number of grounds, including mental disability.
India	Persons With Disabilities (Protection of Rights, Equal Opportunity and Full Participation) Act (1995)	Offers protection to those with a mental disability. The statute definition includes mental retardation but excludes many other mental disabilities.
Ireland	Equal Status Acts (2000–2004)	Discrimination in the provision of goods, services, accommodation, education and the disposal of premises prohibited on nine grounds including disability, defined to include intellectual, learning, cognitive and emotional disabilities. Under this statute, disability includes an existing disability, one that existed but no longer exists, one that may exist in the future, or one that is imputed to the person concerned, a person who is associated with a disabled person.
	Employment Equality Act (1998-2007)	Discrimination specifically prohibited in the workplace and in vocational education. The Equality Authority, set up under the Employment Equity Act, investigates appeals.

(Continued)

Country	Legislation	Description
Israel	Equal Rights for People with Disabilities Law (1998)	Promotes equality for all people with disabilities, including people with mental disabilities. The law prohibits discrimination and requires affirmative action to correct present discrimination, develop programmes to integrate people with disabilities into the open work market and provide diagnostic and consulting services.
	The Rehabilitation of People with Mental Disabilities in the Community Law (2000)	Makes a clear statement that individuals with mental disabilities are entitled to live, work and be educated in the community. People who meet eligibility criteria are entitled to rehabilitation services, including employment and training. Prohibits workplace discrimination on any grounds and makes it clear that setting irrelevant conditions is discriminatory as well.
Japan	Fundamental Law for Persons with Disabilities (Revised 2004)	Prohibits disability based discrimination but does not clearly define disability based discrimination or its remedy.
	Handicapped Persons' Employment Promotion Act (Revised 2006)	Targeted employment rate for people with disabilities, including people with mental illnesses.
	Labour Standards Act	Provides for short-term trial employment (up to three months) for people in need, including those with a mental illness. At the close of the trial, parties can decide whether to proceed to a regular contract. Government incentives provided for every individual who is given a regular contract as a result of this programme.
Lithuania	Law on Equal Treatment	Places duty on the employer to apply equal treatment criteria in hiring and working conditions, take measures to avoid harassment, provide conditions for disabled people to obtain work.
	Law on Support for Employment	Names people with disabilities and outlines special measures to support them in the labour market. Employers are encouraged to hire people with a disability.
Mauritius	The Training and Employment of Disabled Persons Act (1966)	Includes a section on anti-discrimination, which makes it an offence for employers to discriminate against disabled people in any aspect of employment.

Country	Legislation	Description
New Zealand	Human Rights Act (1993)	Defines disability comprehensively and includes psychiatric illness, intellectual or psychological disability or impairment. It also grants protection against discrimination to the disabled person and to their relatives or associates. Also has an Office of Disability Issues that coordinates national disability strategies following a social model of disability, which emphasises the role of the environment in producing discrimination.
Norway	Anti-discrimination and Accessibility Act (2009)	This law was drafted to strengthen existing anti-discrimination legislation to promote full participation in society with equality between people with a disability and other citizens. Disability includes mental and cognitive impairments without specifying the degree or duration, or requiring that the impairment has resulted in consequences for the person concerned. Monitored and enforced by the Norwegian Equality Tribunal and the Equality and Anti-Discrimination Ombud.
	Working Environment Act (2007)	The purpose is to ensure safe working conditions and equal treatment among workers. It protects against labour market related discrimination on the grounds of disability. Ensures that the working environment forms a basis for a health-promoting and meaningful work situation.
People's Republic of China (Hong Kong)	Disability Discrimination Ordinance (1995)	Prohibits discrimination on the grounds of disability with respect to employment, accommodation, education and access to a variety of social and civic activities, goods, and services. It protects the disabled person as well as their associates from discrimination. The Equal Opportunity Commission hears complaints and takes legal action, where necessary. Decisions have been handed down which include discrimination as a result of a family member having a mental illness.
Philippines	Magna Carta for Persons with Disabilities	Allows for the rehabilitation and social inclusion of disabled people into mainstream society, including equal opportunities for employment. Disability includes mental impairment.

(*Continued*)

Country	Legislation	Description
Sri Lanka	Constitution of Sri Lanka	Guarantees freedom from degrading treatment and equality before the law for every person and recognises the right to make special legislation to protect people with disabilities. It guarantees freedom from arbitrary arrest, freedom of speech, assembly, association, occupation and movement.
	Protection of the Rights of Persons with Disabilities Act (1996)	Ensures the promotion, advancement and protection of the rights of people with disabilities. Disability is defined to include physical or mental. The non-discrimination provision in this act applies to recruitment and employment. Otherwise there is no legislation that specifically guarantees the rights of disabled people relating to employment and work. A National Council for Persons with Disabilities oversees the application of the legislation and can file a grievance on behalf of a disabled person.
Sweden	Prohibition of Discrimination in Working Life on Grounds of Disability Act (1999)	Combats disability in working life for people with physical or mental conditions that limit functional capacity. Prohibits direct and indirect discrimination in all spheres of working life. Indirect discrimination refers to practices that appear neutral but disadvantage people with disabilities.
The Nether-lands	Law on Equal Treatment of the Disabled and Chronically Ill (2003)	An anti-discrimination law that outlines obligations concerning necessary accommodations for those with a disability or chronic illness with respect to employment, education and public transportation. Complaints can be filed to the Commission on Equal Treatment (decisions not legally binding) or proceed through civil court.
United Kingdom	Human Rights Act (1998)	This Act made the rights in the European Convention on Human Rights enforceable in UK domestic law.
	Disability Discrimination Act (1995, 2005), Equality Act (2010)	Employers have obligations not to treat disabled people less fairly than others. Disability is defined as either a physical or mental impairment that limits day-to-day activities. The disabled person must demonstrate that the impairment has a substantial effect on activities and this can be difficult to demonstrate. In the 1995 version of the Act, mentally disabled people (but not physically disabled people) had to demonstrate their condition was clinically recognised.

Country	Legislation	Description
United States	Americans with Disabilities Act (1990)	This Act explicitly prohibits discrimination in employment and includes people with a physical or mental disability and their family and close associates. Through a series of court decisions, the definition of disability was interpreted restrictively to exclude most individuals with a mental illness.
	Americans with Disabilities Amendment Act (2008)	The purpose of this Act was to restore the intent and protections of the original Americans with Disabilities Act. It rejected a number of Supreme Court decisions that excluded mental disorders if, for example, they were intermittent or episodic, and departed from the strict and demanding standard of 'severe limitation' that had been applied.

CHAPTER 16
Organisations and Resources

This chapter provides details of organisations and resources of relevance when working to protect, promote and ensure the human rights of people with mental health problems, and to combat the discrimination and abuse experienced by them. All organisations and resources that have been listed are transnational (i.e. they work in, or focus on, at least two countries); we have chosen not to include organisations whose work is focused within one country only. Please bear in mind that our compilation is indicative of the resources available rather than a complete documentation of all relevant organisations and resources. All web site addresses listed were correct and functioning on 1 April 2011.

16.1 Legislation libraries and databases

The resources below comprise databases and online libraries of legislation and policy that address disability, anti-discrimination and health. These databases and libraries can be useful in comparing different countries' approaches to legislative action, and in giving additional ideas of how to develop or transform existing legislation in the country in which you work.

16.1.1 Disability Rights Education and Defense Fund (DREDF) International Directory of Disability Laws

www.dredf.org/international

The DREDF web site provides an international directory of national disability non-discrimination laws.

16.1.2 The Equal Rights Trust Virtual Library

www.equalrightstrust.org/library-introduction/index.htm

This virtual library serves as an educational tool on non-discrimination issues. It includes various materials related to non-discrimination and equality, including international, regional and national norms, case law, policy papers, academic and other articles.

Mental Illness, Discrimination and the Law: Fighting for Social Justice, First Edition.
Felicity Callard, Norman Sartorius, Julio Arboleda-Flórez, Peter Bartlett, Hanfried Helmchen, Heather Stuart, Jose Taborda and Graham Thornicroft.

16.1.3 World Health Organization International Digest of Health Legislation

www.who.int/idhl-rils

The WHO International Digest of Health Legislation comprises an extensive selection of national and international health legislation. Texts of legislation are summarised in English or mentioned by their title. Where possible, links are provided to other web sites that contain full texts of the legislation in question.

16.1.4 International and Comparative Disability Law Web Resources

http://law.syr.edu/library/electronic-resources/legal-research-guides/humanrights.aspx

This web resource, hosted by the Syracuse University College of Law, provides comprehensive bibliographic resources devoted to international and comparative disability laws. The site is organised under three broad categories: international disability laws, regional disability laws and individual countries' disability laws.

16.1.5 NATLEX

www.ilo.org/dyn/natlex/natlex_browse.home

NATLEX is a database of national labour, social security and related human rights legislation. It is maintained by the International Labour Organization's International Labour Standards Department.

16.2 World Health Organization literature and resources

The World Health Organization (WHO) (www.who.int) has, over a number of decades, developed numerous materials of great relevance to those working to combat the discrimination and abuse experienced by people with mental health problems.

16.2.1 Resources specific to mental health and human rights

16.2.1.1 WHO Resource Book on Mental Health, Human Rights and Legislation

Available at: www.who.int/mental_health/policy/resource_book_MHLeg.pdf

The *Resource Book* aims to assist countries in drafting, adopting and implementing legislation that improves the lives of people with mental disorders. It highlights the key issues and principles to be incorporated into legislation and draws on a range of international examples.

16.2.1.2 WHO Checklist on Mental Health Legislation

Available at: www.who.int/mental_health/policy/WHOLegislationChecklist.pdf

The checklist accompanies the *Resource Book on Mental Health, Human Rights and Legislation* and aims to:

- assist countries in reviewing the comprehensiveness and adequacy of existing mental health legislation;
- help countries in the process of drafting new law.

16.2.1.3 WHO–MIND (Mental Improvement for Nations Development)

www.who.int/mental_health/policy/en

The WHO–MIND project supports countries to implement programmes to ensure that effective treatment, prevention, and promotion programmes are made available to all people who need them. One of the four core thematic areas of WHO–MIND is focused around human rights and legislation. The WHO–MIND project also includes Quality Rights, a project to unite and empower people to improve the quality of care and human rights situation in mental health facilities and social care homes.

The WHO–MIND web site provides a range of resources and information sheets, which can be downloaded.

Literature

World Health Organization (2007) Best practices: mental health, human rights and legislation (Best practices, Sheet 3). World Health Organization, Geneva, Switzerland.

Funk, M, Drew, N, Freeman, M, Faydi, E and World Health Organization (2010) *Mental Health and Development: Targeting people with mental health conditions as a vulnerable group*. World Health Organization, Geneva, Switzerland.

16.2.2 Resources Focused on (Mental and Physical) Health Care

16.2.2.1 WHO–AIMS

www.who.int/mental_health/evidence/WHO-AIMS/en

The World Health Organization Assessment Instrument for Mental Health Systems (WHO–AIMS) is a tool for collecting essential information on the mental health system of a country or region. It has been designed to assist in the improvement of mental health systems and is primarily intended for assessing mental health systems in low- and middle-income countries.

Literature

World Health Organization (2009) Mental health systems in selected low- and middle-income countries: a WHO-AIMS cross-national analysis. World Health Organization, Geneva, Switzerland.

16.2.2.2 WHO Mental Health Atlas

WHO (2005) *Mental Health Atlas*. Department of Mental Health and Substance Abuse, World Health Organization, Geneva, Switzerland.

http://apps.who.int/globalatlas/default.asp

The *Mental Health Atlas 2005* is the second instalment from the WHO project to examine and strengthen mental health resources worldwide. The Atlas contains a global overview as well as country surveys covering 16 themes that include: the state of mental health policy, legislation and financing, mental health facilities, numbers of psychiatric beds and professionals, programmes for special populations and the availability of therapeutic drugs. The Atlas can be viewed, downloaded, or used in interactive form. The interactive form allows global, regional and country data to be displayed and compared.

16.2.2.3 WHO Mental Health Care Law: Ten Basic Principles

www.who.int/mental_health/policy/legislation/ten_basic_principles.pdf

This reference document, published by the WHO in 1996, lists and describes ten basic principles of mental health care law, and provides annotations for their implementation in practice.

16.2.2.4 WHO Mental Health Gap Action Programme (MhGAP)

www.who.int/mental_health/mhgap/en/index.html

The Mental Health Gap Action Programme aims to:

- reinforce the commitment of governments, international organisations and other stakeholders to increase the allocation of financial and human resources for care of mental, neurological and substance use disorders;
- achieve much higher coverage with key interventions in the countries with low and lower middle incomes that have a large proportion of the global burden of mental, neurological and substance use disorders.

Literature

MhGAP Intervention Guide for Mental, Neurological and Substance Use Disorders in Non-Specialized Health Settings. Version 1.0. World Health Organization, Geneva, Switzerland. http://whqlibdoc.who.int/publications/2010/9789241548069_eng.pdf

16.2.3 World Health Organization Regional Offices

The World Health Organization has, in addition to its Geneva headquarters, a number of regional offices, some of which pursue extensive programmes and projects that relate to mental health and human rights.

16.2.3.1 African Region

www.afro.who.int

The African region has a focus on strengthening countries' capacity for the development and implementation of national policies, plans and legislation for mental health.

16.2.3.2 Region of the Americas (The Pan American Health Organization – PAHO)

http://new.paho.org

A human rights approach is central to all of PAHO's mental health work. PAHO launched an initiative in 1990 that was designed to restructure psychiatric care throughout the Americas. Central to this initiative was the promotion and protection of the human rights of people with mental disability. Soon after, PAHO gathered legislators, mental health professionals, human rights leaders and organisations of people with disability to advance mental health care reforms throughout the region. This resulted in the Declaration of Caracas. The PAHO web site includes a number of useful resources and documents relating to mental health and human rights. (Chapters 14.3.5.1 and 14.3.5.2 give details of the Declaration of Caracas and PAHO Resolution CD47.R1 Disability: Prevention and Rehabilitation in the Context of the Right to the Enjoyment of the Highest Attainable Standard of Physical and Mental Health and Other Related Rights.)

Literature

Human Rights & Health: Persons with mental disabilities: Pan American Health Organization. Available at: www.paho.org/english/dd/pub/10069_Mental.pdf

16.2.3.3 South-East Asia Region

www.searo.who.int

The South-East Asia Region has an ongoing project about mental health legislation. The Health and Behaviour Unit, in collaboration with the Mental Health Unit at the WHO headquarters, has developed a programme to assist member countries in updating/developing modern mental health legislation, policies and services (www.searo.who.int/en/Section1174/Section1199/Section1570_6726.htm).

Literature

World Health Organization (2004) A Systematic Approach to Developing and Implementing Mental Health Legislation. Report of a Regional Meeting of Experts, 6–8 December 2004. New Delhi, India. http://www.searo.who.int/LinkFiles/Meeting_reports_6-8Dec-04_Ment-141.pdf

Rantala, RE, Drew, N, Pathare, S and Funk, M (2010). Right to Health Through Education: Mental health and human rights. In: Plantilla, JR (ed.) *Human Rights Education in Asia-Pacific*, Vol. 1. Asia-Pacific Human Rights Information Center, Osaka, Japan, pp. 188–199.

16.2.3.4 European Region

www.euro.who.int

The European Region has an extensive portfolio of work that centres around mental health and draws together the promotion of mental health, the prevention of mental disorders and the protection of human rights. At the WHO European Ministerial Conference on Mental Health, held in Helsinki in January 2005, the Mental Health Declaration for Europe and the Mental Health Action Plan for Europe were signed and endorsed on behalf of ministers of health of the 52 Member States in the European Region.

The Declaration, Action Plan and Pact for Well-Being give impetus to the development of mental health care in the European region, and aim to support the implementation of policies and activities to improve mental health promotion, prevention, care and treatment. The area within the Action Plan that focuses on stigma and discrimination includes the following actions for Member States to consider:

- introduce or scrutinise disability rights legislation to ensure that it covers mental health equally and equitably;
- develop a coherent programme of policy and legislation to address stigma and discrimination, incorporating international and regional human rights standards.

16.2.3.4.1 Mental Health Declaration for Europe: Facing the Challenges, Building Solutions

www.euro.who.int/en/who-we-are/policy-documents/mental-health-declaration-for-europe

16.2.3.4.2 Mental Health Action Plan for Europe

Mental health action plan for Europe: Facing the Challenges, Building Solutions. First WHO European Ministerial Conference on Mental Health, 12–15 January 2005, Helsinki, Finland. World Health Organization. Regional Office for Europe.

www.euro.who.int/en/what-we-do/health-topics/noncommunicable-diseases/mental-health/publications/2005/who-mental-health-action-plan-for-europe

16.2.3.4.3 The European Pact for Mental Health and Well-Being

This was launched at the European Union high-level conference 'Together for Mental Health and Well-being' in Brussels, 13 June 2008. It acknowledged the importance and relevance of mental health and well-being for the European Union, its Member States, stakeholders and citizens. The Pact followed the European Commission's Green Paper (November 2005), *Promoting the Mental Health of the Population. Towards a mental health strategy for the EU*. The Green Paper was the first response to the WHO Mental Health Declaration for Europe.

> Also see Friedli, L. (2009) Mental health, resilience and inequalities. Mental Health Foundation/World Health Organization, Geneva, Switzerland.

16.2.3.4.4 European Network for Mental Health Promotion

This is a large network for mental health promotion in Europe. The web site provides information, tools and policy examples relating to mental health promotion.

www.mentalhealthpromotion.net

16.2.3.4.5 The Tallinn Charter: Health Systems for Health and Wealth, 2008

www.euro.who.int/__data/assets/pdf_file/0008/88613/E91438.pdf

In relation to health in general, Member States of the WHO European Region renewed their commitment to human rights norms such as solidarity, equity, participation, transparency and accountability in the Tallinn Charter on Health Systems for Health and Wealth (2008).

16.2.3.4.6 The European Observatory on Health Systems and Policies

www.euro.who.int/observatory

The European Observatory on Health Systems and Policies, which is based within the WHO European Region, supports and promotes evidence-based health policy-making through comprehensive analysis of the dynamics of health care systems in Europe. Its work on mental health policy addresses the continuing move towards community-based care and how barriers to system reform may be overcome (in particular, the resources in Box 16.1). The web site provides a wealth of material that allows readers to compare health systems in different countries, understand the role of European Union law and policy in health system governance, measure and tackle health inequalities across Europe and so on.

Box 16.1 Resources

European Observatory on Health Systems and Policies: Policy briefs on mental health (2004, No. 7). Available at:
www.euro.who.int/en/home/projects/observatory/publications/policy-briefs/observatory-policy-briefs

Mental health I – Key issues in the development of policy and practice across Europe

Mental health II – Balancing institutional and community-based care

Mental health III – Funding mental health in Europe

Edited volume: Knapp, M, McDaid, D, Mossialos, E and Thornicroft, G (eds) (2007) *Mental Health Policy and Practice Across Europe: The future direction of mental health care*. Open University Press and McGraw-Hill Education, Maidenhead, UK. Available online at: www.euro.who.int/en/what-we-publish/abstracts/mental-health-policy-and-practice-across-europe

16.2.3.5 Eastern Mediterranean Region

www.emro.who.int/index.asp

16.2.3.6 Western Pacific Region

www.wpro.who.int

16.3 Other intergovernmental organisations and resources

16.3.1 International Labour Organization (ILO)

www.ilo.org
4 route des Morillons, CH-1211, Genève, 22 Switzerland
tel: +41 (0) 22 799 6111
fax: +41 (0) 22 798 8685
email: ilo@ilo.org

The ILO has an extensive array of documents, guidelines and reports relating to disability, employment and social services. See, in particular, the sections of the ILO web site entitled:

- Inclusion of Persons with Disabilities (www.ilo.org/skills/areas/lang–en/WCMS_DOC_SKL_ARE_DBL_EN/index.htm).

- ILO Social Security Inquiry database (www.ilo.org/dyn/ilossi/ssimain.home?p_lang = en).

  Other resources and reports include:
- *Achieving equal employment opportunities for people with disabilities through legislation: Guidelines (2004).*

  This resource provides extensive guidelines on, and examples of how, effective legislation on the employment of people with disabilities can be developed and implemented.
- *World Social Security Report 2010/11: Providing coverage in times of crisis and beyond* (2010).

  This report provides extensive documentation and analysis of social security and social protection programmes.

16.3.2 United Nations Enable: Rights and Dignity of Persons with Disabilities

www.un.org/disabilities

The United Nations has been discussed throughout this book, and readers should refer to the frequent references and resources scattered throughout this volume. This web site provides extensive material and resources that relate to the UN Convention on the Rights of Persons with Disabilities (CPRD), including the full text of the Convention, as well as up to date details of signatories and ratifications of the CRPD and its Optional Protocol.

16.3.3 United Nations Office of the High Commissioner for Human Rights (OHCHR)

www.ohchr.org

United Nations Department of Economic and Social Affairs (DESA)

www.un.org/en/development/desa/index.html

The Convention on the Rights of Persons with Disabilities and its Optional Protocol are serviced by a joint Secretariat, which comprises staff of both the United Nations Department of Economic and Social Affairs (DESA), based in New York, and the Office of the High Commissioner for Human Rights (OHCHR) in Geneva.

The Secretariat also issues publications and acts as a clearing house for information on disability issues; promotes national, regional and international programmes and activities; provides support to governments and civil society; and gives substantial support to technical co-operation projects and activities.

Literature

Byrnes, A, Conte, A, Gonnot, J-P, Larsson, L, Schindlmayr, T, Shepherd, N *et al.* (2007) *From Exclusion to Equality. Realising the Rights of Persons with Disabilities: Handbook for Parliamentarians on the Convention on the Rights of Persons with Disabilities and its Optional Protocol*. United Nations, Geneva, Switzerland. Available at: www.un.org/disabilities/documents/toolaction/ipuhb.pdf

United Nations Office of the High Commissioner for Human Rights (2010). *Monitoring the Convention on the Rights of Persons with Disabilities – Guidance for Human Rights Monitors*. United Nations, New York and Geneva. Available at: www.ohchr.org/Documents/Publications/Disabilities_training_17EN.pdf

16.3.4 United Nations Educational, Scientific and Cultural Organisation (UNESCO)

www.unesco.org
The headquarters are located in two places in the same area (with one general phone number).
7, place de Fontenoy, 75352 Paris, 07 SP France and 1, rue Miollis, 75732 Paris Cedex 15, France.
tel: +33 (0)1 45 68 10 00

UNESCO is a specialised agency of the United Nations established in 1945 to contribute to peace and security by promoting international collaboration through education, science and culture in order to further universal respect for justice, the rule of law and human rights along with fundamental freedoms proclaimed in the UN Charter.

Education is one of UNESCO's principal fields of activities and action in this field is explicitly set within the 'inclusive education' framework adopted at the Salamanca Conference in 1994, whereby 'schools should accommodate all children regardless of their physical, intellectual, emotional, social, linguistic or other conditions' (Article 3) (see Chapter 6.1). UNESCO has developed a number of guides and toolkits that focus on inclusive education.

Literature

UNESCO (2009) *Policy Guidelines on Inclusion in Education*. UNESCO, Paris, France. These guidelines, as well as toolkits, are available for download from the UNESCO web site: www.unesco.org

UNESCO (1994) The Salamanca Statement and Framework for Action on Special Needs Education. World Conference on Special Needs Education: Access and Quality. Salamanca, Spain.

16.4 Non-governmental organisations (NGOs) and resources

All the organisations included in this section work in more than one country and have a significant focus on combating the discrimination, abuse and social injustice experienced by people with disabilities (including people with mental health problems and people with intellectual disabilities). Many of the web sites for these organisations contain a number of downloadable resources that readers will find helpful both for extending their knowledge and guiding their practice.

16.4.1 Amnesty International

www.amnesty.org
1 Easton Street, London WC1X 0DW, United Kingdom
tel: +44 (0)20 7413 5500
fax: +44 (0)20 7956 1157

16.4.2 Association for the Prevention of Torture (APT)

www.apt.ch
PO Box 2267, CH–1121 Geneva 2, Switzerland
tel: +41 (22) 919 21 70
fax: +41 (22) 919 21 80
email: apt@apt.ch

16.4.3 Basic Needs

www.basicneeds.org
158a Parade, Leamington Spa, Warwickshire CV32 4AE, United Kingdom
tel: +44 (0) 1926 330101
fax: +44 (0) 1926 453679
email: info@basicneeds.org

16.4.4 Disability Rights International (DRI)

www.disabilityrightsintl.org
email: info@disabilityrightsintl.org

16.4.5 European Coalition for Community Living (ECCL)

www.community-living.info
mailing address: c/o National Centre for Independent Living, Unit 3.40, Canterbury Court, 1-3 Brixton Road, London SW9 6DE, United Kingdom
tel: +44 (0)20 7587 3982

16.4.6 ENUSP (European Network of (Ex-)Users and Survivors of Psychiatry)

www.enusp.org
email: desk@enusp.org

16.4.7 EUFAMI (European Federation of Associations of Families of People with Mental Illness)

www.eufami.org
Diestsevest 100, B–3000 Leuven, Belgium
tel: +32 (0)16 74 50 40
fax: +32 (0)16 74 50 49
email: info@eufami.org

16.4.8 Gamian (Global Alliance of Mental Illness Advocacy Networks)

www.gamian.eu
Secretariat: GAMIAN-Europe, c/o 424 St. Joseph High Street, St Venera SVR1013, Malta
tel: +356 21 440456, +356 21 224580

16.4.9 Global Initiative on Psychiatry

www.gip-global.org
GIP-Hilversum, PO Box 1282, 1200 BG Hilversum, The Netherlands
tel: +31 (0)35 683 8727
fax: + 31 (0)35 683 3646
email: hilversum@gip-global.org

16.4.10 Human Rights Watch

www.hrw.org
350 Fifth Avenue, 34th floor, New York, NY 10118-3299, USA
tel: +1 (212) 290 4700
fax: +1 (212) 736 1300

16.4.11 Inclusion International

www.inclusion-international.org
KD.2.034-6, University Way, Docklands Campus, London E16 2RD, UK
tel: +44 (0)208 223 7709
fax: +44 (0)208 223 6081
email: info@inclusion-international.org

16.4.12 International Disability Alliance (IDA)

www.internationaldisabilityalliance.org
International Disability Alliance Secretariat, WCC Building, nos. 153-154, 150 route de Ferney, 1211 Genève, Switzerland
email: stromel@fundaciononce.es

16.4.13 International Disability Rights Monitor (IDRM)

www.idrmnet.org
Center for International Rehabilitation, 211 E Ontario, Suite 300, Chicago, IL 60611, USA
tel: +1 (312) 280 4970
fax: +1 (312) 573 0019
email: info@cirnetwork.org

16.4.14 Interrights (International Centre for the Legal Protection of Human Rights)

www.interights.org
Lancaster House, 33 Islington High Street, London N1 9LH, UK
tel: +44 (0)20 7278 3230
fax: +44 (0)20 7278 4334
email: ir@interights.org

16.4.15 PILNet – The Global Network for Public Interest Law

www.pilnet.org
Paulay Ede utca. 50, 1061 Budapest, Hungary
tel: +36 1 461 5700
fax: +36 1 461 5701

16.4.16 Mental Disability Advocacy Center (MDAC)

www.mdac.info
Hercegprímás utca 11, H-1051 Budapest, Hungary
tel: +36 1 413 2730
fax: +36 1 413 2739
email: mdac@mdac.info

The MDAC web site provides a number of resources for human rights activists, lawyers and academics. These include research reports, legal analysis and training packs and advocacy manuals. It also provides links to relevant international instruments and their documents.

16.4.17 Mental Health Europe

www.mhe-sme.org
Boulevard Clovis 7, 1000 Brussels, Belgium
tel +32 (0)2 280 04 68
fax +32 (0)2 280 16 04□
email: Info@mhe-sme.org

16.4.18 MindFreedom

www.mindfreedom.org
MindFreedom International, PO Box 11284, Eugene, OR 97440-3484, USA
Tel: +1 (541) 345 9106
Fax: +1 (480) 247 5510
email: office@mindfreedom.org

16.4.19 Open Society Mental Health Initiative

www.soros.org/initiatives/health/focus/mhi/about
Public Health Programs, Open Society Institute, 400 West 59th Street, New York, NY 10019, USA
tel: +1 (212) 548 0600 or (212) 548 0100
fax: +1 (212) 548 4679 or (212) 548 4600

16.4.20 World Federation for Mental Health (WFMH)

www.wfmh.org
6564 Loisdale Court, Suite 301, Springfield, VA 22150-1812, USA
tel: +1 (703) 313 8680
fax: +1 (703) 313 8683
email: info@wfmh.com

The Global Online Directory of Mental Health Patient/Service User, Family Member/Caregiver Support Groups and Mental Health Advocacy and Awareness Organisations (available on the WFMH web site) is a comprehensive worldwide searchable directory of existing mental health patient/service user, family member/caregiver support groups and mental health advocacy organisations.

16.4.21 World Network of Users and Survivors of Psychiatry

http://wnusp.rafus.dk
Store Glasvej 49, 5000 Odense C, Denmark
tel: +45 66 19 45 11
email: admin@wnusp.net

16.4.22 World Psychiatric Association (WPA) Global Programme against Stigma and Discrimination because of Schizophrenia – 'Open the Doors'

www.openthedoors.com

Useful literature

Sartorius, N and Schulze, H (2005) *Reducing the Stigma of Mental Illness: A Report from a Global Programme of the World Psychiatric Association*. Cambridge University Press, Cambridge.

The book documents the work of the WPA Programme, and provides comprehensive details and advice about running various anti-stigma programmes in countries that are economically, politically and culturally diverse.

Index

Mental Illness, Discrimination and the Law: Fighting for Social Justice, First Edition.
Felicity Callard, Norman Sartorius, Julio Arboleda-Flórez, Peter Bartlett, Hanfried Helmchen, Heather Stuart, Jose Taborda and Graham Thornicroft.